Most famous for *The Lucky Country*, Donald Horne is one of Australia's best known social and cultural critics. Author of more than 20 books, he has contributed his own brand of informed and entertaining analysis to many print and broadcast programs, and to the magazines he has edited.

He moved from editing to academia in 1973, when he joined the University of New South Wales, of which he is now an Emeritus Professor. Active in public life, he was Chairman of the Australia Council for six years and now chairs the Ideas for Australia program, as well as being Chancellor of the University of Canberra.

This is Donald Horne's fourth book on tourism and how we 'invent' a world when we travel. *Money Made Us* (1976) and *Right Way Don't Go Back* (1978) were followed in 1984 by the internationally-acclaimed *The Great Museum*.

The Intelligent Tourist

DONALD HORNE

MARGARET
Gee

Published by
Margaret Gee Publishing
an imprint of
Margaret Gee Holdings
Suite 2a, 61 Victoria Street, McMahons Point, NSW 2060
A.C.N. 005 604 464

First published in 1992

Distributed by Gary Allen Pty Ltd
9 Cooper Street, Smithfield, NSW 2164

Copyright © Donald Horne
Photographs copyright © Donald Horne

All rights reserved. No part of this publication may be
reproduced, stored in a retrieval system, or transmitted
in any form or by any means electronic, mechanical,
photocopying, recording or otherwise without the prior
permission of the Publisher.

National Library of Australia
Cataloguing-in-Publication entry

Horne, Donald, 1921– .
   The intelligent tourist.

   Bibliography.
   ISBN 1 875574 16 6.

   1. Travel. 2. Tourist trade—Social aspects. I. Title.
910

Edited by Anne Matthews
Typeset by Midland Typesetters, Victoria
Printed by Australian Print Group, Victoria
Production by Vantage Graphics, Sydney

CONTENTS

Preface: Experiencing tourism — ix

INTRODUCTION

1. **Home thoughts from the carousel** — 3
   Why do we become tourists?

PART ONE: THE MAKING OF TOURISM

2. **Inventing Victoria Falls** — 15
   The bridge
   The statue

3. **Magic agendas** — 23
   Casting spells
   A radiance of celebrity
   Exorcising tourism
   The Ozymandias factor

4. **The modern pilgrims** — 41
   Relics
   Faith in the authentic
   Bodies

5. **Civic pilgrims:** *Pradakshina* **on the Tourmobile** — 52
   The mysterious ecstasy of being in Washington

6. **The gods are alive (under glass)** — 57
   A day in the Old City
   Touring the supernatural: a tourist's etiquette
   A traveller's kit of myths
   Tourism as cult
   Art? Or religion?

7. **Interlude: FAMILY HOLIDAY
   (ON AN ENCHANTED ISLAND)** — 79

Family diary
The enchanted island
Travelling into the mundane

PART TWO: A REALITY THAT IS OUT OF THIS WORLD

8. Inventing the authentic 101
Moral torments of the original condition
The authenticity of cities
Creating Old Singapore

9. How to be real 112
Rituals of the camera
Making sure reality is still there
Smelling like real

10. Classifiers of the universe 121
The mystique of museums
Reality guaranteed by the state
Control by classification
The straight lines of progress

11. The principle of intelligent superficiality 132
A cultural genes bank
Specialising in generalities

12. Interlude: THE PALACE-ON-WHEELS 138
Not the Orient Express
Tourists and travellers
The excerpt experience

PART THREE: THE MAKE-BELIEVE OF THE PUBLIC CULTURE

13. Tourism and the make-believe of the public culture 165
Tourist showcases
The formation of public cultures
How to 'read' tourism

14. The public woman 178
Alternative readings

15. Temptations of beauty and nostalgia   184
   A nice day at an industrial site
   Machines as metaphors
   Fanfares of science

16. Looking for 'the people'   199
   Workersland
   Making the invisible visible

17. Breaking into the public culture   212
   Whose heritage?
   Museums in the alternative

18. Revolution as public culture   222
   The Soviet Tourmobile
   The myth of The Fall
   New truths in the public drama

19. Interlude: A MUSEUM OF IMAGINARY LANDSCAPES   237
   The eighth wonder of the world
   'Nature' as experience

PART FOUR: A TOURIST'S GUIDE TO NATIONALISM

20. Them and us   249
   Tourism among the Tarzan Villages
   The Euroracist museums
   Mixing us with them
   Making an exhibit of yourself in your own country

21. The national tourist showcase   264
   National pilgrimages
   Visiting the national capital
   Choosing the nation's story
   The conservatism of the tourist past

22. Patriotic ironmongery   287
   The silences of guns and uniforms

23. The civilisation packet   294
   Staking out the past
   Perils of 'the classical'

Cradles of history
Civilisation in an afternoon

24. Interlude: SHOWS WE SAW THAT SUMMER   306
Aspects of the theatrical

PART FIVE: HOW TO BE A TOURIST

25. Bali now—and what it can teach Third World Britain, etc   325
Has tourism spoilt Bali?
In Third World Liverpool
What do you do for a day in Denver, Colorado?
A belief in people

26. Visitors in our own lives   342
Looking at things
Our own range of experiences

27. Coming out of the culture bunker   350
Turning things into art
The right to look
Wonder, resonance, awe, curiosity, scepticism
A world without art museums

28. How to be a tourist   364
You can't do the world
A place for the intelligent tourist

Keywords   376

Bibliography   385

Index: Places   392
           People and themes   406

Preface:

EXPERIENCING TOURISM

◆ ◆ ◆

This book is concerned with tourism as the greatest continuing mass movement of peoples in human history, and with sightseeing as one of the important conveyors of meaning in our times. It is written for people who would like to consider, critically, how sightseeing can seem to take over some of the functions of religion; of how intimately it is connected with the crisis in authenticity in modern societies; and how easily it can become an expression of nationality. But this book is also written for people who still want to enjoy their sightseeing.

I have not made the structure too rigid—themes are approached from different perspectives. A glossary of keywords is a reminder of the main ideas. Footnotes here and there are meant to be interesting asides. And, since a function of tourism is to provide stories to tell when we get home, I have broken up continuities with patches of narrative, scene-setting and anecdote.

* * *

Two main kinds of academic books and articles are now being written on tourism. One kind provides textbooks for the academic production line in tourism diplomas, but most of these do not confront the paradoxes and fiascoes and spiritual perils of tourism—nor do they contemplate the possibilities of enlightenment, apart from the lighting up of dollar signs. The other type of books, mainly from sociologists, anthropologists and semioticians, is inclined to treat tourism as a disease requiring appropriate classification before being eliminated.

Many books analysing tourism give the impression that the people who wrote them have never been tourists. The best writing on tourism is done by people who respect many of the landscapes and relics of material culture that are on the tourist schedules, but who can also contemplate the absurdities with which tourism can transform them. They can also find an interest in the ambiguities of tourism itself. This kind of writing is intended, as this book is, for those who can gain pleasure from analysing the experiences of tourism and who, for that very reason, can find sightseeing all the more interesting. It accepts that just as some people bring to a ball game or a concert more knowledge and wisdom than others, so some people are better at being tourists.

* * *

As ever, I wish to thank my wife, Myfanwy, for her support and assistance.

INTRODUCTION

♦ ♦ ♦

1.

HOME THOUGHTS FROM THE CAROUSEL

◆ ◆ ◆

After we arrive at Bombay from Singapore at one o'clock in the morning, the conveyor belt at the luggage carousel seems too old to move. A long, thin, black rat scurries beneath it—it is waiting to chew our luggage. My wife and I collect two trolleys. We wait.

In the 1930s, a movie would sometimes end with a woman rushing towards the camera to throw herself into her lover's arms, or to embrace a child, or the lost family dog. If the carousel is slow to start, or if everybody's luggage is coming out except ours, we stand there hoping that two Paklite suitcases will come back to us like lost dogs. At luggage carousels one can question travelling.

* * *

When I was on a university lecture tour in California and found in San Francisco, after a flight from Sacramento, that my suitcase wasn't on the carousel the man in front of me in the queue at the lost luggage desk was sobbing. They had lost his two suitcases and he was off to Hawaii. When my turn came I provided the strap that the suitcase was pulled by, as if this were the collar of a lost dog. "Okay, okay," said the man behind the desk. "Okay." This meant he was writing down at least some of what I said. "Okay," he said. "Okay." He gave me a receipt and a telephone number.

In Sacramento I had been booked into a Spanish Mission motel where I was able to take notes on the culture of the motel strip. In San Francisco I now discovered they had booked me into a flimsy-looking Spanish Mission motel on the border of what seemed a bad part of town. The street was mean and the room was bleak. The light from a neon sign flashed through the thin curtains. When I tried to lock the door, part of the lock fell away. "Okay," said the man at the desk. "Okay." Then I discovered the lavatory was blocked. "Okay," he said, "we'll fix that tomorrow." I couldn't change motels until I had rung the airport but, when I tried to ring, the phone didn't work. By the time the man at the desk agreed that my phone didn't work and allowed me to use his, it was 10 pm. United Airlines had shut down for the night.

I tried to 'secure the door' with a chair propped under its handle, but the handle was too shaky. On public affairs TV, as if it were the beginning of an ethnic joke, there was a discussion between a German, a Japanese and an Englishman. The surrounding rooms creaked and rustled with sexual ecstasies, throat-cuttings and mouth-garglings. At 11 pm there was a BBC repeat. Coughing and death rattles from other rooms accompanied a 'Great Performances' piece. Awake again at 3 am, I wrote out a list of what I should buy to replace my lost possessions.

For breakfast I was put at a table of four 'singles', in which there was a centrepiece with individual mirrors so that we could look at ourselves while we were eating. After breakfast I walked past a major pornography centre to a modest drugstore to buy a disposable razor. At 9 am United Airlines rang. "Professor Horne, your luggage has arrived from Oakland. Okay?"

* * *

We are still at the carousel at Bombay airport. The belt has not moved. The long black rat has not reappeared. Here is another reminder of the days when travel was a test of endurance. I know that. I know that negotiating blizzards through the Straits of Magellan to get to San Francisco was a different kind of inconvenience from standing in the lost luggage queue at the United Airlines desk. And I know that Indians sleep on a railway platform so that they can struggle towards carriages to which they may have to cling from the outside. But the more exact the timetables and itineraries become, the more easily autonomous nervous systems fall into mechanisms of fight or fear, or minds sink into melancholy and doubt—as mine does as we stand here at a quarter to two in the morning at the Bombay airport, waiting for the belt to start moving. The less inconvenient travel becomes, the more we exaggerate inconvenience. The dangers and fears of the heroic days of travel are replaced by irritations with bad management.

The belt moves, the two suitcases appear but we then sit in the hotel bus for three-quarters of an hour. It is 4 am before we are in bed in an airport hotel that has a very used look. (An airport hotel is a kind of hyphen: it is not a true arrival.) When we get down for breakfast at 8.15 am they tell us we should already be at the airport because though it says on our ticket that Flight IC 806 will leave for Delhi at 10.45, IC 806 is now leaving at 9.30. But when we get to the airport we are told it is running late and has been rescheduled for 10.15. We have no decisions in these changes of purpose. They are being done to us. We follow the incremental delays of Flight IC 806 on the departure screen until it disappears from the listing. At the last minute, and by accident, we learn that there is no longer a flight IC 806 and that we are now on Flight IC 187. We leave Bombay at 12.30 pm.

WHY DO WE BECOME TOURISTS?

As tourists we develop programs for tiring ourselves out more systematically than at work or at home, and we risk physical hardships and social dangers we couldn't imagine in our everyday lives.

Just as sport has become a principal festival in the secular modern-industrial societies, so has group tourism. Within its ceremonies of departure and return it is a ritualised break from routine in which, whether they know what they are doing or not, participants are defining certain values in an atmosphere of fellowship (even if the fellowship is officially defined by the tour leader). As tourists we proclaim what matters in existence and we display who *we* are and declare who *they* are (and the 'they' can sometimes include other, but lesser, breeds of tourists).

Tourism can be a ritual in which by moving our bodies from here to there we summon up regenerative forces. It can provide the annual reward for a year's striving; some tourist-journeys can be the event of a lifetime. We can gain prestige from tourism. We can 'find ourselves'. Alternatively, we can come back 'a different person'. Whether physically, intellectually, morally, or spiritually, we can feel better after we have done some tourism.

And it can give us a sense of control. Through strategies of timetables we can organise the world. Through strategies of anecdote we can return with new tales to tell that may affirm old attitudes, or make new affirmations about what life might mean. Through strategies of photography we ensure ourselves a past.

Tourism can provide us with the opportunity of contemplating the marvels of the natural world and some of the greatest achievements of the human species; through it we can consider the complexities of human difference, the puzzles of the past and the transitoriness of all people and all things.

Through tourism we can also make repulsive idiots of ourselves, understanding next to nothing of what we are seeing, despising the people who show it to us and, through travel, narrowing our minds.

Or, from the finest motives, simply because there are so many of us, we can kill the very things we love by treading all over them, cramming them out of view, or fencing them off, so that the only form of preservation is to limit those who can see them. The government of Ecuador set up controls to protect the unique species of plants and animals in the Galapagos Islands, whose strangeness excited the imagination of Charles Darwin. They decided to restrict 'eco-tourists' to 3500 a year. Visitors are now more than 10 times that number. Until recently the 50 national parks of the United States were natural holiday places for 60 million visitors each year. Now, bookings for some campsites, or permits for whitewater rafting or cycling open months in advance and sell out in a few hours. In summer, the floor of Yosemite Valley can be more dense with people than Manhattan.

Venice now has 12 million visitors a year. Like Disneyland, it exists entirely for tourism. How long will it be before it is entered through turnstiles, as if it were a theme park?

However sympathetic we are as tourists, we can change what we look at, so that it becomes something that is *observed*, as if it had no relation to anything else. We create a new culture—the culture of tourist-observed objects and people (in which tourists themselves have been described as being 'in parenthesis'). For example, the fetish markets of West Africa. In West Africa there is an established belief that if a spirit can be enticed into a box, a pouch, an idol, a dead lizard, or whatever, and then 'plugged in', the spirit will serve the person who owns it. Fetish markets became a natural feature of the larger West African towns. Now they can be turned into tourist attractions and the fetishes become curiosities. A guide takes you around and you buy a frog or a skull or a calabash and take it home, where it is no longer a fetish. It is a souvenir.

As Conrad Hilton, a pioneer of the international hotel chain, said: 'Each of our hotels is a little America'. Tourist money can help transform the nature of a country, or parts of it—not just with new hotels or increased pollution. The showcase parts of a country are likely to become whatever it is that tourists expect the country to be, and since nearly all international travel is commanded by the prosperous modern-industrial societies (and more than half of it by Germany, the United States, Britain, Japan and France alone) there is a tendency for the national showcases to become what the tourist business in those countries believes its customers would like them to be. Tourism is a way for the prosperous societies to define the world.

* * *

In the second half of the 1960s a specialist form of tourism developed to serve a particular class of Japanese man. It was tourism for the rice farmers who, because of the Japanese government's protection of rice-farming as a folkloric (and vote-getting) tradition, had more spare money than they had ever imagined. To help them spend some of it, travel agents put together an all-male tourist package covering Hong Kong, Macau and Taiwan. A tour group would fly to Hong Kong to buy presents for their loved ones in the shops with whose owners the travel agents, in their capacity as touts, had made their deals. To cross the mouth of the Pearl River the rice farmers would be put on a ferry with a stroboscopic strip show, and then they would be settled around the poker machines and gambling tables of the casino in Macau, with which the travel agent had also made a deal. The tour would climax in Taiwan, where the farmers would settle down in hot baths with the whores of the sin city of Peitou.

As they travelled on their triple treat they were culturally sterilised and kept under seal. A similar insulation could protect the British lager louts who, on package tours to parts of the concrete Costas* of Spain, enacted what used to be known in the Butlin's Holiday Camps of their parents as 'Cock Week'. Americans can enjoy the beaches, lagoons, lookouts, boat cruises, designer hotels, swimming pools, discos, nightclubs and shopping plazas of Acapulco with scarcely anything to remind them of where they are—apart from the restaurants offering Mexican food, but that is available in most of the motel strips of the United States anyway. (Mexican food is also available in a restaurant in the Marriott Hotel, Cairo, to make Americans feel at home.)

This book is not concerned with people who travel exclusively for one or more of the deadly sins of lust, avarice, gluttony or sloth (lolling around the swimming pool), or, for that matter, shopping, sport or sociability. (To finish the score on the seven deadly sins: *pride* and *envy* can also be connected with sight-seeing tourism, if we come back proud of our own experiences but still envious of the experiences of others; *anger* of course can, for some tourists, be the prime mover.) The book is about tourists who are engaged, at least to some extent, in sightseeing, with an interest in at least some of the following: looking at historic sites and monuments or significant buildings, villages, town squares, boulevards, marketplaces, picturesque quarters, new architectural developments, etc; visiting museums and other exhibitions, and going to theatres, concerts and other kinds of performance ranging from a Palestrina mass to an African rain dance; standing in the presence of (or taking a helicopter flight over) magic landscapes of nature, filled with cultural messages that in Europe go back 300 years, and longer in China and Japan; and getting to know something about the ways of other peoples, whether at the ends of the earth or in the next town.

But sightseeing can be hard to avoid, even if you try. Going to the Kentucky Fried Chicken in Beijing can be sightseeing. If tourists seek sociability outside their hotel, in *taverna, shebeen, danceteria*, or *biergarten*, or the Down Under disco in the floating hotel in Ho Chi

---

* COSTA REPLICA. To attract British package tourists on chartered holiday flights, the Chinese are planning to pour concrete along a seven kilometre crescent of beach on Hainan Island—to turn it into a replica (including neon-lit strips of bars) of the concrete complex of Benidorm on the Costa Blanca, that deals with four million visitors a year.

Minh City, they are sightseeing. Going to a church in someone else's country can be sightseeing. Going to a picturesque market is clearly sightseeing but so, in the Brezhnev era was going to GUM—the 'department store' at one side of Red Square, with its arcades of small shops that became a kind of museum displaying the failures of a stagnant economy. Equally, the invention of skywalks in Minneapolis in the 1960s was a symbol of progress: when you walked the Minneapolis Skyway, a second-level maze of shops, banks and restaurants, inter-connected by walkways, footbridges and escalators floating above the plazas, you were walking into the future.

Even the tourism of *avarice* followed by the Japanese rice farmers can sometimes not prevent sightseeing, While casinos are now even more look-alike than hotels, some remain part of sightseeing. In a place that a little over 100 years ago was only bare rock, with a few goats and scraggly olive trees, the statues and domes of the Casino at Monte Carlo, set on terraces with waving palms, are a celebrated monument to excitement, snobbery and greed. Even gamblers notice where they are when confronted with the glaring neon promises of The Strip at Las Vegas that, again less than 100 years ago, was part of the pale, treeless Nevada Desert. Caesar's Palace is one of the monuments of the Western world.

And the tourism of *lust*? No sightseeing was involved for a Japanese settling down in a hot bath with a whore in Peitou, because the whole arrangement was to keep everything familiarly Japanese. However, a woman visitor to Jamaica who accepts the invitation of one of the male prostitutes to go 'partying', or a male visitor to Bangkok who arranges a package holiday which includes a 'girlfriend' chosen from an album of coloured photographs and, like an Avis car, hired in advance for the whole period, may not be able to avoid some multicultural experience. In some places the red-light district is on the tourist list—as in Amsterdam, where sex shops, sex cinemas and live shows are mixed up with quiet family residences beside picturesque canals while, behind display-case windows with red neon strips, picturesque prostitutes sit on what look like surgical chairs that are good for their backs.

Even *sloth* beside a hotel swimming pool can be a reminder of the swimming pool habits of people from other lands. And as far as sightseeing goes if, at $60 per half-hour, you want to swim with a bottlenose dolphin, it probably doesn't matter whether you do it in the Theatre of the Sea in Florida Keys or in the saltwater lagoon carved out of lava at the Hyatt Waikoloa, Hawaii.* It is hard to go to a beach without realising you are somewhere else.

If you are in Mérida in the Mexican Yucatan, the equivalent of a US dollar buys the cultural experience of an hour's bus trip past fields of the greyish, spiky *henequen* plant that was once the region's main economic support, to an authentic Gulf Coast Mexican beach town that is used by actual Yucatecans. At Progreso you won't enjoy the crystal-clear turquoise water experience of Cancun, Yucatan's commercial answer to Acapulco. At Progreso the water is gritty-green, shallow and warm. But you can eat sweet, freshly caught fish, promenade along the breezy *malecón* looking at the waterfront mansions built by the *henequen* barons in the heyday of this hemp-producing plant, stroll on what was the world's longest pier when Progreso was one of the world's great hemp ports, rest under the *palapa* sun shelters, and walk half a kilometre out to sea without getting your head wet.

(Or so we read in the travel pamphlets. On the day we tried to do all this we spent an hour, in a temperature of 35°C, moving forward in a queue, curled in on itself like a serpent, as buses came and filled up with their patient loads. We felt like people who had saved a dollar to spend a day in Progreso. But when we reached the head of the queue, a couple of impatient Yucatecans broke the barrier, got in ahead of us and took the last seats. In protest, we went back to the hotel swimming pool. We will never watch Yucatecan families eat sweet fish, or promenade along the *malecón*, or wade into the shallow gritty-green sea.)

* * *

A reason for analysing the 'magic' of tourism is that its effects *can* be magical. (That statement is not intended as praise.) I want to suggest that words like 'myth' and 'legend', 'festival' and 'ritual',

---

*SWIMMING WITH HUMANS. At Shark Bay in north-western Australia, humans do not go to swim with dolphins. Dolphins go there and swim with humans. For 30 years, identifiable dolphins have come in almost every day to the shallow water in front of Monkey Mia Beach and visited the swimming humans. Some of them are likely to bring seaweed for dolphin-human games of tug-of-war. A tourist group off Australia's north-eastern coast offers excursions to the Great Barrier Reef to swim with man-eating sharks.

can be as important to the life of the tourist as they were to the lives of the 'natives' whose habits and beliefs were analysed by anthropologists from distant lands, or as they have been in societies in which the supernatural has been the main way of explaining things.

And when we speak of sightseeing tourism we are speaking of art, religion and other entertainments; of the search for the past; the nature of power and the nature of nations; of relations between peoples, of the views they have of themselves, of each other, and of existence in general; of the ways in which humans have devised the realities by which they live—and of the breakdowns in knowledge and understanding that can make fools of us all.

Sightseeing tourism can be part of our search for building up a general intellectual criticism of existence. It can become a liberating and empowering force, rather than a force that can lead to conformity, trivialisation and physical and social destruction.

PART ONE

♦ ♦ ♦

The making of tourism

2.

INVENTING VICTORIA FALLS

◆ ◆ ◆

For most tourists who live outside Africa, the nearly two kilometres of Victoria Falls can seem too out-of-the-way and too expensive to get to, and they do not offer the same celebrity as the falls at Niagara. But they offer a larger curtain of water, and a louder roar. They offer more variety in cataracts and chasms, and therefore a wider range of photographic studies, and they provide a spray 500 metres high that dominates the faded landscape like a forest fire. In the flood season, the mist at a couple of viewing points is so intense that photographs achieve a perfect minimalism. They come out white.

The Falls have offered inspirations for interpreting the messages of nature that range from the heavenly to the infernal. The first Englishman to see them said they provided scenes so lovely that they must have been gazed on by angels. The next Englishman said it was as if streams of brimstone were ascending into the clouds. Apart from a bleak promontory where high winds have reduced the vegetation to sedges and tough grass, the shower of spray has formed two rainforests where one can admire palms and ferns, trees draped with vines and creepers, birds and butterflies in season and, in the morning among the imprints of Reeboks, the footprints of baboon or waterbuck.

And from the bridge that spans the Zambesi and connects Zimbabwe with Zambia, one of the world's most comprehensive views of a romantic chasm offers a range of picturesque clichés—an immense cascade, dark, brooding cliffs, forests of sombre greenery spilling down to the very water's edge and a foaming torrent that swirls into a deadly whirlpool before raging on into a gorge walled by steadfast granite.

For those who do go there, the lack of comparative celebrity becomes part of the magic—you can speak, intimately, of 'Vic Falls', as if it were a member of the family, and you don't have to queue up for the viewpoints. There are no videos of the Falls to look at and there are chances for discoveries. (Thousands may already have made the same discoveries, but that's discovery.) If you get up early enough you can have the place more or less to yourself—along, perhaps, with baboon or waterbuck. And Victoria Falls now has a concern for ecological statements. The cement benches have been replaced by comfortable logs, put beside the track as if they had just fallen there. The metal litter bins have been replaced by upright hollow logs, with LITTER carved into the wood so sympathetically that you may not see it.

A small instant township has appeared—it includes a Wimpy Bar, but not yet a McDonald's. But the Victoria Falls Hotel, in its setting of bougainvillea (from South America), frangipanni (from the West Indies), syringa (from South Africa) and jacaranda (from Brazil), is a rare example of a famous hotel that has been able to create the illusion of the imagined graciousness of the old days (except that the servants no longer grovel), without being authentically seedy (like the Imperial Hotel, Delhi), or anachronistically opulent (like the reconstructed Raffles Hotel in Singapore). It provides comforts unknown in the past, while nurturing an atmosphere reminiscent of the past—although, as with all restored grand hotels, if people from the old days walked in and saw some of the modern clientele, they would think there had been a revolution.

We had a splendid few days at the Victoria Falls Hotel en route from one place to the next. On three successive days we paid our respects to the Falls in three of their moods. We breakfasted on venison liver, lunched beside the swimming pool on fresh fish from the Zambesi River, drank gin-and-tonics in the 'I Presume Bar' and dined on blanquette of crocodile tail. We went on one drive in a Land Rover on which we saw nothing, and another when we watched waterbuck, impala, kudu, warthog, zebra, sable, buffalo and elephant. We visited a well-contrived museum village, run by local people and illustrating Zimbabwe's ethnic groups, and watched two medleys of traditional dance.

We also had the pleasure of not going to the crocodile farm, or the snake farm; of not going whitewater rafting, or whitewater canoeing; and of not booking on the Sundowner Cruise or any of the three Air Safaris. We did have a surreal lunch, though, on a canopied pleasure barge floating along the Zambesi, where it is a smooth-flowing river nearly two kilometres wide and scattered with islands of waving palms. As four of us were served lunch by three Zimbabweans in starched white shirts and black bow ties, a group of hippopotamus drifted with the current on one side—on the other, elephants were eating their way through a small tropical island.

We also had the good luck to be at Victoria Falls when Air Zimbabwe went on strike, so that instead of an hour's flight to Harare we took the night train to Bulawayo and the day train from there—26 hours of reminder that Victoria Falls is a long way from what most people would think of as anywhere. How did this remote place become a tourist attraction? Don't quote figures: the Angel Falls in Venezuela are almost 10 times as high; the Khong Falls in Laos are more than 10 kilometres wide. There are two ecologically unsound intrusions into the sanctity of this nature reserve that give the answer: they are the bridge across the Zambesi gorge, which is now seen as spoiling the view from the Victoria Falls Hotel, and the statue of David Livingstone, 'discoverer' of the Falls. (This statue now seems an assault on a nature reserve where the litter bins are natural hollow logs.) These monuments provide ways of talking about two of the beginnings of tourism.

THE BRIDGE

The railway came to Victoria Falls in 1905, as part of the optimism of the British imperial dream for a 'Cape to Cairo' rail track, which in fact got no further than what is now Zaire. The spanning of the Zambesi gorge became one of the legends of British achievement: in the textbook of imperial geography that I studied at primary school, it was the bridge that was in the foreground of the photograph. That was what one was expected to look at: one of the Falls' cascades provided picturesque background. And it was the coming of the railway that gave Victoria Falls its existence in the tourist imagination.

The growth of tourism in the 18th century began with the improvement of roads and coach services, but large-scale tourism could not have happened without the big railway systems that, by the end of the 19th century, were serviced by 100,000 locomotives. Behind the magic of tourism there were steel rails and iron laws of profit and loss. The first Thomas Cook tour, in 1841, a temperance excursion on England's Midland Counties Railways, was possible only because the railway company wanted to sell seats. Cook's Tours would not have existed without railway companies—and then steamship companies—wanting to do deals.

When the African railway was planned, Cecil Rhodes, who had the tourist imagination of a great empire builder, insisted that the bridge should pass near the spray from the Falls. (The framing of views from railway carriage windows had already become part of tourism.) With the same imagination, the railway company built a small hotel and began to invent Victoria Falls as a tourist destination that would entice bottoms onto railway seats. In 1908, the Durban office of Thomas Cook announced its first railway excursion to Victoria Falls, now 'one of the sights of the world' (for £25). Ten years later, the hotel was working at a rate of nearly 4000 guests a year.

At first, rickshaws and donkeys carried visitors to the Falls; then the hotel constructed a narrow gauge rail track (later dismantled for ecological reasons), with the trolleys pulled on the uphill grade by Africans. 'Curio shops' were established (by Europeans). New artifacts were invented to stock them. In the hotel, electricity and fans were put in. New wings were added. A dance floor was laid down in the centre of a large dining room with pink walls and white pilasters leading up to a high, coffered ceiling (now restored). A swimming pool (with 'azure blue water') was built in 1928, and a large courtyard was planted with ('deep green') mango trees. A room was built in which to drink cocktails; and another in which to play bridge. Terraces were constructed and from these guests could sit in wicker chairs and look out at the bridge and the clouds of spray. By then, Imperial Airways was using the Zambesi as a stopover for its seaplane service from London to South Africa.

Now Victoria Falls is on the promotion programs of international airlines, and the schedules of the coach companies and safari operators. The Victoria Falls Publicity Association, set up in 1967, has added new images to those that make Victoria Falls a holy tourist place—images that also make it an entrancing 'holiday place'. The township now includes hotels, chalets, a caravan park, mini-hostels, tour companies, tennis courts, fishing camps, conference facilities, a golf course and a casino.

* * *

The story of Victoria Falls is a miniature of what began to happen to tourism at the end of last century, as the booming railway and passenger liner services competed in providing safe, fast travel for the comfortably-off middle classes, who could now acquire a taste for holidays by the seaside, at spas, in the mountains, at resorts offering winter sports, or close to romantic landscapes or romantic reminders of the past. Excursions for the common people were also developing in some countries—a new habit that was almost universally despised by their betters. (In England, the word 'tripper' was invented to describe the kind of cheap excursionist, usually out only for one day, who, according to an 1890s critic, was likely 'to leave only desolation and paper behind him'. Almost as soon as modern tourism began, some tourists decided they were better than others.) In both cases, tourism had become possible because people had the money and the leisure, but middle class people were able to travel further and for longer periods because they had more money and more leisure.

By the 1880s, about a million tourists a year were already visiting Switzerland, almost all by train. Grand Hotels were being built (and the humble beginnings of cheap accommodation for trippers), and soon the hotels' illustrated luggage labels and the coloured posters of the railway and steamship companies, along with the new kinds of postcards, would join Baedeker and other guidebooks in categorising the world into a few dozen major clichés. Thomas Cook & Son had become an international organisation, and, although the president of the American Express freight firm had declared that there was 'no profit in the tourist business', other travel agencies had been established.

By the beginning of the 20th century the tourist business had many of its present characteristics—but not its present scale, nor, except for early starters such as Switzerland, the grandness of vision, or the rapacity, that now prompts national and regional governments and the governments of many cities, and even small towns, to establish tourist authorities with the mission of bringing in more tourist money. In most countries tourism is, or is dreamed of becoming, the first, second or third largest industry, with calculations of 'spin-offs' and 'multiplier effects' down there on the bottom line. The people who package tours or run the airlines (or what is left of the railways and ocean cruises); who are the entrepreneurs of theme parks, festivals and other extravaganzas; who control the travel agencies, the souvenir trades, the hotels, restaurants and shops; or dream up the marketing propaganda, may or may not have motives of public edification. But they have one thing in common. They are in it for the money. And, those who have the care of museums, historic sites, zoos, national parks, arts festivals, folk revivals, theatres, concert halls and certain national institutions are now also expected to speak the language of money when they seek government support.

THE STATUE

Near a bank of the Zambesi, just at the point where the wide, leisurely river quickens its pace before becoming 'the world's largest curtain of falling water', a yellowish statue of David Livingstone stands, arms akimbo. Words around the base of the statue describe Livingstone as 'Missionary, Explorer, Liberator', and he is also proclaimed 'The Discoverer of Victoria Falls'. 'Solemnly dedicated to the high Christian aims which inspired Livingstone', the statue was put up in 1955 by the Southern African Caledonian Societies. They got these messages out just in time. We now recognise that the idea of Livingstone discovering the Victoria Falls is ridiculous. The Tonga people who lived near them when Livingstone arrived had their own name for the Falls, and their own idea of the significance of this falling water: evidence of human relations with the Falls goes back to stone choppers and hand axes found in gravel beside the river bank. Some of our Lower Paleolithic predecessors were there more than a million years ago.

Throughout the world there are reminders, like the Livingstone statue, of the imperial magic by which things did not exist until they were seen by a European. On the 'It's A Small World' ride in Disneyland, as you pass the audioanamatronic representations of Europe and move towards Asia, you have been warned that you are departing into 'mysterious Asia . . . the exotic world of the Orient, once remote, strange, little known except to a few of the hardiest adventurers', as if Asia existed only in the European imagination.

In Lisbon, across the river from the monumental statue of Christ the King (1959), there is the Monument to the Discoveries, erected in 1960. Prince Henry the Navigator stands on the stylised prow of a ship, beneath stylised sails and a sword bearing a cross—symbolising both military might and faith in God. He is showing the way to statues of colonisers and warriors, cartographers and cosmographers, sea captains and artists, chroniclers and men of God: magicians all. It is as if most of Africa and Asia were not there until the Portuguese rounded the Cape of Good Hope and moved on to India, China and the Malay archipelago—an achievement that was followed by the Spanish creation of a 'New World' that had been there all the time.*

But, in a sense, Africa, Asia and the Americas were *not* there until they were reclassified by Europeans because, in re-imagining them, the Europeans gave them a new 'reality'. This kind of re-imagining was later to become an essential process of tourism.

* * *

One of the insights of travel can come from contemplating material reminders of the decline of empires, and you can do plenty of that, standing beside the Zambesi looking at the Livingstone statue. But the word 'discovery' goes beyond speaking as if the world's natural features came into existence only when Europeans saw them. In naming this body of falling water after a distant monarch who had never seen a large waterfall, let alone Africa, Livingstone was

---

* **THE 'DISCOVERERS'** may have carried cargoes of bombast, supported by cannons, but their expeditions could not have happened without leaps of cleverness. In the maritime museums in Lisbon, Amsterdam and Greenwich there are wonderful reminders of intelligence and intellectual daring in models of boats such as the Portugese *caravel* and the Dutch *fluyt*. And in old sea charts and almanacs, and all the gleaming compasses, astrolabes, quadrants and chronometers.

engaging in an act of appropriation through *naming*.

When our daughter was in second class she kept a 'nature book' in which she wrote descriptions of things from the natural world that interested her—her first cicada, for example—and then drew them. She took this book with her when we went on a picnic south of Sydney. As we drove out on to a headland, we reminded her that this was the Pacific Ocean. She wrote into her nature book 'TODAY I DISCOVERED THE PACIFIC OCEAN', and coloured it blue. It wasn't the first time she had seen this ocean—she had swum in it from Sydney beaches. But what she had done was to conceptualise it in her own way.

As Paul Carter shows in *The Road to Botany Bay*, when explorers and then settlers moved into the territories of indigenous peoples they drew maps and gave names to certain natural features. By doing this, they (as I would put it) cast new spells over the land and re-created it in the way they wanted it to be. They brought the landscape into a new order of being. To the different kinds of people who lived near this part of the Zambesi River over the last million years or so, the waterfall was unlikely to have had the overwhelming predominance that the European imagination gave it when it was 'discovered' (viz named) by Livingstone. It is now one of 'the sights of the world'. As we follow the maps that the discoverers drew, we risk continuing their acts of conquest.

Naming can be one of the essential ingredients of tourism. The 'discoverers', and then the *savants*, were the creators of a world that was examinable. Before them, what the whole world was like was just a matter of conjecture. Now, if we have the resources, we can go and have a look. And that's good.

But one of the greatest despairs of the critics of tourism (which can make them see sightseeing as senseless) is that they believe we can no longer travel on an 'expedition' in which we can find out something new for ourselves, or do any new 'naming'.

3.

MAGIC AGENDAS

◆ ◆ ◆

CASTING SPELLS

The great namers of tourism were not the explorers, but the magicians of the guidebooks and they had begun casting magic circles in the century before Livingstone 'discovered' Victoria Falls. In the 18th century the first guidebooks were giving instructions about the best waterfalls or town squares or mountains or boulevards to look at, and the best places from which to look at them. As guidebooks developed, they went on from telling people what to look at, and in what order, to telling them also *how* something was to be seen. This resulted in a kind of 'framing', in which whatever was looked at became isolated from the rest of the world.

When they were positioned at the appropriate place and looking at a specified natural scene, sightseers were expected to appraise it exactly as if it were a painting. To begin with, they were required to find in it the 'sublime' (a theatrical sense of awe) or the 'picturesque' (arranging the scene so that it produced simple harmonies). To do this, they could be assisted by engravings and lithographs which told them what to see. Later there were postcards, travel ads and brochures and the whole industry of travel photography to bring the world to your coffee table. Now we are required to photograph the scene so that it looks like a postcard.

Because they told people what to look at and what to see when they looked at it, guidebooks became the principal agency of spellbinding. As they became more complex, following the lead of Baedeker, they were to cast their spells through cabalistic signs—in hierarchies of asterisks and of variations between bold type, capitals and italics. Michelin added colours as an aid to this magic. Signs of green, brown and blue on the map of a whole country could declare what was 'worth the journey', what was 'worth a detour', and what was merely 'interesting'. Most of a country was left blank. In an entire city, or perhaps an entire nation, only a few views and vistas, a few buildings, monuments or museums (and only a few objects within those museums) are all we have to 'do'.

The result can be a miracle in which guidebooks obliterate everything in a society that doesn't get a mention, even in light type, in a guidebook. As Roland Barthes said in his often-quoted essay in *Mythologies* on the *Guide Bleu* to Spain: 'to select only monuments suppresses at one stroke the reality of the land and that of its people'.

To these simplifications were added those of the guided tour. To begin with, guided tours could allow for some personal adventure on the way. But as they became more mechanised, their simplifications made even easier the miracle of passing through a society as if it was not there. Tourists just had to follow the itinerary, with what Erving Goffman described as its 'ceremonial agenda of obligatory rites'; an agenda of magic circles.

Magical landscapes

To give examples of what this can mean, I have chosen three instances of the magical spells that can be performed by tourism. They are the transformations of landscapes, rituals and monuments into tourist spectacles . . .

Tourist landscapes are those that have been clothed with fame and human satisfaction. One should understand that in any case 'landscapes' are entirely a human concept, created out of the conventions of our senses and from the meanings and habits of particular cultures. There are no landscapes in nature, and what is seen as a landscape varies from culture to culture. That is why, if people go for a walk in the country, they may see different things.

But with tourist landscapes we are all expected to see the same thing.

In the 19th century landscapes became 'romantic' and most of the landscapes of European tourism are still creations of this 19th century European romantic imagination. Nature had become a vital force that could instruct and ennoble the human soul. Along with a thirst for the past, this romantic creation of landscape was a principal prompting of the growth of the 19th century tourist business, and, in the United States, it dominated it. Before the romantic movement, the Swiss saw their Alps as a wilderness of ice and snow, haunted by troubled spirits. Then writers found a spiritual quality in the Alps, painters invented their sublimity, and some local doctors began to boost their health properties (especially when taken in conjunction with goats' whey). The Alps were transfused with the human quality of grandeur, and in Switzerland itself they became an expression, in four languages, of the freedom-loving character of the Swiss people.

Throughout Europe, mountains and valleys, woods and lakes, panoramas and ocean shores were 'invented' by artists to celebrate various national souls, first in paintings and drawings, and later in photographs. If you stood in the presence of these views they offered freedom, peace, wisdom, sublimity, and general moral and physical regeneration as well as national definition. Some of these physical features got into national anthems. Some of the great landscape paintings were displayed in museums—sometimes, as with the Tretyakov Gallery in Moscow, in museums founded specifically to show off national art.

If you saw yourself in terms of the soft tones and mists of Lake Baloton, you were a Hungarian; if you seemed part of the land of the ox-cart lumbering along a quiet country road, you were a Romanian; if you lived in a land of perpetual harvest where women worked in the fields, you were probably a Bulgarian. Russia was a land of forests and rivers, alternating between sadness and hope. Especially as nocturnes, in the Scandinavian countries the wilderness of trees and lakes provided symbols of noble simplicity and quiet grandeur.

Such transformation by painting passed on to the New World. In their style of painting landscapes of the Andes, Melchor Perez Holguin and his followers defined the true character of Bolivians, and their paintings still affirm the Bolivian character in the Museo

Nacional de Arte in La Paz. With *plein air* enthusiasm, 'the Australian impressionists' set off a fashion for a sun-washed, faded Australia, through landscapes of light blue hills, yellow grass and the spareness of the eucalypt. In Canada, 'the Group of Seven' found the true Canada in gaudy, robust pictures of raw wilderness. It was a painting of *The Grand Canyon of the Yellowstone*, as an epitome of United States vision, that helped persuade Congress to establish the Yellowstone National Park in 1872, the first of the national parks that have provided metaphors of what it might mean to be an American.

New visions of nature provided new tourist opportunities. By the 1940s deserts had moved into the imagination of Australian landscape painters as exemplifying some of the Australian spirit, and by the 1970s visits to Australia's 'Red Heart', especially Ayers Rock (Uluru), had become part of the pitch of Australia's tourist business. When wetlands became interesting an entirely new kind of national park was created in Florida in 1947, where 400,000 surviving hectares of mangrove swamps, hummocks of matted trees, saw grass marsh, mosquitoes, snakes, alligators and a variety of fish and birds became the Everglades National Park. The park came to provide eco-trails, some by power boat, car or tram—others by canoeing, boardwalks, marked foot trails or guided 'swamp tromping'. Now you can go 'eco-cruising' in a five-star ship for 3600 kilometres down the Amazon and then up the east coast to Caracas, Venezuela, accompanied by botanists, ornithologists, anthropologists, marine biologists and historians who provide a program of seminars, and lead expeditions in Zodiac dinghies. On an Antarctic holiday, inflatable dinghies take tourists, along with their rubbish bags, from the ship, with its icebreaker hull, to the penguin or seal colonies.

At times, physical layout can make any kind of alternative viewing almost impossible. You don't just turn a bend of the Iguaçu River and discover the Iguaçu Falls. The Falls are part of almost all programs for 'doing' South America and when you get there you don't wander around as if you were William Wordsworth or Jean-Jacques Rousseau or Henry David Thoreau. The manner of seeing the Falls is systematised into a series of ceremonial progresses, and how you photograph them is usually predetermined. A web of concrete paths and catwalks leaves a feeling of unfulfillment unless you have been *over*, *under* and *into* the Falls, and seen them in their

Argentinean, Brazilian and Paraguayan manifestations. Along one path there is a building where you can look not at the Falls, but at a video of the Falls.

The Mariposa Sequoia Grove in California is an example of an enchanted wood, tourist-style. Sequoias, among the largest and oldest living things on earth, provide one of the natural wonders of California's tourist industry, but all that is left of the particular kind known as 'giant sequoias', which used to grow over much of the northern hemisphere, are some groves on the western slopes of the Sierra Nevada. The Mariposa Grove is a particular tourist attraction because it contains 'the Grizzly Giant', the second most famous giant sequoia in California, and therefore the world. (Age: at least 3800 years. Height: 61 metres. Girth: 28.7 metres.) I inspected the Mariposa Grove in a tram, passing the tall, fat, rusty-brown trees through a mist of commentary from the driver, in which there were pauses of clarity for photo opportunities with suggestions about photo angles, and occasional stops, because unless you measure yourself against a sequoia you don't recognise how large it is. There was talk of death—of forest fires and snowdrifts—but the tone was mainly upbeat: out of the sufferings of fire and snow comes the giant sequoia. Some of the trees were given human character and a few were given names.

Among the martyred trees that lay there, dead, 'the Fallen Monarch' was especially recommended for photography. A hollow tree is 'the Telescope Tree'. Two trees that have grown together are 'the Faithful Couple'. 'The American Legion Tree' has been dedicated to the unknown dead of the Great War. The central moment in our journey was the act of homage to the Grizzly Giant. When the tram stopped for us to walk down a ceremonial path to pay our respects, one woman hurried down the path without showing much interest. When she reached the Grizzly Giant she didn't look at the tree, but at the large board beside it which gave the description we had already heard from the guide. She photographed the large board.

* * *

Veneration for nature is even older in Asia than in Europe. It is an endemic part of the Indian imagination, in forms embedded for a couple of thousand years longer than European romanticism. The feelings that tourists can have when confronted by famous views may be compared to the Hindu concept of *darshana*, the mysterious ecstasy generated in the presence of a holy place. The holy places of Hinduism are given force by their auspicious nearness to natural caves, groves of trees, hot springs, plateaux, mountain peaks and the sacred waters of rivers, lakes and pools. Retreating to a forest is a force for spiritual regeneration and immersing oneself in the Ganges, a river that fell from heaven as a gift of purity and power, cleanses the souls of the living and liberates the souls of the dead.

It was the Chinese, in the Sung Dynasty 1000 years ago, who invented landscape painting, finding meanings in misty forests, scraggy cliffs, lakes and waterfalls and awesome (sublime) mountains, and the Japanese who meticulously ritualised nature cults, from 'withered landscape' rock gardens in Zen temples to mountain pilgrimages. Now, if you live in Tokyo, hours away from Nature's mystery, you can buy a video of Mount Fuji or some other renowned natural feature and leave it playing as a background image. If you yearn for the sounds of nature, a telephone service provides a continuous recording of bird calls and insect noises at so many yen a minute.

From rituals to cultural shows

In some resort hotels in Fiji, the weekly 'traditional feast' beside the swimming pool often begins with a 'war dance', put on by locals who shake some spears at the hotel guests. Now they are Methodists, but when their predecessors developed the dances of which these shows are relics the main purpose of war was to capture some people—women and children were easier to catch—and, at a very large and lively traditional feast, highly significant in its effects on social stability, to cook them and eat them. Almost all tourist cultural shows transmute into 'entertainment' activities that, in their creation, were meant for something else.

In the nightly cultural show at the Silom Village Trade Centre, Bangkok, the main turn is an episode from the *Ramayana*, one of the world's greatest and most influential epics as one of the bases of Hindu wisdom (which also spreads its enlightenment in Muslim

Java and in Buddhist Thailand in the special Thai form of the *Ramakien*). The episode selected is the one in which Rama captures a deer: they have chosen this episode because part of the hunt is pursued through the audience, and this provides photo opportunities for the tourists.

If it is alive, pageantry can summarise part of a culture. But revived purely as a tourist performance it stands for little more than quaintness. When the Belgian National Tourist Office attempted to package Belgium as the land of the 'festival' a few years ago it produced a brochure, *Belgium: Festivals and Folklore*, listing 260 national or local ceremonial occasions that took in variously bonfires, feasts, processions, carnivals, merry dances, fireworks, torchlight parades, thanksgivings, effigy burnings, blessings, *fêtes*, cavalcades, folk dancing, passion plays, tree plantings, tournaments, floral parades, annual fairs, flower shows, *tableaux* and military marches. But whether it was the annual onion battle at Aalst, the festival of the cats in Ieper, or the charcoal burners' feast at Yvoir, these celebrations were dead—what was reborn was caricature of how colourful it was to live in 'the past'.

The transformation that creates 'landscapes' is value-added. But when we appropriate rituals and ceremonies intended to affirm communal beliefs, and turn them into cultural shows, so much meaning can be drained out of them that they become value-subtracted.

In the same marketing position as the weekly cannibal dance put on at a Fiji resort hotel (although commercially in a different order of magnitude) is the exploitation of royalty in London. Buckingham Palace and the Tower are two of the highspots for something like 150 tourist coaches each day, and the crowds watching the Changing of the Guard are so large that in 1991 the transport authorities asked for the ceremony to be rescheduled, to help improve traffic flows. What were once the symbols of entrenched imperial power, and earlier of the divine rights of princes, now help the balance of payments. And while the royalty in Europe's other six remaining kingdoms can, to tourists, seem merely quaint, in London the Foot Guards at the Palace, the Household Cavalry at the Horse Guards and the Beefeaters in the Tower of London juxtapose old power with the celebrity of the Windsors as the greatest of all family soap operas.

The magic of monuments

A complex of squares in Sofia brings together some of the principal symbolic structures of Bulgaria. In 1990, there were riots demanding that the ruby-red star glowing from the top of one building should be pulled down, and early one morning the body of Georgi Dimitrov, founder of Bulgaria as a people's republic, was taken out of its mausoleum in one of these squares and cremated. Things wouldn't really have seemed to change until the symbols in these Sofia squares had been seen to change. In these squares you can also find preserved, in unlikely circumstances, three old assemblages of stone and tile that nobody is going to pull down: they are as essential to a democratic Bulgaria as they were to a communist Bulgaria and a monarchic Bulgaria—because, although never intended to commemorate anything, they have become revered affirmations of Bulgarian nationality.

One of them sticks up in the centre of a square across from a department store and the Grand Balkan Hotel. It is a red-tiled roof. In the pedestrian underpass you find that this roof is supported by fragments of three walls in the middle of a courtyard shared with an outdoor cafe. This bizarre interruption to the staidness of the heart of Sofia is St Petka, a tiny 14th century church, restored and conserved as a reminder of Bulgaria's creation of Slav civilisation. (Elsewhere in Sofia are reminders of Bulgaria's invention of the renaissance and the reformation.)

Across the street from St Petka and the outdoor cafe, in the courtyard of the Grand Balkan Hotel, is a small, tiled rotunda. This began as a 4th century Roman building, but became a church, then a mosque under the Ottoman occupation, and a church again after the liberation. It stands in the hotel's courtyard as a reminder of the glorious struggles against tyranny in Bulgaria's past.

The third is in the adjoining September 9 Square. When developers started excavating here they found they were digging against part of the old fortified wall that surrounded the town from the 2nd to the 14th century. After a crisis of urban environmentalism (all this happened under the communists) the excavations proceeded but, as a compromise, some remains of the wall were incorporated in a monument. A low relief sculpture in bronze shows Krum, a famous 9th century warrior, approaching the city gate in the historic action in which he added Sofia to the land of the Bulgars.

These three structures have become 'monuments' that stand for something. Objects developed for one purpose are transformed into tourist spectacles that would have astounded, disgusted, amused or terrified the people who created them.*

The enchantment of tourism is to turn inanimate matter into meaning, by transforming it into an historical site or by putting it behind glass in a museum. Whether it is conserving the three miles of elegant facades of St Petersburg's Nevsky Prospect, or purchasing the whole town of Williamsburg, Virginia, a model of 18th century British colonial life in North America. Or transforming the Machu Picchu ruins in Peru into 'the lost city of the Incas' (and the top archaeological tourist attraction in South America until tales of terrorists, pickpockets, hotel lobby con-men and snatch-and-grab thieves frightened people off), or presenting, as sacred trophies of British civilisation, the Parthenon marbles in the British Museum. Or whether it is the processional way and Ishtar Gate built in Babylon by Nebuchadnezzar II, taken apart at its site and put together again in the Pergamon Museum, Berlin . . . all of these become objects that stand for something else.

They commemorate persons, ideas, social classes, events, epochs and styles, and if they purport to be historical they are anachronistic (in the original sense): the present is used to explain the relics of the past. Then the meanings given to the past can be used to justify aspects of the present; in the right season, they might justify beliefs about how things should now change. Recognising the Bulgars as the founders of Slav civilisation can mean that Bulgarians can still act in the proud spirit of Krum.

The temples of the Parthenon were not built as a ruin celebrating

---

* MAKING TOURIST SITES SACRED. In *The Tourist*, Dean MacCannell gives four stages of 'sacralisation' of a tourist site. Firstly, it is named. Then it is 'framed' and elevated (given its status as a site). After that comes 'enshrinement' in which the framing of the site becomes significant. Then comes the mechanical reproduction (postcards, souvenirs etc). After that you can stand in its presence as a holy tourist place.

Western civilisation.* When the first restaurant went up in 1916 on a wharf in San Francisco it was not intended to grow into 'Fishermen's Wharf', so celebrated an emblem of San Francisco that 85 per cent of the city's tourists now go there. Ivan the Terrible, when he ordered a throne plated with ivory, had not intended to provide the Kremlin's Armoury Museum with an example of exquisite 16th century Russian craftwork. The Emir's Palace and the rest of the Old City in Kano, Nigeria, were not built as a monument to the power of the Hausa 1000 years ago; they were built as part of that power, and, at the time, taken for granted. When a moated castle was begun in the 13th century near Maidstone, Kent, it was not intended to become Leeds Castle, number three in the British stately homes business, with a grotto, a golf course and a conference facility. When what became Australia's most hated penal settlement was built at Port Arthur, in what is now Tasmania, it was not intended to provide a monument to colonial architectural style or the occasion for a pleasant day's outing from Hobart.

Even monuments built as monuments can be transmuted in meaning and become monuments celebrating something else. In 1893 a memorial was put up in London to honour the great English philanthropist and social reformer, the Earl of Shaftesbury, for his concern for the poor and in particular his reforms limiting the exploitation of child labour. Its central symbolic device was an aluminium figure of the Angel of Christian Charity. This was transmuted in popular meaning into a statue of Eros and in this form it became a symbol of Piccadilly Circus, itself a symbol of London. So the Angel of Christian Charity became the statue of a god of love that you must 'do' when you are in London.

---

* THE PARTHENON AS A MONUMENT TO POLLUTION. The preservation of the Parthenon has now become part of its meaning—in an epic story of the perils of acid rain, of the encrustation of the marble that came with air pollution, of remedying earlier botched restoration by replacement of the iron clamps which had eroded and cracked the stone, of the gradual making of replicas of all the sculptures and the preservation of the originals in a nitrogenous atmosphere in a museum, and of the reconstruction of the Erechtheion by using new marble to fill out the old.

A RADIANCE OF CELEBRITY

At the beginning of the 16th century, when Kyoto was being rebuilt after being devastated in Japan's most senseless civil war, someone designed a new rock garden for the temple at Ryōan-ji. It was a rectangle of white gravel with 15 stones beside a low, brown earthen wall. There are a number of these austere, lonely gardens—'withered landscapes' (*kare-sansui*)—in Kyoto's medieval Zen temples, and for more than five centuries no-one had any special interest in Ryōan-ji. It was noted only for its pond, a model of late 12th century refinement. Because of the mandarin ducks that lived on the pond, Ryōan-ji became known as the Temple of the Mandarin Ducks. When modern tourism came to Kyoto, although guidebooks did list other rock gardens as exemplars of stillness and simplicity, none of them gave attention to the small rock garden in the Temple of the Mandarin Ducks.

Then, in the 1930s, the Ryōan-ji garden was 'discovered'. It was proclaimed to be famous. It became famous. All the coach parties stop there.

It is now declared symbolic of the withered landscape, symbolic of Zen, symbolic of the simplicity of Japanese taste and, if you wish, of the mysteries of existence. If you are in Kyoto you *must* sit on the steps of the wooden veranda of the rock garden of Ryōan-ji, ponder the garden's or life's meaning, and feel better for it.

On my first visit I had no revelations, but I sat on the veranda steps and enjoyed pale sunshine lighting up patterns in white gravel, noticed shaded intricacies of clumps of moss, and was reassured by the creak of the veranda's dark wooden boards. As recommended, I then considered the garden's relation to modern abstractionist painting. After that, I went on to some other *kare-sansui* gardens and recognised that any one of them might equally well have had the fame that went to Ryōan-ji.

One of the enchantments of tourism is, simply, celebrity. Certain objects and places are framed within a radiance of fame that drives us on, all over the place, to stand in its presence—and, sometimes, to stand on its presence. In 1992 the number of tourist 'expeditions' that climbed to the summit of Mount Everest reached five in one day. The Nepal government decided to increase fees and cover itself for the costs of removing the rubbish—which, by then, included oxygen cylinders, an abandoned helicopter and a corpse.

* * *

The *Mona Lisa*, in its bulletproof shrine in the Louvre, is so famous for its fame that queues make it impossible, in any serious sense, to see it. The *Mona Lisa* is not the world's greatest painting. (What would that mean?) It is Europe's most celebrated painting. Its celebrity was created by 19th century obsequiousness to the renaissance, followed by the scandal of its theft when it disappeared for two years, followed by the fun made of it by the Dadaists and then by later generations of wits and advertisers. And, now, by the sheer momentum of tourist desire.

Near Cairo there are something like 70 pyramids, and throughout Egypt there are countless sphinxes. Yet 'The Pyramids' means the three at Giza, and 'The Sphinx' means the sphinx beside them, with the 230-centimetre incision that is seen as its enigmatic smile (which is simply the standard mouth of Old Kingdom statuary). And what happens to us when we get there? An impression of size and a feeling of fame, but not the fame of the pharaohs. It is the fame of Napoleon Bonaparte, who brought the pyramids into the European imagination, and of Thomas Cook, who helped Europeans get there. Paved roads connect them. Buses take us from one to the other. A visit becomes a preoccupation in defending oneself against the attacks of the peddlers and cameliers, who pester visitors with a force unknown anywhere else in Egypt, so that a visit to the pyramids can be marked mainly by a ride on a camel, or even, more comfortably, being photographed on a stuffed camel—although the camel is not even the typical mode of Egyptian transport. If one wants to be photographed on the characteristic Egyptian riding animal, one should sit on a small donkey.

Less than 30 kilometres further on there is Sakkara, where the richness of tombs is matched only by Luxor, yet the fame of 'The Pyramids' and 'The Sphinx' can dazzle out of consideration the carvings and paintings, hieroglyphs and architectural inventions of Sakkara. Here, one can still see the first pyramid ever built, designed in the third millennium BC, and the first major building in the world made entirely of stone. In Sakkara we are in the presence of the birth of the monumental. From here on a clear day, when the wind is blowing away the muck coming out of the cement factories, one can see straight across to the pyramids of Giza and imagine a whole vast plain of dozens of pyramids, complete and gleaming in white limestone.

It is almost physically impossible to visit Cairo for the first time and not be photographed in front of the Great Pyramid. The coaches now also go to Sakkara, but it is still easy to go to Cairo and not visit Sakkara.

Consider the kind of monument that the Great Wall of China has been turned into. Under the slogan 'Love our Motherland and Restore the Great Wall', a stretch of derelict wall a couple of hours drive from Beijing was chosen for some hundreds of metres of reconstruction, and then put into a tourist package that includes a picnic lunch at the Ming Tombs and a stroll down the Sacred Way. At the base of the wall, near the bus and car parks, there is a nest of Great Wall Souvenir Shops, with a big sign saying, in a number of languages: IF YOU HAVEN'T CLIMBED THE GREAT WALL YOU HAVEN'T LIVED. On Sundays, tourists coagulate into an almost immovable mass as they engage in the ritual essential to 'doing' the Great Wall—climbing to the highest point to say you've been there. Even on days so cold that your camera freezes, the views are splendid, but there are splendid views all over China: what matters is that you have 'done the Great Wall', an act as significant as photographing Table Mountain to show that you have 'done' South Africa, photographing the sunset over Manila Bay to show that you have 'done' the Philippines, or photographing the Obelisk in Buenos Aires to show that you have 'done' Argentina.

There is a regular round-flight tour—Delhi, Agra, Khajuraho, Varanasi, and back to Delhi—which makes it possible to 'do' India in six days. A special promotion in Australia in 1990 allowed for 'doing' the world in 21 days. It included agenda items such as elephant polo in the princely state of Rajasthan, a sumptuous Berber feast in Morocco, a glamour visit to England's famed Royal Ascot, exotic rickshaw rides in Kathmandu, the unique White Nights Festival in Leningrad, adventurous river trips in the wilds of Borneo and a lunch you will never forget with a NASA astronaut at Cape Canaveral.

EXORCISING TOURISM

Criticising the idea of 'doing' the Pyramids, or the Great Wall, or the Taj Mahal, or the Obelisk in Buenos Aires—not to mention 'doing' India or the world—should be carried out with tact. Some people are likely to find it snobbish and selfish if you try to detach yourself from such ambitions, especially if you have 'done' a fair bit of sightseeing yourself. The questions of the awe and resonance with which some monuments can be approached—and what that might mean—is taken up later in this book. What I'll say here is that we can never 'do' a country, or a city, or even a street, and to believe that we have 'done' a monument by standing briefly in its presence and ticking it off on an itinerary is foolish and petty. There can be all kinds of worthwhile reasons for wanting to look at celebrated monuments, but never merely for their celebrity, unless it is the celebrity itself we are studying. (Without their celebrity some are not worth any time at all, except as examples of the folly of celebrity.)

But there is a strategy that can be applied generally in sightseeing. I'll take Victoria Falls as an example. Unless you work yourself out so thoroughly—swimming, playing tennis, kayaking, or game fishing—that you are too exhausted to remember where you are, even a few days at the Victoria Falls Hotel is an example of how difficult it is 'just to have a holiday'. It can also be an example of how one can enjoy tourism all the more if we know how to encourage ourselves to do it critically, taking things as they come, but also thinking about the intellectual shadows that surround them.

If you pay tribute to the Falls by going to the viewing stations, or if you walk through the rainforests, then you are negotiating with the European traditions of romantic landscape. And if you hire a Land Rover to spy on the animals, you are entering the whole dialogue of what it means to be natural, and what our relation is to all the other living things. At a place where the rubbish bins are hollow logs, you cannot avoid being part of 'the environment debate'. By paying even the slightest attention to the Livingstone statue, or the 'I Presume Bar', or the dishes on the menu with Livingstone allusions, you are moving in the margins of historical theorising, and you are in them again if you have any views on the authenticity of the hotel's restoration. As in any other hotel on the international circuit, there can be the interest of meeting people from other places, but there are also the problems of defining yourself in relation to Zimbabweans in terms of curio shops, a museum village, two performances of traditional dances and giving a tip to the doorman in the funny hat.

I don't believe in the occult. Even if there are mysteries,

contradictions and unknowns we don't need gods and supernatural forces to explain them. Yet I use the word 'magic' to describe the transmutations of tourism. This is because since humans can believe in magic it therefore has effects. 'Magic' is also a useful word because mystification and, for that matter, legerdemain exist and there is plenty of evidence of them in the tourist business. I also use the word because of our peculiarly human talent for creating wonder and meaning. But also because if we understand that the wonders and transformations of tourism are nothing more than magic, this means that if we challenge them, they go away.

Intelligent tourists can exorcise the spells cast around celebrated objects or activities and make their own transmutation. Hey presto, you redefine them as you choose. If you stand on the bank of the Zambesi and confront the Livingstone statue, you can look at it with the detachment with which Europeans used to regard the strange objects that had come out of Africa into glass cases in museums. You might see the statue as an imperialist charm, by whose magic the Caledonian Societies of Southern Africa claimed for themselves the world's largest curtain of falling water. One hope for sightseeing as an intelligent and useful pastime is that we can become exorcists—and, paradoxically, by this, add to tourism's charms.

THE OZYMANDIAS FACTOR

Contemplating the actual mysteries of many of the things we look at as tourists can lift us out of the pseudo-precision of magic—including the pseudo-precision of the spiel of the guides. There can be nothing more real than a mystery. The example I am about to give is from the Mayan relics in Yucatan . . .

Progreso, the Yucatan beach town we didn't get to because of bus queue jumpers, was founded as a port for exporting hemp to manufacturers of rope and twine. The hemp came from *haciendas* owned by Spaniards and it made them so much money that, along with the churches and palaces built by the conquerors in the 16th century, the boulevard of mansions created by the hemp barons as 'the Champs Élysées of the Yucatan' is now part of the tourist spectacle of Mérida.

Their wealth came from growing hemp cheaply by using the labour of the despised Maya Indians who were, in effect, as an apparently inferior race, their slaves. Yet, by the middle of the 19th century, European scholars had developed theories that the awesome ruins of the grand buildings that the Spanish had found were not relics of the 'lost civilisation' of a vanished people, but the ruins of buildings constructed by the ancestors of the despised Mayas.

After United States archaeological teams dug away dirt from old sites and excavated new ones in the forests and brushlands (and looters raided other sites, selling stuff to collectors), scholars built up a new field of study from examining the buildings themselves, the calendars and astrological texts, the wall paintings, ceramics and carvings, and, later, hieroglyphs on wall inscriptions and in the four bark paper books that survived out of what must have been thousands. The Yucatan peninsula is a museum of Maya culture. As well as the sites already excavated, the remains of hundreds of other towns and cities are still submerged under earth and forest.

In the Yucatan itself, except for looters and a few others (some of them Yucatan nationalists looking for a past) all this was little more than a matter of curiosity. Now it is a matter of economics. The development of synthetics ended the boom in hemp. The biggest money-maker in the Yucatan now is oil; fishing and fish-processing are doing well, but tourism is moving into second place. Cancun, still only swamp and sand until the late 1960s, is now successor to Acapulco as a growth centre and 'secluded beaches' are available right down the coast, with a spin-off into the adjoining fragment nation of Belize. But the ruins—most notably those at Chichén Itzá and Uxmal and, further south, at Palenque, are now also part of the tourist pitch. In the sun-and-sand belt of the Caribbean, almost every beach resort has at least one Maya ruin. Even Cancun has two small temples and its own small museum of anthropology.

Imagine you don't know any of that. Imagine you go to these three places—and perhaps also to Tikal in Guatemala, the largest of all the classic Maya sites, with the remains of 3000 structures—and just look at them. What do you see? Monumental proof of an abandoned civilisation with a distinctive form of architectural plan. The most obvious elements are the precipitous pyramids, the highest going up to 70 metres, and the arrangement of buildings on stepped platforms to form a plaza. At their most complex (Palenque), these buildings can themselves be a labyrinth of galleries and chambers, patios and inner courtyards, but more usually the individual rooms are curiously small (leading the Spaniards to call some of them 'nunneries' on the assumption, presumably, that there was no living space smaller than a nun's cell). On the upper facades of almost every building, sometimes in stucco, usually in carvings and ornate mosaics, there are exuberant low reliefs of masks and serpents, jaguars and eagles, of sacrifices, battles and other human relations (some impossible to work out) and of brilliant abstract patterns. At Uxmal, in a building placed on a terrace 100 metres long, the famous frieze, constructed from a mosaic of thousands of pieces of delicately interweaving mask motifs and geometric shapes, may be seen as one of the world's most ambitious reliefs. At their most complex, these carvings and mosaics have a vertigo effect, driving the eye along the frieze with a kind of dynamic off-balance. At times there are colonnades. At Chichén Itzá, a hall mounted on a three-tiered platform is surrounded by 50 square pillars.

The architectural evidence is of a civilisation of artistic and intellectual complexity. The scientific evidence is that it flourished over most of the first Christian millennium. What do we know about it? Because cryptographers have now cracked the meaning of most of the hieroglyphs in the four remaining books and in the stone inscriptions, we can know more about the Mayas than about any of the other complex Native American civilisations. But what do we know about the use of these buildings? The stones do not speak to us. They merely echo what we say. This cultural echo is the great echo of tourism.

If we think we have the legs for it, we can pay the tourist's tribute to history by climbing to the top of a celebrated Maya monument to say we have been there—which can mean hoisting oneself up the cliff-like stairs with the help of a steel chain, and then, in a panic of self-recognition, accepting that the only way down is on hands and knees. You descend like a penitent. What do you learn? You hear descriptions such as 'Governor's Palace' or 'House of the Old Woman'. These make no more sense than 'Nunnery'. Even the use of the word 'temple' can be just a guess and the use of 'palace' is also entirely a guess. But the guides go on spinning ludicrous stories which, out of nothing, explain everything.

There is unlikely to be anything more to know about the use of these buildings—just as it is unlikely that there will ever be more than guesses about why these hundreds of towns and cities were abandoned. Nor will we ever know more about the building 1200 years ago and, later, the abandonment of the great *stupa* of

Borobudur in Central Java—a complex of terraces, gateways, niches, miniature *stupas* and staircases providing an upward circumambulation of the longest existing frieze of Buddhist reliefs. Nor why Angkor, a city of 12 square kilometres, was abandoned along with the pyramids and towers of Angkor Wat, Cambodia's and one of the world's most ambitious temples. No more than the traveller in the desert in Shelley's sonnet, *Ozymandias*, knew where the two vast and trunkless legs of stone had come from ('Nothing beside remains . . . The low and level sands stretch far away . . .'), or who was the Ozymandias whose monumental sculptured head lay beside them on the sand, and of whom it was said on the pedestal that this was Ozymandias, king of kings: 'Look on my works, ye Mighty, and despair'.

Scepticism must be one of an intelligent tourist's most useful traveller's aids—taking from tourism its illusionism, one of its greatest commercial and emotional appeals. And since so much of tourism is concerned with looking at the works of the mighty in decay, *Ozymandias* should become the special sonnet of tourists. We should mutter it to ourselves to exorcise the magic of explanation where there can be no explanation. That all things pass can be the special lesson of tourism.

* * *

In fact, scepticism might begin with Shelley's poem. He wrote *Ozymandias* after seeing a head of Ramses II ('Ozymandias' to the Greeks) in the British Museum. It was not true that 'Nothing beside remains . . . The low and level sands stretch far away . . .'. What was stretching far away when Shelley came across the monumental sculptured head were the rest of the British Museum's exhibits.

For that matter, from the Ramses Hilton in Cairo to Ramses's Abu Simbel temple near the southern borders of Egypt (so popular that there is a half-hour shuttle airline service to it from Aswan), the works of Ramses II are essential to the Egyptian tourist industry. Another reason for *Ozymandias* to become the special sonnet of tourists.

4.

THE MODERN PILGRIMS

♦ ♦ ♦

RELICS

The coming of the railways, along with the development of tourist hotels, travel agencies and the rest of the industry's infrastructure, made modern tourism possible. But these were not the reasons why people became tourists. We can understand our modern cult of sightseeing better if we go back to the religious pilgrimage. Central to this was the adoration of holy relics; now, as modern tourists, we find different kinds of 'relics' but, just as the pilgrims did, we can still use them as ways of seeking redemption.

Anyone who is in Southern Italy during the season when, according to local cults, relics of dried saints' blood liquefy according to the calendar can get a feeling for the efficacy of relics—specially in Naples, where the event is now televised. To get into a receptive mood, the tourist should approach the cathedral by the recommended route. This means you must pass by small, shabby *piazzas*, and along narrow streets of decrepit palaces where the washing hangs out above the dark alleys, along which footpads escape after snatching tourists' handbags or cameras. If you do this you become part of a tunnelling mass of people beside cars that creep together, head to tail.

At the cathedral the prime attraction is a skull. You find it inside a silver bowl in a grandiose baroque chapel, flashy with seven sumptuously decorated altars, and formidable bronze grilles flanked by colossal statues of St Peter and St Paul. It is the skull of St Gennaro, beheaded in the 4th century, and inside it is an ampulla containing his dried blood. After the tumult of the street it is natural enough to learn that, twice a year, in mass crowd scenes as agitated as the streets outside (and now in front of millions on television), the blood turns liquid and the people press towards the altar to kiss the ampulla and renew their belief in St Gennaro.*

Smears of dried blood like these, along with old rags, splintered bones, slivers of wood and other relics of Christian saints were among the avenues by which business was done with the supernatural after the Roman Empire was Christianised. The saints had replaced the Roman deities as ways of gaining supernatural assistance. It was their function, along with the Virgin Mary, to make appropriate representations to the ultimate heavenly authorities, and they were best approached in the presence of some relic of a saint's body.

Some churches kept written records of the miracles delivered by the saints whose relics they held, keeping count of the number of cures from sickness or madness, the numbers of lost limbs restored, of deliverances from captivity, of robbers warded off, along with details of resurrections of the dead and of acts of justice and revenge.

Relics were so essential to getting things done that when Christianity spread to the north of Europe some of the bodies and skeletons in the south were dismembered, and parts of them were sent off to the northern churches. Relics looted from the Eastern church also helped make distribution more equal, although there was a continuing fear of fakes. As the churches spread, parts of bodies, like modern power stations, gave an extended service throughout Europe.

As the liquefactions of Southern Italy show, relics can still attract

---

* **BLOODY MIRACLE.** In 1991, Dr Franco Ramaccini, an organic chemist, and Dr Sergio Della Sala, a neurologist, published an article in *Nature*, suggesting that the 'blood' might consist of gels of a kind that turn into liquids when vibrated. In their experiment they used hydrated ferric chloride, to be found in molysite, of which there is plenty around Mount Vesuvius. They pointed out that this technique was known in the 14th century, when the liquefaction ceremonies began.

Christian pilgrims—although the greatest numbers are now drawn to places where there have been visions by children, most of them of the Virgin Mary, followed by healings. Lourdes attracts several million pilgrims a year. (The largest of the Hindu pilgrimages, held every generation, requires 15,000 extra trains.) But what now most attracts European tourists, if they are interested in relics at all, can be the lavish reliquaries in which the scraps of holy rag and bone are contained. A visit to the Treasury of a cathedral can be like a visit to a jeweller's. In modern-industrial societies it is secular 'relics' that prompt the great mass movements of tourists—on a scale unknown in even the holiest of the Christian pilgrimages.

And just as there were self-seeking negotiations between pilgrims and relics, there can now be self-seeking negotiations in which tourists get something out of museum exhibits, monuments, historical sites, historical spectacles and enchanted landscapes (which are a kind of 'relic'). When objects, isolated by the magic circle of tourism, become transfused with power and meaning, what tourists seek from them—one way or another, physical, moral, cultural—is regeneration. Sightseeing becomes a pilgrimage in which certain objects are given regenerative properties. Although Thomas Cook was too much of a Baptist to speak of relics, according to Piers Brendon in *Thomas Cook: 150 Years of Popular Tourism*, right from the start he saw tourism as meaning that 'man has been brought nearer to man and nearer to his Creator'.

Suggestions that tourists are pilgrims have been made since the 1970s. (I made it in *The Great Museum*.) In *The Englishman's England*, Ian Ousby made specific comparisons: religious pilgrims trod a beaten path towards a well-publicised goal. So do tourists. They went in groups under the supervision of a guide. So do tourists. They followed an itinerary in which they stopped at intermediate points. So do tourists. They could buy the church equivalent of souvenirs. (He might have added that there was a period in the middle ages when the pilgrim business was Rome's main industry, with substantial spin-offs for the lodging-house keepers and those who worked for them.) John Sears in *Sacred Places*, after providing evidence that 19th century United States tourists would describe themselves as 'pilgrims', makes further comparisons: pilgrims sought spiritual renewal through contact with a transcendent reality. So did visitors to Niagara Falls. Pilgrims saw their destination as a sacred place where they would experience God more closely. So did visitors to Niagara Falls. It is now no longer God that is sought, but regeneration.

FAITH IN THE AUTHENTIC

The change from religious to secular came when works of art began to be treated like holy relics. The rich and powerful had for hundreds of years been big 'collectors' of relics (properly encased in opulent reliquaries), but when rich and powerful 15th century European humanists began collecting classical statuary as well as holy relics, a shift commenced which reached its decisive moment somewhere in the second half of the 18th century. By then, art objects were also being venerated. It is now a platitude that in modern-industrial societies art museums are seen as places of such inspirational power that they have become the modern cathedrals; it is also a useful historical statement.

The words that hallowed this transmutation came in the first half of the 19th century, specifically in Prussia and Bavaria. An art museum was declared a *Tempel der Kunst*, a temple honouring art, which demanded 'sacred solemnity' (in the words of Frederick William III of Prussia). To this was added the democratic idea, conceived, more or less, during the French Revolution, that works of art belonged to the people. Scarcely anyone believed this, although it was assumed that even 'trippers', if they progressed appropriately in front of objects classified as works of art, might receive some revelation. Since tourist agendas now usually classify a visit to a cathedral primarily as an art experience, not only are art museums cathedrals: cathedrals have become art museums.

The palatial architecture of art museums and their ritualistic arrangement of objects maintained distance and esteem. They are still to be respected as shrines for the spirit of civilisation (although mainly a Western and sometimes a narrowly national civilisation). They now also earn deference, because prices paid for the few 'masterpieces' that still come onto the art market increases the fame of the asterisked objects already in the museum collections (which may be all that a packaged tourist sees). But perhaps art museums are most valued for their *authenticity*. If 'a Rembrandt', admired and famed for generations, is declared to be not 'a true Rembrandt' it can be no longer worth looking at, except, perhaps, for its notoriety as a fake. The long controversy over the refurbishing of Michelangelo's frescoes in the Sistine Chapel (financed by the Nippon Television Network Corporation) was concerned less with the appearance of the finished job than with its 'fidelity', as if this were a question with a final expert answer.

It is the idea of authenticity that unites the different objects from which tourists can seek regeneration—whether in art museums, or other museums, or in the church of St Petka in the courtyard of the Grand Balkan Hotel, Sofia, or in the Mariposa Sequoia Grove, California—but it was in museums that this cult first developed its implacability. It spread beyond art collections in the 19th century when the old 'collections of curiosities' were being replaced by systematised science and history museums, and the acts of magic began to occur that produced one of the most effective touristic transmutations. A stone, a hat, a bone, or a chair, taken from the outside world and put into a museum, ceased to be like anything else. Classified and conserved, it became 'the object'. Put on show, it became 'the exhibit'. As an 'exhibit' it was defined by its detachment from the rest of the world. As an 'object' it entered a realm of extraordinary purity. In an age of growing meretriciousness, it was *authentic*, the real thing.

* * *

By the end of the 1980s, a psychiatric unit in Florence's Santa Maria Nuova Hospital had treated more than 100 tourists for 'Stendhal's Syndrome'—a tourist condition characterised by a loss of a sense of reality and identity, insomnia, paranoia and guilt, and named for the occasion when Stendhal wrote in his diary, after first seeing the Giotto frescoes in Santa Croce: 'I had palpitations of the heart . . Life was drained from me. I walked with the fear of falling'. Authenticity can provide a secular epiphany of meaning equal to a supernatural revelation. We can imagine the past pressing in on us with all its weight.

Faith in authenticity may cast a radiance of value and scarcity that hallows the object-in-itself. A museum can become a collection of isolated objects, each sacred because it is authentic, and, because of their authenticity, offering a unique reality.

BODIES

Another part of the true birth of tourism came when homage began to be paid to the remains of secular as well as saintly leaders.

The bodies of great queens and princes had, of course, been significant in most cultures (thereby, as it happened, providing wonders of the tourist world such as the Taj Mahal, Tutankhamen's treasure, or the tomb of the emperor Qin Shi Huangdi at Xi'an, with its 8000 terracotta warriors). This process reached one of its most complex anatomical forms with the Austrian Habsburgs, various parts of whose dissected corpses are preserved in three different sites in Vienna.

I spent the better part of a day on a pilgrimage to the places where portions of dead Habsburgs are kept. It began in the Kaisergruft, next to the 17th century Capucin church, where there are regular guided tours and explanatory notices in several languages. A monk took us to a crypt where the main parts of the remains of two and a half dozen emperors and empresses, and more than 100 archdukes, lie in coffins of brass or pewter on marble floors, guarded by figures of weeping maidens, mourning eagles, laurel wreaths, angels and trumpets, and crowned skulls. My next way-station was the Hertzgrüftl, a small room behind the altar in the Gothic Augustinerkirche in the enclosure of the imperial palace. I had telephoned to arrange to be shown the silver urns, kept behind the altar, which contained the hearts of the Habsburgs. The last stage of my progress was a three-quarters of an hour guided tour of the catacombs of St Stephen's Cathedral where, stored on shelves, are metal canisters that look like the large mess buckets that armies use to transport hot food. In them are kept the entrails of the Habsburgs—after the bodies were gutted and filled with wax, it seemed improper to throw away the leftovers.

The remains of the Habsburgs were treated with this complex veneration because they were members of a dynasty chosen by God to rule Austria and therefore the world. (In the main part of St Stephen's Cathedral a sarcophagus of red marble, swarming with allegorical figures, proclaims AEIOU, which is not a run-through of the vowels of the Latin alphabet but an acronym for *Austria est imperare orbi universo*—it is for Austria to rule the entire world.) However, a new kind of veneration came to the bodies of princes when they were seen not as dynasts but as symbols of a nation.

One of the first of these symbols was constructed in the 16th century in Uppsala Cathedral. It was here that a showy monumental tomb was built, in what at the time was the latest Flemish fashion, for the body of Gustav Vasa, the founder of modern Sweden, around whom a national cult flourished from the time of his death. A portrait of him as father of his people was invented by contemporary chroniclers and, as with William Tell, the legends went on and on, and could be shifted around to prove anything (although, unlike William Tell, Gustav Vasa had existed). Three centuries after he died, this reformation prince was restaged, in a complex redecoration of the tomb, as a solid 19th century Swedish gentleman.

When the English gave Napoleon's body back to the French in 1840, it was made ready for its last resting place beneath the cupola of the church of the Invalides, where it was given the honours of both Roman emperor and national hero. The body was dressed in a simple guardsman's uniform. The heart, which had been taken out, was put in a silver urn and placed between the legs. The body was then installed inside six coffins, with the whole ensemble encased in a sarcophagus of red porphyry, reminiscent of a piano stool. Upon the marble pavement inlaid with designs of a conqueror's laurels, 12 classical statues proclaim Napoleon's victories, and on the walls 10 large reliefs represent him in the character of a great Roman, builder of roads, canals, and bridges, patron of industry, commerce and education, moderniser of administration, codifier of laws.

By then it was the turn of the nation-founders who had rebelled against princes. In the centennial year of George Washington's birth, Congress wanted his remains implanted in the centre of the Capitol, already a place of tourist pilgrimage. But the State of Virginia possessed the body and, following Washington's own wishes, kept it in the family tomb at Mount Vernon, where it is rather remotely placed for pilgrims, near the slaves' burial ground. However, the granite obelisk and rotunda in Oak Ridge Cemetery, Springfield, Illinois, marking the tomb of Abraham Lincoln (whose assassination symbolises a second founding of the nation) is the climax of a tourist promotion called 'The Lincoln Heritage Trail' which, according to *Birnbaum's United States*, 'blazes 2200 miles along the folkloric roads of Illinois, Indiana and Kentucky, Abraham Lincoln's home states'.

In glorifying nation-founders, however, nothing could match the veneration of the corpse of Lenin at the heyday of the Lenin cult (which also led, later, to the corpses of Georgi Dimitrov, Mao Zedong and Ho Chi Minh being put on honoured display). There was the corpse of Lenin, queues of pilgrim-tourists filing past, laid out in perpetual state at the heart of Russia (except during the annual period of renewal and restoration) in a mausoleum whose understated solemnity, in red granite and black labradorite, contrasted with the excesses of the Lenin cult that dominated the public symbolism of the Soviet Union, as if Lenin were Krishna, or Christ, or Buddha, or Muhammad—which, for a while, he was.*

The idea of resting places for the illustrious dead in general, not only saints, princes and the creators and/or saviours of nations, developed during the renaissance. One of the first centres of the cult was the Franciscan church of Santa Croce in Florence, which, by the 15th century, had become a place of honour for the bodies of Florentine humanists—scholars, biographers, booksellers, translators—to the glory of the age and of Florence. In great funerals, the corpses of now-forgotten scholars were carried into the church with volumes of their own writings in their lifeless hands. When the funeral orations were over, laurel wreaths were laid on their brows; on their tombs were carved words that honoured not God but individual excellence: 'History is in mourning and eloquence is dumb . . . the Muses cannot restrain their tears'. When Michelangelo's tomb, attended by the spirits of Painting, Sculpture and Architecture, went up in the 16th century, Santa Croce had become a pantheon of individual intellectual virtue; Galileo's body was moved in; monuments went up to Machiavelli and, 500 years later, to Dante.

By the 17th century, around Chaucer's tomb in Westminster Abbey there were assembling the beginnings of 'Poets' Corner'. Literary pilgrimages were also one of the precursors of modern tourism. In St Petersburg, the Tikhvinskoye Cemetery became an open air pantheon to many of those who made Russia one of the great centres of cultural achievement in the late 19th century. Maps are provided for pilgrims to the graves of artists and intellectuals in

---

* **THE LAST TSAR.** After the bones of Tsar Nicholas II and his family had been authenticated in 1992, plans began at Ekaterinburg to erect a church to be placed over the entombed bones as the centre of a new tourist complex.

the Père Lachaise Cemetery, Paris. Among the trees in a natural amphitheatre in Oslo, the Norwegians established a Grove of Honour for Ibsen and other illustrious dead.

* * *

The whole dynamic of Christianity was of martyrdom—from Christ's crucifixion, through all those true believers whose mutilations, disembowellings, stonings, floggings, beheadings, burnings, skinnings, clubbings and stabbings provide so much of the content of the paintings of the opening galleries of a European art museum. When Protestants came to be martyred by Catholics in the Protestant revolutions their remains were usually not available for veneration. However, the ground where they were hanged, beheaded or burned could become sacred. In Prague, the executed followers of Jan Huss, the proto-protestant burned at the stake, are commemorated by plaques in Old Town Square at the spots where they were killed; in Edinburgh's Grassmarket a garden, with the cross of Scotland cobbled from old paving stones in its centre, marks the site of the gallows where over 100 Scottish Covenanters were hanged. However, when secular revolutionaries took over from the Protestants as disturbers of an old order there were plenty of corpses.

The revolutions and wars of liberation of 19th century Europe and Latin America provided enough martyrs' bones to fill a chain of ossuaries—even if some are now forgotten, as in the Place des Martyrs in Brussels, honouring heroes of the 1830 Belgian uprising against Dutch rule, a square of shabby houses whose centre is taken up by a mausoleum which, if it recalls anything for divided Belgians, is likely to recall their failures to achieve nationality. There was controversy in Mexico in 1989 about the disposal of the revered remains of the right arm of General Alvaro Obregon, which was severed in battle in 1915 during his campaign against Pancho Villa, and preserved in a jar of formaldehyde in the marble Obregon Monument in southern Mexico City: at the end of the year it was buried with honour. Powerful cults developed around other martyrdoms. The Mur des Fédérés in Père Lachaise, where the last of the Communards were shot in 1871, became such a sacred place for revolutionaries that a radicals' pantheon formed beside it, with the graves of radicals, and of communist functionaries, crammed in among monuments to massacred innocents.

After the slaughter of the 1914–18 Great War and the disasters of its trench warfare (as much symbols of human failure and degradation as the concentration camps of the 1939–45 world war), martyrdom became democratic. War had become, as George Mosse put it in *Fallen Soldiers*, 'an expression of the general will of the people', and, as with the early Christians, anyone, at least any fit male, now had the right to be a martyr. In most of the winning countries, and in Germany in a different way, all dead soldiers became martyrs in a sacred cause. In the old days, to dispose of a battle's dead, ditches were dug as a place to throw the corpses after they had been plundered. In the 20th century the cult of the fallen soldier has provided one of the deepest fountains of human meaning—both of misery and in exhortations of national salvation through sacrifice. Plantations of crosses turned farmers' fields in Europe into some of the most sacred grounds in the world (a process begun in the United States near some of the battlefields of the Civil War, still important tourist attractions). In Russia after 1945, the enormous monuments in granite and bronze to the motherland's 20 million or so dead in the Great Patriotic War developed more meaning than the statues and busts of Lenin.

Usually accompanied by sacred earth from the battlefields, bodies of 'unknown soldiers', entombed in marble or granite within or beside some prestigious national edifice, became places of ordained ceremonies. After 1945, as well as monuments to martyr-soldiers there were also monuments to the massacres by the Nazis of 10 million or so innocents, and some of the concentration camps were cleaned up and turned into museums of aspects of the European potential. In Hiroshima and Nagasaki, Peace Parks mark the epicentre of the atomic blasts. As the bones of the victims massacred by the Stalinists were unearthed, the places where they were shot also became holy ground.

* * *

Even some of the statues put up for the dead can come to life, as if they were shrines periodically enlivened by the return of departed spirits. (In *Feeling and Form*, Susan Langer describes statues as 'the first permanent inhabitants of cities'.) The first time I was in Dublin I remember being taken around the statues in St Stephen's Green and in O'Connell Street, as if these Irish martyrs and heroes in marble and bronze were still alive and still engaged in their melancholy failures. In Cracow, Poland, the statue of Adam Mickiewicz, the 19th century poet-patriot, still breathed enough life to become a symbolic place for the 1970s student protests. When the Nazis occupied Warsaw, they beheaded the statue of Chopin.

Possessions of the famous dead are reverently placed in museums. In Athens, there are pieces from the cloak worn by Patriarch Gregorios V, before he was hanged by the Turks after the Greek uprising of 1821. In Pretoria, there is the suit worn by Paul Kruger at his investiture; in Melbourne, the armour worn by the bushranger Ned Kelly on the day he was captured by the police. South of Mexico City, the desk Trotsky was sitting at before he was assassinated with an ice pick. In Belgrade, notes made by the folklorist Vuk Karadzic, inventor of the modern Serbian alphabet. In Walmer Castle, Kent, the chair in which the Duke of Wellington died. In Washington, DC, the false teeth worn by George Washington.

* * *

Tourism, so embedded in death, can seem to deny it. It can give instead an illusion of everlasting life. Yet, as David Lowenthal suggests in *The Past is a Foreign Country*, many of the charmed objects of tourism should be allowed to show their age. Some of them might be allowed to die. I remember at a conference in London, after Lowenthal had said this, a later speaker told us how concerned she was about *the very chair* in which the Duke of Wellington had died. It was the most popular object on tours of Walmer Castle, but its chintz had faded. They had been conducting research on a small scrap of unfaded chintz and had found a manufacturer who would provide an authentic replica. The chair (unlike the Duke) could be re-covered and live forever. And people would be able to buy the authentic replica chintz in the museum shop.

5.

CIVIC PILGRIMS: *PRADAKSHINA* ON THE TOURMOBILE

◆ ◆ ◆

THE MYSTERIOUS ECSTASY OF BEING IN WASHINGTON

The Hindu idea of *darshana*, a mysterious ecstasy generated by being in a holy place, can be even more useful in understanding modern tourism when associated with another Hindu idea, that of *pradakshina*—the ritual of walking around a holy place and meditating. Isn't this what happens in our ceremonial progress as tourists? We pass from one object or vantage point to the next, in a manner preordained by signposts, labels, guidebooks, audiophones or tour guides. The difference is that our meditation is often done *for* us by tour guides, audiophones, guidebooks, labels, signposts or even public address systems.

Both Hindu ideas can be applied to a Tourmobile sightseeing tour of Washington, DC.

The Tourmobiles, long blue and white train-like motor coaches,

CIVIC PILGRIMS 53

jointed into several parts for manoeuvrability, stop at 18 entrances to some of the most holy places in United States tourism, and make three meditative encirclements—around the Arlington National Cemetery and Capitol Hill, as well as the wider circling of the whole ceremonial area of the Washington Mall and its environs. Your meditations can be provided by the commentaries of 'friendly and courteous narrators who will enlighten and entertain you'. ('If all the telephone lines in the Pentagon were placed end to end they would engirdle the globe seven and a half times . . . Have you heard the joke about why they called it Foggy Bottom?') The whole core circuit takes 90 minutes, but you can get out at as many of the 'sites of your choice' as you wish, with 'free reboarding'—tourmobiles follow each other every 20 minutes (on a good day).

When the city of Washington was conceptualised, it was intended to demonstrate the magnificence of a political concept—the republican ideal. The dome of the Capitol, the palace of the people's representatives, was to dominate the city in the people's name, and this ideal was to be given emphasis by the great vista of the Mall stretching out from the front of the Capitol. Actually, unlike the central axis of the gardens of Versailles, or the landscaped sweep in front of Parliament House, Canberra, or, in another way, the Rajpath in New Delhi, the Mall as vista doesn't come off. If you stand there, it seems strangely rural: you are in the middle of a lot of green grass, with white picket fences from a Reagan election commercial signifying small town virtue. There are also two admirable ways in which it doesn't work as an exercise in republican grandiloquence. One is that it is taken over by the people in their holiday clothes, as if they owned it. The other is that for decades the Mall has been a place where people, assembling at the Lincoln Memorial at its far end, have been able to speak in Lincoln's name (now also in Martin Luther King's, because that is where he delivered his 'I had a dream' speech) and it is where, for most of this century, the people have traditionally protested against actions taken by executive, legislature or judiciary in the name of the people.

However, if republican grandiloquence is measured by derivations from the architectural styles of Greece and Rome (revival, neo, beaux-arts and deco) there are hectares of it around the Mall. Although perhaps the grandest expression of classical grandeur in Washington, and a Tourmobile stopping place, is the Union Railway

Station. A granite edifice based on the Arch of Constantine on the outside and the Baths of Diocletian within, guarded by Stars and Stripes and gilded republican eagles, with patriotic exhortations carved into its facade, and encircled by the flags of all the states, with a statue of Columbus and a copy of the Liberty Bell in the middle, the Union Railway Station looks like the place from which the United States is really run.

But it is principle rather than power that informs the Tourmobile pilgrimage. The four most holy places encompass the four ideals of the United States political system—a system structured in such a way that at any particular time there might be belief in at least one part of it. Capitol Hill signifies the legislature (and, in its colonnades, pediments and ceremonial sweeps of stairs, imperial Rome). The White House signifies the executive (and, in its illusion of vulnerability and accessibility, ordinary folks—the White House lawn is described by the Tourmobile narrator as the place where the president's helicopter lands and as the scene of the annual hunt for Easter eggs). The Supreme Court building, signifying the judiciary, expresses the majesty of the law by summoning so much marble in vast floors and a fortress of columns that it makes Hitler's architectural plans seem modest. But the centre of the political idea is to be found in a temple with awe-producing monumental steps, United States eagles, a symbolic pediment and 72 Corinthian columns. At the heart of this temple, guarded by flags on either side, is the shrine containing in a tabernacle the country's most sacred relic—the United States Constitution, beneath which are the Bill of Rights and the Declaration of Independence. The Declaration of Independence is also celebrated in the Constitution Gardens in the Mall, in a brass plaque bearing facsimiles of the signatures of those who signed it. It was a mark of the times that when the gardens were named they were called 'The Constitution Gardens', not 'The Independence Gardens', thereby perhaps taking the same view of constitutional freedom as that presented by the audioanamatronic vinyl-covered 'Mr Lincoln' in Disneyland, whose view of freedom is that true liberty exists in obeying the law.

The bodies of 60,000 American dead are honoured as the Tourmobile encircles the Arlington National Cemetery, with stopping points at the Tomb of the Unknowns and at the quiet graves of the assassinated Kennedys, with next to each a low wall inscribed with what may or may not continue to be famous words. (In the

United States texts can be as important to politics as they have been to Marxism and theology). In the Mall itself, the United States men and women killed in Vietnam are dignified by the Vietnam Veterans' Memorial, effective even to opponents of the war because of its avoidance of traditional architectural rhetoric and its concentration on the simple idea of death: a sunken path passes between walls of polished black granite, and on these are 58,007 names. Nothing else—until a conventional heroic statuary group was put up nearby for those made uneasy by contemplating death unadorned.

As well as the Kennedys, three other notables among the political dead are honoured in masonry and marble. The Washington Monument is more a monument honouring the idea of an obelisk (of which it is a notably phallocentric example) than the memory of George Washington. The long queues, with waits of up to two hours, for the elevator inside the obelisk are for one of the essentials of tourism, a ritualistic ascent to a panorama—without this the tourist has not 'done' Washington. At the Lincoln Memorial there is no doubt where the honour lies: two rows of columns lead up to a Greek temple where the Lincoln colossus sits in its marble chair, surrounded on three sides by portentous epigraphs, some of them among the most famous texts in democratic rhetoric. The Jefferson Monument is in a colonnaded rotunda in a place of calm, alone, beside lakes and lawns, where the Jefferson colossus stands, surrounded by Georgian marble, Minnesota granite, Indiana limestone and bronze engravings of some of the most famous phrases in liberal rhetoric—in a nation where 'liberal' can become a word of abuse.*

Within the general sanctuary of the Mall, some of its holiest places are four great museums where, according to lowest common denominator hype, you can stand in the presence of authentic objects ranging from the remains of the world's largest elephant to the authentic jacket worn by Fonzie in *Happy Days*. After honouring

---

*THE NEXT MONUMENT. Beyond the Jefferson Monument is the green grass where a memorial to Franklin Roosevelt will go up some day. The words that will be engraved in bronze or granite have not yet been chosen. But how can they not be directed to the particular concern of Roosevelt as one of the 20th century's greatest rhetoricians of humane government intervention, as Jefferson was of 18th century enlightenment and Lincoln of 19th century democracy?

space, history, science and industry you can add learning, by admiring the copper dome and the marble opulence of the Library of Congress. The Tourmobile makes a special side-trip to the Kennedy Center for the Performing Arts, where you can honour civilisation in the Grand Foyer, one of the largest rooms in the world. In the National Gallery of Art, the Hirshorn Museum, the National Museum of African Art and the Freer Gallery you can honour Art itself.

The Tourmobile brochure says: 'With a hundred million museum exhibits, world-renowned monuments and memorials, art and artifacts, you'll need Tourmobile, because only Tourmobile can direct you through the maze of countless things to do and see'. As well as looking at Fonzie's jacket and the world's largest stuffed elephant, the countless things to do and see include pondering the meaning of 18th century enlightenment, 19th century democracy, the arts, science, learning and the principles of good government. Although not even the courteous and friendly Tourmobile operator can get through all that in a 90-minute ride, those principles are there, along with carnival inanities and mindless chauvinism. It is up to the tourists to purify themselves by exorcism and then do their own meditating—and perhaps also recall the Ozymandias factor, that all things pass and all empires crumble.

6.

THE GODS ARE ALIVE (UNDER GLASS)

◆ ◆ ◆

A DAY IN THE OLD CITY

Towards the end of 1992, just as the Arab *intifada* was renewing itself, I asked an Israeli friend to help give us an idea of how a visitor with a few hours to spare might pursue the tourism of religion in the Old City of Jerusalem.

Christians first. We had intended to drive to the top of the Mount of Olives, survey the view from the Intercontinental Hotel, and then walk down the precipitous side of the Brook of Sidron, past the Chapel of the Ascension (built over the footprints left on a rock by Christ as he began his ascent into heaven). Then on past the Church of the Lord's Prayer, the Garden of Gethsemane, the Church of the Agony and the Tomb of the Virgin. We would then enter the Old City itself, inspect the Crusader church of St Anne for its architectural beauty, and walk along the route of the Stations of the Cross (noting the bizarre locations that had been finally established for them by the end of the 17th century). On to the Church of the Holy Sepulchre, built over the site of Christ's cross on Calvary and the site of his tomb after the Empress Helena, Constantine's mother, went to Palestine in 326 AD to specify exactly where these and other holy places were—in the same kind of process, says Eric J Leed in *The Mind of the Traveller*, as that now used in establishing theme parks.

Our friend says it could be risky to drive up to the Intercontinental in a car with an Israeli numberplate, because we might be stoned by Palestinians. So we drive up the Mount of Olives, along a walled lane in which there hasn't been any stoning lately, to a windy spot where we look out over a wet Jerusalem, enclosed in walls built by an Ottoman sultan and dominated by the golden dome of a shrine built in Byzantine style by an Arab caliph.

As recompense for our limited success on the Mount of Olives we drive to Mount Zion, but although a sign says:

THE LAST SUPPER⟶

the Hall of the Last Supper is closed for the day.

Finally, after a walk up through narrow streets, we stoop under a low archway into a small square. Perhaps because we are still stunned by our 3 am wake-up this morning for our flight from Cairo, and are tired and hungry, or perhaps because it is crowded in by other buildings, we don't comprehend that this is the entrance to the Church of the Holy Sepulchre. And it is not clear what, where, or why we are there when we enter the building. What we are aware of is an overall impression of muddle and garishness. We walk up some stairs, past some chapels in appalling taste and then down some stairs again without recognising that that was Calvary—Christ has been stripped, nailed to the cross, died, and taken down again without our knowing it.

We only gain some sense of historical perspective, in this cramped mess of altars, clusters of lamps and terrible paintings, when we are confronted with a pink marble slab. This covers the stone declared to be the place where Christ's body was anointed. We notice it because a young woman lies, prostrated, beside it. We go back to the start and up the stairs again (look; see those incisions in the rock? . . . that's where they put up the cross! . . . and do revision). Downstairs again. We enter a dimly lit rotunda, a basically 11th century structure, on the site of the church Constantine had built after his mother had decided that this was the authentic site of Christ's tomb. Within the rotunda is a small two-room building—the sepulchre chapel, a kiosk in early 19th century Turkish rococo!

In the first room, three clusters of lamps are hanging: the top row is Catholic, the next Greek Orthodox and I know that the third is Armenian—because the Armenians are one of the three principal partners in the sepulchre enterprise. We wait while some people come out of the inner chapel through a very low door. It is our turn to stoop our way into a small room, where we photograph a marble bench. When we come out I contemplate an aesthetically bearded young priest in Orthodox dress, lighting up a new set of candles behind the Sepulchre in the Chapel of the Copts. (The Copts, along with the Syrians and the Ethiopians, also share in the enterprise. The Copts have a prize position because they claim a piece of rock from Christ's tomb itself, the rest of the tomb having been destroyed by a caliph in 1009. But because the Ethiopians fell behind in their dues, they are restricted to only one of the many minor chapels and they live in a set of small cells built among some ruins up in the roof.

We sit for a while in the Franciscan chapel (the Franciscans operate the Roman Catholic concession), which has been done up in a more present-day style. While we are sitting, three censer swingers from three different faiths (none Catholic) stride in and, in turn, and take brief possession, swinging censers noisily, as if fumigating the chapel from the presence of the others.

Our friend says that news in the morning's papers means we should avoid the Crusader church of St Anne and the Via Dolorosa because they are in the Muslim Quarter.

We move on at once to the tourism of the Jewish religion and walk to the Western Wall, a principal tourist attraction to gentile photographers because of it provides opportunities to photograph men in black hats nodding at an old wall. (There is even better photographic game in the Me'a She'arim district— home to most of the ringleted ultra-orthodox *haredim,* with the most extreme wearing striped grey and white robes, with ringlets and white skullcaps sticking out from under their black dress hats. Some of the *haredim* run when they see a tourist photographer, but there are days, especially when they detect violations of the *shabbat* that they can get nasty and engage in some stoning.)

At the Wall there is also an emphasis on sacred rock, because it is related to the Great Temple built by Herod and destroyed by the Romans. It was not part of the Great Temple itself, but a section of the retaining wall of the platform on which the temple was built.

In fact now it is mainly of Muslim stone, from the time the Arabs raised the platform and put some of their own buildings on top, though some authentic Herodian stone is on view at the base. At the time that the wall acquired its pilgrim status for Jews, it was cramped up close to an Arab settlement on an alley only three or so metres wide. However, after the 1967 war, the Israelis bulldozed this Arab area away and laid out a vast paved plaza in front of the Wall, so that its old stones now legitimise an open air space that is both synagogue and religious festival centre—and a triumphalist declaration of nationhood as well.

From the Western Wall we pass down two streets and up through a beautiful old Arab gateway into the principal Muslim site that tourists see in Jerusalem, the Haram al-Sharif ('the Noble Sanctuary'), the only part of the Old City that has genuine international tourist-aesthetic appeal. It takes up about one sixth of the Old City and offers a unique sense of space and proportion. On a level plaza of 14 hectares, raised on its masonry platform, it displays, with plenty of space between, one of the world's most beautiful shrines, a large and elegant prayer house, delicate gateways, minarets, paths, fountains, gardens, old academies and an Islamic museum done in modern-designer good taste.

Its centrepiece is the 7th century Dome of the Rock, a geometrical study in proportions, built as a shrine for the rock from which Muhammad made a quick ascent into heaven on a white-winged beast, to receive a revelation of belief (and where Abraham had earlier prepared his sacrifice). The external decorations of floral-motifed tiles in green, black and yellow, panels of blue and white calligraphy and patterned doors lead up to the gold dome. Inside, the gold and red patterns of the domed roof, the painted glass of the windows, the foliage designs on the panels, the blue, green and gold arabesques, the inlaid mosaics in gold and pearl are arranged with a rationality that makes the rock itself, inside an intricately carved wooden screen, seem the only irregular thing in the shrine.

The nearby prayer hall, with a silver dome offsetting the gold of the shrine, gives an immediate elegant impression of space and light, with long vistas of columns from which one can examine, with some sense of leisure, the marble, the chandeliers, rugs and painted glass. Presentation in the separate museum building projects a confident civilisation of great taste by making much of comparatively little in careful display and lighting. Even a coat of Arab armour is set out like an expensive designer jacket.

All this, along with the fountains, the gates and so forth, suggest a civilisation assured of its mastery. From these aesthetic appeals, a visitor who knew nothing else would imagine that it was Islam that dominated Jerusalem.

I have compressed our experience for this account. We actually spent several days going to different parts of the Old City, with revision periods in between. But what I have described is what can happen and does happen in this old place where, in textual terms, the same God is worshipped in three different ways, and in various relics of rock. I have compressed it because it brings up the two things that can most go wrong when religion becomes the object of sightseeing—there can be an over-emphasis on art, or there can be an over-emphasis on banality.

TOURING THE SUPERNATURAL: A TOURIST'S ETIQUETTE

The Arabs of Jerusalem do not see their 'Noble Sanctuary' simply, or mainly, or even at all, as 'art'. The elegant prayer hall holds 5000 people, but on Fridays the public address systems are at work so that the preacher's message also goes out to the thousands standing on the platform outside, because there is no room in the prayer hall. What is being preached is not aesthetics but religious faith and what they see as ethnic survival. The first things you see in the Islamic Museum are not the aesthetic triumphs of the past, but the blood-stained clothes of Arabs who, in 1990, were killed in a clash with Jews who want to repossess what they see as not the Arabs' Noble Sanctuary, but as the Jews' Temple Mount. Many of the *haredim*, and some other Jews, believe that the shrine and the prayer hall and all of the other aesthetically satisfying objects should be destroyed. Other Jews demand at least the right to pray in the Noble Sanctuary. When my wife was lost in aesthetic contemplation, an old Arab came up and commanded: "Don't pray!"

The largest formalised religious beliefs, that now tell people what the world is and why it is like that, come from words that were put together over 1300 or so years—from the writing of the *Upanishads*, the philosophical disputations and discourses that are seen as the basis of Hinduism, to the revelation in the 7th century of the various truths revealed to Muhammad that were later put together as the Quran. In this time, the Hindus also elaborated the great epics, the *Ramayana* and the *Mahabharata*, and compiled collections of legends and sacred law. The Jews brought together religious historical tales and legal precepts. The Buddha gave his sermons, although it was not until 500 years later that there developed an agreed sacred Buddhist text. Gradually, Christians decided which of a number of small books circulating among them should be brought together as the Christian canon. To all these sacred texts were then added billions of words of explanation and argument in what for centuries was the basic form of scholarship—studying and interpreting a sacred text.*

But the words of religion do not make good tourism. The Protestant Reformation, for example, was mainly about words, yet if you go to one of the famous churches of the Reformation, where rebels began to preach that the basis of Christian faith was the Bible, not the Church, what dominates the nave is not an altar but a lectern, holding a large, open Bible. But, as tourists, we are likely to look at the Catholic leftovers—the friezes, the arcades, murals and stained glass, which we can admire as art.

The Word doesn't make good pictures. Even though, in Islamic culture, calligraphy is seen as the highest of the arts, to the European tourist the Word, the Arabic script of the Quran, flowing or angular, can seem an abstract decoration, part of the general geometry of a mosque. The Word reaches its most commanding expression in the great temples of ancient Egypt. Even if we don't know what they mean we can feel their presence. The first I ever saw of Egyptian temples were the two long colonnades that lead up to the gateway of the Temple of Isis at Aswan, in which there is such an extraordinary sense of movement and life in the stone, with the capital of each column sprouting a different kind of palm frond and all of the columns seeming to 'speak' to us through the hieroglyphs

---

* SCHOLARSHIP. These techniques extended to the scholarship of secular classics (Homer, Shakespeare, etc) which could become equally reverent and arcanely allusive. New scholarly discourses now proliferate in the humanities and social sciences, but they maintain many of the old ways, as if Marx's *Capital* was the *Upanishads*, or Barthes' essays were Ecclesiastes.

and the reliefs cut into them. Egyptian temples had a lot to say. (After several days of 'feeling' their message, at Dendara I dreamed, for a moment or two, that I was a papyrus column, illuminating the world, in reliefs and hieroglyphs, with enlightenment and knowledge.) But we don't know what they are saying. And to people preferring 'the classical' all this scribbling carved into the stone can seem an interruption to the architectural lines.*

The religious word is likely to come off best for us as tourist observers when it is sung. However, whether Catholic or Orthodox Mass, or Buddhist chant, or Protestant hymn, this singing is more likely to come to the tourist in a concert hall than in church or temple. There are places where a church itself becomes a concert hall, but more usually tourists stand at the back of a church waiting for the singing to stop so that they can move in and photograph the altar.

Not always. A New York company, Harlem Spirituals Tours, runs two tours a week offering religious singing *in situ*, and the grandeurs and miseries of a Harlem tour as well. Some of it is historical: we looked at the facades of the birthplaces of famous sons and daughters of Harlem. Some of it was a battlefields tour: of the sites of famous encounters between police and demonstrators. There were also horror stories of unemployment and crack, AIDS and lung and liver diseases, which made an apt introduction to the service in the shopfront chapel where, for an hour, our coach party was spread out among the rest of the congregation. We clapped our hands and enjoyed the eloquence, both biblical and wisecracking, of the preacher; the communal affirmations; and the swaying and clapping and joyous singing of the ARC Gospel Choir in their red and yellow gowns. At the end of the hour we learned that ARC meant Addicts Rehabilitation Centre.

What is usually preferred as religion's tribute to tourism are large architectural statements that dramatise power. When the Catholic

---

* **THE WORD OF LENIN.** Of the secular faiths of the 20th century, communism was the greatest example of a faith whose wisdom was based on the Word—of Marx, ostensibly, but it came to be the Word of Lenin that was put up in bronze or carved into the walls of just about every public place in the Soviet Union. The great words of liberalism and democracy surrounding the colossal statues of Jefferson and Lincoln in their neo-classical temples in Washington do, however, attract some tourist attention.

Church recovered itself after the successes of the Counter-Reformation, the baroque style exulted its triumph. When Sultan Ahmed I decided he wanted a greater imperial mosque in Istanbul than the Emperor Justinian's Haghia Sophia, he founded a mosque (now 'the Blue Mosque') meant to be more magnificent and more elegant. The temples of Kanchipuram, one of the sacred pilgrimage cities of India, are spread throughout the city and are all that is left of the ambitions of three great kingdoms that lasted almost 1000 years. The glory of the pharaohs found its most extravagant expression in the temple complex of Karnak, whose Great Hypostyle Hall is itself larger than any Christian cathedral; whose total spread is greater than that of any other religious centre; and whose fame helps keep 200 floating tourist hotels on the Nile. In the north of India the Mughals marked out what was to become a tourist trail with the architectural marvels of the mosques they built in Agra, Fatehpur Sikri and Delhi. When, in 1778, a Thai general captured a jade Buddha, the Phra Kaeo, from the Lao it was enshrined on a tall, orange pedestal in a cloistered royal chapel in Bangkok, where it became part of the royal cult in Thailand and, as the Temple of the Emerald Buddha, the most 'fabulous' tourist temple in South-east Asia.

Even in the most doctrinaire secular period of the communist regime in Laos, dozens of serene Buddhas, in terra cotta, bronze and wood, were stored in the crumbling arcades of the Wat Sisaket in Vientiane, demonstrating in stylised positions and gestures the potential for goodness and peace that is fundamental to the Hinayana Buddhism of South-east Asia. When, in the late 1980s, things began to free up in Laos and tourist figures leapt to 600 a year, the temple was placed on Laos's highly tenuous tourist route. It was as *art* that the statues were likely to be scrutinised by tourists, even though the ethnic Lao were still so fundamentally Buddhist that you could be awakened twice over in Vientiane—by the national anthem, played on the public address system to welcome yet another glorious morning in a workers' paradise, and also by the drums and gongs of the Buddhist temples.

* * *

Obviously, Jewry is not just a matter of photographing hairy men in black dress hats. In the new city of Jerusalem the Shrine of the Book commemorates Jewish belief in the Word; the Museum of the

Diaspora in Tel Aviv celebrates Jewry in exile as a faith of extraordinary duration; and the Holocaust Museum in Jerusalem's new city recalls its persecution. In the context of the Old City the story is best told in reconstructions such as the Yishuv Courtyard, recalling how, in the old days in the Jewish Quarter, a number of households would turn their backs to the streets and in on themselves, contemplating the communality of their own courtyards. Although the reconstruction overdoes the display of material culture—so that one gets the impression of a comfortable 19th century bourgeois life, when in fact each family was likely to live in only one room—there is a special poignancy in the intimacy of the little synagogues that were integrated with these humble living quarters. (There is also a special irony in the way in which the Jewish Quarter, damaged in the 1947 fighting and partly obliterated by the Jordanians during their 20 years control, has now been yuppified in its restoration. Once a place of poverty, it is now a place of property in which even the excavated Cardo Maximus, the colonnaded and porticoed main street of Roman Jerusalem, has had boutiques, art galleries and jewellery shops installed in some of its porticoes. One restaurant offers 'An Authentic First Century Roman Dining Experience'.)

As sightseers of religion we should never simply laugh it off through unfamiliarity, or—to put it less politely—from complacent ignorance. Apart from the muddle and tawdriness, one of the reasons why Western Europeans are likely to be put off by the Church of the Holy Sepulchre is the predominance of Orthodox sects. *They* shouldn't be in charge of the tomb of *our* Christ. When General Charles Gordon, 1500 years after the Empress Helena made her decisions, declared that Christ's tomb was really in a spot that is now near the East Jerusalem Bus Station its garden setting appealed, in particular to the Anglican imagination, and it still has a following. To Anglicans, it is more *our* kind of tomb.

In a similar mood, many Westerners can dismiss the whole achievement of Byzantine (and therefore Orthodox) art without thinking about it, because its handling of Christian themes is different from 'ours'. Yet the frescoes and icons at Novgorod, say, despite destruction by the Nazis, make up one of Europe's greatest collections of medieval art. And the churches, cathedrals and monuments of the 'Monastery of the Caves' at Kiev provide reminders of almost 1000 years of art.

There can also be problems for Europeans generally in the Mahayana Buddhism of East Asia: some temple styles are so loud, and the statues so ungodlike by Western standards, that they become not art, but 'grinning idols', transmuted to Fantasyland. Nor are Westerners likely to pay even tourist attention to the deities of Hinduism, not even as art—because of all the arms and legs. Certainly not as religion—because they can seem too profuse and too contradictory, although that is part of the point. (Muslims find difficulties in understanding the Christian belief in the Trinity: one God who is at the same time a Hebrew deity, a Son of Man and a Holy Spirit?) Hinduism can offer most tourist interest in the X-rated temple sculptures of Khajuraho, or in the famous rock temples of Ellora, Ajanta or Elephanta, which offer the 'cave' experience as well as the art experience, or simply in a temple or two chosen to fit an itinerary. (Jain temples can be preferred because they offer the spectacle of a monk with his nose and mouth in a fine cloth mask, worn to avoid killing germs.)

* * *

When we are treading through myths of the past as sightseers we are always close to the remains of supernatural beliefs, even if we may not recognise them behind the art museums or the curio shops or the cultural shows. What we can do as sight-seeing tourists looking at manifestations of supernatural faith is to respect them.

By 'respect' I don't mean revere. I mean that we should understand that these things were, or still are, parts of myth-systems and that out of these myth-systems people have tried to make sense of the world. I certainly don't mean that one should believe in them: but we should understand how others believed in them, and perhaps try to find out something about that belief.

For most of human history, central myths making sense of human societies have been myths of the supernatural.* From the creation

---

* RELIGION, FAITH, THE SUPERNATURAL, SUPERSTITION. People sometimes say 'Marxism is a religion'. This confuses two things. Both Marxism and, say, Christianity, are overall faiths that provide a general coverage on what things are, how they got that way, and what to do about them. But a religion is a faith that finds its explanations and its methods of action in the supernatural. Marxism is a secular faith. (A 'superstition' is a religious belief with which you do not agree.)

of the world to what happened yesterday, these myths explained everything. Through astrology, divination, oracles, trances and auspices, they provided information for forward planning. And they provided the most acceptable ways for getting things done—by prayer, sacrifices and ritual dances. And in sheer performance value they provided the most powerful expressions of communality.

Myths of the supernatural were a way of describing the world and a way of expressing individual and communal values. Seeing them in these ways need not be beyond a careful sightseer, although what can be difficult for us, if we are rational Westerners, especially if religious objects seem to involve art, is to remember that they were also ways of getting things done. (There isn't the same difficulty in countries such as India, or some of the African or Latin American countries, where the gods and spirits are still used in daily intercourse.) As the jargon has it, as well as being cognitive and expressive, they were instrumental. It can be hard to keep in one's mind as a rational tourist looking at, say, a statue of the Virgin Mary, or of Jupiter, that one is looking at relics of myth-systems in which the divinities had to be bribed with offerings, frightened with threats, coaxed by dance or song, or persuaded by prayers.

A TRAVELLER'S KIT OF MYTHS

As sight-seeing tourists treading through other people's myths we can equip ourselves with a small travellers' kit of anthropological terms, that may help us tread with knowledge or at least with wonder and not simply, whether amiably or angrily, with nothing much at all in our heads.

Myths

Begin with 'myth', a word I have been using without explanation. By it I don't mean a story which isn't true, but a belief held in common by a large group of people that can, by a kind of magic, explain everything, or almost everything. In the case of religious myth everything is explained and justified in terms of the supernatural.

Legends

This idea of 'myth' is abstract. One of the ways in which myths are given vigour is by story-telling. This was so important in maintaining the intensity of most religious myth that it provided the dominant theme in the development of drama, narrative, dance and song. In tribal or village cultures a whole community might take a part in dressing-up, singing, dancing, miming, chanting and generally acting out stories concerned with gods and demons, heroes and villains. But since these stories were not 'just stories' (no stories are), but supported the principal myths of those societies, we need a word with more magic about it than 'story'. I don't think there is a better word than 'legend'—simple stories (whether true or false doesn't matter) that help perpetuate a myth.

As tourists we can see scraps of legends in the medleys of 'cultural shows', but our most usual confrontation with religious legend comes from visual images in a place of worship, or 'a ruined temple' or a museum. They may be a series of panels, telling the story like a comic strip, but a legend could be so familiar that one painting or sculpture would recall the whole story. When we see depictions of legends from the life of Christ, or of the Lord Krishna, or the Lord Buddha, mighty Zeus, Osiris, or of Ah Kinchil, the Sun God of the Mayas (and at night the Jaguar God of the underworld), we are in the presence of attempts to provide simple but telling tales of the supernatural. The Hindu epics are the richest story-cycles in the world. Christ is presented as a superb storyteller; the Old Testament is, amongst other things, an anthology of short stories. The life of Gautama provides the central sequences of Buddhism, but there also developed a whole pantheon of other Buddhas, and of Bodhisattvas, the enlightened saviours of compassion who work for the welfare of all living things. Legends were built around each of them, as legends were built around Christian and Muslim saints. Saints provide a good story.

When we are confronted with legends in cultural shows, or in museums or on temple walls, we may not know what much, or any of it, is about. In India, legends of the Lord Krishna, as one of the incarnations of the deity Vishnu, so permeate the culture that they are even told in comic books, and provide a continuing basis for movies and television serials. But how do the rest of us react in a museum in front of a low relief when we read a label which says: 'Krishna upturning the cart', or: 'Krishna stealing the butter', or: 'Krishna subduing the serpent Kaliya'? A whole sub-section of Indian painting has been devoted to the theme of Krishna's time with the cowherds, and a sub-section of that is devoted to his particular relations with the *gopis*, the milkmaids. But for those living outside India, and the parts of South-east Asia that are familiar with the great Hindu epics, what meaning is there in a miniature of which, we are told, the subject is '*Gopis* implore Krishna to return their clothes'?

In many secularised Christian societies similar questions might be asked by people passing in front of, for example, paintings illustrating the Passion of Christ. Do they know that the 'Passion' encompasses the episodes of triumph, betrayal and suffering encountered between Christ's entry into Jerusalem and his entombment, and that for centuries artistic conventions made visual presentations of these episodes thick with allusive meanings? To how many tourists do titles on paintings such as 'The Agony' or 'Before Caiaphas', or 'The Mocking' or 'Ecce Homo' mean anything? 'The Last Supper' is probably still widely recognisable, and recognition of 'The Crucifixion' would be wider still. But how many of those who look at 'Crucifixions' in famous art museums, or, for that matter, in the multi-media presentation at the Forest Lawn Cemetery, Los Angeles, could give a five-minute theological account of why that man was up there, or give a one-minute account of who those people are at the foot of the cross?*

In this sense, any antiquities museum or comprehensive art museum is a museum of legends.

---

* **CRUCIFIXION.** The conventions of crucifixion painting involved three scenes—the nailing to the cross, death on the cross, and the deposition from the cross—to which was added the 'Lamentation' over the dead body, or the Piéta, which gave a special significance to the Virgin Mary as mourner. The people at the foot of the cross were some or all of the Virgin Mary, Mary the mother of St James the Less, Mary Magdalene and St John—and sometimes the patrons who commissioned a painting. A Thames & Hudson book, *Encyclopedia of Themes and Subjects in Painting*, can add meaning to visits to art museums, giving the background to everything from Abraham, see *Isaac*, to Zeus, see *Jupiter*.

Icons

And also, of course, a museum of icons. As the third word in the traveller's kit, 'icon' means an image that carries an immediate conceptual and emotional weight to a significant group of people. Although the word has become fashionable among semioticians and advertising copywriters, I use it because, like 'myth' and 'legend', it retains some magic. In the case of religious myth, its specific use in the Orthodox Churches meant images which could themselves achieve some of the sacredness of the holy persons they represented, as any tourist who drops into an Orthodox church will discover.

Making visual images with impelling conceptual and emotional weight seems to have been part of all societies, but there have never been so many of these images as there are in the modern commercialist societies, nor have they been spread so widely—for example, the image of a bottle of Coke can be found almost anywhere. In imagining ourselves in the societies where the only icons were those of the kind now in museums, it can be useful to see the reliefs on Maya ruins as similar to television ads, Christian wayside shrines to billboards and Buddhist chants to singing commercials—although we should remember that they were not produced in such bad faith as most modern advertising.

Festivals

Festivals ('ritualised breaks from routine, defining certain values in an atmosphere of joy in fellowship') can sometimes be best observed in family festivities, but these are not in glass cases to be looked at.

Latin America has a such a harvest of religious festivals that tourist schedules can run to specialties—such as the Holy Week festival in Tandil, Argentina, where, in 1943, a new Calvary was created in marble and landscape gardening by a local businessman. Or All Saints Day in Asunción, when the local rich display themselves on folding chairs outside their large family mausoleums in a cemetery of deceased notables; or any Sunday in Bogotá, when crowds, some carrying crosses or climbing on their knees, pay homage to a revered hilltop sculpture of Christ.

Or perhaps so—I read about these three festivals in a guidebook. Do tourists go to them? Or do they just add spice to a guidebook? What can't be doubted is that the larger the festival, the less likely it is to change because tourists are looking at it. Tourists can be simply part of the scene (except to pickpockets) in an orgasmic show such as Rio's pre-Lenten *Carnaval*.

The festival of Christmas shows how a festival can lose its supernatural reference and change in value. Christmas was a Christian feast joyously reaffirming belief in the legends about the birth of Christ. It later also became, in different Christian countries in different ways, a festival honouring the family. Then, in the prosperous commercialist societies, the originally modest practice of exchanging gifts (as a reminder of the legend of three wise men bringing gold, frankincense and myrrh to the infant Jesus) became the festival of shopping. Honouring the goodness of shopping becomes the most demanding part of Christmas—so convincingly that even in Buddhist (and tropical) Bangkok at Christmas, the hotels and department stores are lit with fairy lights and decorated with images of Christmas trees, Santa Claus and Mr Snowman.

Rituals

'Ritual' is at the base of supernatural ceremonies. It is instrumental, a way of getting things done. It also becomes expressive. People participating in ritual are engaging in a common enterprise expressing beliefs and values. What is the effect of tourists observing supernatural rituals in which they do not believe, and how are they supposed to behave? Of course, if the ritual is part of putting on a cultural show all we need are our cameras.

The tourism of ritual can be most tactfully observed in an archaeological or ethnographic museum, sometimes also in an art or decorative objects museum—statues, communion chalices, masks, bells, sacrificial knives, censers and voodoo images were all made to assist dealings with the supernatural. There are no problems of tact involved in looking at them in glass cases (although there is the problem of having some idea of what it is all about). But a tourist can be involved with watching people engage in rituals in which they still believe—Hindus obtaining purity at Varanasi by immersing themselves in the Ganges; the sick and disabled seeking a cure at Lourdes; Americans buying a fundamentalist's videotape that tells them how to safely rise to heaven when the trumpet sounds for

Armageddon.* (I know that United States Fundamentalist, Evangelical and Pentecostalist churches are not on tourist schedules, but, along with general faith healers and millenialists, they should be.)

An example of how tourists should not behave occurred, when we were in Southern Africa, in the matter of divining. One of the most down-to-earth uses of the supernatural is that it provides a channel for obtaining exact information about what has happened, or will happen, and what should be done about it. There is belief in divining all over Black Africa. There are 60 or so methods of divining carried out in these countries, including *astromancy* (reading the stars), *cleromancy* (throwing lots), *geomancy* (studying lines in the sand), *haematomancy* (observing trickles of blood), *ornithomancy* (observing the flying of birds). Diviners answer questions about health problems, the well-being of the dead, weather forecasts (droughts, floods) farming decisions. But for tourists, this can become just a game. In the Victoria Falls Craft Village there were two diviners, but the tourist pitch reduced them to 'fortune tellers'. In the shop in our Pretoria hotel diviners were reduced to 'witch doctors': you could buy a set of 'Witch Doctor's Bones' and follow the printed instructions to do your own divining. So far as I know, there are no hotel shops in Naples with ampules of St Gennaro's blood and instructions about how to liquefy it.

The rational tourist finds it easier to imagine the instrumental when it comes to the tourism of sorcery. In all religions there has been a continuing struggle against evil forces—devils, demons, witches, gnomes and ghosts, along with more generalised ideas of temptation and desire. (Evil is essential to myths of the supernatural: how otherwise to account for the way things are always going wrong?) For the tourist, there are sculptured temple guardians intended to frighten off evil spirits, horrific carvings and paintings, and in museums, both the charms, amulets and other devices for

---

* SECOND CHANCE. Jerry Farwell preaches that when the trumpet sounds the born-again Christians will instantly disappear, leaving their clothing behind them. 'If you are driving a car, the unsaved person will suddenly be startled to find the car is moving along without a driver and will crash. Stark pandemonium will occur on every road.' But there can be hope for those who are not saved at the sound of the first trumpet. They can buy a videotape called *What to do if you are left behind.*

protecting oneself from evil, and the instruments of black magic of those who want to cause it.

Tourists travelling in parts of Africa and Latin America can read newspaper reports of contemporary sorcery, even if there are no organised tours of evil-doing ceremonies. However, in Western societies sorcery has been abandoned for secular methods of getting things done and has little place in tourism, except, for the period when the Soviet regime installed the Museum of the History of Religion and Atheism in Kazan Cathedral, Leningrad.

What we are left with is the concept of the witch. (Estimates of women killed as witches during the hysteria of the 16th and 17th centuries range from 100,000 to 300,000.) And in Salem, Massachusetts, noted for its 17th century witch trials, there is an illustration of the banality of tourism. After room had been made for the roadways and car parks, the malls and the plazas, what is left of the material substance of Salem are fragments of its period as a great New England seaport that was put out of business by Boston. But the witch experience provides Salem's basic industry. Of the persecutions nothing remains other than some documents of the trials, so entertainments have been invented to make the witch hunts a characteristically trivial tourist pursuit. An authentic 17th century house has been renamed 'The Witch House', and stocked with stuff that might have been in it, and given a history it might have had. The result is an authentic 17th century hand-carved colonial furniture and gleaming pewter tour. A few minutes away on the 'Salem Trolley' (offering a ride through history), a 'Witch Dungeon Museum' has been created around an authentic old beam. The 'Salem Witch Museum', (with the punning slogan 'EXPERIENCE MASS. HYSTERIA' and a large cartoon statue outside of a witch on a broomstick with a cat) puts on a short, spooky sound-and-light show with witch-mood music and a portentous, if well-meaning, warning against the evils of modern witch hunts. Unless you go to Salem to look over what is left of its days as an early New England seaport, you are in for a day of organised fatuity.

TOURISM AS CULT

I will show in Chapter 13 how one can apply this kit of myths to the secular as well as the sacred. But they can also be applied to tourism itself.

One can go further: at least in the most extreme form of tourism—that in which there is a full pilgrim's surrender to the rites of the itinerary. The kit of myths can be applied to tourism as if it were a supernatural cult.

The *myth* of such tourism is the possibility of regeneration through travel to other people's places. Its *ritual* is to achieve this regenerative force by moving our bodies in a predetermined pattern, in proximity to objects or activities that, through the radiance of fame, have been given some of the magical properties of holy relics. The *legends* of tourism are found in travel books, guide books, travel brochures, and in the stories we bring back home.

The *icons* of tourism—the Taj Mahal, the gondola, the Andes, the grass skirt, the Sphinx, the Little Mermaid in Copenhagen, the Beefeaters, the Kremlin, the Statue of Liberty—can all become not much more than emblems of themselves as symbols of tourism, or even symbols of symbols of tourism. The posters can have more meaning than what they are supposed to represent. In a hotel with a big tourist trade, the extravagant photographs in the elevator showing the poolside bar, the dinner-by-candlelight restaurant and the friendly coffee shop offer a great deal more glamour than you usually find at the swimming pool, the restaurant or the coffee shop.

As a *festival*, group tourism declares the difference between *them*, the non-tourist, and *us*, as the tourist, and this can be one of the memorable results of the tourist experience.

It can also lead tourists into becoming the observed and curious *them*, viewed by the natives. Piccadilly Circus is no longer a cosy symbol of what it means to be a Londoner, which visitors treat with awe. The 'Eros' statue became part of a pedestrian zone. A sign was up, in case you missed the statue, saying EROS. On its steps sat the tourists, surrounded by a ceremonial ring of 24 litter bins. Scattered all around were cardboard boxes, half-emptied plastic sacks, empty cans, partly eaten food, sweet wrappings, cigarette butts. The tourist buses encircled this prime tourist site like jackals.

ART? OR RELIGION?

One of the city's main squares is cordoned off and crowds watch the arrival of those who have tickets. Inside, almost everyone stands—1000 or more—for this annual performance in music theatre. When the lights go out a performer in red and gold appears, a kind of human candelabra. As we all shine with light, the dais empties and the people themselves become the show. In a great hall glowing with candles and alive with people kissing and embracing, the chorus sings softly as the main performers, dressed in red, black, green and gold, come and go, singing their parts, appearing and disappearing. When they come together and sing from the centre of the dais, the full spectacle begins: the stunning voices of the chorus, the cross-rhythms of chanting, the shimmering of colours, the theatricality of hundreds of co-ordinated movements and the surges among the people. The story told is familiar, but it is done with beauty and grace.

The square was one of those large public spaces in Sofia that make up its symbolic centre. The auditorium was the Alexander Nevski Cathedral, whose choir was under the patronage of Boris Christoff, Bulgaria's contribution to the international opera circuit. It was during the communist regime. The occasion was an Easter Mass celebrated by the Bulgarian Orthodox Church (open only to special guests).

This is another reminder of the relations between the arts and religion, which should be a concern of any of us if we are in an ethnographic museum, or watch a cultural show, or spend even five minutes in a celebrated religious edifice. We should not let art obscure religion. But we need not let religion obscure art. Even if belief goes, the shapes of belief remain, and some are put into art museums, as the cathedrals of modern-industrial societies. For sightseers the gods are still alive, but they are transformed into exhibits, under glass.

An example of how changes in sightseeing can change the use of objects related to supernatural practice occurred in Australia with Aboriginal artifacts. Until the early 1960s, the material artifacts of the Aborigines were given such an old-style ethnographic approach that a museum visitor would have awarded them no marks for either art or religion. Aborigines were assumed to be so concerned with survival that they couldn't spare the time to 'have' much of a culture, so the concentration was on hunting weapons, spears, boomerangs, and so forth. Few material possessions, therefore poverty of culture. Even the patterns in which these things were arranged under glass remained the same, suggesting that Aborigines would never change, and were on the way out anyway. Then there was an exhibition in 1960–1 of other kinds of Aboriginal things—painted visual images—that toured the State art museums. The idea began to develop that Aborigines *did* 'have' a culture—because Aboriginal things were now being displayed in art museums.

This was followed by another discovery. In the seas of red sand dunes, the wide plains of mulga and spinifex, the salt flats, sandy creek beds, waterholes and hills of purple rock of Australia's enormous Western Desert, Aboriginal people, as part of their ritual, created designs of red, black, yellow and white dots, straight lines, curves and concentric circles of complex meaning, and through these abstract forms they celebrated their creation myths—their 'Dreaming'. They would paint on rock face or sand, on earth, on ceremonial objects, or on their own bodies. When the remnants of tribes settled in impoverished fringe settlements, some, in the 1970s, as a result of the arrival of a white schoolteacher, began to paint their Dreaming in acrylic paints (using the same basic colours and symbols) on paper, plywood, linoleum or canvas. The museum treatment of Aboriginal images as art helped them sell what they were making and there is now a 'school'. People who paint stories that are told in lines and dots and curves, in which they are trying to let other people know about the nature of existence and of human meaning, sell paintings that can be interpreted as a form of abstract expressionism.

Now that Aborigines are seen as having a culture because they produce art, museum ethnographers want (rightly) to present Aboriginal art in a context of supernatural ceremony. The art museums made these things art. The ethnographers now return them to belief.

We have already seen how tourism has taken over some of the role of religion in its concern with pilgrimages, with authentic relics and with regeneration through communion with Nature, Art, the Authentic, the Past and other forms of spiritual refreshment. To this we can add that sightseeing also provides us with the wondrous, using some of the same techniques as religion. This is because many of the objects expressing religious belief also express a wider system of meanings than supernatural myth, because of their imaginative power. It is the phenomenon of imaginative power that adds to the case for seeing tourism as a substitute for religion. Not in terms of supernatural belief: a belief can't be a religion without the supernatural. But in the ways in which religion has been 'expressed'. Whether approached as religion or as art, Aboriginal desert paintings, or frescoes of Krishna stealing the butter, or the singing in the Addicts Rehabilitation Centre, Harlem, or in the Alexander Nevski Cathedral, Sofia, are forms for expressing human imagination.

Images of the crucifixion of Christ, for example, came from artists. We don't know when the cross became the central image of Christianity. It wasn't an image used by the early Christians, who were still looking towards a quick second coming. So far as we can learn anything from surviving scraps of mosaic or illuminated manuscripts, there seemed to be no agreement about how to represent Christ. Tourists looking at the brilliant mosaics in Ravenna, in Northern Italy, find in a 5th century tomb a Christ who is a young beauty, a good shepherd tending his flock. Down the pathway, in the mosaics in the church of San Vitale, they find a young beardless Christ, enthroned between two angels, as handsome as a classical Greek statue. In mosaics from about the same time, in a hall in the Forum of Vespasian, Rome, Christ is a bearded figure of awe, an almighty potentate radiating the majesty of judgment, rather than the humility of crucifixion. Even when the cross began to dominate, it was a crucifixion of lordly triumph, as you can notice when walking through an art museum. In the Romanesque collection, Christ is on the cross, but as a great prince politely performing a ritual; then in later galleries his eyes close and his body curves in stylised suffering; the agony becomes bloodily alive—galleries spout with Christ's blood.

Equally, in representations of the Buddha. At first the presence of the Buddha was indicated only by symbols—a horse, a wheel, a tree, then, perhaps from Greek influences, artists began to depict the figure in stone or metal and the sculptural conventions began of the Seated Buddha, the Standing Buddha, the Reclining Buddha, the Walking Buddha, the Crowned Buddha. The iconic manifestations of stylised Buddha images can take up most of the opening galleries of museums in a Buddhist country, and each combination of posture, gesture and expression has its own meaning. These were all created by artists. And as well as the meanings given to them by theologians (the equivalent of an advertising agency's clients) there were the meanings given by their very design, which we can continue to interpret. Paintings of Christ at the Madonna's breast go beyond supernatural meanings to shaping images of motherhood, of womanhood, of babyhood (and of breasts).

The point is that religions were invented by humans. So were the arts. Which came first? The usual answer is first religion, then art, but one could argue the opposite: that religion grew out of the imaginative capacity of human beings to invent meaning in words and gesture, dance and music, image-making, reasoning and storytelling—that is to say (as we would put it now) 'the arts', and these gave shape to much of the belief in the supernatural. As tourists we can move through a world of wondrous things removed from our everyday lives (not all of them technically art, but that doesn't matter). Some of them had religious meanings. Others didn't. But they can all have an imaginative appeal that distinguishes them from the ordinary.

7. Interlude:

FAMILY HOLIDAY (ON AN ENCHANTED ISLAND)

◆ ◆ ◆

FAMILY DIARY

When our daughter, Julia, was nine, and our son Nicholas six, we took them to several countries in South-east Asia, beginning with Bali. It was 1971, when Bali was already seen as being 'spoilt'. When we got home I stuck the photos in a scrapbook and wrote a family diary in the spaces around them. This is the Bali section of it. The 'D' referred to is me, 'M' is my wife, Myfanwy. The style of the diary was intended to catch the attention of two children.

Sunday

Julia and Nicholas settle down on our MSA flight ML 787 and try out Malay, European, Chinese, Japanese and Indian music. They are listening to *The Waltz of the Flowers* when the hostess brings colouring-in books and crayons. Even one of the grown-ups is colouring in. Nicholas reads all the information in the safety pamphlet and says he wants to know what to do if there is an accident.

We are crossing the Australian desert. (Colour it red.) During lunch it turns brown. (Colour it brown.) Suddenly it's the Indian Ocean. (Colour it blue.)

We're at the Bali International Airport, where it's hot, but the man who meets us from the Segara Village Hotel is very friendly.

On our drive to the hotel at Sanur we see many of the things we had read about in the guidebooks. Tick them off: coconut palms. (Nicholas wants to climb one.) . . . Baffle walls to keep demons out . . . Batik (Julia wants a dress made of batik) . . . Women carrying objects on their heads . . . Green rice paddies . . . Brown drum towers.

OUR FIRST CREMATION. We stop for a small cremation, but it is almost over. It is like arriving late at a barbecue.

OUR FIRST TEMPLE PROCESSION. A temple procession goes by, of women in bright colours carrying intricately prepared temple offerings on their heads—just like in the guidebook.

The Segara Village Hotel consists of a dozen or so bungalows grouped around a courtyard with a garden of tropical flowers. A shrine to the family deities is in one corner, and outside each room there is a small offering of rice and flowers to the gods or the ancestral spirits. The owner takes us around to choose which bungalow we want.

After settling in we walk down to Sanur Beach (only 100 metres away) for a swim, but it is low tide in the lagoon and swarms of children are pestering us to buy things. We all get a bit cranky. Back at the Segara Village Hotel they are putting oil lamps on the little verandas attached to each bungalow. When we have dinner together in the courtyard under a banyan tree, our table lamp is a candle enclosed in a leaf.

We're in bed. It's warm.

Monday

When D wakes up at 5.30 am he hears the birds singing in the courtyard gardens and Nicholas and Julia chattering next door. All three get dressed and walk around (whispering) in the garden, which is purple and mauve and green. M joins them for coffee on the veranda, then for a breakfast of papaya and boiled eggs in the garden.

After breakfast we walk along the beach, where people try to sell us things and a boatman wants to take us for a cruise in the lagoon on one of the outriggers (called a *prahu*). There is a dead cat at one end of the beach.

At the hotel they tell us we *must* be at Batubulan by 9 am to see a *Barong* dance. Perhaps an early *Barong* dance will be better than early morning telly. We hire a car and driver.

THE BARONG DANCE. *Gamelan* music. Fine dancing. Good acting. Amusing clowning. And a *kris* trance dance at the end. Nicholas likes it better than the Margot Fonteyn ballet he saw a couple of days ago in Sydney. The *Barong*, the monster who loves humankind, and the *Rangda*, the witch who is an enemy of humanity, become as real as a fairy story about good and evil. Later, Julia and Nicholas play *Barong* and *Rangda* games.

The actors are ordinary villagers and when the show is over they take off their costumes and go back to work. But the *Barong* mask has magical powers and, to keep its strength, the *Barong*'s beard must be dipped in holy water.

THE ART VILLAGES. We drive off from Batubulan (famous for stone sculptures) and at the first shopping gallery Nicholas buys a monkey mask like the one we saw in the *Barong* dance. We go through several art villages—Celuk, famous for silverwork, Batuan, famous for painting and weaving, Mas, famous for woodcarving. We are approaching Ubud, famous for art.

We have seen: food stalls, village markets, children picking nits out of each other's hair, truckloads of soldiers, rice paddies, women washing clothes in the river, coconut palms, boys flying kites, banana trees, overcrowded buses, children shouting 'hallo', women carrying bricks on their heads, ducks, pigs, men stroking their fighting cocks.

A QUIET VILLAGE. A tyre blows out and we stop to change it. A deep path falls down through the ferns to a rushing brown river. All around is the quiet of a village. Mud walls with thatch on top keep demons out of the family compounds. The village children are shy.

At Ubud we are shown over a palace (*puri*) turned into a guesthouse. It is as dreary as in a boarding house on a wet day but someone tries to persuade us to move here from the Segara Village

Hotel. Julia and Nicholas say: "No, no. We love the Segara Village Hotel".

We inspect the museum, Puri Lukisan ('Palace of Fine Arts'), which gives us the impression that we have had an introduction to Balinese painting.

THE ELEPHANT CAVES. Near Bedulu we fumble around in the pitch dark of the 11th century 'Elephant Cave', perhaps established as part of a Buddhist monastery. There was once a king here whose habit it was to have his head cut off and then put back on every day. One day his head fell into the river and was washed away. For want of something better, a servant put a pig's head on him, but this made him so ashamed that he forbade his people ever to look at him again. He was called 'Bedulu', which means 'He who changes heads'.

When we arrive for lunch at the Puri Suling restaurant we are greeted by the beating of a large gong. Hibiscus and frangipanni hang over our table and as we eat our bean soup, *satay*, grilled tuna and coconut pancakes we look out over a valley of rice fields while music is played from a thatched pavilion on the slope of the hill.

The driver uses his horn against both humans and animals as we drive back to the hotel fast. Then a siesta.

THE MYSTERIOUS FORTRESS. Down at the other end of the beach (which looks very shabby at low tide), the 10 floors of the Bali Beach Hotel tower over Sanur Beach. From where we are, nothing moves. After Nicholas and Julia try out their snorkels in the lagoon we walk along to inspect the hotel, as one of the curiosities of Bali. We find a large chlorinated swimming pool with no-one in it . . . an arcade of shops with no-one buying . . . expanses of polished floor with no-one on it . . . We inspect its mini-golf course: the hazards are authentically Hindu.

At the beach market we buy a bunch of bananas, a bottle of palm wine and a bottle of palm beer and, when the lamps are alight again on the veranda, M and D try these terrible-smelling drinks. The palm beer tastes as bad as it smells: the palm wine is aloof and stringent.

MONKEY DANCE. After dinner we go down to the beach compound to see a *Kecak* dance. The story line is hard to follow because of the program notes and one of the actors keeps snuffling, coughing and adjusting his mask. All the same, the 'monkey chorus' is remarkable. For an hour, 100 men roar, chant 'chak-a-chak-a-chak', grunt and hiss, waving their bodies and vibrating their fingers altogether as if they were a flock of birds. The story is made up of a few scenes from the *Ramayana*, a great Hindu epic that everyone in Bali knows. There is a *Ramayana* film on in Denpasar now and a Balinese girl called Ratni, who Julia has made friends with, tells her stories from the *Ramayana*.

Tuesday

Another early start after breakfast in the garden. The car climbs up into the hills, where the walls are of stone, not mud. Drums and gongs are beating as a long village procession takes offerings to the gods.

OUR FIRST TEMPLE. We knew all about the temples, having read about them. Now, at Pejeng, we go into a temple where there is a large bronze drum, once a moon that fell from the heavens many centuries ago.

A Bali temple is a collection of courtyards open to the sky, where there are shrines and storehouses. Trees and grass grow inside the courtyards and most of the time the temples are empty—people have no use for them except when the almanacs say it is time for some of the deities or ancestral spirits to come to earth and occupy specified shrines. (The shrines are always on the mountain side of a temple since mountains are good: they are where the water for the rice fields comes from. The sea is bad and full of demons.)

When a spirit is marked down in the almanac as due to enter a shrine there is a holiday and all the people bring food. The essence of the food is passed on to the spirit by burning incense and the food itself can then be eaten by villagers in a banquet. The temple is beautifully decorated and the spirit is entertained by dances and drama. Cockfights are held, so that the blood of the cocks will feed the evil spirits and keep them away from the entertainment of the good spirit inside the temple. If the spirit wishes to speak, someone will fall into a trance to provide a medium. When the spirit goes back to the heavens the temple doesn't matter until the spirit's next visit.

Balinese people do a kind of 'trade' with the spirits. They feed and entertain them so that the spirits won't harm them, or might even do them some good. This is how religions began. Since there are a lot of spirits in Bali, keeping them happy takes a lot of time.

In each village there are three main temples, each for different functions. There are also neighbourhood temples for groups of family compounds, and within each family compound there is a family temple. There are temples for public baths, temples for agricultural societies. Near each rice paddy there is a shrine.

TIMES PAST. At Gunung Kawi we are in a very historic part of Bali. We put on temple sashes and walk down 300 and something steep stone steps to see the *candis*, 10 memorials to kings who became gods, carved out of the rock in one night by the fingernails of a giant. A number of Balinese go with us. One speaks English. Two sell coconut milk, one sells walking-sticks. One holds Nicholas by the hand. One just asks for some money. After looking at the *candis* we cross a raging torrent and make an offering of hibiscus in a rock monastery. Then we have to climb up again, some of us puffing and dripping with sweat. The coconut-sellers push their coconuts under our faces as if we were all condemned and they are offering us salvation. At the top D has to decide what each of these men should be paid. M buys some batik and then has a discussion about the price of bananas.

This area, and the other places we go to today, was settled in the Bronze Age (300 BC to 100 AD). New discoveries continue.

OUR FIRST VOLCANO. After a drive to the sacred springs of Tampaksiring we begin a mountain drive, then swing in off the road and stop. What are we supposed to do here? Admire the view? Is it our last stop before the volcano? The driver doesn't speak English.

An orange is thrust through the window and shoved into D's mouth. Julia and Nicholas are trying to avoid sucking oranges. D and Nicholas break free of the orange-sellers and move towards the edge of the road to admire the view. But an orange-seller is following. It is her orange I sucked, therefore it is her oranges we must buy. (Is that little peak down one side of the mountain a volcano? Is that smoke or a cloud? It burps. That *is* the volcano.)

Back at the car, M has a guidebook open at a page illustrating the fruits of Bali. If she has to buy fruit she wants to be rational about it. D's orange-seller demands 300 Rp for 10 oranges: he has sucked one, therefore he pays for 10. He says 150 Rp. She puts two more oranges into the plastic bag and writes 12 in the dust with her toes. Twelve oranges for 300 Rp. (The volcano burps. More smoke. A roar. We hurry back to the edge of the road.) D has settled for 150 Rp for 12 oranges, but as he holds the plastic bag he feels the woman's hand taking some of them out. (Another puff of smoke. Another roar.) Now we are being offered some long, thin wooden carvings, but since we didn't suck any of these there is no obligation. The woodcarvings salesman gives us a short, friendly and lucid lecture on the mountains of Bali.

When we get to the state temple of Bangli, with its enormous banyan tree in the first courtyard, the temple guide tells us we should have been there last week when there was a big festival, with thousands attending. The temple banners have now been washed and put out to dry and the baskets the offerings came in are reduced to a wet sludge.

Back at the Segara, we sit on a shady veranda where M and D drink three bottles of Surabaya beer and Julia and Nicholas drink 7-Up, an exotic drink not available in Australia. Julia and Nicholas go for a swim with some friends they have made and at night we make up two jolly Australian tables, children at one, parents at the other, eating prawn dishes under the banyan tree and talking about things back home.

Wednesday

DENPASAR. Our first stop today is Denpasar, the capital. It was here in 1906 that the Raja of Badung made his last stand against the Dutch, choosing death and honour when he and his court dressed in their finest clothes and jewels and walked into their slaughter.

We visit the Museum Bali for a run-through on Bali's art history, then the palace of the rajas of Badung, just past the main bus station, where some of the pavilions are now used by artists and there is a shop, where Julia buys a *Rangda* witch mask. At the Kokar Conservatorium of the Arts they are preparing for a visit from Queen Juliana of the Netherlands.

ROYAL TEMPLE. Mengwi is where the rajas of a powerful kingdom kept shrines for the visits of their ancestors. The temple is surrounded by a moat made sacred as the bathing place of heavenly nymphs. By now, Nicholas and Julia know that Bali, which is the centre of the world, rests on a giant turtle and that is why there is a turtle at the base of many shrines; we do revision on how the open space above represents the earth and the tops of the shrines represent heaven. On the rough back road between Mengwi and Sangeh there is an explosion. The car lurches. Another blow-out.

Once again we feel we are 'off the tourist track'. Time for lemonade at the village shop.

MONKEY FOREST. When we buy peanuts at the Sacred Monkey Forest at Sangeh we find the monkeys easier to deal with than orange-sellers. After we have run out of peanuts some of the monkeys nevertheless follow us into the quiet grove of nutmeg trees, like guides.

The Sacred Monkey Forest was formed during a great battle in the heavens in which Hanuman, the famous monkey general in the *Ramayana*, was leading a large monkey army. During the battle, part of a holy mountain fell to earth at Sangeh, along with the monkey army, to whose descendants we are feeding peanuts today.

SAILING IN A PRAHU. After an excellent Chinese lunch in Denpasar (steamed crabs, chicken, frog's legs in soy sauce, two soups) M and D sleep it off back at the Segara Village Hotel—until an indignant Nicholas reports that his monkey mask has disappeared—and then reappeared, for sale, in the hotel shop. After this is settled our nerves are still so bad that we get into our swimsuits and find ourselves talked into hiring a *prahu*, in which it is pleasant to sweep across the water, listening to our own rustle, although the tide is out and each whoosh ends with us stuck in a sandbank. From the sea, the slovenly beach looks like a 'tropical beach', fringed with palms.

Thursday

A VOYAGE TO 'TURTLE ISLAND'. Today we take outrigger sailing more seriously. We hire two *prahus* and set off for Serangan (in tourist language, 'Turtle Island'). M and Julia sing as their *prahu* keeps close to the reef. When D's *prahu* tacks out to sea Nicholas finds it a bit scary, as does D when he recalls that Nicholas has not yet really learned to swim. However they both keep up their conversation. When we pass through the Serangan reef, the sea turns from blue to green and we have a long, whispering glide to the island.

On the island, we look at turtles fattening in a bamboo shed, waiting for someone to buy them and turn them into turtle *satay*. Then we go along a dusty track to a sea temple, sacred to the people of southern Bali, where we pause for some 7-Ups. On the way back we stop inside the Serangan reef for a swim in the clear, green water. Off again through sparkling blue water, close together, close to the shore, singing together and very happy. One of the boatmen tells us that the prevailing wind at this very pleasant time of the year is called 'the Australian wind'.

COCKFIGHT. Nicholas has been saying that he wants to go to the cockfight advertised for today in the beach compound. A whole marketplace has sprung up on the fringes of the crowd. In the ring the cocks are being matched: gradually it is agreed which will fight which. When the betting starts, men all around the ring wave money and shout as if they were doing a *kecak* dance. The gong sounds. The owners ruffle the feathers of their birds to make them angry. Then they're at it. For a few seconds the cocks butt each other, then they jump with their steel spurs. The white cock is slashed. Blood spreads on its feathers. Both birds are picked up. End of round. Second round: one cock runs away, the other wins. Julia is almost crying. We decide to go. Now Nicholas is almost crying. He wants to stay.

MASK DANCE. For dinner, we go to the Tanjung Sari, another Balinese-style hotel, stumbling along paths in the dark until we are in a bar overlooking the beach, where each chair is a sculpture. We are here to see a *Topeng* (mask dance) performance but first there is dinner, which is a full *rijstafel* performance, with M and D eating something of everything, Nicholas asking the names of the dishes but accepting only chicken and coconut, and Julia trying a little of everything but not liking it much, although pleased to see that one man hasn't eaten anything.

We enjoy the *gamelan*, and the opening performance in which a nobleman stands in front of a curtain and trembles with threats, doubts, rages and fears. We like the way the main show is done— it's about a war between two rajas—but we don't know what it's about and the program notes set us off on confusing trails. Perhaps they were about a different *Topeng* play.

Heavy rain as we drive home through the dark.

Friday

DAY OFF. We decide to spend the morning doing nothing other than looking around and having a swim. We know and love our hotel and are used to its movements and colours. In the morning, men sweep the paths and pick up the leaves. After lunch they throw buckets of water over the plants. Morning and afternoon coffee comes to the small table on our veranda, and oil lamps are lit in the evening. Offerings to be placed outside each bungalow are carried around on trays like cups of tea. The women wear yellow and the men wear a blue sarong with a fuchsia-pink top, but when we see them arrive for work most of them are in Western clothes. Some of the waiters keep ceremonial garments, glittering with gold, which they put on if guests want photographs.

We are also familiar with the shops made of woven palm leaves in the beach market—batik shops, art shops, and so forth, built around a statue that looks out across the lagoon. Behind them, on the road, are a clutter of food stalls and mini-bus drivers and in front the *prahu* men offer the pleasures of the sea. People seem to know us now. 'Miss Julia', in particular, has been singled out as a significant batik buyer. Nicholas is famed as a kite-flyer, mainly because of the plastic kite he brought from Sydney. At low tide the beach still seems repellent, but at high tide it is as beautiful as a tourist photograph.

After lunch, we walk and shop among the open-fronted shops in Denpasar and look at the traffic, the cinemas and other sleazy signs of the other Bali. Nicholas announces that he will go to bed. While the others have dinner in the garden he eats a *kropek*, four pieces of cucumber and three cheese sticks and by the time we are ready to go to the *Legong* dance he is fast asleep.

COURTLY DANCE. The *Legong* dancers are from the Kokar Conservatorium in Denpasar. D gives a brief introductory explanation that *Legong* and some other performances go back to the palace life. This seems entirely likely when we watch the dancers in their rich-looking costumes perform their precise eye movements, their exact finger movements and their quick shoulder shruggings. For this, and other performances in the beach compound, tourists pay a dollar each for a chair but local people come along (for nothing, with no chair) and, we are told, make learned comments on the performance.

Saturday

This is to be our longest drive. We pass deep river gorges and wide valleys with tracks leading across them to the sea. We pass through a neat, clean, white-looking town with many government offices, but it is not on our schedule.

HELL DISCOVERED. At the crossroads at Klungkung we stop to look at the 18th century courthouse, a reminder of the 300 years when the local Gengel dynasty saw themselves as ruling Bali. Cases were brought here if they couldn't be settled among families or villages. A guide seats us at the judges' table, where there is a flower-offering and some incense is burning, and tells us what the court procedures used to be. The roof shows scenes from hell—the tongues of liars are being pulled out, the hands of pickpockets thrust into flames and the breasts of mothers who abandoned their babies are being cut off. This is the first time Julia and Nicholas have seen hell.

MOTHER TEMPLE. Almost 1000 metres up the slopes of Mount Agung, the home of the gods, Besakih is 'the mother temple' of Bali—30 temples, in fact, laid out over seven terraces. The names and functions of the Hindu deities Brahma, Vishnu and Shiva are now recited daily by Nicholas and Julia. The guide gives us a run-down of the Hindu religion and a description of the volcanic explosion of 1963 which killed more than 1000 people.

A FISHING VILLAGE. We swing east and cross one of the rivers in which the lava flowed down into the sea. It is still a dry land of dead lava. In the next valley we cross a coastal plain of lava, in which the only remains of a village are a temple of the dead, a sacred tree and a few crumpled gateways. Then we drive along a green strip of coast and into the fishing village of Kusamba, with its black sand beach where one of the fishing *prahus* (with an eye painted on it so that it can see in the dark) is being unloaded by women who are carrying the catch in baskets on their heads to the village market. At the end of the beach are thatched huts where salt is dried and sold in Klungkung. Even fishermen in Bali distrust the sea. All the buildings in Kusamba are turned away from it

SMELLY TEMPLE. The driver stops and gestures us towards a temple. Why do we have to look at this? We have seen much better temples. We hear a noise from the cave at the back of the temple. What's that noise? Bats! The driver shoos us in among hundreds of stinking bats. We know what this is now: we have just seen the famous Bat Temple of Goa Lawah.

TOURISTS OBSERVED. Before going on to the Bali Aga village of Tenganan we stop beside the road for a picnic lunch. Opposite are the thatched huts of a Balinese family. (In this part of Bali they don't put walls across a family compound, or even have villages.) A whole family comes out and sits around, watching, laughing and talking, as we take our food out of its pink tissue paper and plastic wraps. They are the tourists, inspecting us.

We attempt contact. D takes out his camera. The husband tells his wife to cover her breasts. M hands out examples of Australian cheese sticks and sultanas. One of the cheese sticks is passed around and nibbled at, with expressions ranging from lack of interest to disgust. Julia and Nicholas then put on a roadside show by pretending to pull off their thumbs and performing other magical devices. M makes a model of a *prahu* out of a paper napkin. Julia does funny things with her hat. They sit, and watch.

THE ENCHANTED ISLAND

The island on which we spent our family holiday was enchanted in the sense that life was organised around ceremonial relations with the supernatural—and presentations of the myth system were easy for visitors to see, in icon, legend and ritual. It was also enchanted because so many of the magic circles of tourism had been drawn around particular objects, activities and places. The coining of phrases such as 'Turtle Island' and 'Monkey Forest' could make Bali seem like a theme park. As we drove along the road to Ubud, concepts such as 'art village' could organise the whole experience. There were shows such as 'the *Barong* dance' that one *must* see, and temples such as Bangli that one must do. As night followed day, a visit to Pejeng was to be followed by a visit to Gunung Kawi. The tourist enchantment was so efficiently prearranged that one of the pleasures of arrival was recognition—look, there are baffle walls, look there is a temple procession, look there is a small cremation. This must be Bali. It was outside these magic spells that we could appropriate some of Bali as our own discovery—when a tyre blew out, for a start, but also getting around by ourselves, and reading a book.

It is almost impossible on a first visit not to move automatically into the programmed tourist image of Bali. You may like it, as we did, but, if you don't, it is still the tourist image you are reacting against. Nor is that image exclusively phony. But it is not exclusively

FAMILY HOLIDAY   91

true. There are other ways of imagining Bali. You can find most of them in Adrian Vickers' *Bali: A Paradise Created*. Earlier Bali was seen as a savage land of widow-burning and slave-trading whose inhabitants, like other Malays, would run *amok* capriciously; it was a decadent and licentious land of royal despotism and warring kingdoms. Then, at the beginning of the 20th century, the Dutch destroyed the Balinese kingdoms. At Denpasar, and then at Klungkung, whole regimes ended with death rushes of thousands of courtiers who followed their rajas in throwing themselves into the gunfire of the Dutch.

The social order was dislocated by Dutch colonial officers with their powers of exile and gaol. The economic order was one of arbitrary forced labour and, for many, impoverishment. It was also a time when a new educated élite began a nationalist struggle against the Dutch and a modernising struggle against feudal traditions. Then came the arrogance of Japanese rule and, after its overthrow, of resistance against the Dutch. With independence, 15 years of political conflict and violent rallies culminated in 1965–6 in the killing of tens of thousands of communists and the educated, with villages burned to the ground and rivers choked with the dead. Six years before we had our family holiday in Bali, a 'discovery' could mean coming across a village revengefully reduced to ash, or a river choked with headless corpses.

The island has its occasional monument to a few of the heroes in these struggles, but they are not on the tourist schedules. There is nothing about Bali's political and social conflicts in the Museum Bali.

* * *

As Adrian Vickers records, it was only after the Dutch seizure that Europeans began creating benign cultural images of Bali. Six years after the last of the rajas' courts had immolated itself at Klungkung, the characteristic tourist phrases were falling into place: 'The enchanted isle', 'The last paradise', 'The island of the gods'. And in the postcards and travel photographs the key visual images had been developed: Bali was a land of rice paddies and waving palms, of bare-breasted tropical damsels and gentle men. Down even to the arrangement of its hibiscus and frangipanni, the setting of the Puri Suling restaurant when we had lunch there would have been familiar to anyone who had seen travel photographs of Bali in the 1920s—except for the lack of bare-breasted damsels. Women's breasts began to be covered, by order, in the 1950s as part of a nationalist and modernising reform. When we were there, some of the conservative older women beyond the concentrated tourist areas still went bare-breasted, but, like the woman in the family scene at our picnic near Tenganan, they would not be photographed. I have always wanted to explain to that woman that it wasn't her breasts I wanted to photograph, but her family.

It was the arrival of the tourist boats (about 250 tourists a month by 1940) that prompted the use of fragments of culture for commercial purposes. Tourists at the Hotel Bali (which the shipping line, KPM, had established in Denpasar in 1925) had to have mementos of their visit. What were they to buy? 'Art' as a separate idea had not been thought of by the Balinese. Wood and stone carving were part of architecture—mainly for palaces and temples—or as decorations on functional objects, or used for guardian figures. Now there was to be 'art', something secular, made separately, and for sale. This produced one of Bali's transformation scenes.

Wood and stone carving had traditionally been robustly ornate evocations of gods, heroes and demons, and, in the case of woodcarvings, brightly painted. But tourists seemed to prefer understated realistic studies, done in polished wood that showed the natural grain. The first art objects to meet this market were carved wooden heads of female dancers; these became the souvenirs that showed you had 'done' Bali. Then followed carvings of girls bathing, of birds and beasts, of women seated quietly in prayer, of old men contemplating life's passing scenes. These were classified as 'characteristically Balinese'. The big leap came at around the beginning of the 1930s: people started carving elongated figures in polished wood, of the kind we had rejected at the volcano site (we were later to buy some garishly painted *Garudas* in the old style). Long, attenuated, stretched-out figures in polished teak became typically Balinese. Stone carvings remained much the same as before: there is not much tourist demand for stone.

By then, Bali was going through another transformation scene. Painting had traditionally pictured (in a style similar to the puppets of the *wayang kulit* shadow play) stories from the *Ramayana*, the *Mahabharata* and other classics. Now tourists wanted works to frame that they might consider they understood. Partly because of the influence of European artists living in Bali, new styles of great imaginative power developed—then imitation drained the life out of them. Such painting was also classified as characteristically Balinese.

At first, only a few small shops sold art souvenirs and they were run by Europeans. These were the precursors of the present 'art villages', the art galleries, the art street stalls—and the art hawker who tried to sell elongated carvings in polished wood to an Australian family visiting a volcano site in 1971.

After tourists had motored from the ship to the Hotel Bali in the 1920s and 1930s they needed some performance to watch while they ate their *rijstafel*. What would they get? The Balinese put together some dance excerpts. A version of the courtly *Legong*, based on several different dance routines, came to be seen as the quintessential Balinese dance and was often presumed to be performed by 'temple dancers', a class of persons which did not exist. The '*Barong* Dance' we saw on our first morning was a medley of bits and pieces: the story line (which is almost universally unintelligible to tourists) came from an amended version of an episode from the *Mahabharata*. The central idea of struggle between good and evil is fundamental to Balinese faith; most of the masks were taken from a sacred exorcism story; there are touches of *Topeng*, *Legong* and other dances; a monkey was added for fun, and a *kris* dance (with a pretend trance sequence) was thrown in at the end. The *Kecak* we saw at the beachfront was also choreographed for tourists, with a fragment of a story from the *Ramayana* (also likely to be unintelligible), played to a background of the brilliantly choreographed 'monkey chorus', which was based on an idea taken from the male chorus of the ritual *Sanghyang* dance ceremony.

It was in the 1950s and 1960s that the bungalow style developed for tourist accommodation, and the magic circles were drawn about the places to visit and the order decided in which they should be visited (and for what purpose). On your eastern tour, see the Hall of Justice at Klungkung, then the Mother Temple of Besakih, then the fishing village of Kusamba. Then you *must* see the famous Bat Cave of Goa Lawah.

TRAVELLING INTO THE MUNDANE

By 1971 Bali was tightly conceptualised into tourist stereotypes that had been developing for 50 years, but on later visits we found that a tourist can become a freer agent by moving outside the narrow tourist structure. If you want to escape the automatic sightseeing in Bali it is particularly easy to do so.

Some possible 'discoveries' are in the guidebooks, but you can find your own way to them and look at them how you want to and in your own time, even those that are alongside the main tourist routes. During the tourist rush-hour, the Elephant Cave has become an adjunct to a large parking lot surrounded by hawkers' stalls, but almost no-one visits, only a kilometre away, the 25 metres of carvings of everyday life that were cut out of the cliff face at Yeh Pulu some unknown number of centuries ago. You reach them by walking between rice paddies and when you get there you take your own time making whatever you want out of this realism carved from rock.

The most effective travelling outside the tourists' schedules can come from something not in the guidebooks—seeking the mundane. This can offset the 'culture' load of dance-drama excerpts, temple visits and artshop haggling, and by putting these activities into context it gives them their proper place in the everyday (and one of the interests of Bali is that its rituals and ceremonies are part of the everyday). Walking along streets in Denpasar can provide the mundane in one go, but, unless you know something about the social innards of Denpasar, looking at its signs of third-rate modernity might simply lead you to believe that Balinese culture has been destroyed and the tourist relics are just a fake. Elsewhere the signs are different.

We had heard that Sebatu, a village not mentioned in the guidebooks, had been awarded a prize as the cleanest locality in Bali so we went to look at it. We found what seemed a long, narrow and—yes, very clean—suburban street of family compounds leading up to the village's principal assembly area, a pavilion done in traditional style, where in pride of place was a motorbike—the first prize in a local lottery. On the way out we stopped to watch a small boy in a T-shirt being taught a *Baris*, a traditional warrior dance. The teaching was in traditional style, in which the student is intended to feel the dance enter his body. The teacher, also in a T-shirt, stood behind the child, body-to-body—forcing the arms and fingers into the correct mode, adjusting posture and tilting the head to match the drum beat of the *gamelan* music that was coming from a tape recorder.

This time, my wife and I were staying on the outskirts of Mas, a largely Brahman village where important elements in modern Balinese woodcarving were invented in the 1930s—groups of young carvers still sit cross-legged in pavilions, working with a master woodworker. There we learned something of the woodcarving business from the inside—the rivalries within and between families, the commissions for coach tour operators, the relations with foreign dealers. We also walked around the lanes of this large village, where we bought fruit from a market under a banyan tree and watched a pig being carried upside down on a pole to the place of slaughter. We looked over the primary school with the red and white Indonesian flag flying above it, walked across the soccer field, inspected the cinema and the badminton court and watched a game of netball being played beside the site of a new *bale banjar* (a kind of neighbourhood clubhouse) that was being built in entirely traditional style. The walls that enclosed all the family compounds gave an illusion of equality, but a Balinese accompanying us pointed to the gold-decorated towers of rich families and other signs of social difference. Back at the place where we were staying we watched the Indonesian evening news on television.

The Balinese like a crowd at the public parts of a cremation, because bustle is auspicious. Within certain confines of behaviour, travellers are welcome to become part of a ceremony instead of being spectators—a rare opportunity in tourism. While the private ceremonies are going on inside a family compound decked out with banners and drapings, travellers are left outside among the motorbikes, the mini-buses and the other tourists, but this gives them a chance to voyage into the mundane.

The Balinese don't usually object to tourists at temple festivals, although they are beginning to expect them to dress at least partly in Balinese clothes that go beyond a token 'temple scarf'. However, the high points happen late at night and may go on until dawn, and can be as hard to timetable as they are to understand in the confusion of incense and sandalwood smoke, tinkling bells, gongs, processions, dances, songs of praise and the sounds of a county fair. All this can seem exotic enough to use up rolls of film, but seeking out the mundane in a festival can bring the Balinese back to the scale of human beings. By daylight you can see the temple transformed by long tapering banners and paintings and brocades brought out at festival time to decorate the shrines, but in particular you can look at the offerings and the women who made them. Balinese women can spend a third or more of their working hours putting together various versions of leaves, flowers, fruits and holy water in combinations of red, green and white to make offerings to spirits of various kinds. One of the first things a little girl learns is how to cut and skewer leaves into elaborate patterns; there are television programs from Denpasar on the making of offerings; and now, with competitions at the annual Bali Arts Festival in Denpasar, the making of offerings has passed from ceremony to art.

For temple festivals women combine fruit, flowers, leaves and a variety of rice cakes, and perhaps eggs or meats, into towers up to three metres high, then dress themselves in ornate brocades and carry these towers to the temple—sometimes in processions, sometimes singly. For the observer of the mundane, single is best. You can stand in a temple and see the women come in one by one, stacking their offerings upon platforms in the temple pavilions—and then walk around appraising other women's offerings, some supporting tradition, some looking for new ideas. A family may come in, parents and children, in their best festival batik and brocade, and you can watch them at prayer, males cross-legged, women kneeling. Incense smokes as they scatter flower petals and a priest sprinkles them from a flower dipped in holy water. When they have been dabbed with damp rice they put their shoes back on, gather their offerings to take home and, if there are other people around, chat for a while in the outer courtyards. To watch one family at prayer is a reminder that this is a religious, not a tourist spectacle. It is also worthwhile to visit the temple when the festival is over. The paintings and brocades and banners have been put away. The visiting spirits have gone. What remain are the stone and moss and ferns of an unadorned temple that is of no significance until the next return of the spirits.

We went to Petulu, a hillside village also not on the tourist itineraries, whose flamboyantly carved, ochre-coloured walls overgrown with bushes give a sense of aristocratic decay, as if one of the baroque quarters of Rome had been overtaken by jungle. It was at the end of an afternoon, at the time when flocks of long, graceful white herons come home, to float above the hill before roosting in the village's trees.

Later in the week we went back at night to a *Barong* performance—to compare the 'real thing' with the tourist performance put on every day at Batubulan. We sat down with the children on the clubhouse floor and listened to *gamelan* music for much longer than we had ever imagined, while in the temple priests were praying and sanctifying with holy water the huge *Barong* mask, the clothes of its body, the dancers who would get inside them and the *Barong*'s ceremonial umbrella, flags and spears. From a child's view from the floor, the *Barong* was both playful and hypnotically formidable, standing in the one spot for an unbearably long time, gaping and jiggling to the drum beat and then, with a change in music, swishing to another spot, gaping and jiggling. Neither the women in their elaborate brocades, nor the men in their casual clothes, seemed to pay much attention to the *Barong*. The part that would interest them would come in an hour or so. In the meantime, the village lane had been transformed with strings of coloured electric lights, shopping stalls and temporary restaurants.

The manager of the bungalow hotel where we were staying invited us for dinner to his family compound. We sat in a small pavilion, from which he pointed to other pavilions that housed his brothers and their families. We weren't expected to eat all of the small feast put in front of us—smoked duck, spiced duck, pork *satay* and a couple of spicy vegetable dishes with jackfruit and coconut. What was left would be served to others in the household. He told us he was short-staffed, bookings were down, servants weren't what they used to be, clearing the swimming pool of insects was a daily problem, and he couldn't do a thing with the waiter.

PART TWO

♦ ♦ ♦

A reality that is out of this world

8.

INVENTING THE AUTHENTIC

◆ ◆ ◆

MORAL TORMENTS OF THE ORIGINAL CONDITION

Why bother to go to heritage sites or museums? A narrow answer is that looking at things that humans have made can provide one of our main entries into studying humanity—in the ways people used these things and in the views of the world implied in their general design.

But other people can look at them for us and write books or produce television programs about them, can't they? So why should the rest of us go to look at old buildings or old things in glass cases? One answer is that you don't really know what something looks like until you see it, and that *seeing* can arouse curiosity in ways that are different from reading.

Objects can't be turned into words—any more than listening to music, watching dancing or looking at visual images can be turned into words. Words are only one of the ways in which we do our thinking.

But, to the people who run heritage sites and museums, there has been a quite different consideration: it has been the cult of authenticity, in which when a thing becomes part of our 'heritage' it enters that realm of extraordinary purity in which, in an age of meretriciousness, it becomes authentic—the real thing.

An example: imagine you are a curator in an industry museum which has acquired a machine that must be turned into an exhibit. How can you present it in an authentic state?

Perhaps you decide to polish or lacquer or paint it to get it back to what it used to be. That will satisfy the nostalgic view of the past as a place of harmony and craftsmanship compared with the shoddiness of the present, and it will satisfy the optimistic view that all machinery is bright and progressive. But, even if it looks like the original, the new decoration is *not* the original. And it doesn't correspond to the present state of this machine. And prettying-up the machine as an aesthetic object gives an inaccurate view of what industrialisation has been like. In any case, the machine will not seem like something old: it will look like a replica.

Make it more complicated. Some parts are missing and the museum director wants a machine in running order. That also offends your sense of authenticity. You argue that it is better to keep the machine as it is and to build a copy or a model to show how it works. Then people can see how the old thing worked when it was young, but the original machine, incomplete, would also be there as a reminder of the Ozymandias factor: that time passes and even machines decay.

You lose that argument. The director tells you to get some replacement parts made so that the machine works. Do you engage in the forgery of making these new parts look old? You don't want to do that. You want to leave the replacement parts looking new, so that people can see how the engine works, but can also understand that it is being kept alive with prosthetic devices. The director says the public won't like that and anyway there is a publicity advantage. He remembers that when the Opel company refurbished its oldest automobile model, built at the turn of the century, their PR people brought out a pamphlet that produced as evidence of authenticity the fact that it had taken 2900 work hours 'to restore it to its original condition'.

You believe that a machine can only be seen as authentic if it is left as it was before it came to the museum—clean it up, certainly, but no more than it would have been cleaned up when it was in use. That means that if it is chipped or scratched or worn smooth by wear and tear, or if it bears corrosion scars, or if pieces are missing, that is now its authentic state. Then the only contrivance is that it has been taken out of the world and put into a museum. You resign.

This catechism of quandaries is not invented. It is based on an article, 'The Restoration of Historical Technological Artifacts, Instruments and Tools' in *The International Journal of Museum Management and Curatorship*, by Herman Kühn, a curator at the Deutsches Museum, Munich. It shows one example of the moral torments of an ethic of authenticity.

* * *

As with machinery, so with Old Masters. It was an authenticity controversy that continued to make the Sistine Chapel something one must *do* when in Rome. This controversy was related to the 16th century Council of Trent order that genitals and nipples should be dug out of the plaster of some of the nudes in *The Last Judgment* and that clothes be painted over nakedness. There was no possibility of 'restoring' what Michelangelo had originally painted because we don't know what it was. Then another question of authenticity came up: should the plaster and paint of prudery remain, since it is part of the history of *The Last Judgment*?

Expectations of the authentic are met by a visit to the Parthenon—because it looks exactly like its photographs. But the Parthenon wasn't built as a half-destroyed outline. It had a roof, parts of it were painted red, blue and gold, and it was dominated by the towering, multicoloured figure of Athena, hung, like some mad witch, in bracelets, rings and necklaces. If the gods restored the Parthenon and confronted us with its authenticity, we would have to admit the bad taste of the Ancient Greeks. Borobudur was painted. Angkor Wat was painted. Many of the Maya buildings were painted. The great temples of India and of Ancient Egypt were painted. Our belief in 'classical periods' as periods of honest stone is unauthentic.

Authenticity can also be found in a sense of communion with 'the people', especially if they can be safely reached by a visit to 'the old town' of a European city (the Plaka in Athens, the Upper Town in Zagreb, the Alfama in Lisbon, the squares and streets around the Domus Cathedral in Riga, the Market Square and its environs in

Cracow, and, for that matter, the Jewish Quarter of the Old City in Jerusalem), or the picturesque quarters of Latin American cities—La Boca in Buenos Aires is a characteristic example. But this can raise some difficulties in authenticity—commercialisation (as with the Plaka and La Boca)—a simple absence of 'the people', who have been replaced by offices, cultural activities and yuppies (in most cases) and the difficulty that when 'the people' are still there, as they are in the Alfama, it is only by contrivance that they are kept that way. Unlike the first Opel car, 'the people' cannot be restored to a replica of their original condition, and there is not much call for organised tours of the Tondo shantytowns in Manila or the *favela* encampments in Rio (although there are now some organised tours of the South Bronx in New York).

A natural feature such as Victoria Falls, the Jungfrau, Mount Fuji, the Grand Canyon, or the Great Barrier Reef is also a kind of relic, in that it provides both an authentic monument offering moral regeneration and also the technical and moral problems of restoration and conservation, which, as at Victoria Falls, can be part of the overall sell. An Antarctic eco-holiday can be a floating seminar on how to conserve the Antarctic. One can approach Nature as a problem in conservation.

* * *

In religious pilgrimages there was always concern about the authenticity of relics, but if there was a problem—the many skulls of St John the Baptist that were to be found throughout Europe, for example, could not all have come from the same body—it was settled as a matter of faith: in this case by proclaiming that the skull was so filled with holiness that it had the power of reproducing itself. But in the tourist pilgrimages the question of the authenticity of historic sites, of museum exhibits and of presentations of folkways can be researched and it can also be subjected to a catechism of moral questioning. I said in *The Great Museum* that authenticity can be the special magic of sightseeing tourism, casting spells of moral as well as material value. I should have gone further. For some, especially those actually in the business, the question of authenticity is one of the inner agonies of sightseeing—added to the fear, among sensitive tourists, that the very act of being a tourist may be necessarily inauthentic.

The tourist experience, that can turn all of Europe into a great

INVENTING THE AUTHENTIC

museum in which to seek an authenticated past, has been part of the same modern crisis in reality that has produced so much writing of history and sociology, and such an appetite for experimenting in literature and the arts. It is part of the flight from what can seem the spuriousness of modernity. As Dean MacCannell said in *The Tourist*, the progress of modernity depended on things seeming unstable and inauthentic. Authenticity was somewhere else—in the past, in other cultures, in the simplicity of other people's lifestyles and (he could have added) in communion with nature.

THE AUTHENTICITY OF CITIES

For the rest of this chapter I will consider the perils of authenticity as revealed in the restoration of cities. If you visit a foreign city, where do you look for the 'authentic'?

If you ask in Bucharest: 'What is typically Romanian?', the answer is that because of fires, earthquakes, politics and other ill-fortunes, practically nothing is typical: most buildings considered 'old' are in a variety of 19th century revival styles—neo-classical, neo-baroque, neo-renaissance and, in at least one case, neo-Tudor—set in leftovers of the framework of a city that is grand in a 19th century way, with wide boulevards, large squares and lavish garden parks. For want of anything better, the 'typical' was taken to be the 'neo-Romanian' style invented in the 19th century, a revival of the 18th century 'Brancovian', which, in its echoing of the slender, soaring quality of traditional Romanian architecture, was also a revival style. Neo-Romanian was a revival of a revival.

Seekers after the Bucharest of King Carol and his mistress, Madame Lupescu, may find authenticity in surviving districts of tree-lined streets with villas in varying shades of brown that recall a briefly assured bourgeois past. In other quarters, where the houses are smaller and shabbier, and the streets narrower, shorter and more straggling, there is a touch of 'the oriental'. The 'oriental' always seems authentic. But perhaps the typical Bucharest is the new city—miles of apartment houses, from six to 12 stories high, set in copious squares and stretches of grass—and the 1000 rooms of the 60 hectare Palace of the Republic. That is the authentic Bucharest of the time of Nicolae and Elena Ceaucescu.

Authenticity can be aesthetically uncomfortable. What is unique about the old quarter of Bern are arcades that run in front of the buildings, with arches so solid that the Bernese do their window-shopping in a complex of caves. From outside, the bulging bottoms look like lumpy boulders and challenge the elegance of the rest of what were once patricians' houses. From the inside, to a visitor, they can seem restrictive and gross. To the Swiss they are the authentic style of the Central Plateau.

Chicago is the world's most comprehensive museum city of modern architecture. The 'Archicenter' run by the Chicago Architecture Foundation offers 70 tours of Chicago, all encompassing buildings that are 'authentic'. The Archicenter itself is opposite the 1890 Manhattan Building, the first tall office block to be entirely supported by a steel skeleton—the first real skyscraper and therefore a greater monument to modernity than Picasso. (Not that Chicago doesn't have its 'Picassos'.) But how will the Manhattan Building and all the other buildings on the 70 Archicenter tours continue to supply authenticity? By being put back to where they were in 1890? How do you do that? You can't restore what went on inside and around them. Will the meaning of authenticity extend to include those buildings that live on, while they change in their uses and physical forms, as life in the city itself changes? What if the buildings begin to rot?

The Bund, the celebrated one and a half kilometres of banks, merchant houses, European clubs and hotels along the waterfront at Shanghai, is a magnificent museum-skyline of early 20th century European architecture, from neo-renaissance to art deco and, with its assured effrontery, a symbol of the confidence of the European occupiers of Shanghai. Although most buildings are now rundown, grimy and overcrowded, it is possible to present the Bund as a nostalgia trip to Noel Coward's Shanghai. Coward wrote the first draft of *Private Lives* in the Cathay (now the Peace) Hotel and the hotel has been renovated in a thoroughly 'faithful' art deco restoration—they even seem to have restored a 1930s jazz band. Restorers could clean up and do over the facades of other grand buildings in a thoroughly 'faithful' restoration of a period of European imperial confidence, but what would this be faithful to? As it stands now, partly restored but mainly in decay, the Bund is a reminder of 20th century China as it moved from the disasters of 'the era of imperial banditry' into disasters of its own.

Some tourist-attracting buildings in Central and Eastern Europe are fakes—and heroically so. They were destroyed in the second world war and replaced by replicas. The most tremendous example is Old Warsaw. As tourists walk along Krakowski Przedmiescie to Castle Square they can admire the 18th century houses (most in various quiet neo-classical forms) now put to modern commercial uses, and the old palaces now serving public purposes. The quiet, shabby elegance suggests generations of adaptation. From Castle Square, tourists move past the Royal Castle along a narrow street to the cathedral, and wander through archways, passages, lanes and small courtyards to the burghers' multicoloured houses in the Old Market Square. Then through the medieval fortress, and past the ramparts of the barbican, to the quieter tones and more pretentious houses of the New Market Square.

Throughout the walk, there are impressions of an enduring and serene continuity of use and adaptation, yet after the second world war none of these buildings existed. The Nazis left only blackened fragments and wastes of rubble. In the most epic reconstruction of an old town that Europe is likely to know, the Poles went beyond pragmatism into an obsessed act of faith. Where there were hectares of wreckage they built hundreds of buildings—houses, shops, palaces, 'ruins' as they used to be. After using X-ray apparatus, quartz lamps and photographic equipment to examine fragments of rubbish and, having studied old records, old plans and old photographs, and 25 landscapes of Warsaw painted by Canaletto in the second half of the 18th century, they prepared plans for hundreds of replica buildings. Some were complete copies inside and out. Some had modern interiors behind the facades (as might have happened anyway). Ateliers were established where metalwork specialists faked old fittings, armour, grids and lattices. Carpenters produced copies of old parquetry and wall panelling. Other craft workers imitated old glass, old statues, old ceramics.

But which Old Warsaw was to be re-created? The Old Warsaw of 1939 was taken as the model and then amended to allow for an equal presence of other and earlier old Warsaws. Squares were opened out to provide better views. The replica cathedral was built without the 19th century improvements. The fortress and ramparts were restored to a wholeness they began to lose several hundred years ago. What was constructed was a museum of alternative authenticities.

CREATING OLD SINGAPORE

Decisions about individual city buildings, or whole quarters of cities, are much the same as those the imaginary curator faced when confronted with the old machine. Do you relacquer or repaint or do you leave the chips and scratches and evidence of wear and tear? If parts are missing, do you forge some new ones or do you just provide demonstrations of how the machine used to work? Two kinds of answers come from programs in Singapore. One is to 'reconstruct'. The other is to leave a few old things standing without any pretence that you have done anything else.

At times it seemed that Lee Kuan Yew's government would obliterate every building in Singapore constructed before 1960—but it decided that the citizens of Singapore, in their amazing transformation, needed material reminders of where they had come from. And tourists might want a touch of sightseeing as well as shopping, eating, resort life, a bird park and a science centre. What was contrived were fragments of 'Old Singapore'.

A Preservation of Monuments Board was set up, and 19 buildings, in Chinese, Melakan, Indian and European styles, were proclaimed national monuments. To promote the idea, one Chinese temple, one mosque, one Hindu temple, and one Christian church were presented in a special issue of postage stamps. The Urban Redevelopment Authority then added an extra colour to the map of its central area structure plan. It had coloured some parts blue for intensive development and others green for parks. Now it declared certain areas 'historic districts', and coloured them orange for conservation.

Two of these historic districts provide a classroom lesson in the perils of attempts at re-creating authenticity—one because past buildings were all there (Emerald Hill) and the other (the Singapore River) because most of its past had been pulled down.

What Singapore did have—like all other cities—was a concept of a characteristic style that was worth keeping for its historic significance. In Bucharest it was 'Brancovian'. For Singapore, it was 'the shophouse'—the terraces of open-fronted shops with living space above that used to make up almost all of Singapore other than the European quarters. Shophouses have now been studied and classified into Early, Transition, Second Transition, Art Deco, Late, Modern and Revival styles, and their facades are analysed in terms of foreign influence—ornate plasterwork ornaments, glazed tiles and fence doors are Oriental; classical columns and louvred French windows are European. There is now an expert vocabulary with which to talk about shophouses.

But which shophouses were to be restored? And where? An outstanding site was found in the terraces of three-storeyed shophouses at Emerald Hill, once a suburb, now part of the Orchard Road tourist, shopping, hotel and restaurant development. They were solidly built and part of a commercially attractive area. ('Own a Shophouse in Emerald Hill—A Chance to Work and Live in a Piece of History.') They provided flamboyant and vibrant specimens of the shophouse as architectural species. And since Emerald Hill was developed as a residential suburb at the turn of the century, mainly for the *Babas* (the Peranakans or 'Straits Chinese'), there was a 'link with history', because there was already a field of scholarship about the Peranakan culture (the Malay way of being Chinese) in the commercial garrisons of Melaka and Penang, and then Singapore. A fashion had developed for collecting Peranakan objects. There was a revival of interest in Peranakan handicrafts and cooking—called 'Nonya' because, while the Peranakans were male (*Baba*) when they were building shophouses, they were female (*Nonya*) when they were producing beadwork or spicy chicken.

As well as restoring the shophouses of Emerald Hill Road, the Urban Redevelopment Authority did up some commercial houses at the junction with Orchard Road: a museum was put in, with some curio shops, some reconstructed colonial stores and a new name was decided on—Peranakan Place.

If you like colour (using that word literally) in a walk through gentrified inner city streets, you can't do better than the restored shophouses of Emerald Hill Road. Refurbishing them like this is the equivalent of relacquering and repainting an old machine in an industry museum but—and this is not true of a museum exhibit if you leave them chipped and cracked and showing wear and tear they will be pulled down. Now they provide pleasant places for some comfortably-off Singapore people to live, and they are reminiscent of the past of this part of Singapore. An intelligent tourist could exorcise false claims to authenticity, and then learn about Peranakan culture by doing a bit of reading, by visiting the house museum in Emerald Hill Road, and then going to the National Museum.*

Like Emerald Hill, the three-kilometre Singapore River is coloured orange for conservation on the map. But while Emerald Hill can appear to be authentically restored, even if this appearance collapses into the usual ironies of authenticity, to restore authenticity to the Singapore River would involve moving the city's warehouses back to the river, cramming its sides with harbour lighters, crowding its banks with tin-sided hovels and hawkers' stalls, and pouring in filth so that it again became an open sewer. With the Singapore River, the Authority had to engage in authentic destruction—of the river's pollution, and of disastrous living areas—although there was also random destruction of old buildings. What was left was a bright, clear waterway, a public promenade with some isolated relics sticking up like stumps of tooth, a few rows of riverfront shophouses (a special style of shophouse), some warehouses (godowns), an old quay, and a former police barracks, 'an architectural gem' that now houses the National Archives.

These relics have become no more than curiosities among the landscaping, the shopping malls, exhibition spaces and residential developments. So why not clear them away? So much had now been destroyed that it might be more authentic to knock down the rest, and allow the river to become an appropriate background to the dreaming towers of the financial centre and the international hotels. The short answer is that there would then be no surviving examples of Singapore's riverside shophouses and godowns—and, as these things go, the former police barracks *is* an architectural gem.

The more important answer is based on accepting that real restoration is never possible. Emerald Hill has not been restored as a suburb for successful *Babas*. It is a splendidly done architectural restoration, which gives pleasure to some middle class Singaporeans and can legitimately interest some tourists as a museum of design. But it hangs together so well that its professional finish and its cohesiveness might tempt the belief that this is what Emerald Hill

---

* **AUTHENTIC BURGERS.** For a while, in Peranakan Place, there was also the Keday Kopi restaurant where the menu had been intelligently arranged as a kind of cultural show of cuisine. Too intelligent. Keday Kopi has shut down and the space has been taken over by 'Delifrance'. However, there is a restaurant that offers 'Nonyaburgers'.

was really like in the Peranakan days. That belief would be ludicrous. (It would be even more ludicrous to imagine that you are walking through history if you walk past the 200 shophouses in the 'Tanjong Pagar Conservation Area' near Chinatown, whose facades have been authentically tizzed-up and whose insides have been so successfully re-done that they now make 'a trendy hub for cafes, pubs, antique shops and professionals' offices'. This used to be the rickshaw drivers' quarter.)

There is no such temptation with the Singapore River. With only fragments of shophouses and godowns surviving, no-one is going to think that this is what the Singapore River was really like. Fragments of streets left standing—isolated buildings now out of context, or fragments of terraces surrounded by contemporary construction—have the saving advantage of making you think. It is as if these leftover buildings have been put into a museum display case, but most of the parts are missing. It can remind the sensitive that these are not 'the past', but relics of the past. If you then want to imagine what things were like back in those days, you do it by using your imagination. Presumably your imagination can establish that the three old godowns that have now been linked in a development called 'Zouk' were not originally built as an entertainment complex with a Mediterranean-style restaurant, cafe, wine bar and discotheque.

* * *

The desire for a pure authenticity conceals the paradox that the authentic must always be contrived. The historic site and the old quarter were not like that when new, and a museum's exhibits can be 100 per cent authentic and at the same time false, in the sense that it is not authentic for things to be taken out of the world, cleaned, conserved, labelled, catalogued, displayed and transmuted into museum 'exhibits'. Authenticity can never be achieved. It is a mirage, part of the enchantment.

It is the *idea of authenticity* that many tourists want. As long as it is confidently asserted and attested by some seal of approval, almost any authenticity might do.

In 1992, a theme park—the Tang Dynasty Village—was opened in Singapore, in which all the replicas are guaranteed to be authentic.

9.
HOW TO BE REAL

◆ ◆ ◆

RITUALS OF THE CAMERA

The appetite for 'authenticity' in tourism is itself part of a wider modern craving—the infatuation with the 'real' and a sense of actuality. There is no better example than the camera—because a photograph can be more real than real, which is what Walter Lippmann had in mind when he told the story in *Public Opinion* of a mother who listens to praise of her baby and then says: 'But wait till you see his photograph'. This belief in the transcendent reality of the photograph has been as important to tourism as the transport revolution that started with the railways. How can we imagine tourism without it? The camera authenticates our journey. It proves we were there.

And while some of the early tourist emblems—the Pyramids and the Alps—were conceptualised in lithographs and engravings, it was the camera that invented most of the sights we were expected to see. Imagine those great moments in the history of standardisation when the first photograph was taken to 'frame' (define) the smiling native flashing her teeth as she held up her happy child, or the peasant craftsman pursuing his traditional craft in the ancient marketplace. In *100 Years in Yosemite*, Carl P Russell describes the process of 'framing' the Yosemite Valley. In 1855 the first lithograph was published, followed by four engravings in an article in *California Magazine*, then 20 glass plate negatives, providing evidence that Yosemite was the world's greatest single Wonder of Nature. Yosemite was declared a public park in 1864, and railroad and shipping companies promoted it as the West Coast's answer to Niagara Falls; trails were built, camping grounds were laid out, hotels went up. A tourist wonder had been created by the camera.

It was this kind of thing that I had in mind when I said in Chapter 2 that, in a sense, Africa, Asia and the Americas weren't there until they were reclassified by Europeans—because, in re-imagining them, the Europeans gave them a new 'reality' and that this kind of re-imagining was later to become an essential process of tourism ('realities' being social constructions that are made up by people to make sense of the puzzles of existence).

When George Eastman invented the Kodak with its roll of flexible film, photography became an art form for anyone with the price of a camera. ('You press the button, we do the rest.') In the industrialising societies, professional photographers were already authenticating events (a wedding wasn't a wedding without a photograph) and solemnising persons, with studio portraits. Now, with easy amateur photography, the family photo album became one of the symbolic bonds of family life. And among the family photographs there began to appear holiday snaps. By the 1920s, Kodak was advertising that 'A holiday without a Kodak is a holiday wasted'. Unless you photographed a view or a famous site you might as well not have been there.

In one of my books, *The Public Culture*, I described how, on my first visit to the Ryōan-ji garden, a group of Japanese tourists participated in a characteristic modern ritual. In turn, each approached their guide and, standing on exactly the same spot, positioned a camera. The guide's lips moved. The camera clicked. I asked my interpreter what the phrase was that the guide was repeating. She said, 'What the guide is saying is "F-stop 2.8, shutter speed 250"'. One of the rituals of tourism is 'doing' the particular sights already defined by professional photographers, and then, like the Japanese tourists in the Ryōan-ji rock garden, photographing these sights in the same way as they have already been photographed in the travel literature, preferably with your companions in front of them. If a group of behaviourists from outer space took notes on what we do as tourists, they might assume that our principal overt purpose was for all of us to take identical photographs of familiar sights.

MAKING SURE REALITY IS STILL THERE

This concern with 'reality' goes beyond framing existence into convenient stereotypes. When the supernatural stopped being the main way of explaining what was going on in the world, a voracious appetite developed for other kinds of reassurances that there really was a 'reality' out there.* Tourism, especially in its concern with authenticity, became part of this fear that unless the world was constantly made 'real', it might go away.

One should see this in context. It was science that made the world 'real'—with its emphasis on the materiality of existence, on empiricism and on the certainties of proof. The most obvious extension of this certitude into tourism was in museums. (See Chapter 10.) Except for art museums, modern museums were founded on the rock of a solid, definable, objective materialism. All the objects in a museum could be taken to represent reality accurately and scientifically. In a museum the very idea of reality as something to theorise about could seem absurd. There were the objects themselves, behind glass, classified and labelled. They were

---

*THE LYING CAMERA. The camera offered the extraordinary assurance that it could not lie. Cameras, of course, 'lie' all the time—in the sense that there is inevitably selection in *what* is photographed (think of the kinds of subjects that are never photographed) and *how* it is photographed. In another way, tourists know this. When they travel in the people-movers on a movie studios tour in Hollywood or Florida, it is the *deceptions* of the camera, the stage secrets, that give them their money's worth. (Unlike Film City, Bombay, for a time the world's largest movie-producing centre, where simple old-fashioned fans wait at the gates to see the great stars and hope for their autographs.)

objects themselves, behind glass, classified and labelled. They were *proof*. There was a reality out there and these objects were representations of that reality.

However, the forms of presentation in museums and historic sites were also related to what was happening in the arts, especially in the thirst to be 'realistic' (a word that did not exist until the 19th century). The concern of tourism with reality can be compared with the 19th century obsessions with naturalistic presentations in painting, literature and drama. They offered more reassurances of the materiality of existence than had ever before been seen as necessary.

Novels created the appearance and the feel of the 19th century in expansive passages of detailed physical description. New types of painting, both in style and content, caused scandal by their concern with 'showing things as they are'. In the fine arts these naturalistic styles were abandoned in the 20th century, but by then for most people what mattered visually was the camera, and the camera offered and still offers illusions of reality unimaginable in any earlier art form. In the theatre, the desire for realism put ordinary language into the mouths of actors and it crammed stages with hoards of real things. This obsession was to disappear, but in the world of drama it was the camera that mattered for most people: movies, television and video cassettes can bring illusions of actuality over the full 24 hours of the day.

And 'travel books' continue the descriptive traditions of 19th century fiction. Ordinary travel books, even those grumpy ones that are concerned with the discomforts and disappointments of travel (such as Paul Theroux's), are exercises in refined sensibility. They provide sensations of acuteness of observation that none of us (including the authors themselves) are ever likely to experience when actually on the trail. A travel book can be, like the mother's photograph of her baby, a 'reality' not available to our experience. Travel writing might be seen as the pornography of tourism: it offers satisfactions that are obtainable only by reading travel writing.

The particular trick of 'realistic' travel writing is to make things seem actual; to make you feel you are *there* (in ways you would never feel if you were there) by the use of material detail. Go back to the paragraph I wrote about Progreso in Chapter 1. Expressions like 'gritty-green, shallow and warm' can make you feel you are there; sprinkling them with words like *henequen or malecón* adds the thrill of the foreign.*

An equivalent in the traditional natural history museums were the 'habitat groups', in which stuffed animals were placed in 'real' settings—producing real stereotypes: the gorilla forever pounding his chest . . . the bear with paws forever raised . . . the deer forever poised, his delicate nostrils picking up a scent . . . the predatory jaguar forever surveying the scene for prey. (You don't see animals in such conveniently photographable poses on, say, a game drive at Victoria Falls.)

This search for authentic things could reach the heroic in a museum such as New York's American Museum of Natural History. The process would start with a field trip to a location. Drawings and paintings were made. Photographs were taken. Samples of plants, soils, rocks and barks were packed and labelled. Sometimes a whole tree was taken back to New York. In the laboratory some of this stuff was preserved with chemicals and painted to make it look real. Some of it was reproduced in wax or cellulose acetate. The original soil and small rocks were used. For the larger boulders, casts were made and reproduced in plaster and then treated to look exactly like the real thing.

SMELLING LIKE REAL

At least the habitat groups were made up of real things or imitations of real things, even if assembled stereotypically, and you could look at them in your own way and at your own pace. Now there are attempts in some museums to turn your visit into a total illusion of reality of the kind you get from a movie. (In some places, of course, they just put on a movie.) Such attempts try to leave nothing to the imagination. For a start, there isn't much time for imagination. You can't look at things at your own pace and in your own way. You

---

* **TRAVEL JOURNALISM.** Travel writing uses techniques of fiction-writing to project illusions of travel. But travel writers are not usually crooks. In this they are different from travel journalists, almost all of whom are corrupted by free trips and the need to attract advertising. They sell clichés in ways that make the travel supplements one of the single most dishonest aspects of journalism.

can't feel your way around an object. You are taken through, with no choices. And, as attempted representations of reality, the more detailed they become the sillier they are.

One example—one of the silliest serious museum presentations in the world—now despoils the reputation of the city of York, in the north of England. York has a famous cathedral—Britain's largest Gothic church. It has city walls, and streets of largely medieval buildings, as well as attractive Georgian facades and one of Europe's most elegant railway stations. But that is not why the streets of York are now awash with tourists. A profitable hysteria came from a new marketing hype: York has a cult tourism trap—the Jorvik Viking Centre, which tuned the enticements of realism to a new pitch by offering authentic Viking sounds, authentic Viking sights—and authentic Viking *smells*. I think it was the extra appeal to reality offered by the authentic Viking smells that made Jorvik Britain's top-rated new tourist show of the 1980s. One of the sights of York is the faithful queue outside the Viking Centre, spaced with notices telling people how long they will have to wait before they can experience a Viking smell. The sales pitch worked so well that 'the traditional celebration of Jolabcot' has been invented to bring life to the deadest part of the winter season. For the three weeks of this pseudo-event 'the ancient streets of York ring to the sounds of Viking cries' with Viking feasts, longship races, traditional processions of Vikings and Anglo-Saxons, and fortunes told in Old Norse.

Come with me to the Jorvik Viking Centre. Stand in the queue for half an hour, or even an hour, then; having bought your ticket, shuffle forward under flickering lights through a semi-darkness of black and red, hearing simulated sounds of distant thunder and reading portentous messages about the arrival of the Vikings (as if this were the biggest thing before the Second Coming). Then find yourself loaded into a time-car which, when full, moves backwards—passing in reverse chronological order through centuries of York civilisation, represented by dummies, which don't represent much because you are moving too quickly. The time-car's personalised soundtrack announces that you are about to enter the ancient city of Jorvik. It is a typical market day, late one October afternoon in the year 948 AD.

The personalised soundtrack tells us to listen (hear the children squabbling in ancient Scandinavian tongues), to look (now we pass

Svein's leather shop and the shop of Snarri the jeweller), and to smell (the stench of the pigsty and the salty tang of a boat that comes in from the sea). What we are passing through is a lifesize mock-up consisting of dummies and simulated houses, shops and lanes, passed so rapidly and in such confusion that all I could coherently remember was a dummy of a man in deep meditation inside what seemed to be a large basket. (When I bought a guidebook to find out what I had seen, I discovered he was using a latrine.) Our time-cars then take us to the site of the excavations that had prompted the guesswork for this confused dream, but all the rotted wood and old fish bones and other relics have been so thoroughly conserved, before being put back where they were found, that this seems just as phony and unmemorable as what we have already passed. When the personalised soundtrack tells us our time-car journey is over we walk through a simulated archaeologist's laboratory, so furnished with lifelike dummies of archaeologists in front of high-tech equipment that it is not possible to also look at the specimens. The vertigo of simulated reality diminishes only when we reach the Jorvik Centre shop.

It wasn't even the simulated reality of the habitat groups in the natural history museums. Tawdry invention seems a better description—an appeal to commercialised fantasy rather than to the imagination. Because one is hurried through, with no control over pace or perspective, what becomes remarkable is not what is seen: what matters is the working of the contrivance.

I looked back from this nonsense to remember the sense of wonder and illumination that came, years ago, when we visited the Viking displays at Bygdöy, near Oslo, and Roskilde, near Copenhagen. In Oslo, the ships were venerated in a cruciform building the size of a cathedral. Each of the three ships, of old, blackened oak dug out of burial grounds and in differing states of wholeness, was displayed in its own 'chapel' of rounded white walls and stone floor. You could spend the whole day looking if you wanted to. One was probably a ceremonial ship, restored, with elegantly carved serpents' heads and intertwined beasts; one, also restored, was sturdily useful; one had partly rotted away, but that meant you could see how it was made. In the fourth 'chapel' were goods found in the burial sites, including a chariot, and in the Historical Museum, iron ingots and smithies' tools presented the Vikings as a kind of early industrial society.

At Roskilde, the Danes chose a relaxed rather than reverential presentation (in Norway, the Viking finds and the construction of the museum had helped expressions of national pride in a glorious past). At Roskilde, the display hall was like a small shipbuilding yard, not a cathedral, and it was set beside the fjord where the conservators had gathered the thousands of pieces of oak, pine, lime and birch that were slowly being turned back into five ships—most of the work being done in front of visitors to the museum, with tools left around when no-one was working. As each ship was put together, they did not replace the missing bits; they just sketched out with thin struts what the rest of the ship might have looked like. Back-up models gave an idea of the vast trading operations of the Vikings: one ship was presented as a transatlantic cargo carrier, another as a coastal merchant vessel. The Vikings were shown as farmers and as a merchant society. Among the models of casks and chests were little Viking figures, wrapped soberly in long cloaks, as grave-faced as 19th century exporters and importers.

I compared and contrasted the two styles of museum presentation, the one reverential, the other open, and thought about how both museums allowed for the speculative element in museum display. I read up on the Vikings and even thought for a while of planning a trip concerned with the tourism of relics of the Viking Age, as one of the first periods when Europeans could see the world as theirs by navigational right. (This trip would have taken us from the Caspian and the Black Sea to the Eastern Mediterranean, England and Ireland, and then west to Iceland and Greenland.) What I am saying is that going to those two museums was a big experience. Being moved back through history in a time-car in the Jorvik Viking Centre with a personalised soundtrack was a very small experience.

At about the same time as the Jorvik Centre was opened (note the pseudo-scholarly phoniness of the word 'Centre'), the Yorkshire Museum re-staged its presentation of antiquities, telling a story of Roman, then Anglo-Saxon, then Viking life in York. If any of the fragments from the past appeal to your imagination you have time to look, and register your own impressions. Models, graphics and words are also there, telling a story. It is quite clear what is authentic and what is reconstructed. There is no attempt to fabricate 'reality'. In the manner of the Singapore River development, if you want to reconstruct the past you have to use your imagination.

People should understand that, along with 'real things', some imaginative devices may be needed to release a visitor's imagination. But reconstructions should contain visual hints within them: dummies can be faceless; a reconstruction of a dwelling place can be incomplete; audioanamatronic dummies can show some of what is going on under the vinyl skin. Museums simulating naturalism should admit the uncertainties of what they are doing in the display itself. If that is done, they cease to deceive. They help the presentation of the hypothetical nature of 'reality'. And they are of more moral and intellectual use to us than fantasy-'reality', the fast food of the imagination.

* * *

In London's Museum of Natural History there is a room where you can imagine that you are in your mother's womb. It is assembled around a recording of the sounds in the uterus of a pregnant woman, and you can hear the pumping of her heart. This can appeal to the imagination, but it is unlikely that any of the hundreds of thousands of tourists who stand in this room each year actually believe they are back in their mother's womb.

10.

CLASSIFIERS OF THE UNIVERSE

◆ ◆ ◆

THE MYSTIQUE OF MUSEUMS

In one of his books of wonders, *L'Assommoir*, set in the slums of the developers' Paris of the Second Empire, Emile Zola tells an anecdote about a visit to the Louvre that provides a perfect text for a sermon on the creation of the 19th century museum, and what went wrong with it.

A party of slum dwellers celebrating a wedding are left with a few spare hours between the ceremony and the modest celebratory supper at a wine shop. To get up an appetite, they decide to take a long walk, but, when the rain comes, the party know-all rolls his eyes and declares: 'We could go to *the museum*. There are antiquities, drawings and paintings, all sorts of things. It is most instructive . . . Oh, it's something worth seeing, *at any rate once*'. None of the others has heard of the Louvre, but off they go, reflecting that if they are all dressed up they might as well go somewhere.

In the Assyrian gallery, chins up, eyes burning, they find the colossal stone figures ugly. ('Stone carving is a damn sight better done these days'.) The presence of a haughty attendant in red waistcoat and gold-braided uniform causes them to walk as quietly as they can, non-stop, through the French Gallery, their eyes dazzled by the gold of the frames ('Must be worth a mint of money'). They stop only at *The Raft of the Medusa*, the most famous picture of the age, where they are struck dumb and motionless by a lecture on its importance.

In the Gallery of Apollo, the high polish of the floor particularly impresses them, but in the Salon Carré, where they are told in hushed tones that everything is a masterpiece, they stop and look. Some ask questions. (What is *The Wedding at Cana* about? It's silly not to write the subjects on the frame.) Others make comparisons. (The *Mona Lisa* is like someone's aunt. The golden hair of Titian's mistress is like that of one of the women in the party.) There is sniggering as, surreptitiously, they indicate the naked women. In the Long Gallery they are silenced as 'centuries of art pass before their dazed ignorance'. Already weary, they begin to drag their hobnailed boots and clatter their heels on the noisy floors. Two of the women complain that their legs are giving way.

The know-all drags them through eight cold and empty galleries, and then among the drawings, on and on, through room after room of 'sheets of paper with scrawls', none even 'amusing'. They tear up a staircase and find themselves in the Maritime Museum. After a quarter of an hour's tramp, they find another staircase—and are back among the drawings. Attendants and other visitors watch them and marvel. They are afraid they will never escape.

Restored to their umbrellas in the courtyard, they breathe again. Oh yes, they were glad to have seen it.

* * *

This anecdote illustrates five functions of the museum as initiatory rite in the 19th century, when the modern-industrial societies were forming. It shows *awe* from contact with a palatial building and from being in the presence of the celebrated, mysterious and costly objects within it; it shows *baffled reverence* for scholarship or, alternatively, *baffled contempt* for scholarship; it provides *titillation* from seeing nudes, dinosaurs' bones, Egyptian mummies and other marvels; and it provides somewhere to keep out of the wet.

REALITY GUARANTEED BY THE STATE

Modern museums acquired their authority from the state. They were forming at the time that new nation-states were being created, and existing states, when they could, were re-creating themselves in terms of 19th century nationalist arrogance. As part of newly forming public cultures, museums were naturally among the places that defined, and then guarded, the body of national knowledge and the national past. In the most powerful nations, museums became grandiose declarations of imperial power.

Collecting had gone on before this time—hoarding things seems to be part of the human condition—but modern museums began in the sense of power, order and democracy of the French Revolution. At this time, in the name of the people, the new French State proclaimed four museums—in which, unlike the princely collections, the objects on show were the property of the people and displayed for the edification of the people. In 1793 the Louvre became the Musée de la République Francaise (and in 1810 the Musée Napoléon). Captive works of art were brought to Paris in Roman triumphal procession, escorted by cavalry and infantry, drummers and bands, with actors chanting hymns of joy.

The British did not show off in this way, but their sheer spread of empire threw out a net which gathered in the world's largest composite collection of archaeological, ethnographic and natural history objects. It was sorted out and displayed in buildings of pomp that confirmed Great Britain's superiority over the rest of the world. Britain dominated the globe: now it was settling down to making an inventory.

In Bavaria, from the 1820s, the king began establishing museum temples in Munich that were dedicated to the greater glory of art and of Bavaria. The Prussian king then opened a monumental construction program of five museum palaces with colonnades and rotundas, that on completion would be celebrated as Museum Island—a holy place of civilisation. Vienna's great boom of reconstruction began in the late 1860s, with the removal of old walls and bastions and the building of the boulevards of 'the Ring'— as large a development project as Haussmann's transformation of Paris. Then two domed, symmetrical museums went up, in the official Ringstrasse style, where art and nature were to be ordered for the benefit of the peoples of the Austro-Hungarian Empire.

Imperial museums in Tokyo, Kyoto and Nara demonstrated the modernisation of Japan; the process was later extended into a wider system of national museums. In a similar demonstration of progress in St Petersburg, the tsar opened to the public the Hermitage collection, which was deemed to have reached perfection in a museum building of Roman palatial style built by the architect of the Munich art temples. In Moscow, the Alexander III Museum of Fine Arts (later, the Pushkin Fine Arts Museum) followed, with its 22 light-grey granite columns exhibiting the virtues of classical civilisation. Then, in the Red Square, a History Museum in turreted redbrick—an attempt (that didn't come off) to capture in a modern 19th century building the virtues of Russian civilisation.

In Washington, as the Tourmobile demonstrates, the museum-palaces representing civilisation took their place beside the buildings of the Executive, the Legislature and the Judiciary. When the size of Beijing's Tiananmen Square was quadrupled in 1958, making it the world's largest square, a whole side of it was given over to two vast museums.

The imperial countries also had halls of conquest, usually in the form of maritime museums, as in Lisbon, London or Amsterdam, and trophy halls, called ethnographic museums. In Madrid, the Museo de America is both. The Ethnographic Department of the Russian Museum (which became Leningrad's Museum of the Peoples of the Soviet Union) assembled such an enormous collection of mementos of conquest (from Latvian coloured glass to Siberian shirts made from nettle), that one of Russia's biggest exhibition spaces was built for it: its centrepiece a great hall faced with pink marble. Rome, like Brussels, established an African museum; an East Indies museum was built in Amsterdam and, in Paris, an African and Oceanic museum, assembled from the leftovers of a colonial exhibition. In the United States, and in Britain's 'white dominions', the indigenous people were usually disposed of, along with fossils, rocks and stuffed animals, in the museums of natural history.

Along with all this (later sometimes providing new parthenons for housing new museums) were the gargantuan displays of the benefits of industry and art in the international expositions that followed the Great Exhibition. They were there to demonstrate the national vigour, and the energy and triumphalism of the age.

* * *

In territories where nationality was still being assembled, national museums became part of the process of nation-building.

In Hungary's period of 'National Renewal' the National Museum, founded in 1802, was a centre of definition of a Hungarian nation, as defined in a mood of enlightenment. At a mass meeting in front of this museum's eight formidable Corinthian columns and its facade (bearing a tympanum in which Hungaria relaxes among figures symbolising the sciences and the arts), the lyric poet Sándor Petöfi proclaimed the 'Twelve Points' that symbolised the beginning of the Hungarian revolution of 1848. The National Museum still stands as a monument to liberal reform—some of the Hungarian intellectuals who combined in the 1956 uprising called their group 'the Petöfi Circle', in honour of that mass meeting in front of a museum.

The Slovene National House was established in Ljubljana in the 19th century on the proceeds of a 'penny collection'. Its intention was to help systematise a Slovene national culture, and now that it has become the Slovene National Gallery it still displays proof, in canvas and paint, of what it meant to be a true Slovene. Similarly, the National Museum in Prague, in its 1885 revival palace, became a centre for recovering fragments of peasant folkways, and, as part of the 'Czech National Awakening', putting them together as Czech culture. At its heart is a national pantheon, and the museum can still provide a backdrop for demonstrations of the liberal spirit. The very structure of the National Museum in Helsinki (built in 1902 at a high tide of romantic nationalism) became a museum of Finnishness—evoking, all in one facade, a Finnish castle, a Finnish palace and a Finnish church.

The new nations that came out of the destruction of the Spanish and Portuguese empires in Latin America, and out of the departure of European empires from Africa, if they established national museums, did so after liberation, but they could still be seen as essential to nation-creating. The National Museum formed in Mali in 1982 was given the task of defining the nation by documenting Mali's entire material culture (in a country where there is little glass for museum cases or for anything else). Museum policy in Nigeria is directed towards 'anchoring' national identity—bringing under one roof objects from different ethnic groups to demonstrate the possibility of unity in diversity. The resurrection of Shona soapstone sculpture, that became one of the symbols of a new Zimbabwe, was promoted from the National Gallery in Harare.

All of the national museums, everywhere, became cathedrals of national belief. They were special places set apart by the state for a particular kind of contemplation in which the people might experience sensations of beauty, goodness and truth. And schoolchildren were later to be taken to museums as an initiatory experience, in which they were confronted with official views of the objective reality of existence. Those who found doubt in the churches could find certainty in the museums.

CONTROL BY CLASSIFICATION

Although the dignity of the nation was behind them, museums were, on the whole, a force for change. The authoritative mystique of museums, their palatial character, their confident ordering, their laconic labelling, their command of the mysteries of authenticity, and, above all, their solid, positivistic irrefutability could make them part of a modernising process—the development of an authoritative organisation of knowledge along thoroughly modern lines.

In tourism, they became the hyper-example of a reality that was out of this world. Partly, of course, because once you entered one of these palaces you were already, literally, out of the ordinary world, and all of the things that had been put into them had also been taken out of the ordinary world and put together in extraordinary juxtapositions. And partly because they became the temples of the cults of authenticity and reality. Nothing was more 'authentic' than a museum exhibit.

But to the tourism of actuality and authenticity they added another cult—the tourism of classification. They had secured a rational control over the universe by classifying it. They became the largest physical demonstration in the modernising societies of what classification looked like—and, to some tourists, all the muddle outside was not as well arranged as the careful ordering of a museum.

By the time modern museums were being invented there seemed to be so much more to classify. It was not only captured art trophies that could be led in triumph to Paris. Plants and botanical specimens collected in the West Indies by Nicolas Baudin, the naturalist-cartographer, were also paraded in the vanguard of one of these triumphs. As a result of the invention of the 'scientific expedition' which Eric Leed, in *The Mind of the Traveler*, sees as unique to the 18th century, with its 'intense hunger for data, measurements, facts and observations', the drawings and specimens of plants and animals sent back by the maritime adventurers had become 'natural curiosities', exciting the rationality of *savants*. Soon they were to come into Europe in their hundreds of thousands. Strange things from the east coast of Australia raised more questions than the rocks that, a couple of centuries later, were brought back from the moon. The sheer novelty and variety of these things demanded new classifying systems.

But classification was extended to any group of things that museums collected—from painting (classified into four great 'schools' at the Musée Napoléon) to human pre-history (classified into three great 'ages' of Stone, Bronze and Iron at the National Museum in Copenhagen—a subdivision made almost 200 years after the concept of geological eras had been put in place by an earlier Dane). The result was that to move through a museum, from scientific order to scientific order, from one 'school' of painting to the other, or from one 'age' of history to the next, was a declaration, made with one's own body, with tired feet, exhausted brain, and aching back, of the belief that existence must be classified.

Classifications could impose such a systematic pattern on a visit to a museum that visitors might not see much of what they were supposed to be looking at. Once a museum's particular ordering had become familiar, returning to it could be a revision course in the particular classifications expected from that kind of museum. Bronze Age/Iron Age; Reptiles/Mammals; Jurassic/Cretaceous; Baroque/Rococo. If you were in a communist society, Feudal/Bourgeois/Socialist. If you were in Mexico, Michoacán/Cuicuilco/Tlaltilco. That is why a visit to a museum became like a visit to a cathedral. It was a reminder, in memorable surroundings, of the immutability of knowledge.

* * *

But by then, the classifiers of the collections were taking over all existence and systematising it into separate parcels of reality, each of which made up a subject, with one subject per museum, or department of a museum. This process was only part of the wider affliction of intellectual disintegration into specialisation, and was in contrast with what had happened before. Pre-modern museums were collections of unordered curiosities. In Teylers Museum in Haarlem, set up by a rich 18th century Dutch merchant, you can still find fossils in one room, astronomical instruments in another, drawings in the next. And there could be a whole 'museum' in one cabinet of wonders. Then came the resolute division of museums and museum departments into particular 'subjects'—archaeology, art, antiquities, natural history, ethnography, science and industry and, in one way or another (from artist's birthplaces to army museums), history. Accompanying this was the setting up of imitations of the Royal Botanical Gardens at Kew and the Jardin des Plantes in Paris—two great achievements of 18th century enlightenment—and the regularising of royal menageries into scientifically classified zoos.*

Although it can now be more fruitful to see the relations between things, rather than to sort them out into separate parcels, we should accept that the museum obsession with classifying could serve important purposes in the modernising cities of the 19th and early 20th centuries, especially in the natural history museums. What was most damaging were the divisions between types of museums. Even

---

* THE FATE OF ZOOS. Both zoos and botanical gardens became places of amusement for the public, although research was also an important element. In the case of zoos, the shopfront concealing the backroom research could become, in effect, a freak-show presentation in which the most celebrated animals (often given funny human names) were something one had to 'do'. In China one had to 'do' the pandas; in Australia, the koalas. Itineraries for Japanese tourists to Australia can be partly determined by the opportunities to photograph koalas. At tropical Cairns, a centre for trips to the Great Barrier Reef, the authorities imported some koalas from the south to put in the Wide World Animal Park, on the assumption that this might extend the stay of Japanese tourists by one more night. Fresh eucalyptus leaves are flown up from the south every second day, the koalas are regularly sprayed with water to keep them cool, and a special fence has been put up to protect them from being swallowed by pythons.

While animal liberationists want zoos abolished, the zoo controllers, especially in the United States, can reassert moral purpose by re-stagings in which the main function of zoos are seen as preserving endangered species, presenting complex environments of plant and animal life in 'habitats', and cultivating community values towards conservation. In 1993 the four zoos in New York were renamed Wild Life Conservation Parks. Seeing animals other than on television can still provide one of the childhood wonders of urban life.

as divisions they were not only arbitrary, they were silly, because they left so much out. Compare museums with scholarly books. These books may be limited by being chopped up into 'disciplines', but by reading widely you can get a range of perspectives on how humans live, and the world in which they live. Traditional divisions between museums did not allow this. These divisions left out most of the social environment. They ignored the complexities of a modern-industrial society, indeed of any society, and indeed of the very idea of 'society'. Archaeological museums presented the past as if it were art. Art museums presented their exhibits without reference to the societies from which they came. Military museums presented war as if it came from somewhere outside society. Science and industry museums left human beings out of their presentations.

If you wanted the feel of the material culture of a particular society at a particular time, and went to a European city's grand museums—its art museum, military museum, ethnography museum, natural history museum, science centre, industry museum and whatever other expositions were around—how would you fare? Not very well. There were no connections between the objects, and many kinds of objects were not there at all. In this sense, museums became anti-'social'. Since it is our social and cultural behaviour that distinguishes us from the other animals, that was a disaster. The 'objectivity' of museums produced a reality in which there was no place for the social.

There was nothing in the nature of material culture that demanded museums should be set up as they were. If there were to be divisions, why make them art, industry, the military, the peasantry, etc? There were other piles into which material artifacts might have been sorted: the material culture of a particular period, for example, with everything running together. But whose interests would it have served if a society had been presented in terms of diversity? Museums made society seem safe by suggesting that differences were not there.

And if the great tasks in a museum were collecting things, classifying them and conserving them—and its principal moral drives were those of authenticity and scholarship—dedication to collecting, classifying and conserving things could become so significant that trying to arrange these things so that they might attract the curiosity of visitors could seem a betrayal of their 'objectivity', and an affront to reality.

THE STRAIGHT LINES OF PROGRESS

Not only were museums categorised into patterns that could be more demanding on the attention than the exhibits themselves: all these patterns could seem drawn together by a straight line. Museums could be *linear*, leading the visitor inexorably from rotative steam engine to spaceship, from amoeba to Man, from archaic to classical, from Stone Age to Iron Age, from entrance to exit.

The straight line policy pushed towards progress. In natural history museums, sometimes after bitter contention, one of the museums' roles became to epitomise Darwin's theory of evolution (and, in that, they performed one of their several very useful popularising functions). In art museums (until the turning upside down of the 'modern'), displays of European paintings emphasised the superiority of renaissance and post-renaissance art by labelling what went before as 'primitive'.

In the museums of the Soviet Union, and subsequently of the other communist regimes, the push was that of dialectical materialism. In the Museum of Chinese History in Beijing you not only moved from one Dynasty to the next: on the first floor you also moved from Primitive Society to Slave Society to Feudal Society. This is just as in the State Historical Museum in Moscow, where you moved from 'Production relations in tribal society' in Room 3, to 'Conditions of erosion of feudalism' in Room 22. Whether in the dioramas in the basement of Jakarta's National Monument—or the relics of the War of Independence in the Museo Historico Nacional, displayed in the very house in Lima lived in by both José de San Martin and Simón Bolívar—museums in 'new nations' were used as demonstrations of the benefits of liberation.*

There was another effect. Since museums displayed material

---

* **PAST GLORY.** Not all museums offer arrows pointing to progress. The main exceptions are those that recall past glory. Recalling civilisations that preceded the Spanish and Portuguese conquests became significant in museum policy in some Latin American nations. In African states, attempts are made to put evidence of pre-conquest culture into museums. In industrial societies there can also be a specific nostalgia for some aspect of the past—usually a belief that the nobility were true aristocrats in spirit, or that the peasantry epitomised the virtues of the simple life. And in art museums, the 'primitive' could seem to have qualities denied to much of what followed.

artifacts, cultures could be valued by the extent to which they produced things that were suitable for display in a museum. Walking from a Stone Age display to a Bronze Age display, one saw an increase in the range of things to look at, and this was likely to suggest a progress from reminders of a primitive, propertyless society to reminders of a culture in all ways superior. This could seem so obvious that it was assumed that, as 'Stone Age Man', the Australian Aborigines didn't really have a culture: there was not enough in the glass cases for them to be thought of as developed human beings.

* * *

We had arrived in Cairo overnight from Singapore, and after a mixed day had gone to bed early and slept right through. Now it was 6 am and I had been working for an hour in our room at the Meridien Hotel (which offers a view of the Nile from every bedroom, and without any traffic din). City lights were still on, but the sky was moving to a lighter blue and there was a light mist over the river. We would soon be travelling along the Nile, looking at temples and tombs, and my early morning thought was that the Nile was not very rationally laid out. So much work had gone into classifying nearly 4000 years of Ancient Egypt into nine periods and 33 dynasties, yet the Nile itself is not a straight line leading us from pre-dynastic to Roman. The beginning of the historical periods is towards the end of the river; Middle Egypt and the Middle Kingdom don't synchronise; periods and dynasties are up and down the river and all over the place . . .

Why can't the Nile and its monuments be laid out rationally, as if they were a *museum?*

11.

THE PRINCIPLE OF INTELLIGENT SUPERFICIALITY

◆ ◆ ◆

A CULTURAL GENES BANK

What do we do as tourists confronted with old stuff from the past or, as the *Cassell's Children's Book of Knowledge* of my schooldays would have put it, the strange ways of other lands? An enlightened answer, going beyond tourism, but including it, would be to marvel at the cultural storehouses of modern-industrial societies—the historical sites, the libraries, museums and archives, the reprints, reproductions and compact disks, and the places used for re-presentations of performance—all of which we can use as we wish. They offer us more varied repertoires of what it might have meant to be human than could ever before have been imagined. They are one of the greatest wonders of our age, and they are one of the greatest justifications for sightseeing.

In these narratives, philosophies and ceremonies; these restorations of dance, music, drama, rhetoric, poetry and visual images; of bodies of knowledge, wisdom and speculative inquiry there is a kind of cultural genes bank. As beings with the power of imagination, if we come across these works we can take them out of the world of isolated, enchanted things and bring them into our own world—so long as we do something with them (enter into a cultural engagement with them) and don't just say: 'Oh, I like that,' or: 'Oh, I don't like that'.

But if we want to, we can also stand in an historical presence. Even if we know nothing about the work, we can at least feel the instructive tremors of our own ignorance of whatever great myth structure this thing was a part. And we know that, if we want to, we can go away and read about it.

If we have learned a lot about whatever it is we are looking at— about the people who produced it, the kinds of meanings that permeated the society in which it was produced, and the different kinds of meanings given by succeeding generations—we can feel what Stephen Greenblatt calls, in *Learning to Curse: Essays in Early Modern Culture*, its 'resonance'. We can reach beyond its formal boundaries and imagine a world of complex, dynamic cultural forces for which we can suppose it to stand. Then how lucky we are.

And it isn't all that hard to give ourselves this kind of background. It doesn't require a PhD, for example, to discover that religious images are not necessarily naturalistic. Statues of Hindu deities are not sculptures of people, but of ideas. They are likely to have lots of arms, legs and heads—not because they look like that, but to communicate their superhuman qualities. The heads may indicate multiple and contradictory expressions, referring to powers and qualities. The hands may be making significant gestures, or holding significant emblems. Buddhist statues have a whole language of postures and hand gestures (*mudras*), just as Christian Orthodox icons have a language of intimacy in facial expression and hand placings, and paintings of Christ's passion have their own language. The techniques of Aboriginal religious art can be entirely abstract.

I noticed in the Boston Fine Arts Museum an 'Activities for Young People' fact sheet, that in a few hundred words made a good start in helping young people approach Buddhist and Hindu statuary. When we read a few things like that we can at least stop laughing at strangeness or being put off by it. We can begin to look. And if we don't see *looking* as part of being a tourist, why be a tourist?

SPECIALISING IN GENERALITIES

Why don't more tourists take an intelligent interest in preparing themselves for sightseeing; and why don't more of them do some reading, or whatever, after they have done their seeing? Why should they want to deny themselves this widening of experience, in which they can break out beyond the confines of classification and authenticity?

One reason is that although they may live in suburban houses or city apartments they may maintain a peasant suspicion of those who regularly enter the specialised world of the intellect—which is to say those who, self-consciously or not, speculate about existence and develop techniques of criticism and knowledge-building. Even many who have obtained the certificates of a university education are likely to have contempt for this world of the intellect, or to feel uneasy in it even though, by missing out on an important and liberating part of the human potential, they are limiting their own freedom. It is one of the great marvels of the world that, having been blessed with a potential for intellectual curiosity, our species has, as a whole, been such a washout.

Other, more specialist, reasons come from several kinds of treachery within the camp. Treason may come, for example, from those intellectuals who argue that all that distinguishes 'high culture' from 'popular culture' is the esteem in which it is held.* We should remember that some of the participants in the activities of 'high culture' haven't just paraded their high culture around as a status sign. They have enlarged their lives by using their access to whole ranges of knowledge about the human potential and what our

---

* THREE CULTURES. The phrase 'popular culture' suggests a voluntary, participatory activity—but this is usually not the case. It is better to use two phrases. POPULAR CULTURE can be thought of as a repertoire of activities that do originate among particular groups of people. But MASS CULTURE can describe the mass standardisation of cultural products and services, with its centralised control, almost universal reach and low levels of participation. To complete the set, there is HIGH CULTURE, which is *not* the culture of a ruling class—most of whom prefer the mass culture repertoire (which can be partly a declaration of their worldview). High culture is not the old ruling class culture. It is a particular characteristic of modern societies, referring to the specialised world of the arts and the intellect, at its best with a special and self-conscious concern with being a critic and seeking meanings. CULTURE? *A repertoire of collective habits of belief and action that give meaning to particular groups, or a whole society.*

physical environment might be, and they have used their access to various techniques—abstract thought, critical analysis, etc. Most people don't have these resources. This means that a small proportion of people can use the repertoires of both high culture and popular culture, but most people have access only to popular culture (much of it highly-commercialised mass culture).

But the principal treason that can inhibit people from getting more out of their sightseeing can be a *respect* for scholarship. Respect for a specialist scholarship, that is—in which intelligent interest can seem superficial, compared with the profundity of the experts. When scholars have devoted a lifetime to the study of the *mudras* of Buddha, how can a visitor to the Boston Fine Arts Museum imagine any point in reading a gallery note?

Becoming a generalist—acquiring an intelligent superficiality—is a specialism of its own. In tourism, if you want to be enlightened you have to learn how to be a sightseer. But then if you want to know how to make spaghetti, you have to learn that too.

* * *

In a tribal culture, everyone is expected to know the same things, except those things restricted to sex or age groups, or which are mysteries available only to the specialists who deal with the supernatural. There is a common language and a common body of knowledge. In a complex modern-industrial society, 'cultural literacy' (a common body of knowledge) has been fragmented. Or so they say, especially in the United States, where political battles are fought over whether there are some things that everyone should be taught in schools.*

---

* **CULTURAL LITERACY.** E D Hirsch, in his bestseller, *Cultural Literacy*, includes, as an appendix, 5000 names, phrases, dates and concepts that every young person in the United States should learn. His supporters greeted this as a return to the sound values of the past. His detractors attacked it for the same reason. To them it represented a dominant white, middle class male culture, to which they juxtaposed other cultures. They were not usually prepared to consider the possibility that a general body of knowledge can be *amended* and made more diverse, and that various groups can learn it (some of it as a kind of second language), although also maintaining their own special knowledge. The alternative is that only the future élites learn this more diverse body of knowledge, which they use in running the United States.

The problem is badly stated. For one thing, although modern-industrial societies don't have the cultural literacy of traditional tribal or regional societies, they do have the mass media—which can provide such a uniform teaching of what life is supposed to be that it can pervade a whole nation, or many nations. There are also the many common wisdoms of modern-industrial life—workplace habits, shopping habits, transport habits and so forth (although one should recognise that these wisdoms may not be shared by the chronically workless and those who don't get around much).

And there is another part of the problem that hasn't been talked about so much. This is that élite experience has changed. In past societies of relative complexity, the educated classes would learn the same sacred texts and secular classics, and among themselves they might even read an élite language (Sanskrit, Latin, Persian, Mandarin, Arabic, etc). They could then share the allusiveness of the legends and beliefs expressed in that language. Walking through an art museum, educated Europeans were likely to know the legends of the oath of the Horatii, the dream of Jacob, the supper at Emmaus or the rape of Europa—they had a shared body of knowledge.

As a result of the specialised division of knowledge (and also because of the increase in what can be known), educated Europeans walking through art museums are now likely to reduce paintings on biblical or classical themes to words like 'oath', 'dream', 'supper' and 'rape', without the addition of the strange names of the paintings' subjects. (Well, then, so what? Even if knowledge is fragmented, we can mend it. If we are interested, there are books.)

Modern societies may seem too complex for a common body of knowledge, even within our own time and within our own place, let alone a shared knowledge that helps when flying all over the world, looking at one nation after another as if they were exhibits.*
How, when we know so little about even our own culture, can we ever know much about people of different cultures—even when they are alive, let alone dead and fragmented into a mysterious past?

---

* AN EMBARRASSMENT OF EMBARRASSMENTS.
For example, in the Thai language there are 300 expressions for various types of embarrassments and anxieties. There are separate phrases for worry about loss of face, worry tinged with suspicion, worry that too much is going on around you, or worry that things are not going your way. A casual visitor is not going to know anything about that.

That is no reason for not trying. Second, or tenth, best can be better than nothing. We can learn to accept with stoicism and irony the fact that existence is mysterious, and that knowledge has always been fragmentary and speculative. We have to understand the virtues of superficiality. There can be advantages in knowing a little about a lot. The alternative is to know nothing about a lot.

And there can be a particular virtue in an intelligent, sensitive superficiality: it can create new 'realities' by taking imaginative leaps in seeing connections between things that the vision of an expert— even the people who live in a particular place—cannot achieve. Travel necessarily makes us superficial observers, but cannot that mean that we have the chance to see things that the experts, including the people who live in the place, may never see? Intelligent travellers may have a sharper concentration of observation, a more innocent eye and may make comparisons with other parts of their experience that the experts, or the local people, may never have thought of. And what's more, they know what they are looking for. They are trying to make sense of the world in their own particular way.

It is in the sense that travel is used as part of our general view of the world, of what might be thought of as our own particular criticism of existence, that it can be said most convincingly that travel broadens the mind.

12. Interlude:

THE PALACE-ON-WHEELS

◆ ◆ ◆

NOT THE ORIENT EXPRESS

I had never been a tourist. That is to say I had never been on an organised tour, apart from the comparatively short guided tours of castles, factories, harbours, palaces, birthplaces, performing arts centres, parliaments, craft workshops, town halls, dungeons and other locations I could get into only under supervision. To write this book I thought we should spend a week or so on an organised tour. Since we were going to India at the time, it would be in India. Someone told my wife about the Palace-on-Wheels.

We sent for the illustrated brochure, itself part of a tour. It promised a royal vintage train to take us from Delhi through the heartland of Rajasthan, India's most colourful state, in a unique collection of coaches, each built for a maharaja and with a royal coat of arms guaranteeing its authenticity. Along with burnished teak and gleaming brass, antique lamps casting a warm glow and gently-swaying tasselled draperies, there would be bathrooms of modern design and each saloon would have a mini-bar. Our schedule, we were told, would unravel like silk in seven days through seven cities, while we wondered at forts and palaces, bazaars and camel-trains. We would eat banquets in five-star palaces, served by attendants magnificently clad in flowing coloured turbans, ever-smiling, infinitely courteous . . .

* * *

The adventure begins

When we arrive at the Cantonment Station in Delhi to board the Palace-on-Wheels, in our hand luggage we have duty-free vodka of the kind we carry to avoid the high price of mini-bars, and eight reference works; *The Penguin Guide to the Monuments of India* (in two volumes), *The Traveller's Key to Northern India*, a Penguin history of India, a Thames & Hudson art history of India, a popular illustrated guide, a photocopy of the chapter, 'Rajasthan: Pleasure Palaces and Desert Villages', from *India in Luxury*, and photocopies of relevant bits of the 22nd edition of the classic *A Handbook for Travellers in India*.

I have a small nervous breakdown when, still wearing our welcoming garlands, we find our sleeping compartment is as cramped as a dugout. Dinner is on, but when we walk along the track we find the restaurant cars are full, and the club car is enforcedly chummy. It is not known when the second sitting will begin. Back in the carriage we have a couple of vodkas and then look at the 'bathroom of modern design'. It is a tiny space with a lavatory, a basin and a shower hose through which the water doesn't flow strongly enough for a shower.

In the morning we are passing alongside a road busy with heavy trucks and camel-carts. In the bathroom of modern design I steady myself against the train's movements by holding onto the basin. Like someone watering a shrub, I hose myself down.

Oblivion

Our carriage, built in 1936, is called 'the Jaipur coach', although the connection with the Maharajas of Jaipur is not explained. Its two attendants are in 'colourful turbans' but, fortunately, in manner they are not unctuously 'ever-smiling and infinitely courteous': they are pleasantly direct.

Breakfast is taken at one end of the carriage in a saloon so small that two of us have to eat off our laps. Two solid Scots, man and wife. An elderly, moustachioed stage Englishman. An Australian couple from Melbourne.

In the introductions, the Melbourne couple explain that they are not married, but when the man is told that the only place with a power point for his electric shaver is the saloon, he says he would be too embarrassed to shave in front of us. I make my first note: group tourism provides personal observation of changing social mores in one's own everyday life.

When the train is moving there is no link between the carriages. The seven of us are held in each other's embrace as the 'Jaipur group'. Our senior attendant tells us we are a family.

* * *

We are now passing through a mess of apartment houses and thatched huts. The train's public address system comes alive. It is time for our rose-coloured glasses, we are told. We are about to enter the Pink City of Jaipur. Luxury buses await to whisk us off to the colour and glitter of earlier days. We will thrill to the richly decorated apartments of women of the royal household. We will stroll across emerald-green lawns where peacocks strut. Through the train windows we see rows of Indians squatting, their bare brown bottoms facing us as they get on with their morning shit.

Transformation scene

Eighty of us walk through a drab grey shunting yard, sprinkled with armed guards. We wear badges of pink, yellow or blue, corresponding to which of the three luxury buses we have been assigned. As well as being part of the Jaipur carriage we are now also part of the pink group.

To the sound of gleeful music, we walk towards a sun framed by two richly caparisoned elephants, whose trunks are raised and curled in salute on each side of a banner proclaiming:

JAIPUR
WELCOMES
PALACE-ON-WHEELS
Rajasthan Tourist Dev. Corpn. Ltd.

As we pass between the elephants we are garlanded with wreaths of marigolds then, as the cross-legged and red-turbanned musicians repeat the same few bars as if they are a hurdy-gurdy, we watch the other Palace-on-Wheels tourists walk through the arch. At the very moment that the pilgrims are garlanded they leave the realities of the shunting yard. They enter the world of tourism.

Study in the picturesque

Ahead lies the promise that at Amber, the ancient capital seven miles out of Jaipur, we will ride on elephants past honey-coloured ramparts up to the renowned Old Palace that shelters beneath the famed Jaigarh Fort. But in Jaipur we are driving through drab morning streets that are coming to life with motor scooters and camel-carts; shopkeepers are taking down their shutters. I want a brief lecture on the socioeconomic significance of what we are seeing. Grubby pink patches appear, then a shabby pink wall, encrusted with old posters and advertising signs. "Now we are in the Pink City," says the guide. He recites a travel writer's ode— we are soon to see the 953 small casements, set in a graceful curve, five storeys high, of the Palace of Winds, built for the ladies of the harem and now one of the most picturesque sights in India.

We are given a photo opportunity, but you cannot get a picture that looks like a postcard if you are standing beside your luxury coach in the middle of the road, bewaring of pickpockets, watching the traffic, and attempting to photograph a pink sandstone facade over the top of passing pony-carts, buses, bullock-carts, trucks, camel-carts and motor scooters, while trying to frame out an electric light pole and three shops because they are untrue-to-period.

(How many of our pink group know that the Palace of Winds is celebrated? As a schoolboy in an Australian country town I memorised a photograph of it in one of the eight volumes of *Cassell's Children's Book of Knowledge*, my most comprehensive window on the world. I have been waiting to see the Palace of Winds all my life.)

Dream run

We move on to a tourists' dream run. We enter a valley through a narrow pass and are given a photo opportunity for a long shot to the yellowed grass of distant hills. Then at Amber we are positioned, four on each elephant, on the elephant shuttle-service to the palace. Halfway up the hill we are photographed on top of our elephants. The photographer will have the prints ready for our walk down.

At the entrance to the palace a yellow-turbanned *bhopa* welcomes us, singing and dancing as he plays his *rawanhatta*. I have noted these words. *Bhopa*: itinerant balladier. *Rawanhatta*: stringed instrument played with a short bow tinkling with bells.

In the palace we can take postcard shots of 'one of the finest gateways in the world', rich with delicately coloured mosaics and lattice screens, and follow this up with pictures of:

- sunken gardens with their bursts of colour
- white marble and floral ceilings
- fine views from delicately carved windows
- the soft greens and pinks of the private apartments
- galleries latticed in alabaster, doors lined with sandalwood, arabesques inlaid with ivory.

I focus on these views, although I don't press the camera button. It is a way of concentrating on what one is looking at, out here on the fringe of the stragglers of the pink group. The indomitable verbiage of our guide, alienated by the cruel traditions of his occupation, has put me into a panic. Unless I take care, I might hear what he is saying. The pink group is forming its first unspoken alliances—a quick exchange of sceptical glances with one of the German-speaking Singapore businessmen, a sharing of raised eyebrows with the Londoner whose face is so composed we call her the Governor's lady (a young Governor's lady in a 19th century portrait).

I imagine myself as a guide: having studied in depth the Penguin *History of India*. I would talk for a minute or two about the rise and the struggles of the Rajputs and then explain that the essentials in this part of the Rajput narrative is *the fort*, facing external threat, and *the palace*, offering an inner, aristocratic civilisation.

'That's all you have to know, for the moment', I would say to the pink group. 'Have a look around. Enjoy yourself. If something arouses your curiosity, ask me a question.'

Economic multiplier

In the palace's Hall of Mirrors a man in a blue denim jacket, and a woollen neck scarf of Scottish tartan design wrapped around his head, stands with two candles in each hand, which, at the guide's request, he lights to show special effects. Our guide tips him three rupees. Throughout Rajasthan, some of the 13,000 rupees we have each paid, on average, for seven nights and six days with the Palace-on-Wheels filters out. To this man, the Palace-on-Wheels is worth three rupees a week for the 26 weeks of its season.

At the Rajasthan State Handicrafts Emporium we watch villagers working at the ancient crafts of handblocking and carpet-making. Then, in the exhibition hall, we are spread in a semicircle to hear a sermon from a white-bearded patriarch on the artistry and moral goodness of making carpets.

The cracking of carpets fills the air, as they unfurl like sails in the wind and are offered for purchase. The patriarch calls out prices. 36,000 rupees! 12,000 rupees! 2000 rupees! Calculations click in our heads. We convert these figures into DM, £ stg, Fr ff, ¥, L, Pt, Skr, Sch, Gld and $US, $A, $C and $S.

The camaraderie of the tourist group explained

At the end of the afternoon the pink group, now thoroughly bonded, is the first to reach Nahargarh (the Tiger Fort), an 18th century hilltop citadel overlooking the city from a ridge of rock. Waiting for the other groups and the promised dinner and cultural show, we wander around rooms that have the atmosphere of a rundown hostel for distressed maharajas, and then cluster along the ridge to watch a lustreless sunset and listen to the sounds of the city rising from the plain. We all agree that the afternoon was a failure. Too much to do. Too much talk from the guide.

We thought the physical surroundings for lunch were all right. The gardens of the Rambagh Palace Hotel, with wandering minstrels, and the hotel's marble verandas, with turbanned waiters and deep cane chairs, gave us our first five-star luxury—in a 20th century palace built by one of those Rajput maharajas who, after the Mughal decline and the failure of the Mutiny, decided to do well out of the British. And, when the British left, to do well out of the hotel business. What we sat down to was third-rate coach party food.

There had been a potential for *wonder* in the first 10 minutes at Jantar Mantar, an observatory park built in the 18th century by the enlightened Sawai Jai Singh II (founder of Jaipur and inspirer of a rational town plan). What we saw was abstract, surreal . . . large sculptures of stone and brass, of triangles, semicircles and spheres. It was like being inside the notebook of some giant geometrician: reason was being brought to the heavens. But there was no chance to stand and look. The poor guide yammers on, passing from one geometric object to the next for almost three-quarters of an hour, as if when next we want to find the position of the Pole Star at night, or measure the altitude, declination, azimuth, zenith or distance of the stars, we will use as our reference this 18th century observatory park in Rajasthan.

Then to a museum honouring the opulence of women's dress and men's weaponry. Then an art museum. The guide gathers the more obedient members of the group around a set of very routine Western-style oil paintings of Rajput notables, but this keeps them from the splendid display of Rajput miniatures, which I look at disconnectedly, moving whenever an attendant comes up to give me a lecture.

The museums were part of a palace providing studies in pink, but no-one in our group wanted to 'do' two palaces in one day. Moments of rest were spent in the courtyard photographing the palace guards in their white uniforms and red turbans. The last of these moments went on the longest—when a guard unwound his 10-metre turban, then wound it up again and, when finished, said: "That is over". One of the German-speaking quartet from Singapore turned to me: "What a pity!" Our rest period was over.

The camaraderie of group tourism comes partly with the alienation of the group from what is offered to them.

Character studies

One of the functions of a tour is to arouse an interest in our fellows, similar to the 'character' interest provided by a 19th century novel. We have added two more to our developing repertoire of stereotypes.

The loud-mouthed Yank is an old American in a baseball cap with a big belly hanging over his belt, and the slouch of a cowboy ready to reach for his six-shooter. While we waited for the cultural show at Nahargarh he dominated the first three rows with anecdotes of the inadequacies of every country he had visited during his retirement. He travels to remind himself of the world superiority of the United States.

The affronted Canadian is a freedom fighter who is threatening to sue the Rajasthan Tourist Dev. Corpn. Ltd. for false advertising. For him, the tour has become a parable of injustice.

In legendary Chittaurgarh

I am so overwhelmed by *ennui* and sleep between leaving Jaipur and, 300 kilometres later, waking for our cups of early morning tea, that there is no time to read about Chittaurgarh, today's first stop. I know that the word 'garh' means 'fort'.

Apart from a sign, CHITTAURGARH WELCOMES PALACE-ON-WHEELS, our only greeting at the railway junction comes from two orange-turbanned horsemen carrying spears. As we walk to the luxury coaches, the moustachioed Englishman tells us that the steam engines are temporarily gone and the train is now drawn by diesels. He is a train buff. He has had a good look at each of our 24 carriages, and when the steam locomotive rejoins us he hopes to tread its footplates.

In our pink group coach we seem to have already shared a great deal of experience. Two of us haven't made it this morning. The American couple who are always late are here. Who's missing? The pompous little English prick with no neck and his long-suffering wife? That's his voice laying down the law from the back of the coach. The Australian opera singer with the blonde hair? She's there in the front with her husband. The Singapore Four are sitting in one row, speaking German. That's the voice of the North Country surgeon behind us. It is the French couple who are missing.

To renew our camaraderie, we make sardonic jokes about what today might bring. No-one has heard of Chittaurgarh.

As the coach climbs the steep, rocky hill to Chittaurgarh, the guide counts off the reigns of the maharanas of Mewar whose capital this was, then gives structural details of each of the seven gateways, and statistical information on the great immolations that occurred here. Inside the last gate we pass through a small village onto a long mountain ridge of dried grass and scattered ruins. We are guided through a ruined palace, with which is associated a long legend—a short version of this is lettered on a signboard.

When the coach stops beside some Hindu and Jain temples (our first temples) and a 15th century Tower of Victory, we are let loose for 12 minutes to do what we like. The Tower of Victory, nine levels of open balconies and pierced stone screens (commemorating a great 15th century victory over the Muslims), becomes something to climb—a staircase winds through the centre and out into the galleries. Or it becomes architecture, marvelously intricate when close; simple and controlled from a distance. The temples, dancing with anecdotes in luxuriant carvings, become art—or superstition, as they obviously do to the loud-mouthed Yank who moves among the ruins like John Wayne hunting bandits.

Consolations of travel

At breakfast in the restaurant car, with the train still at Chittaurgarh Junction before starting its voyage to Udaipur, the two of us enjoy several of the delights of travel. This isn't the Orient Express, but the polished teak is shining and the brass is gleaming, as promised in the brochure, and, an unusual luxury on such a tour, we have most of the restaurant car to ourselves. We have been unbonded; restored, temporarily, to ourselves.

Our breakfast consists of stuffed *paratha* and *poori bhaji* because, determinedly, we prefer the breakfast of the country. Dinner on the first night had been 'Indian Continental', meaning that the attendants offered successive dishes of both Indian and European cuisines, placing dollops of this and that on our plates. Not good enough. We want to know from which Indian cuisine each dish comes. Mughal? Gujarati? Kashmiri? Banarsi? Maharashtran? Goan? The breakfast waiter has taken a diploma in catering and now wants a diploma in tourism. We tell him that when he is a director of the Palace-on-Wheels, he should see to it that there are background briefing sheets to tell people what they are eating.

The greatest delight is that over breakfast we are able to read about a place we have just seen—not in the Penguin guide, but in *Chittaurgarh, Land of Chivalry and Heroism* by Suresh Goyal, Chief Editor of the *Daily Pratahkal*. It is a flimsy pamphlet on thin, grey paper, bought for four rupees from a boy outside one of the Jain temples who couldn't believe it when I gave him a five rupee note and said he could keep the change.

The first chapter, 'A Golden Page of Mewar's Glorious History', tells us that 'the history of Chittaur continues to be an attraction to every tourist and every Indian who values the independence of his country; no place in India has been the scene of such a noble readiness to die; it is unparalleled in the history of the world'. Over the second cup of coffee we read details of the immolations of 1303, 1535 and 1567 when, defeated after a siege, warriors put on saffron robes and sacrificially threw themselves onto the enemy, and the women and children went up in flames in a *johar*—altogether, more than 100,000 lives sacrificed for honour.

Fairytale palace

When Chittaurgarh was abandoned after the immolation of 1567, the next part of Mewar's glorious history began with the establishment of Udaipur as the capital. Five centuries later, Udaipur has been transformed by the magic of tourism into 'one of the most romantic and evocative cities in India, surrounded by incandescent blue lakes with fairytale palaces of outstanding beauty'. At the Lake Palace Hotel—'one of the most beautiful hotel-palaces in the world, set in the centre of a lake like a serene ocean liner moored in an azure sea'—we have a lunch almost entirely without taste.

Devised in the 18th century as 'a summer palace for the maharana to frolic with his ladies'; commemorated in *Cassell's Children's Book of Knowledge* as 'Like a Cluster of Pearls on a Crystal Mirror'; and now promising terraces for sunset cocktails, the palace has acquired subsidiary fame as a setting for the James Bond movie, *Octopussy*. As we move around marble halls, courtyards and terraces—avoiding the loud-mouthed Yank, the affronted Canadian, the Englishman with no neck and other hazards of the voyage, but gossiping with sympathetic types such as the Sensitive Frenchman, whose long hair is frizzed out in retro-Afro, and the Quiet Commander, a gentle old American whose baseball cap is fringed with naval officer's gold braid—we define our slight sense of confusion: we are used to hotels built like palaces, but not to palaces become hotels.

Volume Two of *The Penguin Guide to the Monuments of India* heaps uncharacteristically purple prose on Udaipur and the Lake Palace Hotel, but *India in Luxury* quotes a comment that the recent reconstructions are in 'Trust House Forte Motorway Style'.

The real India

As we leave the coach to visit a folk art museum, the Governor's lady (who has told us she is a barrister) says the pink group's Udaipur guide is a treasure. He also approaches my ideas of what a guide can be. He gives us lecturettes on Udaipur's zinc industry, its local farmers, the kinds of paintings now selling in the galleries. He comes out with a critical five-minute analysis of the caste system. He speaks conversationally, as if something interesting has just come into his head from looking out of the window and seeing a bank or a cinema, the passing traffic or a temple. He tells us how the Udaipur yuppies are moving into the *havelis*, the traditional apartment houses of the inner city—that is a tour I would like to go on: a visit to a yuppiefied Udaipur *haveli*. I now recognise that the Governor's lady, like most of the younger people on this trip (who make up about a quarter of its number), is a yuppie.

Each time we get in or out of our bus, or arrive at or leave a railway station, assemblages of beggars and trinket sellers remind us that 'this is India'. On a photographic tour of the green lawns and fountains of the 18th century Saheliyon-Ki-Bari (translated as 'Garden of Concubines' by our guide), young women in saris are ready, for a tip, to pose against statues, fountains, kiosks and clumps of bougainvillea to help us produce a postcard picture. Back in the coach, we watch as a woman holds up a little girl beside my window; they both flash their teeth in charming smiles. For a tip, I could take their photograph to demonstrate that I know the real India.

There is a fuss at the front of the coach. The opera singer's son wants to buy a bangle from an Indian boy, who half steps into the bus. Swelling with memories of Empire, the Englishman with no neck stands up, red-faced, and shouts at the little boy: "If you come into this bus I will throw you out!"

* * *

Instead of the promised boat ride on the lake, we are to go to the West Zone Cultural Centre, a 'model village' of dwellings characteristic of the four states of West India, where village craftworkers, dancers, singers, musicians and puppeteers can spend a period replenishing their skills and, incidentally, provide something that tourists can visit. The Singapore Four, previously paragons of discernment, complain that the brochure had advertised a camel ride, an elephant ride and a *boat ride*, but now we are missing the boat ride. Others are afraid there will be another cultural show.

We have an English afternoon tea in the courtyard of a replica of 'a typical middle class household in a Rajasthan village'. When we are standing on the roof, watching some tightrope performers, a strange procession dances towards us, led by a woman capering with a couple of metres of pots balanced on her head, and followed by groups of musicians, each prancing around, playing its own tune, and groups of dancers—each dancing its own thing, some forwards and backwards, some in circles.

They dance off to an amphitheatre—with only the two of us following. The rest of the Palace-on-Wheels crowd are putting their feet up in the courtyards of replicas of typical middle class Rajasthan households, or getting on with their shopping.

After a welcoming roll of Rajasthan drums, the villagers enact for us excerpts from their legends—bits of local dance dramas that can last for days, passages from songs about local deities that can last all night, episodes from the story of a village divinity, danced and sung in front of an iconic painting telling the main story of his life. One group plays desert notes in praise of the trappings of a camel.

The light is fading across the valley when other Palace-on-Wheels people begin to appear at the rim of the amphitheatre. As night falls, one by one, they sit in the upper rows.

The Canadian couple

As well as belonging to the Jaipur carriage and the pink group, we are now part of an unspecified restaurant car group that contains elements of pink, but in which there are also traces of yellow and blue. A large proportion of them are younger people, two of whom are tonight sharing a table with us and, as with the Governor's lady and the Singapore Four (until they showed that they preferred a boat ride to the West Zone Cultural Centre), we feel that somehow they share something with us.

They are Canadians, living together but not married, although with wedding plans. She is in marketing. He is in computing. They tell us that there is some resentment among the carriages because this is not an Orient Express luxury experience. So, in an impromptu marketing conference, we decide the Palace-on-Wheels promotion should not be selling luxury, but the comfortably exotic, with a touch of adventure travel. We go on to plan group therapy sessions to enable the resentful to help each other overcome their disappointments. (Do *they* feel that somehow they share something with us? Or are they just being polite to older people?)

Free time

This morning, still at Udaipur, we have a 9.30 am start for another palace, the City Palace, providing further photographs of brilliant blue mosaics, balconies with carved screens and walls inlaid with glass and porcelain. This brilliant decoration provides a chance for the little Englishman, when we are standing in the women's quarters, to scowl at the group and say: "No wonder they lost their empire," thereby confusing the Rajputs with the Romans. (Of all of them, followed by the loud-mouthed Yank, he is least like us.)

On the itinerary, an hour is marked down as 'FREE TIME'. The two of us enjoy our freedom beside a marble-lined swimming pool in an early 19th century palace now turned into a hotel—swimming, sunning, drinking tea and reading through Indian newspapers and parts of a book called *India 1990* which gives us the figures.

Further consolations of travel

When we had looked at the itinerary, the 22 hours between Udaipur and Jaisalmer had seemed a blank, but as we move into drier and drier country the journey is providing some of the delights of railway travel. The long lunch in the restaurant car, for example. We spend it with the Melbourne couple (who have become our best friends). He talks about his escape across the Hungarian border in the late 1940s and how he built up a textile business in Australia. Then gossip: about the other three in the Jaipur carriage, about some of the leading characters in the pink group, even about a few of the more remarkable stereotypes from the worlds of yellow and blue. The Melbourne couple met each other on a tour of Latin America and since then they have been conducting an *affaire*. They offer rumours that some women who travel alone on the Palace-on-Wheels invite attendants into their bunks. We seem to have been travelling together for weeks.

THE PALACE-ON-WHEELS 151

Back in the Jaipur carriage comes the pleasure of framing genre paintings through the train windows—railwaymen on small tree-shaded stations, a row of women in saris walking across an empty field, clouds of pulverised limestone shrouding a village cement works. Followed by the pleasure of an afternoon nap, and of waking up, wondering where I am, and of reorienting around a conversation. The train is at a station. My wife, sitting comfortably on the bottom bunk, is talking through the opened window to some Indian children. "Where do you come from?" "Australia." "Is Australia a 'mocracy? India is a 'mocracy." "Yes," says my wife. "Australia is a democracy."

As the train climbs pale, desolate mountains, the seven of us take afternoon tea in the saloon at the end of the carriage. Whenever the train stops for the brakes to cool, armed guards get out to patrol the line.

In our saloon, we of the Jaipur group have never felt closer. We gossip while the sallow sky fades into dusk. The moustachioed train buff—'a determined bachelor'—tells us that shortly after he retired, a remote cousin (another bachelor) died and left him a small fortune and a villa on the Riviera. He used to be a railway porter. The attendants, who have both taken tourist diplomas, join us and tell us their ambitions.

Yesterday, the Governor's lady said that she and her companion were planning marriage. We all had suggestions about where they might go for a honeymoon. Around us we hear about work problems, emotional problems, retirement problems, honeymoon problems. The tour is partly a guidance clinic.

* * *

In a break from gluttony, we have a supper of bananas and apples back in the carriage while the rest of the Jaipur group has dinner in the restaurant car. In an Indian magazine I am able to read about the designer bathrooms of leading families in Delhi, about communal slaughter in the Punjab and Kashmir, about life in the fast lane of the Bombay advertising agencies, about the failure of the literacy program and about some of the good shows that have been on recently in Calcutta.

Although the attendants had battened down windows and doors to keep out the sand, when we wake for breakfast the carriage is misty with dust. Outside is the Great Thar Desert, stretching from here to Pakistan with plains of rock and sand, scattered with gorse and small thorn trees, shifting dunes and hills in pallid yellow.

The whole thing

From the first sight of the sandstone walls of this fortified desert city rising up out of the wasteland, Jaisalmer ('the Golden City' in the tourist spiel given to us in a coach lined with synthetic leopard skin) has been, for me, the principal sightseeing event of the voyage. It is not a question of detail but of the general effect of wandering through the steep, narrow streets of an old sandstone settlement that came out of the desert trade routes almost a millennium ago (and is still unified by honeycombs of delicately carved facades). And of finding bazaars in small squares, goats tethered in back lanes and, permeating the city, the sweet smell of fresh cow dung.

Over lunch with the Canadian couple I decide Jaisalmer's attractiveness comes partly because we have not been made to look at things out of context. Its people are not *out there*, detached. Everything and everyone in the town is assumed to be worth seeing—rich, poor, palaces, hovels, Jain temples, cheap tourist hotels, delicately carved stone screens, pats of cow dung.

The craziness of the Jaipur observatory provided wonder. I hadn't seen anything like that before. In a sense I have seen everything at Jaisalmer before, but it comes together with poignancy. The Canadians found their wonder in the train journey from Udaipur to Jaisalmer. They had never seen that kind of country. Now it is a highlight of the tour. However, they felt its special features should have been noted on the itinerary for people to know what to look for. We move on to what has become one of our most pleasant pastimes—replanning the tour. We discuss an inexpensive reconstruction of the bathrooms, distribution of fact sheets after each day's tour, a shelf for each upper bunk, fewer forts and palaces . . . (Are they just being polite to us because of our age? Are we keeping them from their real friends?)

* * *

Why am I riding towards a desert sunset sitting on the back of this farting, lurching camel whose stomach is rumbling like a river in flood, with nothing to hold on to except my wife (and I won't hang on to her, because when the camel throws me off I will bring her

THE PALACE-ON-WHEELS 153

down too)? Because in the itinerary it said: '1700 hrs. Camel ride'.

When it is over and the camel is kneeling down, a photograph is taken of me, arm akimbo, looking as if I could ride a camel.

* * *

At tonight's dinner and cultural show—a languid event put on by a couple of performers thinking of something else, but admired by some of the pink group as a really comfortable evening: "Not too challenging"—I ask people what they thought of Jaisalmer. "Good." "Fine." "I liked just walking around," say the wise ones. Complaints about the drains and the smell of cow dung come from the foolish ones—including, to our dismay, the Governor's lady, for whom the lakes and gardens and marble palaces of Udaipur are holiday dreamland. (The Governor's lady is not, after all, one of us.)

In my bunk I read that Jaisalmer continues to look like a community although it is no longer a great centre of trade routes, because of the boom that came from the wars with Pakistan, and also because now, after big tourist promotions, it has become a tourist town. I have 'discovered' a tourist town.

End of rendezvous

After the 10-hour overnight journey to Jodhpur ('the Sun City') we are greeted by a swarm of shoeshine boys, but before we file into another coach lined with plastic leopard skin the train's public address system reminds us that it is only a short time now before the end of our rendezvous with history. Today there is another palace-fort to be taken around and another palace-hotel in which to have a swim and some more coach party food. Tomorrow, after a bird park at sunrise and a visit to the abandoned city of Fatehpur Sikri, we reach our climax in front of the Taj Mahal.

As we again climb a steep zigzag through the seven gateways of a fort, a guide again gives us dates, measurements and architectural details. It occurs to me that I have not been so familiar with the sight of people from the rear since I marched behind all those familiar backs in the army. But, whereas what I was looking at then were mainly the neat rears of young men, now, mostly, these are very broad backsides—Rubenesque men, as well as Rubenesque women, old and young. We are a very well-fed lot, with wide bottoms.

Memories

For several days after the Palace-on-Wheels tour I would wake up with the comforting sensation of being gently rocked by the movements of the train. What then drifted into my mind was not a memory of the journey's 'highlights'—the abstract craziness of the 18th century observatory park in Jaipur, the procession of medleys dancing through the West Zone Cultural Centre at Udaipur, and the fable of a desert community at Jaisalmer; nor the symbolic composite palace-fort-hotel constructed in my imagination as a summary of the successive reigns of the Rajput maharajas. Nor images of yuppies from the Udaipur fast track gentrifying their *havelis* in the CBD; nor the voice of the little boy from the railway siding in the middle of nowhere wondering if Australia was a democracy.

What first drifted across my memory, morning after morning, were our shifting bondings and regroupings and 'the characters'—the loud-mouthed Yank, the Governor's lady, the sensitive Frenchman, the little Englishman with no neck. Sometimes their faces. More often the broadness of their backsides.

TOURISTS AND TRAVELLERS

In his book *Abroad*, Paul Fussell made a distinction between explorers, travellers and tourists, which has now become an analytical device likely to be used by people who write sociological accounts of tourism. The book is a brilliant study of a certain period of travel-writing, but what it has to say about contemporary tourism is both scanty and, in certain ways, snobbishly overstated. Nevertheless, it appealed to an important body of scholars—those who like to divide things by three. His distinction is something like this: Explorers (characteristic of renaissance society) went in search of the 'undiscovered'. Travellers (characteristic of bourgeois society) moved within a territory already made part of history, but could make discoveries within it. Tourists (a product of mass culture societies) seek an experience entirely structured by the tourist industry.

One can rewrite this to make a useful distinction between those who seek experiences that are entirely structured by the tourist industry, and those who make 'discoveries' (an activity not restricted to Vasco da Gama and a few other renaissance sea captains, nor defined by the belief that a place didn't exist until a European saw it). I think one might leave the word 'tourist' with the more open meaning it has had for a couple of centuries, while recognising that the tourist experience can be enlightening, silly, deadening or depraved, according to circumstances. If you need a term of abuse to distinguish between the authenticity of tourists, I suggest 'autonomic tourism'—a kind of tourism that is as involuntary as the functions of the autonomic nervous system of the human body. We become 'autonomic tourists' if, in our sightseeing, we don't move beyond whatever the tourist industry has prefabricated for us, in conceptualisation and itineraries.

A deadly symptom of autonomic tourism is an over-riding interest in travel facilities for their own sakes—freeways, service stations and motel strips; or airport VIP lounges and luxury hotel shopping arcades; or the set meals and air-conditioned coaches of a group tour.* (Paradoxically, to those who most detest the inauthenticity of mere tourists, compared with the great travellers of the past with their heroic discomforts, the delight of true travel [now unobtainable] was also an over-riding interest in the processes of travel itself, although, in this case, in its bracing adversities.)

The idea of 'discovery' remains useful, so long as it is understood that even on group tours we can see ourselves as capable of curiosity and, insofar as the physical conditions of travel allow, of setting a course of our own, or at least thinking for ourselves even if we are thinking within boundaries set by others.

It is too early in this book to sketch out a trial balance on tourism, but one of the things most worthwhile in travelling is the possibility of a sudden exciting of our knowledge or imagination when we see something for the first time that, in our general criticism of existence, can make the world seem that much wider. Sometimes

---

* AUTOBAHNIA. In his *Room Service*, which includes some of the funniest prose sketches written on tourism, Frank Moorhouse puts together the magic land of 'Autobahnia'. In Autobahnia, you can tell what country you are in by whether the roadway is called *autobahn, autopista, autoroute* or *autostrado*, although the music on the radio is always the same.

only a little wider, sometimes with such a change in perception that it becomes a life experience. We can have a feeling of revelation that enlarges the appetite for curiosity or wonder.

In *Learning to Curse*, Stephen Greenblatt writes of moments of 'wonder' when what is seen 'stops you in your tracks', 'conveys an arresting sense of uniqueness', or 'evokes an exalted attention'. He was writing about what can happen in art museums, but it can also happen in the West Zone Cultural Centre or the Jaipur Observatory Park.

* * *

The people most disappointed by the Palace-on-Wheels were those anticipating the Orient Express experience at reduced rates.* They expected vehicular luxury itself to provide the principal pleasure of the voyage. Rajasthan was to be there as well, but as a background of pleasant shopping experiences, picturesque photo opportunities and a prearranged set of delightfully exotic travel posters framed by the carriage windows. It was at Udaipur, with its lakes and marble palaces, that the journey most met such expectations. While the rest of us slept in the train, the Singapore Four lost marks by spending the night in a suite at the Lake Palace Hotel, and when they rejoined us the next day, at the swimming pool of the City Palace Hotel, their imaginations still swam across gleaming marble floors.

The moustachioed English train buff got his money's worth because he was on a train ride; he was able to wave at the other trains—and greet them by turning himself into a train whistle. He spent some time upfront with the engine driver and, instead of seeing the Taj Mahal, he had a smashing day wandering around the Agra City Railway Station.

---

* **A FIVE-STAR PALACE-ON-WHEELS.** The physical side of the Palace-on-Wheels has since been transformed. There are new coaches, with 'five-star cabins'; each coach has its own 'cosy lounge with a television and VCR'; there is a bar and library saloon; and on the last night you get fireworks. But I have been told that its spiritual side remains unaltered. However, the question comes up, for those of us who were on it in the old days before 1991: has the Palace-on-Wheels been spoiled?

THE PALACE-ON-WHEELS 157

THE EXCERPT EXPERIENCE

As we circled within Rajasthan on our pilgrimage, a large minority of our sisters and brothers didn't want to eat the Indian food. A few thought it was not true Indian-style cooking, because it was not the same as the narrow selection presented as Indian in their home countries. If they had meant the buffet lunches at the palace-hotels they were right. With one exception, these were true group tour Indian cooking. But on the Palace-on-Wheels itself the Indian food was better, as Indian food, than the 'continental' fare was as European food. It was not a health question. Most of the abstainers did not like eating foreign food.

Yet the kinds of food eaten in countries one visits as a tourist can be more interesting than a ceremonial agenda of obligatory sites. My wife and I, and our son and daughter, have had several holiday stays in Singapore which have been partly built around eating and looking. The variables have been differing types of cuisine and differing types of social settings. The breakfast-time *dim sum* experience in an old timers' place in a relic building in Chinatown; the steamboat experience in a suburban housing development; the luxury Hainanese experience in a pricey restaurant; a self-consciously arranged English afternoon tea (an ethnic experience) at Raffles. Or a sampling of the Teochew revival in a new and slightly yuppified eating place; Hakka and Hokkien cuisine at two restaurants, side by side, that are museum pieces of an earlier Singapore; a big feed of chilli crab at the seafront; Taiwanese cuisine in a second-rate hotel; congee from the breakfast buffet at our hotel; and famous Singapore street food dishes in a coffee shop, in upmarket hawker centres and in downmarket hawker centres.

If you are interested in the self-images of a nation, characteristic dishes can mean as much as characteristic landscapes. Even when I found myself in a Californian motel strip, it was an illuminating part of the motel frontier experience to go to the eating places scattered among the motels. One could write a book on the declarations of freedom and of cultural diversity in United States eating. 'Fast foods' make certain declarations of freedom. 'Health foods' or 'soul foods' make different declarations again.

There are regional declarations, as in eating shoofly pie on a Dutchland Bus Tour in Pennsylvania, or ordering a steak at the Cattleman's Cafe near the City Stockyards in Oklahoma City. There are the 'Little Italies', 'Chinatowns', 'Mission Districts', 'Japantowns', 'French Quarters', etc. Consider the declarations of eternal regional verity made by ordering clam chowder, or red flannel hash, or spareribs, or Indian pudding; southern fried chicken or Virginia ham or pecan pie; hominy grits or sourdough bread. The 'Vienna Hot Dog Stand' in Chicago serves Italian beef, Polish sausage and 'kosher hot dog'.

People have the right to decide what doesn't go into their stomachs. But what about not only distrusting a nation's food, but also laughing at it? It was when listening to some English tourists in a Bangkok hotel mocking Thai food (the English laughing at Thai food!), that I decided to write this book. Not that one should pick on the English. When I was last in Singapore, I read in the *Straits Times* how there were countless stories of Singaporeans who insisted on eating Chinese food throughout their three-week trips abroad.

* * *

Another good reason for wondering if some Palace-on-Wheels pilgrims might as well not have left home was their attitude to 'cultural shows'. It was dismal that the cultural show that went down best was the lethargic performance at Jaisalmer: its vapidity was, I suppose, what made it acceptable. Like a video of Mount Fuji running as a background image in a Japanese home, it provided a tolerated background to conversation.

What I had wanted was more enthusiasm for the evocative excerpts from village cultures that were put on for us in the West Zone Cultural Centre at Udaipur. This seemed tourism at its best: people from a host country showed visitors things about themselves that they thought we might find interesting. Anyone able to listen and look could make 'discoveries': they could find the dance and the music, in themselves, enlivening, and the commentary made the villagers 'real' and distinctive.

For visitors with imagination, curiosity and goodwill, it could mean something to be told that the singing and dancing in front of a large narrative painting was an episode, lasting a few minutes, of a ceremony enacting events from the legend of a local deity that, back in the villages, might last for days. If they wanted to, they could recognise that the painting of iconic episodes from the legend of a local deity's life was the same kind of thing found in the reliefs and murals of famous Buddhist or Hindu temples. Or in the stories told in stone, paint or leaded glass in celebrated Christian cathedrals. If you used your imagination, what you could see on this stage, performed in front of a setting sun in the hills outside Udaipur, was a reminder of how presenting a divine legend by singing and dancing was one of the beginnings of the arts of performance.

In such encounters with the principle of intelligent superficiality, what is abstracted is an aspect of a familiar cultural form—just as in an art novel, in which style is almost everything, you can gain a feeling for its reality-construction just from reading parts of it. The ending doesn't matter. What we had done at the West Zone Cultural Centre was to examine some 'excerpts'—which, in tourism, are the performance parallel of the 'exhibit'. Performing an 'excerpt' can put a circle around it, as we put a circle around an object or a monument. And, equally, this can be good or bad.

After the Palace-on-Wheels tour was over we went to a short concert of Kathak dance in the Kamani Auditorium in New Delhi. The movements were dazzling—swirling pirouettes, incessant footwork with its intricate patterns, jangling anklet bells, the rapid changes of gesture and glance, the insistent multiple tones of the *tablas*, a build-up of dance out of the sounds and movements of the audience itself—and running through all this I knew there was also an intricate coding, even if I didn't know what it was. The next day, some people in the Department of Culture told me how unauthentic it had been: there shouldn't have been an introduction in English, there shouldn't have been a stage, or electric lights—and what we saw were *only excerpts*.

Yet it was 'only excerpts' of Chinese opera (by which is meant a Chinese singing, dancing, acrobatic, recitative and sword-fighting drama) that gave me the first idea of how this complex symbolic system could be a connoisseurs' art form. I knew that there were facial conventions to identify character, stylised body movements, modulations of voice, 50 significant sleeve movements, hand gestures, finger movements, key conventions of gait, waist movements, 20 kinds of laughing or smiling, costumes and face-painting, each with its own meaning. All of these were stylised to indicate essentials of emotion, movement and language. But to know all that can cramp the experience, so that to see a full performance was all parts and no whole. Then several years ago, when we were in China as part of a cultural mission, the Nanjing authorities arranged a special showing—four of us in armchairs with antimacassars in an empty hall. They put on a collection of opera excerpts, each of a different regional style, and gave us hints about what to look for. One of them told me that when he was watching a classic he looked for the best bits, as if they were excerpts.

In Japan, 'traditional theatre' has already declined into such a rare species that even Japanese themselves, if they see it at all, may see it in excerpts. *Noh*—the medieval song and dance masked drama— is now the world's oldest living drama form, but only just: it survives partly through state subsidy and partly through the help of rich families. There is only one fully-maintained theatre (in Osaka), for *Bunraku*, the unique form of puppetry in which three puppeteers handle each puppet. And *Kabuki* is running out of performers: the National Theatre has had to take over the training of boys to play the minor *Kabuki* parts (playing the major *Kabuki* roles is an inherited right for certain families), but there are only a score or so applications a year.

For a tourist, *Noh* can be hard going. It is concerned more with mood than with incident and it is performed in one of the world's most allusive systems of stylisation. Since it is performed in an archaic literary language it could be hard going for almost all Japanese, if they went to it. The convention is that during the interval what is happening is explained by one or more comics (wearing yellow ceremonial socks, as distinguished from the white ceremonial socks of the principals). The explanations can add to the puzzle, but a visitor doesn't really have to understand what is happening: the style is almost everything. The day we went to the National Noh Theatre, a Japanese in Western dress (wearing brown department store socks) lectured in Japanese on, our interpreter told us, the principles of *Noh*, about which, she said, some of the mainly Japanese audience did not necessarily know much more than we did, since we had just read a book.

We had to leave early and what we saw, again, was only an excerpt, but that seemed enough to demonstrate the style—and how useful it was to keep these fragments of *Noh* alive in the cultural genes bank. Benjamin Britten, for example, after seeing a 15th century *Noh* drama, composed three music theatre parables, which had their own style, but a style he would never have thought of if he had not been to a *Noh* theatre. A background booklet brought out by the Bunraku Association in Osaka records that: 'on June 14 1947, *Bunraku* enjoyed *the greatest honour in its entire history* in the form of a command performance for Emperor Hirohito'. (My italics.) Having made this grovelling statement, the booklet went on: 'Every effort was made to show the art at its best'. The program consisted of two short excerpts.

Kabuki can still draw crowds, although not, of course, crowds as large as those in the porno quarters in Tokyo where, stacked side by side, are the blue-movie houses offering their peculiar combination of frankness about female mutilation and modesty about female pubic hair. Being one of the audience of 2500 in the Kabukiza Theatre in Tokyo provides no problem for a tourist who has learned the skills of intelligent superficiality. All that is needed are a few minutes of background reading, and one of the small radio earphones through which a voice murmurs information. *Kabuki* lends itself to the excerpt approach because, again, style is everything, whether in a dance, a song, a famous soliloquy, or even in a sidelong glance. In any case, what the audience are waiting for are favourite *scenes*—love scenes, breaking-off-an-affair scenes, murder scenes, fight scenes, extortion scenes, parting scenes, exit scenes—and if a scene comes off particularly well, a cry from the audience of 'That's it!' becomes part of the act. (Calling this out requires knowledge, timing and judgment.) The performance we went to was all excerpts, one of which was entirely of a memorable exit.

PART THREE

◆ ◆ ◆

The make-believe of the public culture

13.

TOURISM AND THE MAKE-BELIEVE OF THE PUBLIC CULTURE

♦ ♦ ♦

TOURIST SHOWCASES

The visitors pass through the entrance and walk along cheery, commercial Main Street, USA. They approach the snow-capped Matterhorn. To the right, they see promise of a shiny future of science, technology, and space travel. To the left are adventures among tropical jungles and islands. Further ahead, they glimpse the mythic past of the American frontier, bordered by a land of bears and a quaint New Orleans square, replete with pirates and a haunted mansion. The visitors sense that beyond the mountain, between the American past and the shiny future, waits a fantasy land of fairies and witches, princes and princesses, talking animals and a world-famous mouse.

These visitors stand in the heart of a special universe. They are in the 'happiest place on earth', begat by Walt Disney.

Michael Real, in his *Mass-Mediated Culture*, found a pilgrim's progress through Disneyland a programmed introduction to a living utopia. He also compared it, in terms of being a world apart, with *The Divine Comedy*, in that just as Dante summarised the spirit and worldview (viz the myths) of 13th century Catholicism, so Walt Disney's work typified the myths of the public culture of 20th century United States capitalism. Japanese schoolteachers recommend that their students visit the Disneyland in Tokyo (about 10 million visitors a year) as one way of trying to understand the mores of the inscrutable Americans.

On my day there, the most 'real' thing was a superb, much larger-than-life, audioanamatronic Donald Duck that I followed, marvelling, as he quacked his cantankerous way down the street. I had never thought I would live to see the real Donald Duck.

* * *

In the less than half a year it was open, the Great Exhibition of 1851 attracted six million visitors (165,000 of them on excursions to London organised by Thomas Cook). This is a greater average daily rate of visitors than Disneyland has achieved since Walt Disney opened it in 1955. Despite the super-colossal importance of Disneyland to the tourist business, the Great Exhibition was even more important. It was the first place in the world where enormous numbers of ordinary people paid entrance fees to mill around together in a place of radiant fame, in order to experience the mysterious ecstasy of *darshana* as they stood in the presence of a myriad of amazing magic things, brought together for the purpose of being wondered at. The Great Exhibition gave birth to the international expositions that prompted the first mass tourist movements, and that later developed into international trade fairs and world expos that still provide some of the biggest stakes in the tourist business. Disneyland should put up a statue of Prince Albert, the begetter of the Great Exhibition, honouring him as the precursor of Walt Disney.

A visit to the seven hectares of the Crystal Palace where the Great Exhibition was assembled was a visit to a Fantasyland. 'A rare pavilion such as man saw never since mankind began,' Thackeray said of this tremendous palace of prefabricated plate glass and iron, with its statues and waving palms. But it was the 100,000 exhibits, useful things from Todayland, that people came to see—and the promise that they gave for Tomorrowland. Like Disneyland, this was a special universe and, as with Disneyland, a tour of the Great

Exhibition was a thoroughly programmed introduction to a living utopia—in this case made up of the myths of 19th century British capitalism. It was not, like Disneyland, 'the happiest place on earth'. It was the most progressive place on earth, separated into the six main divisions (divided into 30 sub-divisions) of Raw Materials; Machinery; Textile Manufacturing; Metallic, Vitreous and Ceramic Manufacturing; Fine Arts and Miscellaneous. As visitors walked past these proofs of 'visible progress' (from the great hydraulic press and the giant locomotives to the machine tools, the ornamental cast iron and the new United States invention, the sewing machine), they paid regard to optimism, power, work, wealth and the possibility of endless material improvement.

The profits from the Great Exhibition were used to buy, again with Prince Albert's guidance, the land at South Kensington on which was later built a complex of museums, colleges, libraries and one of the world's largest concert halls, representing the voice of enlightened middle class wealth,* buoyant with optimism and reason and a faith in improvement. Education, science, art and technology would bring light. Business would bring abundance and eternal progress.

Like Disneyland, the Great Exhibition (if briefly) and the South Kensington complex became tourist showcases. As such, they became part of the public make-believe of a modern-industrial nation-state.

THE FORMATION OF PUBLIC CULTURES

The modern-industrial nation-states that began forming in the 19th century were too complex for people to understand. Without a

---

* PRINCE ALBERT AND THE MIDDLE CLASSES. The term 'middle class' here represents a frame of mind, rather than an exact class definition. Although a grand aristocrat and consort of a queen, Prince Albert, in his role as guardian of the Great Exhibition (and in many other ways) was an epitome of the enlightened Victorian middle class mind. In his *Iron Bridge to Crystal Palace. Impact and Images of the Industrial Revolution*, Asa Briggs juxtaposes two group portraits—one of Prince Albert chairing a meeting of the Commissioners of the Great Exhibition; the other, *Men of Progress*, a group of enlightened Americans. Visually, the two groups are interchangeable.

simplified mirage of national life, a special kind of national 'reality', a modern nation-state could not be seen to exist.

The mirage (call it 'the public culture') is of a society in which true citizens share common values and a common life. Other kinds of residents may not appear at all (or only as enemies or misfits). On the Tourmobile in Washington we were given an image of United States history which excluded women, African-Americans and immigrants. The only mention of organised labour came when passing the marble building of the United Brotherhood of Carpenters and Joiners of America. We didn't see the homeless dossing down in Lafayette Square on the other side of the White House. It is not surprising that the 'reality' created in a public culture is likely to reflect the interests of many of the powerful, and sometimes not at all the interests—or even the existence—of the majority.

In Poland, at the end of the 1970s, I felt I was walking through an hallucination. In its public culture, Poland was a successful people's republic in which, as vanguard of the working class and under the outstanding direction of Edward Giereck (the 1970s were 'Giereck's decade'), the Communist Party was playing its historic role of leading the Polish people along the road to socialism. *Everyone* I spoke to said this was rubbish. But that was the make-believe of national life in the public culture of Poland at the end of the 1970s. Then, in the 1980s, year by year, a society began to appear in which there were trades unionists, Catholics, students, intellectuals and farmers. As these groups fought for public space, Poland began to seem to be another country. And when the whole sham of the Soviet Union fell away it was discovered how little most people had believed the public fictions. (Although it has been a great deal harder to throw off the set-up which affected the economies of those countries.)

In the communist regimes, private belief was optional (although, at times of terror, public conformity was enforced). What was compulsory was that, in its public culture, a communist nation should appear to be communist and the bureaucrats of party and state should speak communist.

In autonomic tourism, with its full surrender to the rites of the itinerary, we may see nothing of the society we are visiting, other than a few selected elements of its public culture. We become accomplices in an illusion.

* * *

TOURISM AND THE PUBLIC CULTURE 169

A public culture purports to represent the national life of the state, and to provide the national version of the certainties of existence. You might therefore think of it, in a complex modern society, as a pretence at a shared tribal culture. In analysing it, the traveller's kit of myths introduced in Chapter 6 can again be used.

The national 'tribe' that the public culture projects has certain *myths* (simple beliefs that give meaning), celebrated through familiar devices. There are *legends*, as in soap operas, school history books and 'the news' (which imparts the same kinds of wisdoms by telling us different stories every night). There are *icons*, as in swastikas, hammers and sickles, stars and stripes, Big Macs and stock national types. There are *rituals*, as in voting on election day, or visiting museums; and *festivals*, as in Christmas shopping or sporting grand-finals. (The opening of the Olympic Games demonstrates two of the common causes that unite humankind—a reverence for celebrity and a reverence for gold.)

To our traveller's kit of anthropological terms can be added *lore* and *ceremonies*. All tribal societies had a comprehensive body of wisdom (*lore*) about the nature of the world and how to get things done, passed on orally and by demonstration. Now we use lectures, instructional videos and books (economic textbooks, for example), and, as a substitute for initiations, we award degrees and diplomas and certificates. *Ceremonies* (celebrations in which institutions parade and display their glamour) can be central as value-definers in a secular society—as in Oscar awards, Nuremberg rallies, May Day marches and Changings of the Guard.

The public cultures of the various kinds of modern-industrial societies have as many myths as a tribal village. By a kind of magic, they can banish contradictions and confusion, and make things easier to understand. One way of being a tourist is to use the sightseeing experience to look for some of a country's most public secular myths. It was no accident that the Great Exhibition glorified material progress. In modernised societies, the over-riding myths tend to be industrial and economic. Zealots (both communist and capitalist) have seen history as essentially driven by economic forces. There is a creed of in the materiality of existence. There is belief in industrial growth as the principal engine of a society. There is a creed of waged work as the principal source of human dignity and welfare—to the extent that in the communist societies, instead of 'Enjoy Coca Cola' they were likely to put up 'Glory to Work'.

Now, confidently precise forecasts are made about what will happen next, not by throwing 'witch doctors' bones', but by consulting economic principles or statistical tables. If you want something done you don't offer a prayer, or take part in a ritual dance, or make a sacrifice. You prepare a plan for economic action. If you are seeking communal expression, you may find it in a shopping plaza rather than a cathedral. The Eiffel Towers and Empire State Buildings of tourism are as much expressions of economic myth as a visit to a factory.

The other myth likely to be found projected in the public culture of any industrialised state is the myth of modernity, and in particular the myth of progress, so evident in the Great Exhibition and its heirs. This is the faith that universal human and physical improvement can be obtained by rational action, and that to achieve happiness one does not have to wait for paradise.

Myths of industrialism and progress are part of the definition of a modern state.* These myths may look different in different public political cultures, but they tend to be alternative versions of the same myths. Apparent differences come from attempted 'legitimations' of power.

This is because power needs its magic. It is not sufficient unadorned. 'The strongest man is never strong enough to be always master unless he transforms his power into *right* and obedience into duty', said Jean-Jacques Rousseau in *The Social Contract*. All nations have simple and telling justifications and explanations ('legitimations'

---

* THE POSTMODERN. It may seem perverse that I merely repeat the myths of the modern, and do not acknowledge that, according to prescription, we are now in the era of the 'postmodern'. As it happens, I think there are a lot of valuable perspectives in postmodernist viewpoints—the chimerical nature of reality, the dominance of 'the image', the concern with contextualisation (even if it seems much the same as late 19th century German *historismus*, or for that matter the beliefs of the Ancient Greek sophists). I haven't used postmodernist language, because I seemed to have known all this before the word came into currency. But when it comes to suggesting, as some postmodernists do, that we have reached the end of the 'grand narratives' of progress and rationality, enlightenment and development, an answer would be: 'Look around you'. 1989 was alive with myths of grand narrative. Grand narrative is unavoidable. The question remains: 'Whose grand narrative?'

in Max Weber's term) for why some groups hold political and economic power and others don't.

If we are admiring historic sites and monuments, or walking through museums, we are likely to be looking at relics of the old ambitions and the old justifications of those who were then the masters. But we can also look around and see the justifications of those who are the masters now. Rule by divine right is not claimed for any modern-industrial state (although relics of that belief in art and architectural treasures make up the largest part of some kinds of sightseeing). But there are other potent legitimations—the revolutionary principle, the principle of economic growth, the leadership principle (Hitler's *Führerprinzip*), the liberal principle, the principle of the rule of law, the principle of equality, the capitalist principle, the nationalist principle (*Number One!*) and a number of varieties of the democratic principle, invoking the name of the people. Apart from the *Führerprinzip* (at present remembered in art deco ruins, conserved concentration camps and resistance museums), all these principles come into play on the Tourmobile tour, from the Washington Monument (revolution) to the dome of Congress (democracy)— and a fair bit of *Number One*.

In presenting both national life and the general human condition, myths of the 'nation-tribe' also claimed to explain why one or more races and/or ethnic groups were better than others, why men ran the place, and why one or more economic classes were more important to the public good than others. In ethnography museums, or the Jungle Cruise in Disneyland's Adventureland, demonstrations of race or ethnic superiority can still be made directly: this is us and that is them. It can seem natural that art museums put on such a show of women's groins, and that it is male mastery in history that is taken for granted in Disney's Frontierland and in most national museums. And it is as natural to exclude all mention of wage earners from industry museums, as it is that Main Street, USA in Disneyland ('everyone's home town—the heartline of America') is 100 per cent middle class.

Celebrated clerics used to be essential characters in the 'national tribe': now, where they still have reserved seats in the enclosure, they are only some among others. Guardians of morals and manners are more likely to be personal advice specialists in the press or broadcasting, or authors of sex manuals or instruction videos (earlier, of etiquette books), than ecclesiastics (although God can still seem a player in United States politics). As tourists, we go to religious edifices to see architecture, paintings and sculpture. It is only religious pilgrims (at Lourdes, Varanasi, Mecca, Jerusalem, etc) who are likely to return to the origins of tourism.

The nobility used to command the public scene, but in modern societies, if the royal dynasties have survived at all, they have become 'colourful' and, except in England, the remnants of the nobility mean less than the palaces and art treasures left by their ancestors—which still make up so much of European sightseeing. But remaining in Europe—like smoke in the air after an explosion—are some remnants of the attempt to mobilise the masses around the solid virtues of imagined ancient traditions that was part of 19th century conservatism. Pseudo-traditionalism seems a better word than conservatism and since then it has become a kind of neo-pseudo-traditionalism, a revival of a revival. The tourism of past splendours is its greatest strength.

What was new—it was one of the greatest novelties of the 19th century—was the development of an industrial proletariat. This also had to be accommodated in the public culture. The general abstraction of 'labour' developed in different forms: the Labour Front of the Nazis (well-muscled young men in singlets, singing love for fatherland and Führer); the concept of a liberating working class that provided the increasingly rusty dynamo of rhetoric in the communist regimes (men in singlets, joined by women in sensible blouses); and the trades unions and labour/ socialist/social democratic parties (men in suits), which could be both hope and threat in the liberal-democratic societies. However, with all the communist regimes gone from Europe, tourists can find it hard, often impossible, to celebrate the proletariat: what is usually on offer is nostalgia for the material culture of the powerful.

As another novelty, there was also thrown up, out of humanism and the enlightenment and then the liberal and radical movements of the 19th century, a 'critics' culture'. Its principal myth is that criticism is an essential force for the health of any society, with effects that are both liberating and rational. Since this is a book about tourism, I should say that the critics' culture is one of the few antidotes to those movements that debase, by trivialising, organised sightseeing. The critics' culture reached one of its many flowerings in the revolutionary year of 1989, in the overturning of so many communist regimes, but in all modern societies, including those that are liberal-democratic, the critics' culture can be suppressed, in varying degrees, by the impresarios of the public culture.

Whatever the political regime, whether capitalist or communist, liberal-democratic or fascist, militarist or cronyist, statist or vestigial-monarchic, these illusions of a 'national tribe' permeate the public scene. They do it in Independence Days for example, or parliament openings and presidential inaugurations; in boulevards and office-palaces; in law courts, army parades and police stations; or in the style and rhetoric of political leaders and other 'public figures' (offset in liberal societies by some of 'the critics'). There are the propaganda industries, including advertising, the news and entertainment industries (with their 'celebrities'), and the culture, arts and education industries. In the prosperous societies there is also the enormous importance of the shopping experience. There are the 'leisure' activities, in particular the communal enthusiasms of spectator sport, now turned into television spectaculars. And—whether in the Louvre, or the Tourmobile, or the Palace-on-Wheels, or the *Barong* dance at Batubulan, or the Victoria Falls Hotel—there is tourism.

In this book I have used tourism to provide examples of the myths of the public culture—race and ethnicity (Chapter 20), religion (Chapter 6) and neo-neo-traditionalism (Chapter 21). In this part of the book I provide examples of myths of male sexism (Chapter 14), of the economic and of modernity (Chapter 15), of class (Chapter 16) and of revolution and the critics' culture (Chapter 18). The myths of legitimations of social and economic power are everywhere.

HOW TO 'READ' TOURISM

In any society, tourism is likely to reflect many of the values of the public culture. The magic circles drawn around the objects of modern sightseeing were usually put there by much the same people, mainly middle class, as put together other parts of the new public cultures of the modernising states. They came from similar dreams of public virtue as those which produced the setting up of schools, the declaring of 'national days', the establishing of grand squares, or the designing of dignified post offices. When it was to be decided which sites were historic and should be preserved, which landscapes offered moral improvement, and which relics of the past should be displayed in museums, it was the guardians of the new public virtues who were likely to do the deciding.

In deciding what went where, it could seem natural to display the objects of natives or heathens in special museums—since these backward people were not like us. When history museums or historic sites were organised, and when ordinary things were being transmuted into monuments of new meaning, it could seem equally natural for them to present the prevailing view of the progress of a nation's history. It was equally obvious which landscapes truly expressed the best of the nation's character. Unless the 'critics' had established niches in the public culture, the possibility of presenting contrary views was close to nil.

In the 20th century, both fascist and communist regimes continued the work of edification. A Department of Tourism was set up within Goebbels' Ministry of Propaganda, and his Department of Fine Arts threw out of the German museums similar 'works of decadence' to those that the Stalinists took off the walls of Soviet museums and put into store. In the communist regimes, tourism became an expression of faith in improvement, although, in Moscow, you were more likely to find crowds in the Kremlin Armoury with its treasures of the tsars, or at the Borodino Panorama celebrating the famous victory over Napoleon, than in the Museum of Marx and Engels.

A central ethos in the public culture of fascist or communist societies affected their tourist practices. In the commercialist ('consumer') societies tourist practices were also affected by a central ethos. It was the consumer ethos: tourist sights could be presented as a range of commodities to be bought one by one, or in a package. What this meant was that in the more ebullient commercialist societies, tourism, as well as celebrating the public virtues of edification and regeneration, could also celebrate the public virtues of spending money.

In *Sacred Places: American Tourist Attractions in the Nineteenth Century*, John Sears describes how, even in the 19th century when the sublimity of Niagara Falls was expected to bring the tourist pilgrim closer to God, each designated point of interest was fenced off by a private showman, like a gold claim, with a ticket booth for entrance to a particular view. 'Doing the Falls' was something you bought, commodity by commodity, ticket by ticket, each with its own hype in the guidebooks. All around were sideshows, souvenir shops, brass bands, fireworks, rope-walking and other amusements. By the 1860s, these diversions were seen as a threat to God's wishes in creating the Falls. In the 1880s the surrounds of the Falls on both the United States and Canadian sides were bought back, cleaned up and landscaped into the unnatural beauty of a State Park. (However, for those still interested in tradition, there is plenty of authentic huckstering and tackiness in the two nearby towns, where people continue to make money out of the Falls, especially on the United States side.)

The idea of tourism as a way of buying bits of cultural experience, piece by piece or in packages, is one of the basic marketing strategies of autonomic tourism in commercialist societies. It is also the source of one of the greatest criticisms of tourism from sociologists—that it 'commodifies' sightseeing, turning it into a buying experience. For autonomic tourism, that can be true. And not only can tourists buy cultural experiences as if they were making purchases in a shop, they can also spend a great deal of a tour *shopping*.

(It can be illuminating to look for similarities in the shopping and tourist experiences—but these comparisons should not just be made snobbishly. They are related to the whole experience of looking at things. Walter Benjamin said that the art gallery of the working class can be a department store: along with shopping centres, malls, boutique arcades and so forth we can see them as filled with visual messages alive with meanings, glowing from the products themselves as well as from the merchandising. Magic meanings have been transmuted to the products by advertising and marketing, in much the same way as being on show in a museum transmutes objects with the magic circle of new meaning.*)

* * *

It is not likely that capitalists met secretly to decide that tourism would become a vehicle for the ideologies of the commercialist society. The theory of a public culture does not depend on unmasking conspirators. What is usually done seems the perfectly natural thing to do in maintaining a perceived public good. Prince Albert saw the Great Exhibition as an event that would make better people of his wife's subjects. Walt Disney saw Main Street, USA as an inspiration for his fellow citizens. When the Southern African Caledonian Societies decided to commission a statue of Livingstone and put it on the banks of the Zambesi, it seemed the most natural thing in the world to proclaim white superiority.

Sightseeing can show us for ourselves what the things we read about are 'like' (and then lead us to some more reading about them). It can also help us discover new kinds of things. Why shouldn't we also have some theory about the public cultures of which these things have become a part—and, by cracking some of the codes, recognise that things may not be as 'natural' as they look? What do the Maya ruins stand for in modern Yucatan society? Why did the Bulgarian communist regime sponsor such lavish Easter Masses in the Alexander Nevski Cathedral? Who gains when the legend of the

---

* SEIBU TRANSFORMATIONS. In one of the more ambitious Japanese department stores you can see both these transmutations. If you visit, for example, the Seibu Department Store in Tokyo's Ikebukuro district you can develop museum eyes in Seibu's art gallery (which puts on shows that go to national art museums in other countries), its Studio 200 (with its art films, theatre, music and symposia), its 'creator's' galleries for innovators, its 'hobby house', its gallery for traditional Japanese crafts, its large 'book centre', its salons of antiques, interior design centres, craft centres, living advice centres and its consumer advice centres (these centres have some of the atmosphere of the old museums of applied arts and sciences). Having acquired museum eyes with all of this, it is then easy to turn the rest of the store into exhibits. The 'USSR and Eastern Europe Centre' and the 'Chinese Products Market' become *ethnographic*—strange products from other lands. With a similar framing of the imagination, the centres for Scottish kilts, French perfumes, Italian silks or Swedish glass also become ethnographic reminders of the folkways of distant peoples.

explorers is epitomised by placing the Livingstone statue to mark the designated beginning of Victoria Falls? Who gains from the legends of nation-making revealed in the encirclements of the Tourmobile, or from the emphasis on the pleasures of princely palaces on the Palace-on-Wheels tour? Who gained when the possessions of natives or heathens were given special museums and treated differently from objects from Western societies?

Tourism can become more intelligent if what we are looking at, including relics of an imagined past, can be seen in relation to the myth-system of the society in which it is presented. To do this requires lavish use of the principle of intelligent superficiality.

14.

THE PUBLIC WOMAN

♦ ♦ ♦

ALTERNATIVE READINGS

When we were in Manchester in 1987 we were taken around the Manchester City Gallery to admire the way in which it had been tizzed up, in what was presented as a period decoration style. No-one explained, though, exactly what period, or whether the building had looked like this in the 19th century, or why this new decorative scheme made it a better place in which to hang pictures. What I was looking for was the shop. I had been tipped-off to ask for a pamphlet, *A Feminist Looks Round the City Art Gallery*.

This pamphlet gave a warning that might be lettered above the entrance to any art museum—that art can be treated as having a social function. It also said that art pictured the world for those who paid for the art, and made sense of the world in ways that confirmed the place and power of those who had done the paying.

It didn't allow for exceptions. Artists can play tricks on those who pay them—some artworks sell only after the artists are dead; artworks can have different social functions from one period to the next. But, in the case of the presentation of women in European art museums, there is no need for qualification.

Some assumptions run so grossly through a public culture that they impregnate everything. The presentation of women is one of them. Stereotypes of women mark tourist presentations of almost everything: from buxom young women on the travel posters, to representations in virtually the whole repertoire of 'the past'. Detecting this can be one of the easiest exercises in 'reading' tourism and there is no better place to start than an art museum.

A Feminist Looks Round the City Art Gallery pointed out that the gallery owns more than 90 paintings by women artists, but that only four of them were on the walls. It then referred to paintings on show and analysed them as studies in the legends and icons of the myth of femininity—women as mothers, as decorative objects, as submissive, as dynastic possessions, as fashion plates, as victims, as sources of goodness or gentleness and, in contrast, women as sirens and sluts. An apparently 'innocent' picture by Thomas Gainsborough, *A Peasant Girl Gathering Faggots in a Wood* is analysed so thoroughly from this perspective that for a male even to look at this painting after reading the alternative guide becomes an act of child sexual abuse.

A Feminist Looks Round the City Art Gallery doesn't investigate the most obvious use of women in art tourism—as nudes. But in European art museums one of the main functions of the female body is to be exposed to the male gaze, so that women are not simply naked, but naked as men see them. As John Berger put it, in his often-quoted study in *Ways of Seeing*, nakedness is not supine in Indian art, Persian art, African art or prehistoric art in the Americas, as it is in museums of Western art. Here, bodies are displayed for male use—in nude poses and gestures that have lived on in the pages of *Playboy* and its imitators.

Playboy, *Penthouse* and so forth are carrying on a renaissance tradition. From the renaissance onwards, artists used anecdotes from the Bible, the lives of the saints and the Greek and Roman classics as excuses to display female breasts, buttocks, thighs and groins (although not pubic hair). There were *Venuses* from all angles, beginning with Botticelli's *The Birth of Venus* (1485), the first of the celebrated nudes, and *Eves* by the thousand. The female nude crossed the Alps from Venice, when Lucas Cranach established a workshop at Wittenberg that specialised in *Eves, Venuses*, and *Lucretias*. Lucretia was chosen because she stabbed herself to death, and Cranach could depict her running the dagger into her naked chest, an act that classified her with Cleopatra, who clasped an asp to her naked bosom; with St Agatha, whose breasts were cut off by order of a lecherous Roman governor; with Juno, whose spouting nipples produced the Milky Way; with Mary Magdalene, whose breasts were often used as a jeweller's showcase; and with the Virgin Mary, who, in Madonna and Child studies (the most popular of all renaissance themes), could be shown with one naked breast revealed as she fed the infant Jesus.

The naked Bathsheba was spied on by King David (Samuel xi). The naked Susanna was peered at by two lecherous elders (Daniel xiii). The naked Daphne was pursued by the lustful Apollo (and saved when he was about to rape her by being turned into a laurel tree). Jupiter, as a shower of gold, impregnated the naked Danae; as a swan, he penetrated the naked Leda; and, as an eagle, the naked Europa. Paintings of *The Judgment of Paris* and *The Three Graces* presented full frontals, full dorsals and full laterals of naked women.

There are theories that Nature (in the form of Nature tourism) joins Art in being sexist. In *Sacred Places*, John Sears argues an opposite case—that the national scenery which became a feature of the United States public culture in the 19th century was never 'gender identified . . . Niagara Falls, for example, represented the seemingly inexhaustible resources of our continent, but with its walkways, staircases and shops was highly domesticated . . . Tourism seemed to offer a cultural check on aggressive fantasies of exploiting American resources . . . ' It's not much of a case. There can be shared Nature worship, but the whole language of Nature tourism can become drenched in images of masculinity and femininity. In an essay, *The Outback*, on the growing cult of the Uluru (Ayers Rock) monolithic rock as a national icon of the Australian people, the Australian historian, Ann McGrath, points out that while 'New Age' movements and others see 'the Rock' as a kind of spiritual centre transcending merely human values, it is normally interpreted in masculinist language as symbolising 'a man's country'. To this there has been a feminist reaction of seeing 'the Olgas', a nearby collective of smaller monoliths, as having rounded, breast-like shapes and 'vulval ravines'.

Sightseers can set themselves exercises in 'reading' tourism by looking out in particular for the treatment of women in history, beginning with the 'primitive'. Native Americans were presented in the ethnographic departments of natural history museums in the United States' west as hunter-gatherer societies, with men doing the hunting and women doing the gathering. There were likely to be two lifesize dummies—one male, one female—with the male dressed in all the finery and surrounded by the most spectacular artifacts. The female would be in humdrum clothes, and set among a few leftover things. This did not reveal that the women did some hunting too, if for smaller animals, and that, while the males may have dominated the flashier kinds of hunting, warfare and ceremony, it was women who kept much of the show going.

In museum presentations of the mixed farming economies of Black Africa it doesn't clearly come out that women worked harder than men, and did almost all the work in cultivating crops, although it was the men who owned the grain when it was harvested. In the folk theme parks of Europe and the pioneer theme parks of the New World, a woman's place is usually found in the kitchen, showing off the pots and pans, despite the fact that women could be as essential as men to the economy of a farm.

Even in the tourism of aristocratic houses women are to be remembered mainly for their pedigrees or their pretty portraits, or for reminders of the clothes they wore. Yet as Trevor Lumms and Jan Marsh show in *The Woman's Domain*, a study of seven English country houses, women could be more important than men in developing these mansions or giving life to them. The mistresses of the seven households surveyed ranged from a lady of the court of Elizabeth I, who built two famous country houses and bore on her tomb the epitaph 'Renowned, magnificent builder', to a blue-stocking leader of 19th century radical intellectuals, who used her country house as a base for questioning some of the old order. Of servants in the houses, one, an 18-year-old dairymaid, married her 70-year-old master; another, a career servant, was the mother of the writer H G Wells.

The most significant reminder of women's roles in the National Museum of American History, Washington, is an exhibition of the ball gowns of the First Ladies—but then this museum of United States history doesn't mention in its permanent displays that the United States was a slave-owning society.*

It is only in projections of *social* history that women are likely to make a significant appearance. However, they may make that appearance only, for the rich, through their wardrobes, and, for the others, because of their cooking and cleaning.

* * *

A general feature of the 'nation-tribe' projected in a public culture is that whole classes of people may be portrayed as simple loyalists, or harmless clowns, or sinister threats to the natural order. Or they may not be there at all. This is one of the 'silences' of the public culture: any serious reading of tourism must include attention to these significant silences. Art museums have a special role for women, and historical sites and general history museums may place them in the kitchen or the ballroom, but in much sightseeing tourism women are not there at all. In an historical industrial site, say, or in a war museum, there may be no women, or only women defined in some particularly narrow way.

There are now a few remedial attempts to make the invisible visible. There is the new National Museum of Women in the Arts in Washington, DC, and the Women's Rights National Historical Park has been established in the west of New York State in the declining industrial town of Seneca Falls, because it was a mid-19th century centre of the early women's movement. However, museums, historical sites and tourism generally can be one of the

---

* THE PERILS OF NOSTALGIA. The museum now runs some excellent special exhibitions—such as 'The Road to Independence', 'A Far Better Union' and 'From Field to Factory'—but the regular displays are a fatuous hodge-podge that add up to a proclamation that there has not been a United States *society*. Despite its tendentious messages, the History Museum in Moscow's Red Square was, by comparison, an example of scholarship. Defenders of the National Museum of American History might say that this is just a place 'filled with all the things Americans love too much to throw away'. But nostalgia can be one of the most good-humoured devices of reaction.

slowest-changing parts of a public culture. Consider the changed presentation of women in, say, fiction or movies, television drama or telecasts, in the last 25 years and compare that with the almost complete lack of change in how women are presented in historic sites, museums or other kinds of sightseeing. The invisibility of women is not something that can be overcome by bits of patching in existing museums and historic sites, nor by starting a few specialist shows about women. It is a matter of transforming views of society and history. That can be done in a new book or a new play or a new picture, but tourist sights are so cumbersome that there are very few easy avenues of transformation. They become reminders of what was worth looking at a century or half a century ago.

15.

TEMPTATIONS OF BEAUTY AND NOSTALGIA

◆ ◆ ◆

A NICE DAY AT AN INDUSTRIAL SITE

Until recently, touring the English countryside was mainly a matter of admiring the scenery, photographing picturesque villages, visiting every cathedral in sight and, above all, paying admission fees to the mansions and palaces that the English call 'country houses'.

Now there are theme parks and new museums all over the place, and the stately homes are often part of an 'amusement centre'. But there has also been an intelligent development that no-one would have imagined until 'industrial archaeology' came in during the 1950s, at the very time when the government was paying people to destroy obsolete machinery, and a great many former industrial sites had been obliterated. At that time it was country houses that were to be protected because, to England's enormous moral loss, they were seen as the principal part of the 'soul' of Britain. (Imagine whose interests are served if the soul of Britain is found in a national past inhabited entirely by the monarchy, the nobility and the gentry?)

Now, old mills and foundries, canal basins and coal pits can also be seen as part of the national heritage. Even old slag heaps. Now, some of the top items on tourist agendas are relics of the industrial revolution.

What kind of an industrial revolution do these relics in Britain and in other countries 'represent'? What part do they play in the public culture? What do they 'tell' us about industry and science? (The answer will be: not as much as you might expect, because sometimes a public culture functions most significantly in its silences.)

The leader of this new style was the Ironbridge Gorge Museum in Shropshire, which opened in 1973.* The video in the Visitor Centre, set up in a restored warehouse beside the river, explains that this valley in the Coalbrookdale coalfield was 'the Silicon Valley of 18th century England'. It was the place where the Quaker, Abraham Darby, leased the blast furnace and became the first person to make iron using coke instead of charcoal. This new way of doing things was to turn Britain into the world's ironmaster, and Coalbrookdale into the centre of Britain's ironmaking—both in the quantity of what was produced, and the innovation with which it was made: iron cylinders for steam engines, iron wheels and iron rails, and then the first steam railway locomotive, iron barges, iron plates for iron ships, and, in 1781, the iron bridge (the first in the world) that gave the valley its name. Not only was this the first iron bridge: it was also the first substantial iron structure. It was followed, in 1796, by an iron aqueduct, and in 1797 by a flax mill that was the first building to have an iron frame.

---

* **PATRIOTIC FURNACE.** The United States was 40 years ahead of Britain in restoring an old iron-making site, with the restoration of the Hopewell Furnace, Pennsylvania. This began in 1935 as one of the Depression programs of the Works Progress Administration and was taken over by the National Park Service in 1938. Hopewell was not one of the starting points in legends of the industrial revolution, as Coalbrookdale was, but it is a highly patriotic industrial history site. As a reminder of Britain's attempt in 1750 to stop the American colonies from producing finished iron products, it is seen as part of the legend of the American Revolution. On Independence Day each year, a Continental Regiment Drill team celebrates the loyalty of the Hopewell Furnace during the Revolutionary War.

When innovation moved on to other places and other countries, Ironbridge had a late flowering as a centre for decorative tiles and fine porcelain, and extraordinary art castings in iron. The most ambitious ornamental ironwork at the Great Exhibition came from Coalbrookdale, and some marvellous examples of this now-abandoned art have been brought back to the Ironbridge museum. But as art began to flower, furnaces and forges were abandoned, and factories and mines crumbled. Abraham Darby's blast furnace was left buried among the rubble of foundry shops.

The ruins of the Old Furnace were uncovered in 1959, renamed 'the Darby Furnace' and made into a sacred site. It is now protected by a reliquary of metal and glass, and honoured by catwalks and a sound-and-light show sponsored by a commercial company. A scale model makes it easy to use one's imagination in transforming this great lump—back into the days when it was such a portent of new times that artists went to Coalbrookdale to make paintings of it. The development corporation of a new town, Telford (named after a great 18th century engineer), has now sacralised the gorge as a monument to industrialism, with the Darby Furnace as its altar.

It is an intelligent development, leaving plenty to the imagination, even if, in recalling the industrial revolution, Ironbridge overdoes the Darby Furnace as a 'cause'. At least this legend of iron makes a change from the legend of steam as 'cause' which, in Britain, prevails, although there is also a strong line in railway museums. This is the legend in which James Watt is hero. At his most legendary he first contemplates the power of steam as a boy, watching a kettle boil in his mother's kitchen; as part of a lesser legend, a boulder on Glasgow Green marks *the very spot* where Watt first thought of the idea of a separate condenser. This is 'the birthplace of the industrial revolution'. (Like Glasgow Green and several other sites, Ironbridge is also a birthplace of the industrial revolution.)

The legend of steam attains its most far-reaching expression in the Science Museum in London: for 50 years the first sight most people had in the museum was of the stately 18th and 19th century machines, powerful in their shrine in the East Hall. Entry was down a broad flight of steps to where a visitor could see the rotative steam engines—their metal gleaming, their wheels large and leisurely. After modernisation of the building in the late 1980s, the first thing the visitor is now likely to see is an information desk of plate glass and stainless steel, lit from below, so that it seems about to rise into space like a flying saucer. But the steam engines are still there, if now more theatrically lit and set among fashionable quarry tiles and royal-blue carpeting. Nearby, still, is James Watt's transported workshop, with its 6000 components in the positions they occupied in relation to each other on the day the genius died.

* * *

In Pittsburgh, where 80,000 people once worked in steel mills on the banks of the Monongahela River, and only 4000 do so today, a Steel Heritage Task Force is attempting to conserve the Homestead works, once the biggest in the valley. In Sweden, industrial site museums may finally equal in number the open air peasant museums of an earlier fashion. One, Bergslagen, spreads over 100 kilometres, 50 sites and 2000 years of ironmaking. In the town of Kristiansund on the Norwegian coast, a 130-year-old shipyard has become a living museum. In Kyoto, the Keage Power Plant, one of the world's earliest hydroelectric plants, has joined temples and palaces as a tourist site and part of Kyoto's architectural heritage: it is in the 'Meiji style'—redbrick with stone facings, in the pseudo-French renaissance fashion that had a season after the Meiji restoration.

In the manner of tourism, these restorations or conservations of industrial relics have fed a thirst not only for history, but for the beautiful. Critics of Ironbridge are likely to say that there is too much rural bliss—the Severn Valley offers leafy English beauty and, apart from the sanctified ruins, the reconstructed buildings commit the sin of being admired for their architectural style: where is the clatter and stink, the smoke and fire? Well, what do they want? Jorvik? The sights and sounds and smells of the industrial revolution? They have plenty of aids there to help the visitor imagine what it was like.

In Britain, the traditional historical emphasis has been on textile mills, since they used steam engines (even if, at the start, the power came from waterwheels). And, as buildings, some of the textile mills were (from the outside) as rational and elegant as the 'halls' of railway stations or the Crystal Palace—this means that the industrial revolution can beguile visitors with the aesthetic.

When we drove from Glasgow to see New Lanark it was because I knew that by the end of the 18th century the biggest cotton mill in Britain was there, drawing its power from the picturesque Falls of Clyde. I knew that later, as a mill village of 2500 people, it became the site of Robert Owen's experiment in what Marx would dismiss as 'utopian socialism'.* And I also knew that when it was established by Owen's father-in-law it was mostly children who were the mill hands. But although I had all this in my head as we walked along the footpath, I was taken over by the charms of beauty in this formidable juxtaposition of nature and culture—in a romantic chasm with a raging torrent, where, among the green and pleasant trees there suddenly appear tall buildings of severe beauty, arranged with cold rationality. However, it is possible to admire a tourist view like this, but also enjoy it as an historic site—and to consider how its history continues. Behind the shell-facades of what were tenement houses, where each family had a single room, there are now self-contained, centrally-heated modern apartments for Scottish yuppies.

It is nostalgia, not beauty, that is the enemy. At Ironbridge, something very sickly got into them when they made such a mess of the Blists Hill Open Air Museum that is part of the complex, although not in the gorge itself. Blists Hill was a mining village with three blast furnaces and a brickworks. There are relics of these noisy and noisome activities, but a 'model village' has been set up, containing quaint structures from other parts of the country—a butcher's, a baker's, a candlestick maker's (literally) and other shops reminiscent of cottagey calendar illustrations. Instead of flames shooting up and illuminating the village twice a day when the furnaces were

---

* **UNITED STATES UTOPIAS.** The other part of the tourism of Robert Owen is to visit New Harmony, Indiana, where Owen attempted to establish a commune, lost most of his fortune, but increased his fame. It is listed among 'Utopias' in *Birnbaum's United States*—and now offers a symphony of polished woods in a rich architectural experience and, at the New Harmony Inn, a unique glass-roofed swimming pool, with health spa and sauna, and excellent meals at the Bayou Grill.

tapped, there are now cosy fires in the grates of nice little cottages, with cats dozing in front of some of them. One doesn't want the Ironbridge authorities to simulate a satanic industrial village, but they might be expected not to 're-create' what didn't exist. It is as if all this industrial activity had been performed not by 400 to 500 employees living in an industrial settlement, but by the worthy shopkeepers and their cats.

And nostalgia fogs the Beamish Open Air Museum. This is of much the same vintage as the sacralising of Ironbridge, set in 80 hectares of woods and farmland in the north-east of England— one of those parts of Britain where steel mills, mines and shipyards are all devastated. A turn-of-the-century past has been invented, with authentic structures moved in from all over the place—a pit-top wheelhouse, a Georgian terrace, a railway station, a signal box, a row of pitmens' cottages, a collection of farm buildings, enough cottages and shops to suggest a town— and it is, inevitably, nostalgic. Nostalgic for what? The certainties of a century that was going to provide the Western Front, the concentration camp, the atom bomb and the destruction of the industries of north-eastern England? Unlike Ironbridge or New Lanark as historic sites of early industrialism, but like the butcher's, baker's and candlestick maker's of Blists Hill, Beamish offers an invented past of cosiness. The nostalgia has been built into it. The nastiness has been left out.

The Quarry Bank Mill at Styal, in a valley near Manchester, is an example of how one can have a nice day at an industrial site without excess. Begun as a water-powered cotton-spinning mill in the 1780s, and one of the most successful early factories based on Arkwright's machines, it displays an interesting piece of machinery and, if you like things that move, you can spend some time wandering around it and looking at it from different angles. This is its Great Wheel—in 1819 the largest prime mover in the world, and mover of 10,846 spindles. Styal also offers all the leafy pleasures of a green valley and the harmonies of Georgian architectural styles, along with a medieval village and home-cooked food in the Mill Kitchen. In the Mill Shop there are goods woven on machines powered by the Great Wheel. But, as well as having your nice day doing all this, by looking around you also get an idea not only of 19th century spinning and weaving and counting house procedures, but of how people worked and lived together in a rural factory-colony. And since they still have some very noisy machines, you can ask to have one of them turned on and get some idea of the hideous clatter of the past.

MACHINES AS METAPHORS

One of the roles of the old Science and Industry Museums in the public culture has been to become projections of national styles. Le Musée National des Techniques, Paris, was established in parts of a commandeered priory as one of the democratising museums of the French Revolution. It is now a museum of a museum—but it is a museum of a *French* museum. From Pascal's 17th century calculating machine onwards, with special honour given to Lavoisier in the gleam of brass, the sparkle of glass and other relics of his laboratory, you know, as you stand among all these old appliances, that you are in a monument to the intelligence of the French. Similarly, in the Science Museum in London you can feel the nostalgic beauty of the Old Masters—Watt's rotative steam engines, Arkwright's first spinning frame, *Puffing Billy*, Stephenson's *Rocket*, Davy's safety lamp and other achievements from the people who brought you the Industrial Revolution.

In another stalwart—the Deutsches Museum in Munich, Germany's oldest and largest technological museum—some of the prize pieces are reminders of how clever the Germans were in recognising the relation between science and industry—the instruments of the founder of Germany's first physics laboratory; the vacuum gauges of the initiator of modern vacuum techniques; the large calorimeter used by the enunciator of the principle of the conservation of energy; the frictional electrical machine built by George Simon Ohm, formulator of Ohm's Law; and the original apparatus used by W C Röntgen for his discovery of X-rays.

The Swedes have made Stockholm's National Museum of Science something of a monument to Sweden's brilliant entry into the industrial revolution. There are displays of venerable objects like turbine dynamos, electric blast furnaces and metallurgists' equipment, along with Swedish masterpieces of iron and steel, telephone systems and other achievements of the people who gave us Linnaeus, the great scientific classifier.

There is self-effacing whimsy in the Science and Technology Building of the National Science Museum in Tokyo. Here you are in the capital of the world's industrial beehive and the treatment given to industry is mainly at the level of demonstrations of the ancient craft techniques of making *urushi* (Japanese lacquer) and *washi* (Japanese paper); a presentation of the Irishima salt farm techniques; along with traditional hand looms, traditional kilns and traditional house-building methods.

Brezhnev's Moscow made a recognisable statement in its largest exposition space, spread over 216 hectares and through 80 pavilions—designed in the various national styles of the Soviet republics, with dozens of fountains and statues (one of them the famous *Worker and Collective-Farm Woman*, designed for the Soviet display at the Paris World Fair of 1937). This exposition was entitled 'The Exhibition of the Economic Achievements of the Soviet Union'.

But in all of these industry museums almost everything connected with industrialism is missing—except machines and apparatus. As Kenneth Hudson says in *Museums of Influence*, we have museums of industry, but they are not museums of industrialisation. They are museums of machinery. And this says something about the projection of industrialism in the public cultures of modern-industrial societies.

In the Science Museum in London there is a series of 81 small displays, brightly presented, to tell a story of the development of science and technology that begins with neolithic flint mining. In these 81 episodes the factory system gets one mention (Episode 59). Yet if one were silly enough to put up a case for one single 'birth' of the industrial revolution, the development of the factory system might make more sense than the development of furnace processes or steam engines or spinning frames. Machines did not produce the factory system. It was a human invention. The phrase 'the factory system' was being used to point to one of the new signs of the times by the 1830s, but there were rationalised workshops before then. Michel Foucault notes in *Discipline and Punish* a phenomenon he calls 'the normalisation of individuals', that emerged strongly in the 17th century in the development of institutions such as workshops, asylums, hospitals and gaols. He argues that it was a prefiguring of the 'accumulation of labour' which, along with 'the accumulation of capital'* (reinvestment of the cash flow from slave-trading, for example), makes up a large part of the definition of industrialism. He sees these 17th century developments as a precondition of industrialism: the bodies of workpeople had been disciplined into readiness before the industrialising of machines began.

It is social reorganisation—a redisciplining that works most effectively in forms of social self-control—that is essential in the formation of a modern-industrial society. Bradshaw's national railway guide, first appearing in 1841, should also be an exhibit in the Science Museum: the railway timetable is an important symbol of the basic orderings essential to industrialisation (so that to be held up at the luggage carousel at Bombay airport can seem a flight from reason).

A 'true' industry museum would also have reminders of the development of 'consumer societies'—gasoliers, sewing machines, egg-beaters and carpet-sweepers—and brand names should appear in these museums, encircled and distanced, for observation. The arrival of the phenomenon of window-shopping, the people's

---

* **BEYOND ART.** In a couple of rooms in the Correr Museum, Venice, in objects recalling the advance in bookkeeping techniques, the inquisitive traveller can find another of the preconditions of industrialism. Capital accumulation (investment) is not likely to work unless someone is keeping the books. These documents are the mathematical measure of all the trading and looting, the warfare and financing, carried on by one of the most isolated and money-driven communities Europe has known. The Doge's Palace at the other side of the *piazza*, with its gold-encrusted ceilings and gilt panellings, symbolises more than art: it can make more sense as a reminder of a moneyed ruling class, whose self-perpetuating oligarchy depended on an accurate keeping of accounts.

Another cradle of modern capitalism can be found among the art treasures of the Flanders towns: the first 'urbanised area'. The famous replica of the cloth hall (*Lakenhalle*) of Ieper is not only an 'architectural gem', it is a reminder of how a few rich men controlled the whole operation of the cloth trade—importing raw materials, employing an urban proletariat, owning the facilities and arranging exports in the world's first large-scale capitalist production.

museum, should be given some of the emphasis that we give, say, to the Bronze Age.

One of the most effective (and false) demonstrations of machines as metaphors of general improvement can come from a factory visit. In 'Toyota City', out of Nagoya, a showcase assembly plant has been transformed into a museum of enterprise. Here, 2000–3000 tourists pass each day from exhibition halls to a triumphal parade along the catwalks, admiring the putting together of 'cars that are loved the world over', as part of the building of 'a better tomorrow'. Yet factory visits can be even more misleading in their silences than the arrangements of machines in a museum. The success of Toyota comes from its design and marketing programs, not from its assembly techniques, and not at all from its manufacturing techniques—which in fact it does not have. Toyota subcontracts out all manufacturing of the parts that make up its cars to a line of subcontractors, subcontractors' subcontractors and subcontractors' subcontractors' subcontractors, some of whom run sweatshops that are a marked contrast to the exemplary paternalism presented by the central Toyota works.

If handled with intelligence, the best on-site museums—places like Ironbridge and Styal—must be better at presenting machines in a social and economic context than are the grand national museums of machinery. They don't have too much machinery, and what there is can be seen in its own setting. There is plenty of space for providing background to the objects on show. And you have a chance to think about what it might all have meant.

My favourite memory of this kind of tourism is a visit to Österbybruk ('bruk' means ironworks estate), a small Swedish industrial town of 3000 or so people north of Uppsala, where it was easy to pick up reminders of the old social order. The ironmaster's elegant manor house was now a conference and seminar centre. But there it was still, this mansion, set in a commodious park, from which the ironmasters controlled, in a post-feudal manner, forests, mines, smelters, forges and workers. And there remained two streets of low, white-plastered cottages, now turned into modern dwelling units, where the ironmasters' workers had lived, with, behind them, the now-restored barns in which their wives kept the family's animals. Even though the tourists at Österbybruk used it for swimming, you could see an example of the system of dams, races and locks of the kind introduced into ironworks estates in the 17th century, that powered the ironworks and the hammer shops and for a while made the Swedes the biggest iron producers in the world. An old mill and a hammer shop had been restored to an imitation of their early 19th century condition when they were worked mainly by child labour, 24 hours a day. As well, there was the 1902 mill that was the first place in the world to carry out high-speed steel production, and the rolling mills and forging shops that still produced specialist steels.

And, in one last historical note, there were also the 20th century unemployed who had been used to restore the manor house, the old hammer mill, the workers' cottages—and what had become a Tourist Information Centre.

A good museum of industrialism must also be a social history museum—which does not avoid the embarrassments of industrialism. History museums under some of the communist regimes were efficient in assembling objects from the period of early industrialisation in a way that presented social complexity—although they became trite in the room where 'the revolution' was declared to have occurred. But in capitalist societies, apart from several exemplary treatments of everyday life, mainly in Scandinavian countries, there may be only one museum that has told a serious, adult story. This is the Municipal Museum at Rüsselsheim, known as 'Opel City' because of the dominance there, since the 1870s, of the now mainly automobile Opel manufacturing plant. The town council appointed a young director in the early 1970s to establish a new museum. He decided to go beyond setting up a motor museum and adding a few old sewing machines to show the original basis of Opel's success. He understood that an industrial museum must also be a cultural history museum, so he showed, in a wide range of objects, what the Opel factory did to and for people living in Rüsselsheim—the good and the bad together. There were machines, but there were also trades union documents, works of art, pay packets, domestic furniture, group photographs and Nazi flags.

FANFARES OF SCIENCE

The triumphalism of industry museums, with their fanfare of progress as one machine begets another, can seem modest compared with the propaganda of the science centres that sometimes supplant them in appeal.

The first of these came when the Chicago Museum of Science and Industry was revamped in the 1940s to sell science with hands-on techniques, and to sell itself to industrial firms for sponsorships. Bizarrely housed in a beaux-arts palace built for the 1893 World Exhibition (one of the most lavish successors of the Great Exhibition), this trade fair of science and industry became, with two million visitors a year, Chicago's highest-rating tourist show. Later, the Ontario Science Centre (1969), which abandoned the whole idea of a museum (not that there is anything wrong with that), was to become an advanced model for the four dozen or so 'science centres' in North America, of which perhaps only the Exploratorium at San Francisco offered any sensitive approaches.

The idea of science centre as propaganda device reached a climax in Disney's EPCOT Center in Disney World, Orlando. 'EPCOT' stands for Experimental Prototype Community of Tomorrow, a title that is ludicrously irrelevant for a an educational-entertainment enterprise that makes money out of giving a glossed-up presentation of a hi-tech present. The success of the Great Exhibition was followed by one of the world's largest museum complexes, at South Kensington, dedicated to classification and authenticity, but with a chance for an inquiring mind to find wonder and make discoveries. The success of Disneyland at Los Angeles was followed at EPCOT by super-reality and commercialised fantasy in which the wonder is prepackaged.

The most dazzling of today's science centres is the billion dollar Cité des Sciences et de l'Industrie on the edge of Paris. It has an excellent shop and other reference back-up, and some good special shows—'Les Savants et la Révolution' was one of the most intelligent exhibitions of the 1989 bicentennial manifestations—but, overall, it is a kind of cantata in contemporary display technology praising the wonders, and the immutability, of science. Something as costly and smart and celebrated as La Cité des Sciences can also suggest that the nation that has it must itself be a paragon of technology.

In a suitably more modest way, the Singapore Science Centre can also produce an aura—of a confident, technocratic Singapore—that goes somewhat beyond Singapore's actual scientific capacity. And what of Washington's National Air and Space Museum in its tremendous hangar of glass and steel, with its greater-than-life simulations, its five-floors-high movie screen and its 10 million visitors a year? It might suggest that the United States has an option on the universe.

There is nothing wrong with being titillated into an interest in the latest theories that have come from scientific inquiry, but this doesn't happen in the science centres. The technique becomes the message. 'La géode', a movie theatre in La Cité des Sciences with a 1000 square metre hemispheric screen, is a medium that puts people inside the message. The message is one of glitzy presentation. As Neil Postman said in *Museum News*: 'We do not need museums that dazzle us with modern electronic equipment (our culture already dazzles us with electronic equipment to the point that we are all but blind) . . . At the very least, we need museums that provide some vision of humanity different from the vision put forward by every advertising agency and political speech'.

Beyond the glitz, the message is a positivist one of passing on knowledge about which there is no dispute. Yet the assuredness of these billions of dollars of entertainment devices is at odds with the speculative uncertainties of science (and with the complexities of science). In that sense, these centres tell billions of dollars worth of lies about science. Contrast all this assertive, showy stuff with an exhibition put on in the Natural History Museum, London, about Charles Darwin's theory of evolution by natural selection. It didn't gloss the theory up in high-tech presentation. (In fact, most of it was done through recycled stuffed animals.) It suggested modestly that Darwin's theory is 'a convincing way of explaining how evolution might have occurred', and it maintained throughout the hypothetical approach of science ('Seems to offer a good explanation' . . . 'May be used to explain').

By denying science's hypothetical nature, these science centres give false ideas of how scientists work. There is no recognition that making science involves a complex of activities within a society, and that it is not just an activity performed by hands-on machines. And the people who run the centres can become so obsessed with the idea of a uniform body of simple bits of knowledge, that have to be passed on in an attractive way, that they ignore the lives of the people who go to the centre. I haven't visited it, but I have read that the Maison des Sciences et des Techniques in Montreal is required to take into account the social dimensions of science and technology in Québec, so that its presentations will be related to what is happening among the people who visit it.

For me, the science centres are so triumphalist and so faked that even pushing their buttons can be an act of collaboration with a powerful enemy. However, I can enjoy looking at the machines in an industry museum, although, given that there are usually far too many, not all of them. The Great Wheel in the Quarry Bank Mill at Styal held charm because it was the only one, and we were able to walk around it and brood over it, without having to hurry to look at the next Great Wheel. And, despite myself, I can be drawn in by the glow of authenticity when I stand in front of a relic such as Arkwright's first spinning frame—which I first learnt about from photographs in *Cassell's Children's Book of Knowledge*. ('After much patient work Arkwright made the little machine shown above, which he patented in 1769. Many millions of bales of cotton are now spun every year thanks to the splendid pluck of a man who never went to school.') But we should recognise that by showing such a restricted range of objects, almost every museum of industry, by its 'silences', tells two enormous lies: that the control and operations of industrialism are of no particular interest, and that industrialisation does not have effects on how we live, on how we relate to each other and how we see the world.

Industry museums and science centres are sacred to two urgent myths in a nation's public culture—a faith in progress and a faith in industrialism and the economic. Their triumphal celebration of the merely mechanical and their 'silences' on everything else can seem perfectly natural. But industry museums and science centres can provide a clinically exact example of how guardians of a public culture can operate negatively, with what they leave out—because to widen the presentation of how science works, and how industrialism has worked, could be contentious, divisive, partisan or freakish. And unless there is to be a miraculous spread of enlightenment, the fact that in the commercialist societies company sponsorship of industry museums is becoming stronger makes movements for reform of these museums seem, at present, hopeless.

* * *

In 1990, members of the newly-formed USSR Consumer Society in

Moscow took over a pavilion in the Soviet Union's Exhibition of Economic Achievements and staged a display called 'The Exhibition of Poor Quality Goods'. Among the economic misachievements were cross-eyed teddy bears, rotten food, chipped stew pots, oblong volleyballs and a bottle of mineral water with a small dead mouse inside.

16.

LOOKING FOR 'THE PEOPLE'

◆ ◆ ◆

WORKERSLAND

The Stockholm City Museum includes a modest section consisting of a simulated factory of the 1890s, a stylised working class street, and a cross-section of a tenement containing two naturalistically presented working class households—each of them a single room with a sleeping alcove.

What is remarkable about that?

What is remarkable is that it is a museum portrayal of the creation of the industrial proletariat—the 'working class'—and it is only recently, and still in small rations, that visitors have been likely to see anything about the industrial proletariat in the tourism of non-communist countries. The Labour Museum in Copenhagen also contains an evocation of how working class life was created in the 1870s, when peasants were attracted to Copenhagen by new kinds of jobs and became 'workers'. What is there elsewhere? Not much. There isn't a Workersland at Disney World.

But, in Europe, there is still plenty of room for peasants. At the time when peasants were coming to the cities and being transformed into workers, with results described by Zola in *L'Assommoir*, an enormous diversion effect was being performed. Peasant music, peasant dialects, peasant songs and dances and peasant tales were being recorded and, at the very beginning of their decline, peasants began to be presented in literature, in painting, and in museums and the general tourist experience, as 'the people'.

Artur Hazelius, the Swedish creator of this new tourist form, was the first to collect barns and cottages as well as furniture and folk dress. After he founded the first open air folk museum, Skansen, in Stockholm in the 1890s, the idea that an open air museum typified the people spread from Cardiff, Wales, to Riga, Latvia. The process continues. When the first Korean Folk Village was put together in 1974 at Yongin, 41 kilometres south of Seoul, the buildings and the items within were assembled for the same reason that Hazelius invented the idea of Skansen 83 years before—industrialisation meant the end of an old order. It was time to put what remained into museums.

What went wrong is well known. The concern with everyday life provided an admirable contrast to the grandness of museums, but in most open air museums there was no concern with what was changing out there among the people. The peasant cult resulted in wonderful collections of houses and furniture, and for those who knew the sincerity of a wooden beam there was a realisation of the idea of the cottage beautiful. But they made the peasants seem to be the only true 'people'.*

In the English-speaking New World and in parts of Latin America, there was a similar diversion—in the form of the *pioneer*, presented as a simple stereotype in the nationalist tourist pilgrimage. In white South Africa, the essential element in any outdoor celebration of national spirit was the Voortrekkers' wagon. In Australia, when open air museums finally developed, the true Australia was likely to be celebrated in the virtues of the *bush* (without presenting those social

---

* MAKING POVERTY REAL. There are now complaints from earnest visitors to Skansen that the poverty is not presented authentically. But when these buildings were first erected many of the people who visited Skansen could imagine the sounds, sights and smells of rural poverty from their own experience. According to some critics, even Skansen is now becoming just another fairground and theme park. Over every open air museum hangs the potential of the hyper-real rose-coloured clouds of Disneyland.

conflagrations between whites, and between blacks and whites, that marked the realities of European settlement). In Canada, pioneers came in two languages. (The Homesteaders Village in Austin, Manitoba and the Village Québécois d'Antan in Drummondville, Québec, belong to two different worlds.) In the United States, many reconstructions honour the continuing wisdom of the pioneers.*

As with women and industrialism, the concentration on peasants or pioneers and the ignoring of a proletariat was a prize example of how a most effective form of representation in a public culture can be that of *non*-representation—when whole classes of people, even majorities, are ignored, or may be present only in ways not related to their own views of themselves. If they suddenly appear in their own terms, it can seem like a revolution. (The appearance of the previously invisible can be an aspect of revolution.) These silences in the public culture, transposed into the silences of tourism, provide visitors with a national past of the country they are visiting in which practically all the characters are missing, and in which there is virtually nothing of the country as it is now.

An industrial proletariat *did* form in the industrialising cities of Europe, and an enormous number of material objects *did* come out of this process. Yet, for a time, only in the communist countries did anyone systematically collect remains of this material culture and put them on show. What they put into their museums was arranged as propaganda—but wasn't it, in effect, propaganda to have industry museums in the capitalist societies that had no relics of working class life?

All of the history museums in the communist countries presented 19th century working class life through relics ranging from workers' humble furniture to policemen's uniforms and simulations of dingy lodgings and poor working conditions. But you didn't have to be communist to do that. The images that these things projected were nothing more than what you might read about in any conventional social history of a liberal-democratic capitalist society, such as

---

* IN LANCASTER COUNTY, which is the centre of the tourist experience in the Pennsylvania Dutch Country because it specialises in the Amish sect, five million tourists bring in more than $400 million a year. And also crowded roads, motel strips, filling stations and a pushing-up of land prices—so much so that those Amish who want to go on being Amish may have to move out.

England. The industrial proletariat was invented in England. Yet you didn't find anything like this in museum England. Why was that?

There are two answers, both illuminating in the relation of tourism to a public culture. The first is obvious. It came from the museum's traditional role of abolishing the idea of 'society'. As Baroness Thatcher realised when she said there was no such thing as 'society', without a society a nation can seem much safer. At the time that museums began and historic sites were pegged out (and for most of the time since), major museums and historic sites in capitalist societies (including the liberal-democratic) were servants of the state (whether directly or indirectly), and the people who ran them were not interested in simulations of poor working conditions. So far as public money goes, any offsetting is now most likely to occur in places, such as the Scandinavian countries, where an idealised capitalist myth has been compromised by social-democratic influence.

The second answer is connected with the nature of museum presentation. In this, the invisibility of whole economic classes (and of ethnic groups) is excused by the tradition of 'objectivity'—as if objects selected themselves. This could mean that any arrangement of objects that overtly told a social story might be seen as propaganda, while at the same time the presentation of certain other objects could seem so 'natural' that they did not appear as class assertions. It was natural for a national museum to display aristocratic elegance, bourgeois comfort and peasant sincerity—but not working class anything.

In 1969 a functionalist building was opened in Paris, in the Bois de Boulogne, to provide a permanent home for the formidable collections of the most intellectually ambitious of the folk museum organisations, the Musée National des Arts et des Traditions Populaires. Its Chief Curator, Georges Henri Rivière, one of the 20th century's most innovative museum directors, had put on an enlightened show that allowed what was, at the time, the most intelligent and the most varied use yet of a famous museum collection. The exhibition was restricted, however, to the rural and the pre-industrial. That seemed natural enough. It would have been unimaginable to restrict an exhibition to the urban and the industrial proletariat.

There is now an occasional liberal push, such as the move to present turn-of-the-century Manhattan working class life in the

Lower East Side Tenement Museum in New York, a project assisted with money from Phillip Morris, the National Endowment for the Humanities and the Ford Foundation. But some of the reasons why this can now happen show how, in a sense, it has happened too late. The project was 'ethnic', and United States intellectuals can be more comfortably concerned with alleviating ethnocentrism (and racism and sexism) than in thinking about class. And it was presented as a success story in which immigrants were (correctly) given 'pioneer' status. But what may be decisive is that being working class can now seem a comfortably long time ago.

Presenting the formation of the industrial proletariat can be a nostalgia trip. There has always been a distinction between 'working class culture' as an ideal, and the cultures of the working class— the actual ways in which wage earners and their families express meaning and, in general, behave. Even for those speaking up for it, 'working class culture' can represent *the other*, sentimentally presented and not taking into account what actually happened. It may necessarily become nostalgic. One day, there may actually be a Workersland in a theme park.

* * *

Perhaps there already is. Despite its commendable turning away from the nostalgia of the country house and its other admirable achievements, the Beamish Open Air Museum shows how industrial workers can be 'peasantised' by the opening of an industrial theme park. They have become part of someone else's nostalgia. Presentation of working class life at the time that the industrial proletariat was forming can become merely cosy, unless it recognises that conflict was part of that story.

In a few rooms, the Copenhagen Labour Museum achieves a better presentation of class conflict than Beamish achieves in 200 acres. The Municipal Museum at 'Opel City' also recognises industrial struggle as a natural part of industrialisation. In the stylised working district at the Stockholm City Museum there is a 'window' to look through to see a distant procession with a flag: the flag is red, the procession is an Eight Hours Day demonstration. And, in the cross-section of the museum's working class tenement, one of the dummy figures is of a worker writing a letter to his brother in the United States, telling him how he was blacklisted by the employers after the Great Strike of 1890; now he can't find even casual work and depends on what his wife earns as a servant of the rich.

Class conflict was, of course, the lifeblood of history museums in the communist regimes. Presentation ran, intellectually, very thin after being strained through the legendary moment of 'revolution', but in the earlier stages, before the revolution was invented, material relics of the forming of trades unions and political parties could be turned into interesting stories (except in the Soviet Union, where the Lenin cult didn't leave much room for the workers).

With notebook and pencil, I visited the history museums of all the communist capitals of Europe (apart from Tirana, Albania). The objects on show gave me an authenticated sense of the beginning of the workers' movements—the rubber stamps and the membership tickets and the long columns, packed with small type, of the illegal newspapers. The iconography of the hand-made flags of street battles (symbolising class rather than nation), posters (fat rascals in top hats; monocled murderers in generals' uniforms), banners (women breaking their chains and looking to the new dawn), and the photographs of working class leaders—many wearing pince-nez, making speeches, writing pamphlets and, when in prison, playing chess. Some museums contained the chairs on which the leaders sat to write pamphlets, and the chess sets they took to prison.

I spent ages in Sofia's Museum of the Revolutionary Movement looking at the worthy face of early socialism shown in group photographs—one photograph was of genteelly dressed men, posing formally at a secret conference in the Balkan mountains. The same display case presented the athletic singlets and gymnastic equipment of the Young Bulgarian Social Democrats' Athletic Movement, and the music score for *The Working Class March*, along with an accordion used to play it at a social democratic picnic that was held in secret.

And while in the West the peasants were presented in the folk museums as the most stable element in society, in the communist countries they were turned into the most healthily troublesome—as a kind of permanent resistance movement. In the folk museums of the West there could develop around the idea of the peasantry the warm glow of dreams of *Gemeinschaft*, an organic unity of people and place (even if the re-erected buildings had come from places that might have been hundreds of kilometres apart, and whose people would never have met each other and might not even have understood each other's speech).* But the communist regimes wanted a history of peasant rebellion. Peasant relics were put into national historical museums and displayed at historic sites, and, just as golden ages had been visually re-created as part of the national past, sculptors and painters were set to work to create an oaken age of agrarian uprisings. The true spirit of the country could be found in old peasant tools and weapons, remnants of peasant clothes and standards, ancient remonstrances and maps and other leftovers signifying rebellion. Particularly useful were engravings of floggings, dismemberings, bone-crushings, hangings, burnings, impalings, disembowellings, nose-slittings, beheadings, skinnings and tearings-apart of defeated peasant rebels.

(From late medieval to modern times there were thousands of uprisings among the European peasants—some of them social earthquakes. They displayed a cheeky, democratic, levelling temper in the peasantry and also a sense of God-given right. The communists were working from evidence usually ignored by the people who put together history museums in the West. That the communist countries had no evidence for linking this peasant resistance to their own regimes is another matter.)

Even something as safe as popular agitation for universal suffrage doesn't get a run in the tourist nostalgia business, and only recently have there been attempts to celebrate one of Britain's most long-lasting 19th century inventions—the trades union. After the collapse, through factionalism, of a modest museum experiment in London, a Museum of Labour History was established in a former courthouse in Liverpool, a city that is itself a living museum of the sickness of labour. It was, designedly, more of a social history museum than a labour history museum—partly as a strategy of

---

* **THE TRUE THAILAND**. It was the glorification of the peasantry as embodying the true spirit of Sweden, or Wales, Latvia, South Korea or wherever, that gave folk museums their special aura. For example Muang Boran, the 'Open Air Museum of Old Thailand', 33 kilometres from Bangkok and, at 500 square kilometres, claimed to be the world's largest of its kind, has put together the public culture's whole nostalgia show. There are reconstructed market towns, hamlets and villages, all in honest teak (and in themselves well done), as well as replicas of Thailand's most instructive historical monuments and seven gardens with patriotic and sentimental statuary to remind us of the great myths of Thailand.

survival, to avoid offending a new Council, and partly because the very idea of 'labour history' puts people off. So far as I know, the only declaredly trades union museums are in Scandinavian countries, and with one exception they are very small. In 1990 a National Museum of Labour History was opened in Manchester, whose most publicised activity became the restoration of a collection of old trades union banners. (In treasuring trades union banners there is always the temptation to reduce the labour movement to folk art.)

* * *

The concept of a single working class which would bring a liberating revolution is now 'history'. If it is history, it should be able to be safely put into a museum—but a Museum of Class War! Hundreds of military museums all over the place—thousands if you include small local collections of swords and bugles—commemorate, in a largely inept manner, military engagement. Far more significant than many of the battles that provided the old flags, weapons and uniforms was the period in history when the great issue that seemed to determine the future of humankind was the struggle between Capital and Labour. We could now recall some of its symbols.

MAKING THE INVISIBLE VISIBLE

I have a three-point remedial program for people in the tourist business that might bring into tourist visions clearer suggestions that there have been people in 'the past' who were neither peasants nor princes. The first of them is that they should develop a sense of the importance of 'the everyday'.

The Shitamachi district was Tokyo's 'old town', trailing into the Meiji era many of the ways of life of Edo, the Tokyo of the shogunate. Along its main riverside streets were wooden merchant houses—shops in front and behind them tiny tenement houses, their thin walls crowded into a disorder of alleys. Much of the Shitamachi was destroyed in the Great Earthquake of 1923 and the rest was blown up or burned down in the bombings of 1944 and 1945, yet its way of life lived on in people's minds, and many of its material objects remained with its families. When a museum of the Shitamachi was planned in the 1970s for the edge of Ueno Park, the site of Tokyo's biggest museum complex, people brought along

IT'S AUTHENTIC

◆ ◆ ◆

—BUT IS IT REALLY AUTHENTIC?

In the 19th century, fossickers in the Roman Forum found some broken pieces of a colossal statue of Constantine the Great — the head, a foot, other bits. These relics of old magnificence were taken over to the Capitoline Hill and arrayed in the interior court of a 15th century palazzo. They're still there, surrealistically juxtaposed, as many tourist objects are, and a reminder of one of the paradoxes of tourism—however great the authenticity of historic sites or museum exhibits, when they are taken out of context they become, in a sense, false. As tourists we must inevitably use the past in ways that were never intended.

NO TIME FOR THE VIEW. In the Topkapi Sorayi in Istanbul, one of the grandest palaces in the world, the Ottoman sultans built a marble terrace with elegant pavilions in which they could dine at sunset. Now it is a place where tourists regroup before moving on to the cafeteria.

BEING NORWEGIAN. The Norwegians dug out three Viking ships in the 19th century. Amidst quivers of national fervour a cathedral-like building was constructed as the last resting place of the ships so that Norwegian children could learn what it was like to be a true Norwegian.

ANCIENT BACK LOT. The temple of Abu Simbel, one of the greatest monuments of Ancient Egypt, is not as authentic as it looks. To preserve it from the waters of the Aswan Dam, it was cut up in a $US 40 million program and reassembled on an artificial hill. Now you can walk into the vast concrete dome that backs it and see it as a movie set.

AUTHENTIC HYPE. The Tang Dynasty City, opened in Singapore in 1992, is an authentic replica of parts of old Xian. But since authenticity can be boring it also offers computerised palm-reading and instant concubinage.

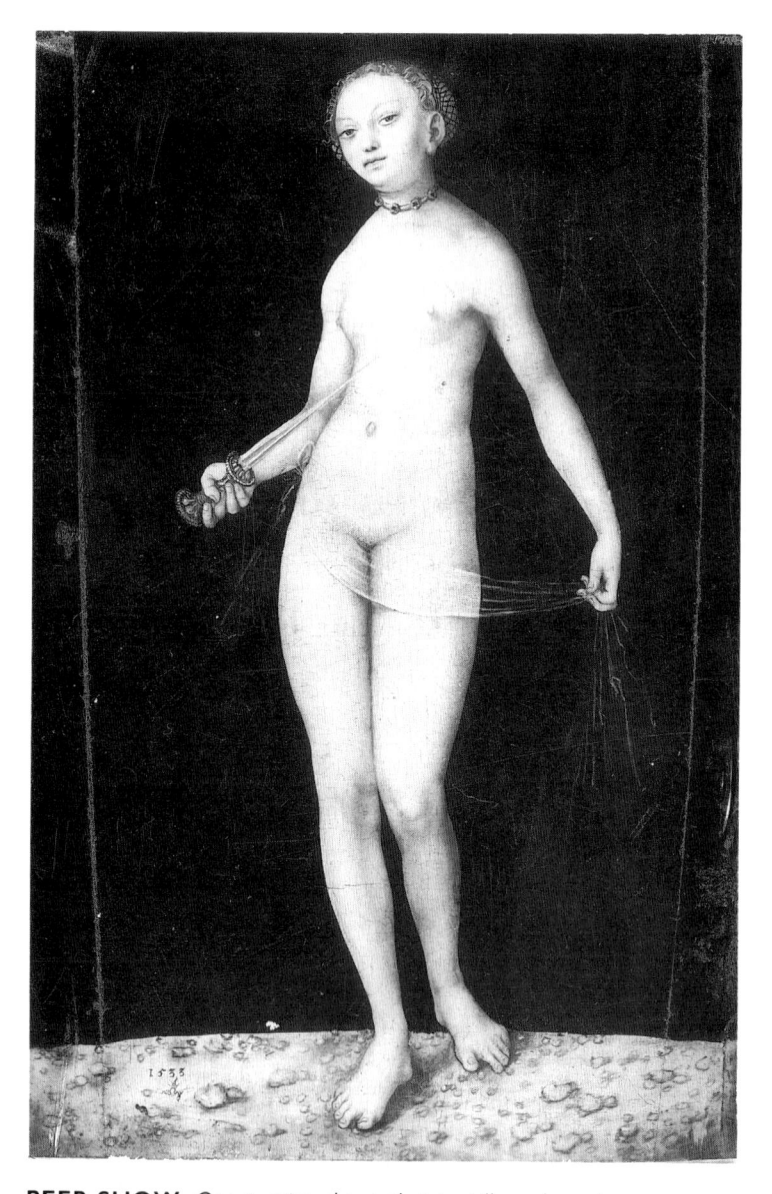

PEEP SHOW. One tourist object that is still used much as it always was is the nude. Lucas Cranach, who established a workshop at Wittenberg in the early 16th century, built up a profitable sideline in nudes, such as *Lucretia*, which gave men a chance to look at a display of naked women—something they still do.

THIS WAY TO THE BUDDHA. One of the greatest transformations of tourism is to turn religion into a curiosity spectacle—even more curious for westerners when they have to take off their shoes.

SECULAR RELICS

◆ ◆ ◆

Religious pilgrims would undertake long journeys in order to stand in the presence of holy relics. Tourists are the modern pilgrims, still seeking relics, but the relics are now secular.

BEGINNINGS. In England the Darby Furnace (above) in Shropshire has become a place of pilgrimage. It is seen as the beginning of the British revolution in ironmaking.

IN VIENTIANE, LAOS, the Town Foundation Pillar (below), believed to be the first building in Vientiane, has been spruced up because it represents 'the Spirit of Laos'.

HERITAGE. Some of the most important secular relics are heritage buildings—such as this peasant cottage in the open air Village Museum in Bucharest.

FOUNDATIONS OF REVOLUTION. When the Bastille was destroyed in the French revolution almost all of its masonry was turned into souvenirs. What now remains of the Bastille are these revered foundation stones piled in a small monument in a little park near the Seine.

REGENERATION. It was the redevelopment of the big, old and partly abandoned market buildings of the Quincy Hall area in Boston, along with the rejuvenation of nearby Faneuil Hall, 'the cradle of liberty', that made Boston a cradle of urban regeneration. New respect for old buildings necessarily gives them entirely new purposes.

NATIONALIST RELIC. The reconstruction of the Rila Monastery in the 19th century was an important expression of Bulgarian nationalism. The monastery is now the destination for the most popular coach tour from Sofia.

ALTERNATIVE KYOTO. Kyoto is famous for temples, gardens and villas. But another respected heritage site, given its tourist authority marker, is the Keage Hydroelectric Power Station, one of the world's first hydroelectric power houses.

DEATH RELIC. This row of pleasant bourgeois residences is in fact one of the streets in which the officials of Auschwitz lived their own comfortable lives. Concentration camp sites are also part of the cultural heritage of Europe.

NATURE AS HERITAGE. Famous nature tourist sites are also 'relics'. At Victoria Falls (below) much is made of the conservation plan. Even the raincoats (above) handed out to sightseers seem relics of an earlier time.

BORDERS

◆ ◆ ◆

Some border crossings (above) still have an 'authentic' (viz old-fashioned) flavour. But in Disneyworld, Florida (below), you can cross eleven 'borders' like this one as you visit eleven countries in a morning—or, if you are in a hurry, in less than half an hour.

STATUEMANIA

◆ ◆ ◆

In any capital city there is likely to be an outburst of public statuary, purporting to give the authentic history of the nation—almost always misleadingly.

Under the Soviet Union there were thousands of statues of Lenin (right) such as this stereotyped one in Leningrad, each of which told an exemplary story.

Brussels offers Mercator, the famous geographer (below), as a famous Belgian—although Belgium was not to be invented until 230 years after his death.

In Dublin, Wolfe Tone (left), leader of a late 18th century uprising that failed (because of informers), killed himself—a fact suppressed in Irish myth.

Almost every Italian city has statues to forgotten heroes of 19th century uprisings—this one (below), in Florence, commemorates a fiasco.

A statue of Columbus arising above the traffic and the smog of Barcelona presents Columbus as a great Spaniard, when he was an Italian.

MEETING 'THE PEOPLE'

◆ ◆ ◆

One of the most 'authentic' experiences of travel can be to meet local people—but not if one treats them as museum pieces.

THAILAND. A boat ride along one of the klongs of Bangkok is a highlight in a trip to Thailand, but we shouldn't imagine we have learned anything about the Thai people by staring into their backyards. And we should understand that the woman who rows up to the boat with drinks (above) is paying commission to the boatman.

OLD TOWN. A walk in the Alfama, the 'old town' of Lisbon, and one of the most picturesque quarters of Europe, can seem very authentic. But not by accident. The 'old town' of almost any city is likely to be artificially maintained—there is an Executive Commission for the Upkeep of the Tradition and Character of the Alfama.

SOWETO. Almost all 'people tourism' has been concerned with preserving the past and the picturesque. In the late 1980s some South African blacks began to arrange half day tours in which the group would assemble to take an overview of Soweto (above) and then meet some of its realities (below).

MEETING OURSELVES. Some of the best memories in travel can come from meeting ourselves. One of my favourite travel photographs (above) is of our son, aged 13, helping with the luggage as we change platforms on a provincial branch line station in France on a cold winter afternoon—and a photograph, taken ten years before, of me sitting in one of the most hackneyed settings in world tourism (below).

foot-warmers and chests of drawers, votive cards and photos, cash boxes and cooking pots, bamboo flutes and hairpins—to produce a treasure house of 50,000 ordinary things.

A superb example of how to preserve the everyday is found in Glasgow, a city whose industrial base was annihilated, thus reducing its population by a quarter, and much of whose society was destroyed by erasing almost all existing tenements and replacing them with what are called 'the schemes'—plans for better housing that, like 'the projects' in New York, were named for intention rather than achievement. The municipally-backed People's Palace Museum became a point of continued definition for the victims. As the 'Old Glasgow Museum' it had fallen into limbo, a kind of rubbish dump, but its awakening began in the mid-1970s. A new curator, Elspeth King, knew that museum collections could be built up by redefining bits of rubbish as 'material culture'. Despite lack of money, lack of space and lack of faith by the City Council, her employer, she opened up the idea of a new kind of museum with a series of everyday-life-in-Glasgow exhibitions. The first of these drew 80,000 people in a year, and annual attendance moved towards 500,000 (almost entirely local).

As the Glasgow slums were emptied of people, she and her assistant searched the demolition sites for old things left by the deported. Through ordinary objects, the People's Palace provided a story of Glasgow social history since the 18th century 'tobacco lords' laid a basis for its material prosperity. The permanent collection (perhaps Europe's largest assembly of ordinary items) was augmented with special exhibitions (the suffragettes, the temperance movement, the Celtic Football Club, the textile trade, the Scottish Labour Party, etc, etc). Glasgow people brought objects along to it, to build up the collection. When they visited the museum, they knew where they were. There was material to read about the exhibits, but the people who went there also carried their own explanations. Edinburgh decided to set up a similar museum, called 'The People's Story'.

Another example comes from Luxor, risen from 18th century insignificance when it was the forgotten mud-hut village of al-Uqsur ('the palaces'—whose only remnants were the tops of a few pharaonic columns that still stuck up out of the sand and rubble). As the Europeans rediscovered Ancient Egypt, al-Uqsur was identified as ancient Thebes, for 500 years the capital of the Egyptian

Empire. It was transmuted into an archaeologist's dreamworld and again transformed when the Thomas Cook cruises began to call there. Now, with airline, railway, car and coach connections with Cairo and as a stopping place in the circuit of all 200 of the Nile's floating hotels, it is one of the tourist dreamworlds of the late 20th century, resurrected as a wonder of temples and tombs. All the temples are royal and the tombs are those of kings, queens and dignitaries. There is an exception. Near Deir el Medina, the remains of a village of approximately 80 houses were uncovered by the French Institute of Oriental Archaeology about 50 years ago. These were the houses of a social hierarchy of 80 families of designers and scribes, of artists, painters and draughtsmen, of quarrymen and masons and of porters and diggers, with their various foremen. From the 40,000 pieces of pottery and papyrus that they unearthed, the Institute staff have built up a social history of this community, running over several centuries—their class relations with each other, their married life, their diversions, their labour disputes. More is known about them than we know about most contemporary neighbourhoods . . .

So far, the story is true. What is also true, unfortunately, is that there is no exposition of these findings. If you have a good guide you'll get five minutes or so and a few more minutes to look around. Then it's on to the funerary temple of Queen Hatshepsut. When I visited the site, some of my fellow pilgrims said they found this village one of the most interesting things they had seen in Egypt.

The second part of the remedial program would be to recognise that life is social. I think I agree with Kenneth Hudson's praise in *Museums of Influence* of the Museum of German History, set up by the German Democratic Republic in 1952 in the largest and showiest baroque building in East Berlin. (The Federal Republic of Germany shut the museum down in 1990, but, after a lot of argument, reopened it with exhibitions that are less triumphalist than had been feared—an early one that opened in 1992 gave a from-both-sides presentation of the propaganda of the Cold War.) With a combination of separate objects and room restorations (a worker's living space, 1901; a concentration camp living space, 1941) it put forward a thoroughly familiar view of German history since the French Revolution. I liked it for the reason that Kenneth Hudson did: because it was 'designed to present German history *as a whole*— the politics, industry, literature, empire-building, science, wars, music—as a series of mighty decade-by-decade sweeps'.* The story it told by its style was more important than the story it told by its content. In its style it said that life is complex, and *social*—a story that museums have found hard to tell.

The third element in the remedial program is that in tourist treatments of 'the past' there should be a policy of *pluralism with everything*. It would be a shabby kind of history-writing that didn't recognise that social division and social conflict exist. But it can still be easy in heritage sites and history museums to get away with presenting a past without social divisions.

Heritage sites and museums that already recognise the usefulness of social history are halfway there. But for reformers, the approach should be general, and intrusive. Get into everything. It should become 'natural' that economic, social, regional, gender and ethnic divisions are kept in mind by the people who decide on heritage sites and their treatment—and on what objects to put into museums and how to arrange them. Otherwise they can be seen as cultural genocidists.

But museums are collections of objects, not collections of words (unless the words are treated as objects). How do you provide reminders of social difference through objects? I will consider the example of economic class—how people gain their incomes, and/or how they work—because now that the history museums of the communist regimes are themselves history, this kind of museum concern may go out of fashion. How would one follow a policy of *class with everything*?

In 'In the Land of the Dispossessed', Charlie Leadbeater suggested a five-fold segmentation of the modern labour market—between the long-term unemployed, the short-term unemployed, the peripheral workforce, the unskilled and semiskilled employed, and the skilled employed. How could you match each of those segments with different kinds of objects? Imagine distinguishing in terms of what they had in their households between the 'peripheral workforce' and 'the unskilled employed'.

You don't have to be as exact as that. A museum is not an

---

* WHOLES. I know that there are dangers in speaking of a society 'as a whole'. What I mean is that societies are complex, both in inter-relations and differences, and *never* exist simply according to some specialist academic or museum perspective.

algebraic representation of a society. You don't have to get everything in. 'Representation' is not possible. The story of social difference can be effectively evoked from a generalised juxtaposition of objects. There is a very simple device for doing this. I came across it in Switzerland in the 1970s, although it was already established by then. It was notable, because some students had kicked up a fuss by demonstrating against the conservatism of the Bernese Historical Museum, and the authorities responded by putting aside their orthodoxies and agreeing to indicate, through objects, differences in social life in the first half of the 19th century. The centrepiece was an arrangement, of a kind we all know about now—a contrast in living room conditions. In three naturalistically arranged living rooms (one patrician, one middle class, one peasant) there were contrasts in a variety of objects—tables, eyeglasses, reading matter, walking-sticks, etc—at which the citizens of Bern could look, and consider museum presentations of history in a new way.

In an early attempt to reform the Nordic Museum, its top floor presented historical contrasts in Swedish living conditions—between a room from a two-room peasant's cottage, a 17th century nobleman's bedroom, a reconstruction of the town hovel in which a tobacco spinner had died, and a rich brewer's drawing room. Before that, the Museum of German History in Berlin had already made comparisons of room reconstructions to indicate the different modes of living in the same era. Some of what is done may be by reconstructions, since the poor don't leave much behind them. But there are records of the poor, kept by their masters. The Nordic Museum's reconstruction of the tobacco spinner's hovel was based on an inventory made in 1769, after the tobacco spinner had died.

Juxtaposition seems to have become a routine technique in some community museums. At a seminar I attended in Norrköping, Sweden, one regional museum director told how ordinary objects were being collected and displayed in set pieces to help children understand differences in social class. Another regional museum director said she was planning an exhibition contrasting, from material culture, the peasant migration to the cities at the beginning of the industrialisation in Sweden and post-war immigration. A third director told how, through assembling objects, again from community collecting, she arranged a display in her museum indicating how, in that particular region, (a) a lower middle class 'housewife', (b) a male industrial worker, and (c) an upper class person on vacation might spend a day. Her museum had published a regional history for schools, with a presentation of the different social classes.

If a concern with social difference became important, people who run museums could develop and systematise formulas of juxtaposition so that they became common museum practice, recalling diversity. Juxtaposition is also, incidentally, a way of meeting the basic purpose of a museum in arousing people's curiosity by encouraging them to look. In cities with extensive collections of both 'art' and 'folk' objects, a grand reform would be an interdisciplinary revolution, in which the contents of both 'art' and 'folk' museums were put together, in themes. Those afraid that this would mean the end of the appreciation of the fine arts would not be showing much confidence in the inherent worth of these arts.

* * *

Tourist trails with everyday dwellings, or museums with everyday things, can be declarations that anything can be worth looking at if we know how to look.

It is only one more step—although the greatest—to a community where people develop a taste for preserving and honouring their own things.

17.

BREAKING INTO THE PUBLIC CULTURE

◆ ◆ ◆

WHOSE HERITAGE?

A wide red line runs for three miles along the pavements of Boston, sometimes painted, sometimes done in red brick. Where the pavement is itself in red brick, the line becomes grey stone. It is the route of 'The Freedom Trail', a device whereby visitors to Boston can see most of the buildings, graveyards and monuments that have a connection with the American Revolution and (optional) with the concept of liberty. Boston isn't rich, like Philadelphia, in relics of the Declaration of Independence and the invention of a new kind of state (although one-day coach tours from Boston to Plymouth take you to the site of a creation myth), but the Boston Tea Party is an essential legend of the Revolution.

For those who can walk, the 'Freedom Trail' of 16 sites allows a couple of days if you want to stray into the downtown business district, or what are seen as the Irish and Italian neighbourhoods. Although most buildings on the trail have been remodelled, they provide gossip about Boston's past and a range of architectural styles. There are diversions: at several points, chatty lectures; in the Old

South Meeting House, taped recitations of 18th century oratory about liberty; several small museums; lunch in the Quincy Hall complex; and, at the end, a lavish multi-media presentation. If you want a hands-on experience, as a side expedition, you can visit a replica of one of the Boston Tea Party ships and throw a dummy chest of tea into the harbour.

From examining the Freedom Trail one can see both the limits and the potentials of tourism.

Firstly, what do the legends of the Freedom Trail stand for?

Protest, demonstrations, outspoken intellectuality, independence, freedom, liberty, boldness, bravery, rough debate and the curative power of the public meeting. The patriotism of freedom, not of nation.

What does this have to do with the contemporary United States?

It has much to do with the 1960s protest movements, and their continuations. Nothing much to do with the rule of law. Nothing to do with the 1980s faith in greed—it was not taxation that the colonists were against, but taxation without representation. And it has a great deal to do with the turnarounds in 1989 and 1991 in Europe.

What 'statements' does it make about 18th and 19th century Americanism?

When the red line took us into Faneuil Hall, a monument to the salvationary role of the public meeting, we listened to a chat from a National Park Ranger (female and black) who ended her talk with the question: "Who were the people who went to public meetings?" We put up our hands. Men? Yes. Whites? Yes. Protestants? Yes. In speaking for all of the United States, the Freedom Trail spoke for white, Protestant males.

In that sense, it can be seen as a WASP Freedom Trail.

That is the limitation. But the potential is that there could be alternative tourist trails. As it happens, another story is told in Boston—in the Black Heritage Trail, devised by Boston African-Americans as an alternative walking tour, and now also assisted by the National Park Service. The pivot is the African Meeting House—opened by African-American Baptists in 1806, and now a National Historical Site as the oldest-standing African-American church building, and restored to an elegant version of its 19th century condition. The legend told by the meeting house and other stopping points is of a minority staking a claim to also being American. Some of the reminders are mainstream: an 18th century house built by a black colonel who led a black company in the Revolutionary War; a memorial to the blacks of a regiment that fought in the Civil War; the meeting house itself is part of the concept of democracy as a public meeting.* Other buildings recall struggles for a different kind of freedom: safe houses in which escaped slaves were hidden; meeting places for Abolitionists; schools for African-Americans.

Boston remains one of the most segregated United States cities. But the Black Heritage Trail does show one way out of the grossest stereotypes of public culture tourism.

In 1990, Boston gained a third heritage trail, the Boston Women's Heritage Trail (actually four trails), honouring women artists, women professionals, fugitive women slaves, suffragettes, women philanthropists, religious leaders, art patrons, abolitionists and union organisers. Many stories are told here, other than those pointed to by the red line of the Freedom Trail.

There could be other heritage trails. An Irish Heritage Trail would be obvious. A reconstituted brick tenement or two in the North End could recall the earliest Irish refugees from the potato famine of the late 1840s, who began to take over an area which was declining from gentility into what was becoming Boston's principal slum. Perhaps something is left somewhere of one of the old mills to which the Irish looked for work. Replicas of the 'No Irish Need Apply' signs that went up in the panic following the Irish invasion

---

* AFRICAN-AMERICANESS. The Anacostia Museum in Washington DC put on an exhibition in 1989, 'The Real McCoy: African-American Invention and Innovation, 1619–1930', that celebrated black inventors and innovators who added to the inventory of United States technology. Included was Elijah McCoy, a 19th century African-American inventor whose hydrostatic oil lubricator is believed to have provided the basis for the expression 'the real McCoy'. Like the Dusable Museum of African-American history, Chicago, and, often more modestly, the 100 or so other African-American museums established since the 1950s, it shows how the *Americaness* of African-Americans can be demonstrated. (A counter-stragegy, of showing the Africaness of African-Americans, has also been established.) Similarly, the Indian Pueblo Cultural Center, near Albuquerque, New Mexico, showed the Americaness of the Pueblo Indians. The Pueblo uprising of 1680 against the Spaniards is presented heroically as 'the first recorded revolt for freedom in the United States, a fact little known to Americans today'.

could mark the beginning of the Irish Heritage Trail. A large part of the trail should be the Irish neighbourhood, a trolley journey away in South Boston ('Southie') among the triple-decker apartment houses ('the Irish battleships', which took three to six families) and in the Catholic churches and parish halls in 'Southie' that provided a Catholic alternative to the WASP Meeting Houses, churches and Masonic lodges. Mementos of old police and fire stations could be added as a reminder of the early talents of the Irish as cops and firemen, but the transformation scene would be the Old City Hall, in showy Second Empire style, as the place where the Irish mayors took command of Boston. It symbolises the peak of Irish achievement.

The Irish Heritage Trail could conclude at the modest two-and-a-half storey wooden house in Brookline, now restored as it was when John F Kennedy, grandson of an early Irish mayor, was born there in 1917.

The 'North End' provides both a problem and an opportunity in possible heritage trails. In the guidebooks it is disposed of as the Italian quarter, and so it has been for 60 years, but, apart from a bust of Dante outside the library and a summer fiesta tourist season, as a tourist Italian neighbourhood experience the North End tends to range from pasta to pizza. Only about half of the North End people are Italian and the gentrifiers are moving in and exposing the ancient beauties of 19th century brick. But in the North End one could work out a trail policy that paid tribute to one of the most remarkable of the many United States ideals—if the broad red line of the Freedom Trail crisscrossed specially marked trails of the many ethnic groups that had their turn at living in the North End. The Irish Heritage Trail would pass through it and of course there would be an Italian Heritage Trail. But there would also be a Jewish Heritage Trail, and Swedish, Russian and French-Canadian Heritage Trails. As a kind of side salad there could be pointers here and there to exhibitions from immigrant groups who never made it to the North End because it was becoming too pricey—Chinese, Puerto Ricans, Arabs, Hispanics and other varieties of true Americans, whose rights the 18th century Boston ascendancy could never have imagined as part of their historic cause.

Another tourist trail that might be added to Boston is that of what Oliver Wendell Holmes called 'the Brahmin caste of New England'—the 19th century merchant princes and shipbuilders whose clippers sailed wider than any Venetian oligarch could have imagined. A Brahmin Heritage Trail would run past the elegant row houses of Beacon Hill with their curving bowfronts and wrought-iron trim, and the Back Bay mansions in brownstone or brick, in almost every revival style known to 19th century architects, along with the classical portico of the Museum of Fine Arts, the Richardson Romanesque facade of Trinity Church, and other public palaces. But it would go beyond architecture and provide little lectures here and there about the social and economic base of the Brahmins in their time as the rulers of Boston.

And, as a contrast, there could be a Boston Poor People's Heritage Trail.

Part of this would need little more than rewriting the Freedom Trail labels to include the poor as well as the rich. Faneuil Hall labels could be expanded to explain that part of the democratic significance of town meeting politics was as a means for the rich to maintain their domination. At the principal places of revolutionary disturbance there could be proper tribute to 'the Boston Mob', which was useful in the American Revolution, as the Paris mob was in the French (although more under control). Sometimes this usefulness was direct, as when a Boston mob provoked the British into shooting at them in March 1770—on the Freedom Trail, a circle of paving stones on a traffic island commemorates 'the Boston Massacre'. More usually, it was a result of the Puritan élite turning the class anger of the street gangs to the purposes of patriotic fervour. Using street violence was a different process from the rational call for liberty that runs on the tapes at the Old South Meeting House.

Paving stones could record more modern street incidents on the Poor People's Heritage Trail—tear gas battles between police and the marching unemployed during the Great Depression; days of rioting following the welfare sit-ins of the 1960s. A Trades Union Trail might be included as well.

There isn't much tourism of Native Americans in New England, although Plymouth has a reconstruction of the domed dwellings of the Wampanoag people and enactments of their crop-raising, meat-drying, weaving and other activities. When the Puritans settled Boston there were Wampanoag camps on the south shore of Massachusetts Bay. They were in the way, and they were trading land to other settlers. The Puritans set on them. When it was over,

600 English and 3000 Wampanoags were dead. What Boston also needs is a Wampanoag Heritage Trail.

* * *

In *The Heritage Industry*, Robert Hewison said: 'Heritage, for all its seductive delights, is bogus history. It has enclosed the late 20th century in a bell jar into which no ideas can enter, and, just as crucially, from which none can escape'. This might be so in England, where so much of heritage has been that of the nobility (there is no Freedom Trail in London or a Tourmobile commemorating civic virtue), but the legends of the Boston Freedom Trail can expand in meaning. The heritage of protest, demonstrations, outspoken intellectuality, independence, freedom, liberty, boldness, bravery, rough debate and the curative power of the public meeting can be anybody's.

The myths behind the Tourmobile tour as a pilgrimage through the symbolic layout of Washington is the myth of the state as a political contract, and of the United States as a nation created by the decisions of its citizens, who are Americans by choice, and free to change. Against the monumental Roman declarations of power in Washington's masonry there are the Lincoln Memorial and the Mall as protest place, transformed, by 'the people' (or some of the people), into symbols of freedom for dissent.

In many ways this is humbug. Things don't happen as simply as that. But it is good humbug, and relevant humbug. We have moved back to a revival of claims for ethnic political self-determination that can become so great they can destroy nation-states without achieving 'ethnic cleansing'. (Only Hitler provided a final solution to that problem.) One can recognise ethnic diversity in a nation-state that is defined not *ethnically* but *politically*, as a liberal democracy formally dedicated to toleration and to the electoralisation of politics (representative democracy).

What was democratically dangerous in the Tourmobile experience was that so many ways of being an American were missing from it, and none of our Tourmobile guides was as enlightened as the National Park Ranger in Faneuil Hall, who ran us through her pluralism quiz.

To define any nation in terms of a single identity is a lie in which, as tourists, we can become collaborators. Nations are not personalities; they are political units encompassing many different classes of people—and, ideally, they should be living together in toleration. That is not a perfect state of affairs, but it is a start.

By walking the Freedom Trail and not seeing the poor, the women, the African-Americans, the Irish, the Italians, and the other ways of being a Bostonian, one walks over the memory of these people. But if they gain a place for themselves in the public culture, by widening the tourist definition of the past to fit them in, then one can walk the Freedom Trail and recognise that the patriotism of liberty can also belong to *them*.

MUSEUMS IN THE ALTERNATIVE

Can museums also learn the language of diversity? The only way is to recognise that realities are up for discussion. The grand museums presented narrow, selective and monopolistic views of existence and there weren't alternatives to them. What would be a liberal-pluralist museum policy?

Yes, more museums. But more museums that offset existing perspectives and conceptions of reality—and new crops of these are arriving: heritage centres, regional museums, community museums, museums reconstructing everyday life (ranging from everyday life in the 1950s to everyday life in the Stone Age), eco-museums (in theory the most democratic and participatory of all), museums run by indigenous people (a few), minority ethnic museums (in the United States: African-Americans and Hispanics), craft centres with an economic function in Third World countries, living museum foot-trails, social history museums, working life museums, and a range of segment-of-society-museums—from museums of the post office to museums of food.

There has been some democratisation in siting museums, most obviously in Japan, where they are found in department stores, in office blocks, in railway stations, and—since developers can be required to allow for museum space in construction plans—in shopping plazas and city centre complexes. Industrial sites are opening up—one at the site of a Bronze Age copper mine in Tonglushan in China. The French have developed a theme park around the megaliths of Karnac in Brittany; you can go on a 51-kilometre dinosaur drive in the Dinosaur Park in the Alberta Badlands. In India, the National Council of Science Museums developed a number of buses as 'museums on wheels', and, from these, science centres (that are seen as possible sources of illumination) were established in many rural districts. As in the Museum House of Tacubaya (a socially devastated district on the edge of Mexico City), a main museum can set up an outstation among the kinds of people it is least likely, otherwise, to reach. Even in the field of war museums the old 'realities' can crack. In 1992 a new museum, the oddly-named Historical of the Great War, opened in Péronne among the sacred soil of the battlefields of the Western Front in France, that shows what the Great War did to the societies on both sides of the Front.

Should the immense misers' hoards of the grand museums—the stuff you usually don't see—be taken out of store and spread throughout the land into regional museums or even community museums, to see what different interpretations might be given to these hidden treasures? Until it was decided in 1990 to found a National Museum of the American Indian, something like 80 per cent of the Heye Foundation collections were kept in store by the Museum of the American Indian in New York. Imagine how many of these objects could have been given back to the native Americans so that they could make their own displays.

Can bias be offset *within* museums as well as between them? In the past, the idea of diversity of approach within one museum affronted the authoritative traditions of the museum profession. In any case, the costliness of museums has meant that institutions controlling their money have usually been conservative. And their bulk and complexity has meant that when change was wanted it could be ponderous. Now both curators and controllers are likely to want refits (sometimes out of concern for the tourist trade), but when the last glass of champagne has been drunk at the reopening, the reconstructed museum may end up not being any more pluralist in approach than what it replaced. One type of museum mystification is likely to remain ingrained: it is that museums provide a definitive reading. The reconstruction of a museum may simply mean a change in definitive readings.

The pluralist answer would be to encourage alternative readings *within* the one museum. How can people be led to understand that, within one museum, there can be as many different museums as their own knowledge and imagination and experience might lead them to invent? Easily. Encourage the publication of more alternative readings and sell them in the shop. That is one suggestion: alternative guides.

At the Musée en Herbe, during Paris's 1989 bicentennial carnival, there was an exhibition, *Uluru*, that gave quite a good presentation of Australian Aboriginal life. It was presented as culture—as distinguished from Aboriginal life as ethnographically-classified hunting equipment, suitable for glass cases, or Aboriginal life as art objects and curios, suitable for sale in galleries. An anti-racist organisation, Survival International, had also been given some space in one corner of the museum to present an alternative, or supplementary, view in a small exhibition of their own, *Australia— the Aboriginal Land*, with the theme of Aboriginal prior ownership and of Aboriginal 'misery in a country of abundance'. There is another suggestion: making space for a counter-exhibition.

But can't a recognition of the hypothetical nature of any exhibition become ingrained into museum practice?

My ideal museum is a small establishment that has put together some things I hadn't imagined being put together, or a small museum that has put together some familiar things in a way I wouldn't have thought of.

But if a museum is large, I would answer this question by saying that museums could present themselves in three parts.

At the beginning there would be a special display intended to encourage visitors to understand how objects, like anything else in existence, can be interpreted in many ways. One arrangement might be contrasted with another, to demonstrate how different arrangements of similar objects can tell different stories. Or one object could be presented with a variety of labels, to show how it might be read in different ways by different people. Or the museum might indicate how, in its history, it has had quite different styles of presentation of the same things, giving them different meanings. There are dozens of other ways in which, to use a 1960s expression, museums can be 'de-mystified' and 'realities' can be demonstrated to be hypothetical.

Then there would be the centrepieces of my ideal museum— 'signed exhibitions'. These would be theme shows presented by curators with relevant tricks of the trade, and with a clear statement about why these particular objects were chosen instead of others, and how this was only one of many ways in which they might have been presented. To suggest how this was only one possible 'reality' among many, some of the objects rejected by the curator might also be displayed, with statements about why they were rejected.* And, as suggested in the last chapter, if it was a social history presentation, there would be an inbuilt policy of displaying difference.

A museum, initially, was both a scholars' storehouse and an exhibition space. The storekeepers were scholars who decided what to collect and how to collate and interpret it; along with the collectors were the housekeepers with the skill to make sure that everything stayed in good order. Neither that kind of scholarship nor those kinds of skills necessarily went with a flair in arranging exhibitions. For that, creative people were needed who could put together a good show which, through its themes and presentations, would arouse curiosity (as happened with the great 19th century International Exhibitions). Scholarship is necessary in arranging exhibitions. Without it, they can be fatuous. But with it they can also be fatuous. As well as scholarship, there must be the kind of conceptualising drive that can produce an exhibition appealing to the imagination.

But in my ideal museum, instead of all the rest of the collection being locked up in a store, most of the things would be put on open display in a kind of Museum of Wonders and Curiosities so that people could browse among unrelated things as they wished. They could look at them, picking and choosing, reacting to them in those idiosyncratic ways in which human minds can work. They could make discoveries of their own. Then, if they wanted information, they could get it and, having made up their own museum, they could make up their own catalogues.**

---

* A MUSEUM AS EXHIBIT. In 'Always true to the object', Susan Vogel describes how Washington DC's Center for African Art put on one exhibition that used objects to demonstrate how Europeans project their needs and fantasies upon Africa, and another to dramatise how arbitrarily some African things become 'arts' and others 'artifacts'. Both exhibitions examined Americans rather than Africans.

**VISIBLE STORAGE. The University of British Columbia Museum of Anthropology at Vancouver became a museum-world leader in the experiment of 'visible storage', when much of its collections was placed in open storage in the galleries of a new building. The main criticism is that the presentation may be too intelligent for the visitors. An alternative is a less austere presentation, with evocative groupings of 'treasures', of the kind that the Western Australian Museum experimented with in a show in Perth in 1991.

18.

REVOLUTION AS PUBLIC CULTURE

◆ ◆ ◆

THE SOVIET TOURMOBILE

In the spring of 1918, Lenin announced a policy of 'monumental propaganda'—67 sculptures, each to be unveiled in a significant ceremony. They would be of 18th and 19th century Russian heroes, of international revolutionary celebrities such as Danton and Garibaldi, and of artists, writers, composers and thinkers, along with symbolic works such as *Monument to the Soviet Constitution*, all 'connecting the past, the present and the future'. This epidemic of statue-making was the Bolsheviks' reply to the Tsarist monuments that had dominated public space. There would also be a new kind of public holiday—a revolutionary holiday, on which public places would be transformed with bright flags, festive and witty panels, triumphal arches, garlands and obelisks, and with figures made of cardboard, plywood or cloth.

As part of this cultural push, a section of the Winter Palace in Petrograd was taken over in 1920 for a Museum of the Great October Revolution. Into it were put objects that had become framed as part of 'history'—pamphlets and rubber stamps of the early workers' movements, red revolutionary banners, manuscripts of great revolutionaries, maps showing city strongpoints, celebrated photos such as that of 'the July massacre', sketches for the first uniforms of the Red Army (designed after a competition by an artist who specialised in Russian fairytales), ration cards from the 1918 famine, a hangman's noose used by the Whites during the Civil War and a tree trunk on which they had notched the number of those they had executed. These objects were grouped around events now transformed into national legends and icons, telling the heroic story of the revolution. The Soviet Union was producing its own national past. Several years later, another Revolution Museum was put together in Moscow, in what used to be a nobleman's club. Then others, in other cities.

Lenin's body came the 85 kilometres to Moscow, from the country house where he died, by train (the house became the object of a half-day group excursion). The carriage and the engine that pulled it seemed too sacred to be used for anything else and were enshrined at the Paveletsky Station as the 'Train of Mourning', part of the Moscow tourist pilgrim experience of what became the 20th century's biggest and longest lasting (and most picturesquely terminated) personality cult.

When Petrograd became Leningrad, magic circles were cast around 253 sites in that city dedicated to the memory of Lenin. Statues and busts of Lenin went up in their hundreds and thousands throughout the Soviet Union. Starting with his arrival at the Finland Station, his 1917 activities were divided into a series of legends that made Leningrad, for its season, the Jerusalem of communism. Each legend provided a basis for paintings and sculptures which had the same function as those that in the days of Christendom commemorated major scenes from the last days of Christ. As a basic part of the cult, another kind of museum was invented—the V I Lenin Museums, with their white marble and red velvet, were established in the major Soviet cities so that Soviet citizens could know the mysterious ecstasy of *darshana* as they stood in the presence of the memory of Lenin. The grandiose Lenin Memorial in Ulyanovsk, Lenin's birthplace, spread over so many streets and squares that several of the buildings in which Lenin grew up had to be demolished. Most original Lenin objects were in Moscow and Leningrad, but off to the other V I Lenin Museums went replicas of Lenin's manuscripts, the chairs he sat on, the tables he worked at, the green-shaded lamps he read by, his pens, pencils, pen holders and glue pots.

After the 1939–45 war, the Soviet regime instituted tourist pilgrimages. They were built around a national showcase of Revolution Museums, V I Lenin Museums, History Museums (often quite good) and Museums of the Great Patriotic War, along with specified cultural treasures. These became basic to the itineraries of people who were given free trips to the Soviet Union and to internal autonomic tourism. It was a national tourist circuit as preordained as the Washington Tourmobile, but compulsory. Soviet citizens who went on Intourist tours of other countries would also find revolutionary monuments in their path. A Soviet tour of London might include Highgate Cemetery, for the opportunity to pay one's respects in front of the colossal bronze bust of Marx, above the august grave to which his remains had been moved from the humble original burial place in another part of the cemetery.

The 'peoples' democracies' of Eastern Europe also established revolution museums and they became so stereotyped that, whether you were in Prague or Sofia or Bucharest, you could walk around them and pick out the main story without needing to read the labels. In China, North Korea and Vietnam adjustments were made to include the wisdoms of Mao Zedong, Kim Il Sung and Ho Chi Minh. In Eastern European capitals, if some local relic established a connection with Lenin, there was also likely to be a V I Lenin Museum. The Museum of the Revolutionary Movement in Sofia exhibited a note from Lenin to his secretary: 'Get me a Bulgarian-Russian dictionary'. That represented Lenin's personal connection with Bulgaria.

By 1990, as the revolutionary statues were pulled down and the revolution museums were closed, new kinds of exhibitions were arranged in Eastern Europe. The Museum of Contemporary History in Budapest had a show in the winter of 1990–1, 'Propaganda and Reality in the Fifties'. Exhibits included fragments from the plinth of the giant Stalin statue (pulled down in the 1956 uprising), a mock-up of the interrogation room of the State Security Authority and a suitcase sealed on the arrest of one of its victims. In east Berlin, the former Ministry of Security was opened as a horror museum. In Warsaw there was talk of assembling some of the erstwhile props of the revolution cult for a project to be called Stalinland. (After Phnom Penh was cleansed of the Pol Pot terror, a museum was set up in the high school that the Khmer

Rouge regime had turned into an interrogation—viz torture and execution—centre. A mosaic of victims' skulls are formed into a map of Cambodia and among the torture tools and mug shots there are copies of the rules for the interrogated—Rule 6 said: 'While getting lashes or electric shocks, you must not cry'.)

In Moscow, three-hour tours are now offered of the KGB headquarters. In one hall of the Museum of the October Revolution there were put together relics of the August 1991 struggle—banners, tins of baked beans, graffiti, Molotov cocktails and photos of Yeltsin climbing onto a tank. Lined up outside the museum were some of the street furniture of the August days—a tank, pieces of barricade, a bus. The events of the civil war were re-presented in a tragic style and the stagnation of the Brezhnev era as a black comedy. In the Central V I Lenin Museum they inserted photographs and documents showing the physical and mental collapse of Lenin in 1923–4 from successive strokes—the kind of presentation for which, earlier, one would have been shot.

THE MYTH OF THE FALL

It would have been surprising if there had been no tourist revolutionary pilgrimages. Like nationalism, the revolutionary myth was a European invention, and it has been one of the most often-used devices in the public culture to justify new power. In its wilder reaches it took its shape from some of Christendom's best stories—a martyred god, offering salvation through his martyrdom; a primitive church that grew powerful enough to overcome Rome; and a belief in the liberating conflagrations of an apocalypse. In its strongest form, it is the belief (whether secular or supernatural) that evil will be purged through an apocalyptic period of chaos; goodness will then forever triumph, thereby ending history.

If in nostalgic form, as a creation myth it is part of the legendary history of almost all nations. Whether you are buying a lottery ticket in the Plaza Bolivar, Caracas, beneath the statue of the Great Liberator, or queuing for the elevator in the Washington Monument, or, as part of a coach tour of Old Delhi, visiting the Raj Ghat (where Gandhi was cremated), or inspecting the clock museum in Topkapi Soraya, where all the clocks are set at 9.05 (the very moment when Kemal Ataturk died), you are in the presence of sanctifying memories of revolution, even if associated with the characteristic banality of tourism.

In the 19th century, and up to the October Revolution, the United States was seen as the archetype of the successful founding of a state through revolution. Successive US governments were likely to welcome, if patronisingly, almost any anti-imperial or, in general terms, liberal, uprising, even if, in style and drama, the French Revolution also maintained imaginative power.* It was only when the Soviet Union took over from the United States as the holder of the revolutionary ideal that certain kinds of revolutions were seen as repressive rather than liberating. (Although there was never any doubt in the United States itself about its own revolution, in tourist terms rebellion is more specifically celebrated in Boston than in Paris.) But the idea that there were revolutions in Eastern Europe in 1989 and in the Soviet Union in 1991 can mean, in the liberal-democratic countries, that revolution can again seem, in the long run, on 'our side'.

However, there can be difficulties in determining when a revolution actually occurs. The idea of revolution was central to the public cultures of the communist regimes. The principal legitimation of their power was the inevitability that a proletarian revolution would provide the liberation of humanity (this belief was Marx's greatest error), and the Communist Party was its unique vehicle (this belief was Lenin's greatest error).** In Eastern Europe, there were problems in deciding

---

* REAL REVOLUTION. The American Revolution was not really a 'revolution' that offered a new society. It was an uprising that led to secession. The French Revolution was correctly seen as the first secular uprising leading to a whole new order. That is why it fascinated Marxists. Consider Zhou Enlai's celebrated response, when asked what were the effects of the French Revolution, that it was too early to make a judgment.

** MARXIST–LENINIST ERROR. In the *Grundrisse* and later works, Marx argued that proletarianisation would produce a proletariat 'conscious of its being'—that is to say, it would be forced by circumstances to become what it had to be (which was a class uniquely equipped to overcome the problems of production). As it turned out, that was not what happened. Lenin perceived that if the working class was left to itself, the best it could produce were trades unions. In *What is to be done?* he argued that what was needed to give workers the consciousness to play their role in history was a vanguard party (led, as it turned out, by him). This arrogance provided the legitimation for abandoning democracy and triumphantly moving on to so many disasters.

when these revolutions were supposed to have happened—to which different answers (all phony) were found in different revolution museums. But in the Soviet Union there were no doubts. Made word in the brain of Lenin, the revolution was made flesh in the drama of the fall of the Winter Palace. This was to be the key theatrical episode in the legend of the Great October Socialist Revolution.

Lenin held the Jacobinical idea of revolution as insurrection. From the French Revolution and the fall of the Bastille onwards, the symbolic conclusion of a revolutionary insurrection came with successfully storming a public building. As Mikhail Bakunin once said with anarchist wit: no revolution could be counted successful until the revolutionaries had gained possession of the town hall.

The fall of the Winter Palace was a simple and memorable tourist story. Near a bust of Lenin, beside the entrance to the symbolic centre of Leningrad's Revolution Museum, was a map of Petrograd on the night of the October coup, with the government strongpoints shown in black. You were expected to stand beside the map and listen to a lecture on the topography of the revolution and the seizure of the strongpoints. Then you moved to the centrepiece: a diorama of the storming of the Winter Palace. The lights dimmed. The 'shot that went around the world' sounded from the cruiser, *Aurora*. Lights flashed. There was a clatter of gunfire. Then the triumphant roar of workers and soldiers. The Winter Palace had fallen.

The lights came back on. The *Internationale* was sung to proclaim humanity's most impressive victory.

The facts wouldn't have made such a good story. The Bolshevik *coup* in Petrograd ('the Great October Socialist Revolution') had already happened by the time the Winter Palace was occupied. Although Lenin (in hiding, in the suburbs) had forced the decision to attempt insurrection, he was out of touch when it began. Disguised with a wig, he caught a late night tram into the city to find out what was happening. Unlike the famous Eisenstein movie, *October*, there were no bands of workers, streaming forth, fulfilling their destiny as liberators of humanity. What had happened was that groups of soldiers and Red militia had gained control of the Petrograd bridges, and several hours after Lenin arrived similar groups had replaced the government guards on the telephone exchange, at the power stations, the telegraph agency, the state bank, the railway stations and other buildings on their list. On one building all that was needed was the breaking of government seals. There were some arguments and a few shots. No-one was hurt. But by breakfast, Lenin had written a proclamation affirming that there had been a workers', soldiers' and peasants' revolution.

A couple of hours later, this proclamation was telegraphed to provincial centres and scattered in thousands of handbills in the streets of Petrograd. But the Winter Palace was still in the hands of government forces and the government was sitting around a table inside the palace. The 'fall' of the palace was supposed to be arranged by noon, but nothing happened. At 9 pm, to speed things up, Trotsky suggested that the cruiser *Aurora* fire off a volley of blanks—he didn't want the fabric of the building damaged. That set off real shooting, for an hour or so, and 14 people were killed. By 1 am, Red militia, soldiers and sailors were wandering through a Winter Palace in which the lights had failed, and they lost their way. The Provisional Government had to be found before it could be arrested. Another hour passed. It was discovered in a small dining room.

* * *

Now that the entire legend of the October Revolution has been destroyed, the Fall of the Bastille stands alone.* Compared with the great moments of the revolution in 1789—the opening of the Estates-General, the tennis court oath, the abjuration of feudal privileges, the Declaration of the Rights of Man and of the Citizen— what happened to the Bastille was, in itself, an accidental and insignificant incident, but it was given enormous theatrical power because it was turned into a good story. The government had intended to demolish the Bastille (in its place there would be a public

---

* THE FALL REVISITED. We were walking along the Boulevard Henri IV in Paris in 1989, the year of celebration of the bicentenary of the fall and demolition of the Bastille. A young woman stopped us and said in American–French: "Pardon, monsieur, où est las Bastille?" I explained in Australian–English that the reason many of us were here this particular year was because the Bastille had been destroyed in 1789. We told her that some foundation stones of one of the Bastille's towers were piled in a small monument in the Square Henri Galli, near the river. She went off to view them, but she seemed put-out by this French destruction of their own cultural heritage.

square, with a column praising Louis XIV as the restorer of freedom) and the building was attacked for the gunpowder stored in it, not to release the prisoners, of whom there were, anyway, only seven. But that doesn't prevent the story from remaining one of the principal legends of the modern world. And it is a story that provides a lesson in the tourism of revolution.

I remember my disbelief in the early 1950s when I first went to the Musée Carnavalet and saw part of its big collection of leftovers from the tourism of the Bastille. (In telling the story of Paris through objects, it was the first such social history museum I had seen—I didn't know that people were allowed to do things as interesting as this in museums.) The relics showed how the legend of the Bastille gained much of its instant strength by instant tourism. Prints went on sale showing the people rising, inspired by the Spirit of Liberty. Equally symbolic prints went on sale showing the building's demolition, with a whole skyline of pick-swingers. Visiting the ruins became a tourist attraction. There were guided tours. A travelling show of Bastille curiosities toured France. There was a big souvenir trade—in scaled models of the Bastille, inkwells made from prisoners' chains, paperweights and other nick-nacks carved from its stones, representations of its storming (in stucco, porcelain and faience, and on barometers, medals, commodes and playing cards). The demolition of the Bastille marked the beginning of the tourism of revolution.

There was also an almost instant tourism after the failures of the many European revolutions of the 1848 *Volkerfrühling*, the springtime of the peoples (or of nations, depending on how you translate *volk*). It was not on-site tourism—all the sites were back in the possession of the enemy—but of revolutionaries. Revolutionaries, especially those who had failed, could become celebrities, with big sales of engravings and of seats for their performances in public halls. When Louis Kossuth came to England in 1851, Thomas Cook ran two excursion trains for people who wanted to look at the famous Hungarian revolutionary.

But 1848 marked, in particular, the elevation of the *barricades* as being as significant a symbol of insurrectionary revolution as the Fall of the Bastille. Used in uprisings in Paris in the middle ages, barricades had come back into favour with the 1830 Revolution, and in 1848, in Paris alone, 4000 trees were chopped down to provide the trussing for 1500 barricades. They then arose throughout the streets of Europe. By then the barricade had received its definitive symbolic treatment—in Delacroix's *Liberty Leading the People*. This painting was at first notorious because Delacroix had given Liberty a suggestion of underarm hair, but when it was hung in the Louvre in 1874 it began its career as a glorification of the barricade. As countries gained their independence and/or certain freedoms, barricades entered tourist pilgrimages in paintings, monuments, on-site plaques and history museums. While no building 'fell' in the Moscow turnaround of August 1991 (in fact it was the resistance of the 'white house', the Russian parliament building, that provided a central part of the story), barricades were an important part of the whole television spectacle—and almost instantly took their place in the Revolution Museum in Moscow.

Delacroix's painting provided not only the most famous barricade. It also provided the most famous definition of Liberty as a woman—a concept that, with *the fall* and *the barricade*, became one of the principal icons of revolution as insurrection. What worked best in the French bicentenary celebrations of 1989 were exhibitions presenting the Revolution as if it were an iconographic study in famous advertising campaigns, and of these the best was *When Paris danced with Marianne, 1879–1889*, at the Petit Palais. It was a silly title, but the exhibition had a sensible purpose—to show examples of the epidemic of statue-making that broke out when the government of the Third Republic cleaned up the revolution and made it theirs, with the *Marseillaise* as national song, the tricolore as national flag and Bastille Day as national day (projecting the spirit of public holiday chauvinism). The statues were mainly those glorifying great men, arms outstretched in great-man poses, but the central concern was the continuing representation of France as a woman—either as La République, filled with national purpose, or as Marianne, France in a red cap, Delacroix's Liberty, if with her underarm hair shaved off—and used as events demanded. She was later put into the helmet of a Gaul to fight the Hun in the Great War, then put back into a red cap as a socialist, then as a communist, then as a member of the resistance and later as a symbol of liberation.

Rescheduled as Democracy, she was last seen as a styrofoam improvisation in Tiananmen Square, but as a tourist spectacle she has been reduced to ultimate meaninglessness in the Statue of Liberty in New York Harbour. This mammoth gift from France began as a crowned Liberty, Enlightening the World. She then became, for a period, the Mother of Exiles after Emma Lazarus wrote her a poem as part of a funds drive. Now she has decayed into a national monument that has to be 'done'—'Two hours from here to the Crown' says a sign on the line where people queue so that they can 'do' Liberty.

NEW TRUTHS IN THE PUBLIC DRAMA

What can be said for the tourism of revolution in the future?

The first thing one must say is that it should be *there*. Much sightseeing, especially in Europe, is of palaces, or of churches controlled by the kinds of people who lived in palaces. The result of this is that tourists are haunted by relics of the showing-off used by Europe's former masters to assert and justify their power. This can be one of the most reactionary elements in the public culture of a modern-industrial society, and one which makes no allowance for the mysteries of social change. Memories of revolutions can help redress the balance.

Nostalgia for expired ruling class artifacts can seem so natural that a routine presentation is missing of the nobility as, among other things, one class dominating others, and doing it partly by the very display of these palaces and their treasures.

(The way out is being able to 'read' an English country house, a Rajasthan palace, a *schloss*, a *château*, a *palazzo*, a *palacio*, or a Balinese *puri* in the knowledge that things weren't like that at the time. These grand buildings don't even 'represent' the rulers. Those who lorded it in such surroundings were not necessarily 'cultured' because they lived in buildings that we now see as art.* Chicago is a living

---

* GOOD TASTE IN DISASTROUS TIMES. Ginkaku-ji, the retreat of the 15th century shogun, Ashikaga Yoshimasa, is seen as one of the finest manifestations of good taste in Kyoto. The garden is probably the best preserved of the period. The frail four-and-a-half-mat tea room provided the standard for the teahouses of Japan, and the simplicity of the 'Silver Pavilion' is one of Japan's tourist symbols. Yet Yoshimasa was a warlord, who built a retreat at a time when the brutality and incompetence of his shogunate had produced such disasters that most of Kyoto was in ruins. A more accurate representation of Kyoto at that time would be a load of rubble.

museum of some of the finest expressions of several generations of modern architecture, but what do you learn of the masters of Chicago by admiring the emphasis on light in the window arrangements of the Manhattan building, the uncompromising simplicity of the Monadnock Block, or the elegant tranquillity of the Federal Center? (Do we remember Mayor Daley because the Daley Center is in the international style?)

However, revolutions might now be taken more seriously than in romantic ideals of *the fall*, *the barricade*, and a female Liberty who has shaved off her underarm hair. As an example of how these approaches can become exhausted, consider the basic failure of the bicentenary of the French Revolution in 1989.

Apart from some minority shows, almost all the Revolution had gone. Things were already moving that way in 1889 when, with the Universal Exposition, the Eiffel Tower and a thousand banquets, the centenary was a great tourist occasion that merchandised Paris as capital of the world. But then the Revolution still also had some political use, the new anti-clerical, republican government presented it as the liberal event that began modern French history, so that summoning the States-General in 1789 began the process that led to the opening of the Eiffel Tower in 1889.

The 1989 celebrations, however, sold Paris as the *cultural tourism* capital of the world, and the city of the world's most celebrated new or refurbished museums. It was more as the national day of France than as Bastille Day that July 14 was made such an ambitious television event. The 'Joy of Celebration' procession of songs, oddities and dances put on by foreign and ethnic contingents could have been celebrating anything and the climax—a celebration of the *Marseillaise*—was of the anthem as the world's best-known national hit tune.

The collapse of the communist regimes can suggest a different story. The revolutions of 1848 all failed. The revolutions of 1989 all succeeded, at least in the sense that old regimes were overthrown. A way of looking at this change is to ask: how can museums and other tourist programs handle the revolutions of 1989?

Except for Romania, which provides, on video, a record of the decline and fall of the tyrant Ceaucescu for which Shakespeare could have written some splendid lines, there was no violence in Eastern Europe in 1989 that left behind a litter of museum exhibits. Citizens did not arm themselves. They did not take to the barricades. No town halls fell. What did fall was the Berlin Wall. Unlike the attack on the Bastille, which was of no significance, or the occupation of the Winter Palace, which was a revolutionary formality, the demolition of the Wall, and the demolition of the whole frontier fortification structure of minefields and barbed wire and control posts of 'the Iron Curtain', was a real symbol that people were no longer prisoners in their own countries—they would no longer be imprisoned or shot or blown up if they tried to get out. One of the most sudden and profound political changes in Europe's history had occurred and also one of the most poignant symbolic changes. Neither the Bastille nor the Winter Palace were over-riding symbols of oppression, except retrospectively. The Berlin Wall was.

Yet it was not stormed. And its fall cannot really be commemorated by souvenirs of bits of brick or snips of barbed wire. It was peacefully demolished in a kind of festival. What fell were regimes, but not because they were stormed. What the people did was to assemble in the streets and threaten the regimes by singing and chanting, and with signs. As Timothy Garton Ash puts it, in *We the People: the Revolution of 89*, in the endgame in Poland the symbol of change became 'round table talks' between the former prisoners and their gaolers. In the German Democratic Republic it was Monday night demonstrations in Leipzig, following peace prayers in the churches. In Budapest, the funeral service for Imre Nagy, held in the square where a monument celebrates the arrival of the Magyars; while in Prague it was the debates in the Magic Lantern theatre, along with the rebel-rattling of 300,000 keyrings. When police got rough, demonstrators tried to hand them flowers or to place lighted candles at their feet. With their control of terror disintegrated, the rulers went because even they were no longer convinced of their right to be there. At the very period that postmodernists were proclaiming rejection of 'the grand narratives' of history, people in all the capital cities and many others in Eastern Europe were engaging in acts of street theatre based on one of the great legends of the *liberal*-revolutionary myth—that the people should take to the streets and *argue*, and that reason would then prevail. It's all on video.

In industrial societies with strongly developed public cultures (whether communist or liberal-democratic) the great social changes of the last three decades have been dramatised not on the barricades or by seizing strongpoints, but from the street theatre of public 'demonstrations'—the civil rights movements, the women's movements, the green movements, various ethnic movements, the gay movements and (in the communist regimes) pluralist movements against a state policy of monopolising the whole society. All the demonstrations have been from movements trying to gatecrash the public culture and play out new dramas that would project new icons and legends and assert new myths against the old. They are appeals for the 'demonstration' of new truths in the public drama. If the battle to become part of the public drama succeeds, the objective is not to seize the telegraph exchange but to get on to the television 'news'. The revolution museums of the future may be collections of demonstration symbols and television news programs. During the 'Round Table' drama serial in Poland, according to Timothy Garton Ash, a Party official said: 'We'll give you the riot police before we give you television'.

There could be revolution museums and other tourist programs that were not built on lies: they could be museums of the *symbols* of revolution. After all, what museums can do, by placing objects in context, is not to bring back the past, as if a museum were a spiritualist séance, but to evoke aspects of past imagination. If they were seen as museums of symbols, industry museums could join them: they could uniquely present some of the significant sizes and shapes and meanings of industrialisation and revolution.

Also war museums. War museums can't really give you the sounds and sights and smells of war. But a lot of the material that they already have (weapons, flags, uniforms), arranged and labelled differently, could provide a sense of the symbolic meanings of military organisation. My memory of being in the army is of a life encompassed by regularised shapes (specific kinds of weapons and vehicles) and regularised symbols (acronyms, badges, shoulder patches, uniforms). These were the 'language' of the army and we all had to speak it.

For human society to exist, we must invent the signs of our culture and these then become the social world. (This is of course the approach of semiotics, but then so is much of this book, although I have used my own language. To argue against the use of semiotics as an analytical device is to argue in favour of a deprivation of the senses. It is not only in tourism that meaning is a kind of magic, producing continuing transformation scenes.)

Apart from changing the guards on the public buildings, an

insurrection becomes a 'revolution' only if it provides a theatricalisation of sudden change—the substitution of one lot of signs for another makes the difference between a revolution and a *putsch*. Even occupying the public buildings was part of the act. A revolution is supposed to make the world feel different. The Bolsheviks carried out a *putsch*, but within a few hours Lenin had drafted a proclamation defining it as a revolution. Through this imaginative action, it then became a revolution—until, in 1991, it was redefined as a *coup*, and it was Yeltsin addressing the masses from the top of a tank, rather than Lenin addressing the masses from the top of a tank, that became a symbol of revolution.*

If 'revolution' means more than insurrection, we should be looking to it for symbols of the great social transformations of the modern age (as distinguished from political change). A museum presenting these would be a real tourist presentation of change. The growth of science. The arrival of toleration and of the secular state. The beginnings of the liberation of women. The development of the nation-state. The rise of the industrial society, and the effects on the imagination of the shapes and symbols of industrialisation—the factory chimney, the business office, the assembly line, the automation console, the balance sheet, the stock exchange, the graph, the labour exchange, the flow chart, the boardroom, the picket line and the icons of merchandising. Two group photographs in the Rüsselsheim Museum of Opel factory workers—one taken in 1876, not long after the factory opened, and one in 1902—show a contrast between a comfortably grouped collection of self-confident artisans and a regimented group of piece-workers, most of them in uniform. Their descendants could be photographed shopping in a supermarket.

None of these changes happened in sudden, apocalyptic insurrections, in the social equivalent of the astronomers' big bang.

* * *

---

* **LENIN** had the advantage that there were no videos of his famous speech from the top of a tank when he arrived at the Finland Station—an established icon in the repertory of Leninmania. When Yeltsin climbed onto a tank to address the masses outside the 'white house', we saw his backside poking towards the camera as he clambered up, and his unsteadiness and uncertainty when he got there. Not much of a statue.

236 THE INTELLIGENT TOURIST

When I introduced the idea of a 'public culture' I referred to its ambiguous relationship to the 'critics' culture' that was thrown up out of the humanist, enlightenment, liberal and radical movements of earlier centuries. In the critics' culture the principal myth is that criticism is an essential force for the health of any society—and for the whole human condition. Is there a tourism of the critics' culture (which itself contributed so much to the events of 1989)? To its credit, no. There isn't a critics' Tourmobile, with stop-offs at the Erasmus House in the western suburbs of Brussels, at the Spinoza statue outside 72 Paviljoensgracht, The Hague, or at Mary Wollstonecraft's and William Godwin's tombs in St Peter's Church, Bournemouth.

It is in their work that the critics are to be respected, not their monuments. The work of the critics' culture can now be seen to include widening the public culture. The critics can be important to tourism, not just by mocking the absurdities of autonomic tourism, but by respecting the potentials of looking at things afresh and meeting new kinds of people—and by including the 'new truths' of the public drama. By widening the public culture, the critics could help save tourism from itself.

19. Interlude:

A MUSEUM OF IMAGINARY LANDSCAPES

◆ ◆ ◆

'THE EIGHTH WONDER OF THE WORLD'

On the Zambesi River four of us enjoyed a surreal lunch, floating on a canopied pleasure barge, served by waiters in starched white shirts and black ties, while elephants ate their way through a small tropical island. It was a send-up of the travel experience. At the same time, we could enjoy the sights.

It was also a reminder of how most tourist experiences are necessarily put into a frame, and that the way you travel does part of the framing for you. The Rajasthan we saw from the Palace-on-Wheels was partly framed as a pseudo-luxury train experience; for those who remained on board at all the 'tour-sites', the Tourmobile defined Washington as a set of designated snapshots taken from a shuttle bus.

I decided that this book needed a chapter on Nature tourism, to be placed after some chapters on the public culture—because when God gave us the industrial revolution, she also invented the romantic

Nature movement to distract our attention. Why not the story of a small expedition which would provide examples of how the method of transport can become part of the tourist experience, even the main part? We could also contrast what happened (our 'discoveries') with the clichés in the brochures and guidebooks, and I could include some musings about similarities between Nature tourism and art museum tourism.

New Zealand seemed a good place. Close to Australia where we live, it is a kind of art museum of scenery, and having been only to its cities we had seen nothing of the New Zealand Nature collection. We could turn some of it into 'exhibits'—and reach a climax at Milford Sound.

I had always wanted to visit Milford Sound since I first heard of it, which, since it is in New Zealand, was much later than I first heard of the Zambesi River Bridge, or the Maya ruins, or the Palace of Winds in Jaipur. (The only photographs of New Zealand in *Cassell's Children's Book of Knowledge* were of a Maori ['Costumes of the World'] and the foot of a kiwi ['Telling a Bird's Fortune by its Feet'].) Milford Sound as an antipodean fiord, beset by steep and often snow-capped mountains, its dense forests dipping down into clear, deep waters, has symbolised what, if I was back at high school producing essays on romantic poets, I would have described as 'majesty' and 'peace'. It is hyped as the 'eighth wonder of the world'.

We had an instructive time with brochures, guidebooks, fare schedules and timetables. If we had simply wanted to send-up New Zealand we could have done the whole thing from Rotorua, the principal New Zealand tourist showcase. The Rotorua tourist people offered seven forms of transport in one ad: *rafting*, with 'all its surprises and excitements', along the beautiful Rangitaikei River; *float-planing*, 'flightseeing at its best'; *cruising* on the lake in the Southern Belle-style paddle steamer, or skimming the soft waters of the lake on *water-skis*; a *skyline skyride* in a spacious gondola, leading to a superb meal in a hilltop restaurant; *scenic helicopter flights* with individually crafted rafting and jetboat combinations; *bushwalking* beside gentle trout streams, with pet animals and underwater viewing facilities; and gaining an insight into the world of kiwifruit by travelling into Kiwifruit Country in the unique *Kiwifruit Tram*.

That was Rotorua, but Queenstown, the Nature tourism showcase of New Zealand's South Island, went one worse. In an excess of autonomic tourism, it offered 'THE QUEENSTOWN FAMOUS 5 IN ONE DAY' (*Queenstown's five most famous popular attractions, including famed Milford Sound, packaged together with connecting transport*). This is an example of how the autonomic tourist industry can 'commodify' Nature. You buy some bits of Nature, in a convenient five-pack.

After a couple of weeks we had assembled our own package: seven different types of scenery and seven different types of transport—a beach bus, a train journey, a desert ride, a mail-run, a nature drive, a ski-plane flight (with a heli-hike alternative), and the Milford Track walk.

1. The Beach Bus Ride

At the furthest tip of Cape Reinga, at the top of the North Island, there is a sacred place of wild, desolate beauty where the blue South Pacific Ocean meets the turquoise Tasman Sea. A lone, gnarled *pohutukawa* marks, according to Maori legend, the place where the spirits of the dead begin their long homeward journey. It was here that we would begin our spectacular ride in a Beach Bus along the gently-curving Ninety Mile Beach, a magnificent unbroken arc of whiteness that forms a beautiful natural highway, where we would churn along the sand accompanied by the roar of the surf.

2. The Silver Fern Ride

Travelling through the North Island by the fast, air-conditioned Silver Fern rail car, we would sink into the comfort of a sheepskin seat where our complimentary meals and our complimentary newspapers would be brought to us as part of the silver service. Settling beside our panorama window, we would enjoy photo opportunities and spectacular views, while listening to the on-train commentary. We would see raging rivers cutting through hillsides like slices of crystal, bridges that would launch us across ravines and gorges in one breathtaking span, tiny communities set in the brilliant greens and the black, loamy soils of some of the world's richest farmland, and vast pine forests stretching far out to the horizon.

3. The Desert Ride

I thought we needed to 'do' one other North Island destination by leaving the Silver Fern Rail Car for a day or two, for some place which would provide a colour that wasn't green. The first thought was to experience the naturally sculpted Waitomo Caves and their entrancing glow-worm grotto. There we would drift in a silent barge through twinkling caverns and enjoy the unique blackwater rafting experience, floating through caves and over small waterfalls in rubber rings.

The other possibility was the Desert Road: a windswept dramatic interlude through loose sand and gravel, bare of vegetation except for spiky bush and red tussock. We would pass across a volcanic plateau within sight of snow-capped Ruapehu, with its simmering crater lake warmed by volcano steam, then smouldering Ngauruhoe, belching gas into the sky and triple-peaked Tongariro, with its serene lakes and springs.

4. The Mail-Run

Several places in New Zealand are noted for a scattering of islands. For a while we contemplated the Bay of Islands—144 islands set in deep water, famed for a graceful fusion of sea with land, and an adjoining coastline indented with secluded coves and unspoilt beaches backed by verdant native bush. The form of transport could be the day-long 'Cream Trip', chugging in and out of tiny, isolated inlets delivering milk, mail and newspapers. However, the tourist literature described the 'Cream Trip' as the most famous launch cruise in the country and that suggested a very low authenticity rating.

We decided on the mellow beauty of Marlborough Sounds, 1000 kilometres of sheltered waterways at the top of the South Island. There we would find a labyrinth of myriad islands and engimatic coastline, the emerald sea clawing with long fingers into the green land, creating innumerable little coves and blissful vistas of vibrant greens beneath deep blue skies and puffs of white cloud.

At first, the only two forms of transport within this idyllic environment of secluded coves, pristine beaches and blue inlets seemed to be float-plane or water taxi. Then we learned that a launch did a mail-run to bays, homesteads and farms. That it was called the 'Royal Mail Cruise' questioned its authenticity, but the alternative was the 'Beachcomber Fun Cruise'. In any case, you had to bring your own lunch for the Royal Mail cruise, and make your own tea on board—and that sounded real.

5. The West Coast Ride

The West Coast of New Zealand, of course, had to be visited. But as a journey of hundreds of kilometres it couldn't be done simply by rafting, skyriding, water-skiing or floating in a rubber ring. We would hire a car and try to get something extra out of it by writing about road signs, viewpoints and local guidebooks.

So, through verdant rainforests we would snake across rugged mountains and turbulent rivers to the jagged west coast, where the Tasman Sea crashes into limestone cliffs that have weathered the storms of time. There the sun comes flashing down a wall of green; river voices break through the stillness of forest-fringed lakes as smooth as mirrors; and the snow of the distant alps is tinged pink in the aftermath of the day, while all around is the clean fragrance of the bush. Then, pausing to stroll along an all-weather walkway and, in the early morning when the breeze is still, to glide across a mirror lake, we would drive on past moody lagoons and deserted beaches fringed with vibrant humming forests, then across wide river mouths flanked by pockets of lush green, until finally we would turn inland for primeval drama, and slowly wend our way through massive granite mountains blanketed in black-green forest. At the end of each day we would relax over trout, lamb, kiwifruit and tamarillos—New Zealand specialities in tune with the surroundings—washed down with one of the finest of the New Zealand whites.

6. The Ski-plane Ride

During our drive along the West Coast we would stay at one of the two glacier settlements. In visiting the glaciers we would sample an essential part of New Zealand Nature tourism, the ski-plane, by flying to the Franz Josef Glacier. There we would land on the giant tongue of pale green ice, framed by valley sides of native rainforest thrusting towards the sea, and wonder at this peerless alpine panorama.

We thought we would also put our names down for a 'walk tour' on the Fox Glacier after reading an advertisement which promised *alpenstocks* and hobnailed boots and a guide who would cut steps put into the ice. But we decided not to go on the fly-in, fly-out heli-hike in which the helicopter would circle over the boiling spume of a beauteous waterfall before landing on the glacier, even though the guide would lead us to safe positions for photographs before the helicopter flew us to our next stop—for drinks on the centre of the main ice. (But all too soon the helicopter would take us on a last, farewell swoop over the marvellous amphitheatre.)

7. The Milford Track

In all six of these episodes, the clichés, done in the international language of instant *darshana*, would add zest to the wonder of what we ourselves would discover and talk about over the trout and the tamarillos. What required tact were the choices of conveyance. We were satisfied with a range that lay between the West Coast drive, in which we could do the framing ourselves (with the illusion that there wasn't a frame) and the Silver Fern Rail Car, where the framing would be done by the panorama window (recognising that railway windows were one of the first travelling sightseeing frames of modern tourism). On the Beach Ride the frame would be more important than the picture.

But how do you arrange the framing when you are about to go to a place you have been wanting to see all your life, because it will connote 'majesty' and 'peace'? When I read the Milford Sound brochures they offered short launch trips as part of a tour. On the longest (two hours) we were invited to 'count the waterfalls while eating a lunch of chicken and champagne'. But what I wanted was to find peace and majesty by staying at Milford Sound for several days. We would go for walks. We would hire our own boats, at dawn and midday and dusk. If viewing scenery can be like visiting an art museum, this would be like walking around a sculpture and assessing it from different angles—although as yet you do not have to count the masterpieces in an art museum while eating a lunch of chicken and champagne.

Another essential part of the regenerative pilgrimage to Milford Sound was getting there, not by luxury coach or float-plane, but by walking the Milford Track. This was also something I had wanted to do since I first heard of Milford Sound.

The Milford Track is a trail about 55 kilometres long, between the head of Lake Te Anau and Milford Sound, punctuated for the people who go on 'Conducted Walks' (in groups of 40) by warm, overnight lodges with piping-hot showers, comfortable bunk rooms and 'farmhouse-style meals'. 'Freedom Walkers' (whose numbers are controlled) have to make do with huts in which they look after themselves.

The people who sell the Conducted Walk suggest training for it by tramping over hills in a good, strong pair of boots, with a pack on your back. They provide bedding, food, towels and eating utensils at each lodge and the food comes in by helicopter—you carry the rest in your pack. If you get sick they fly you out by helicopter.

If you had broken in your boots and your body, the first day of 'the finest walk in the world', 16 kilometres through native beech forest beside a river, would be relatively easy. The next 15 kilometres, taken on the second day, would be tough climbing. Up past riverwood trees along rocky tracks, and then, above the bushline, climbing against strong winds, probably rain, perhaps snow, into a mountain pass with an awesome view. Then down a steep, stony canyon and into a valley, with one of the highest rates of rainfall in the world, surrounded by mountains and with one of the world's highest waterfalls. The third day would be a 21 kilometre trek, mostly downhill, alongside a river and then beside the long lake that leads into Milford Sound. There are two other days on the Conducted Walk—one, at the beginning, for a launch trip to the head of Lake Te Anau; the other, at the end, for the launch cruise of the Sound, the coach drive back to Te Anau and then the ceremonies of group farewell.

It was reassuring to read that you could set your own pace and that all 40 people didn't have to walk together in a group. But as I read on, something began to seem familiar. What lay behind the statement: 'After dinner there is a short briefing session before the social activities'? *What* social activities? And why would the first day begin with a group photograph? What if on the last night, at Milford Sound, at the celebratory dinner when the souvenir books and certificates of achievement were distributed, I didn't get a certificate? What does it mean when it says that, after the group photographs had been purchased, trekkers would be given names and addresses lists of their newly-found friends? What if my name wasn't on anyone's list? Was it compulsory to have a newly-found friend?

And what if, as with the Palace-on-Wheels, there drifted across my mind each morning, when the Milford Track was done, memories of the broad backsides of my fellow pilgrims?

'NATURE' AS EXPERIENCE

This is not an attack on nature tourism, but a defence of it from the two great perils of the commercial 'packaging' of nature—the peril of 'the view', strong since the 18th century, telling you what to look at and from where; and the peril of the billionth repetition of 19th century romantic nature clichés (to which there are now being added late 20th century ecological clichés).

I don't believe in any mystic or redemptionist approaches to 'Nature' with a capital N, because Nature, imagined like that, does not exist. It does not 'speak' to us; it speaks only in echoes of what we say. That is why looking at a natural scene can be one of the greatest joys of sightseeing, partly because you can look for yourself. You can engage in acts of creation and make up your own 'scenery' as you go along. However, you can do that even better if you have some idea of what you are looking at.

We spend a fair bit of time in the Blue Mountains, about an hour and a half away from where we live in Sydney. Five minutes from where we stay is a 'view'. It is not a commercially celebrated Blue Mountains view where tourist coaches line up, but it is an immense view, over the tops of eucalypts to great plateaux with their steep falls, some so steep that they are stripped to bare sandstone; wide, forested valleys in a haze of blue that, somewhere beyond the horizon, drift back into being a normal, inhabited Australian countryside.

When we are in the Blue Mountains I walk every day to look at this view, even when the valleys are filled with cloud—and feel better for it. I can't really say why, but I know that contemplating the view provides enormous choice, from the whole panorama to looking at just a single tree, and that it becomes more complex because I know something of the geological history of the whole formation. I can imagine the waterfalls and ferns hidden in the general view; I know about some of its uses by Aborigines (relics are still there) and of how, if they were going to represent it, it would be in the abstract, as a 'dreaming'. I also know of how its crossing by three European explorers was seen as an early widening of a small colony's limited, paranoid perceptions, and of how, later, it was celebrated in the European style as 'sublime'. I know about its bushfires and its tourist industry and the social structure that now lies behind it, just along there, just down the road. And I can still go back and look at the view, or at something as solitary as a single tree.

PART FOUR

♦ ♦ ♦

A tourist's guide to nationalism

20.

THEM AND US

♦ ♦ ♦

TOURISM AMONG THE TARZAN VILLAGES

In the 1970s the Greek Orthodox Church recommended a new prayer, which asked Christ to save Greece from the scourge of worldly tourism and the modernistic spirit of the contemporary Western invaders. Following that, a group of churches were so concerned about the threat to Third World countries presented by 'golden hordes' of tourists from rich industrial societies, that they met in Penang, Malaysia, in 1975 and set up an Ecumenical Coalition on Third World Tourism. The coalition declared that tourism, as it exists, is a 'violation of human rights and the dignity of people'.* Another church body, the Christian Conference of Asia, condemned tourism as wreaking havoc because it was totally unmindful of real needs in Third World countries.

---

* SOCIAL SCIENCES AND TOURISM. This and several other points raised in this paragraph come from an excellent run-through on the anti-tourist literature of anthropologists and sociologists—'Representations of International Tourism in the Social Sciences: Sun, Sex, Sights and Servility', by Malcolm Crick, in *The Annual Review of Anthropology*, 1989. Crick reviews 214 books or articles on tourism and concludes that in their treatment of tourism the social sciences have failed.

Others have criticised the destruction of physical environments and the growth of prostitution and drugs. Critics can also cut down the belief in the economic benefits of tourism. These benefits can partly dissolve because of vertical integration (airlines owning hotels and car firms, for example), transnational oligopoly (16 hotel chains own a third of the hotels in Third World countries), all-inclusive package tours arranged before tourists leave home, the occasional dominance by expatriate management and the development of facilities that are of no use to local people.

One of the strongest concerns can be that tourism can marginalise people in their own country. At Victoria Falls we were enclave tourists living in leftovers from the colonial world. The real attractions were natural views, resort diversions and wildlife. The Zimbabweans came in as providers of curios and dance medleys and as waiters, entertainers and people in junior positions. The same applies to the Yucatecans at Cancun, although when the latter are guides among the Maya ruins they become controllers of the secrets of the past. The Palace-on-Wheels was an example of the 'framing' effect of Third World tourism: it suggested that all that mattered in Rajasthan were colourful relics. Apart from our guide at Udaipur, who gave us some of the local socioeconomic gossip, modern India was a threatening intrusion. When the little boy wanted his money, India was ordered out of the air-conditioned coach. But in our coach journey into Harlem we were touring the Third World present.

The vice-president of Edgar Rice Burrows Inc once said his firm would consider purchasing The Gambia. (Maximum width: 50 kilometres. Population: approaching a million, who are spread around the Gambia River.) He was considering building a series of Tarzan Vacation Villages there. This is simply an extreme example of how the rich countries can 'define' what Third World tourism will be, and, for the tourist, what that nation then becomes. (The Gambia is defined simply as a cheap-package-holiday beach resort for the European mid-winter. But Togo, eight countries to the east of The Gambia, 50 kilometres wider than it and almost twice as long, enjoys the slogan 'All of Africa on a small scale' and is presented as an intimate treasury of scenery, wildlife and folkways.) The travel industries in the rich countries will also define the people of the poor countries stereotypically. Naturally. That is what they do to themselves.

An extreme case is Hawaii. The native Hawaiians, having been dispossessed by United States sugar cane growers and pineapple planters, partly obliterated by introduced diseases and then almost bred out of genetic existence by imported foreign workers, became useful as a holiday-makers' caricature. Turning Hawaii into a tourist paradise required selecting a few fragments of local culture and then reconstructing them as the whole thing. As in Bali, the commercial stimulus came from the arrival of cruise ships. On 'steamer days' in Honolulu there was *lei*-making at the hotel, and a performance of a simplified and sanitised revival of the *hula*, danced in grass skirts that were neither grass, nor Hawaiian. (The idea came from the Gilbert Islands.) Music could come from a ukelele, a musical instrument that the Hawaiians devised from a Portuguese original. The *luau* was reconstructed as a tourist feast and the *aloha* shirt was developed so successfully that it was transferred to other Pacific islands. In Fiji the *aloha* shirt became the *bula* shirt ('bula' being Fijian for 'aloha').

Most tourists in Hawaii still show no evidence of giving a damn about the Hawaiians, beyond the *aloha* caricature, which reaches its pits in the so-called 'Polynesian Cultural Center' (run by those authentic Polynesians, the Mormons), 'a scenic hour's drive from Waikiki', where you, too, 'can meet the people of Polynesia, learning their crafts, their music, their dance as you tour authentic reproductions of their villages'. The Polynesian Cultural Center reduces living people to bad reproductions of audioanamatronic models—a process essential to its particular sort of authenticity.

More than a million tourist-collaborators go there every year. Many fewer tourists visit the Bishop Museum, which has the world's largest collection of Polynesian material. Its Herbarium Pacificum contains more than 450,000 preserved plants. Its Pacific land snail collection of four million specimens is the world's largest. It is big in Pacific vertebrates, and more than 12 million insects are mounted on pins or slides or stored in alcohol. Research staffs working with these collections feed scholarly presses, including the museum's own. In addition, the 100,000 ethnographic and historical objects from the Pacific, half Hawaiian, bring scholars from all over the world. But so far as the tourists go, most of this need not be there. It is not on show—and what tourists do see does not reflect the wisdom and knowledge built up in the research papers.

What they see reflects commercial guesses about what tourists really want—which, in the Bishop Museum, is believed to be 'The

Hawaiian Hall', built at the end of the 19th century in the Richardson Romanesque style out of lava rock quarried nearby, and furnished with stately display cases in the local *koa* wood. This is the stopping place for coach tours.

What does The Hawaiian Hall say about the Hawaiian people? Its vestibule is dominated by dark depictions of the dwelling places of mysterious gods, models of whom can be bought in the shop. What dominates the hall is the hall itself, with its polished woods and colonnades and asserted sense of occasion. The proclamation is not *Here are the Hawaiian people*, but: *Here is The Hawaiian Hall, a highlight in your exclusive coach tour*. There are some delightful things to look at—the long feather cloaks and helmets of the most powerful chiefs, in red and yellow, trimmed with black and green; polished calabashes that would go nicely in your home; and there are the curiosities of the Hawaiian monarchy, established by Kamehameha out of warfare and maintained for a century—the oil portraits of Hawaiian monarchs in their European-style military uniforms, glittering with the Orders they had invented, their silver tableware, their thrones, the Royal Crown of Hawaii. The museum offers a simple story of progress, from 'The Legacy of the Past' on Level One through 'Conflict and Consonance' on Level Two to the successful conclusion of 'Living in Harmony' on Level Three. The souvenir booklet says the most famous single exhibit in The Hawaiian Hall is the specimen of a sperm whale, 55 feet long, suspended from the ceiling. It is at this that the coach parties are told to look.

The museum's research departments of history and anthropology know a great deal better than this—both of the fate of the Hawaiians as natives, and of the Japanese, Chinese and other labourers who were brought there to do the rough work. But The Hawaiian Hall is seen as the main selling feature. We were taken around by one of the people that run the museum, and I had to insist that half an hour be cut out of a program designed entirely around the conservation and research departments, so that we could go up front to have a quick look at what visitors could see. When we went into The Hawaiian Hall, our guide said: "I haven't been here for years".

* * *

However, I don't believe that everything about tourism is always bad for Third World societies. In Chapter 25 I will write about Bali, to present a different example—of how, in balance, tourism may have assisted the Balinese to enter the modern age. The negatives in Bali are outweighed by positives—so far. And even where tourism degrades Third World societies, one should make distinctions. A famous example of devastation in South-east Asia is Pattaya, on the Gulf of Thailand, which, initiated as an R and R station during the Vietnam War, was upgraded, then sank into the mess of its own sewage, drug deaths and sexually transmitted diseases.* But is there anything particularly Third World about that, or is this just one of the general disaster stories of tourism?

One should also recognise that environmental disaster and economic disappointment can come from tourist programs anywhere, although perhaps their effects are worse in Third World countries. In discussion about Third World countries degraded by tourism what becomes more particular are two fears—that old cultures are being destroyed and that old imperialist stereotypes of inferiority are being revived. One should be cautious in making too much of these two arguments. In both cases—yes, that is what can happen. But old cultures are disintegrating (or responding) everywhere—and not just because of tourism. It is ethnocentric to see Third World people as so stupid that tourism uniquely threatens their culture.

In the industrial societies all kinds of material forces changed traditional cultures. It wasn't tourism that devastated Harlem. And in Third World countries what are the specific disasters of tourism, compared with the initial social destructions of colonialism, the pushing together of peoples into rubbish-heap life in shacks in improvised cities, the population eruptions, the downfall of traditional economies, the unemployment and other debacles in attempting to invent new economies, the triumph of television, transistors and general mass culture, and the flirtations with the images of consumer goods?

---

* A THAI TRADITION. The disasters of the Thai sex trade, with its child labour, its condom-free sex and an average of an extra 200 HIV-positive infections per day, are based in the traditions of the Thai male culture, not the tourist culture. Most of the 250,000 prostitutes serve Thai men, not tourists, and while the use of condoms is spreading in the more expensive brothels used by tourists, prostitutes who attempt to use condoms in the cheaper brothels are as likely to be beaten up on the job as Thai wives who made the same suggestion at home might be.

However there is no doubt that while the distinction between *them* and *us* occurs in all tourism, in Third World tourism it can hold a sharper edge. Here is a *they* who are characteristically inferior to *us*. In private—like those Palace-on-Wheels innocents abroad, the Englishman with no neck and the loud-mouthed Yank—tourists may dismiss the natives as sly, perfidious, lazy and happy-go-lucky. But in public presentations the only hints you can now get of servility are likely to be promises of service—such as the threat of ever-smiling courtesy in the Palace-on-Wheels brochures. Come and be pampered by ever-smiling menials. The real distinction between *them* and *us* is that *they* are presented as a people of the past who can't make the present work. We can downgrade them as human beings for the very reasons—their markets, their palaces, their curios, their dances, their ruins—that make them worth visiting. Yet if they make the present work in our terms they are likely to be seen as having degraded themselves by abandoning their own culture.

* * *

On one matter there should be no ifs and buts—and that is that an indigenous people who have been displaced, however long ago, by invaders should not be turned into a freak-show in their own lands.

At least one live native was actually put into a museum. Ishi, 'the last of his tribe' (which means that the rest of the tribe was destroyed), was placed in the University of California's Anthropology Museum in 1911, where for five years he was observed, and exhibited. Usually, whether in the Nordic Museum with the Sámi, in the Auckland Museum with the Maori, the Hakodate City Museum with the Ainu, or the South African Museum with the Khoisan, relics of the natives were placed in general museums, as fascinating lumber among a lot of other, unrelated, stuff. The natives were encased and framed as primitives in what had once been their own territories.

Reducing people to insulting stereotypes is a process that comes naturally in the tourist trade, but it is particularly repellent when applied to the dispossessed. The Auckland Committee on Racism and Discrimination has put together a list of 'grossly offensive' souvenirs sold in a country where words like *haka* and *tiki* have become part of the tourist pitch, and where Maoris have become extra curiosities among the natural curiosities of boiling lakes and steaming geysers. In a leaflet, *The Souvenir Trade: Debasing a Culture*, the Committee says:

> 'Maori culture has been swept into the souvenir shop. However, it is a grotesque, plastic Pakeha (white) version of the Maori. These so-called 'Maori' souvenirs are designed, devised, made and sold by Pakehas and the profits go into their pockets. The souvenir trade uses sacred objects . . . and belittles their importance and specialness. The souvenir trade often depicts the Maori people in an insulting and racist way. They are ridiculed as figures of fun, as mere children. Maori women are portrayed as 'dusky maidens' in European models of what Maori women should look and act like.'

The example is given of how in Maori society the human head, particularly a chief's head, is considered sacred, yet images of chiefs' heads are printed on souvenir cushions, to be sat upon, or on souvenir handkerchiefs, on which you can blow your nose.

THE EURORACIST MUSEUMS

On the way to Harlem for the Harlem Spirituals Tour, the coach passes a statuary group in front of a granite palace. At the centre of the group is a white man on his charger. On one side of his horse is a Negro (I am using the language of the time), on the other a Redskin. They are both on foot. "That is the American Museum of Natural History", says our African-American guide, "and in front of it is the most racist statue in New York." The mounted conqueror is President Theodore Roosevelt, and inside the museum the whole front area is a memorial to him. One of the first things you are likely to see is a lifesize diorama, 'Old New York', in which two Dutchmen with guns stand firm as the Redskins approach, bearing gifts. A line in the caption says: 'The ancestors of Theodore Roosevelt settled here'.

Unreconstructed, the American Museum of Natural History is a museum of the colonial kind in which dinosaur bones, stuffed animals, minerals, gems and meteorites are placed side by side with relics of the past material cultures of non-European peoples. The Hall of African Mammals is alongside the Hall of African Peoples; the Hall of Asian Peoples is between Asiatic Mammals and Birds of the World; the Hall of Pacific Peoples is opposite North American

Birds. In a city where 'Black' and 'Hispanic' are words of pride and terror, all that is presented of Africa are curiosities of the past—ostrich feathers, spears, dance costumes, headdresses—and of Latin America, reminders of the splendours of lost civilisations and of the quaint ways of primitive tribes. The Native Americans of the United States are also presented as a people of the past, in totem poles, thunder pipes, fish hooks, and so is 'Asia'—in the golden wares of Samarkand, the shamans of Central Asia, the temple trumpets of Tibet, an ornate Chinese wedding chair. In a United States that continues to live partly on Japanese money, the Japanese section is devoted predominantly to the Ainu. It is a textbook example of the error that reality (in this case, whole civilisations) can be 'represented' by a collection of objects.

Museums like these don't provide any of the ambiguities that face someone criticising the effects of tourism in a Third World country. They exist in advanced industrial societies and, as they stand, they should all be abandoned.

They started to develop at the time when the imperial adventurer-collectors began to send home what they called 'artificial curiosities' as well as 'natural curiosities'—bits and pieces of this and that from the material cultures of peoples seen as primitive. Some ended up as oddities in the houses of the rich. Some were added to the collections of the *savants*, to illustrate theories about how cultures developed. But many were classified and placed behind the glass of handsome museum display cases, where they could seem a natural part of the European inheritance. In the 19th century, things from 'primitive' societies gained extra attention among the common people when Native Villages and Colonial Pavilions were added to the International Exhibitions that, for many, were the true museums of the age. And there were displays of live 'natives' as curiosities.

What was being established was the basis of the museum classification called 'ethnography' or 'ethnology' or 'anthropology', which could also have a section concerned with India and China and societies influenced by them. These were not seen as primitive, but as 'oriental' and in some instances they went off to another museum, sometimes an art museum. However, often it was all there together, from Aboriginal boomerangs to samurai swords, from saris to fetishes—the ethnographic, distinguishing *them* from *us*. In one of those surreal juxtapositions that museums can make normal (if there were to be a patron saint of museums it should be Salvador Dali), relics of European peasantry were sometimes added to relics of the primitive peoples and orientals, but these were displayed with reverence and nostalgia, since they evoked various kinds of European national character. However, I shall ignore the peasants and skip over a definitional difficulty by calling the museums that I have in mind the 'Euroracist museums'.

'Euroracist' because these museums, whether in themselves, or as departments of general museums, represented alien culture with a vengeance (the vengeance of the European imperial imagination). Japs, niggers, chows, abos, hottentots, redskins, wogs, etc—the Euroracist museum lumped them all together, as if they were all the same because they were all different from us. In the former colonies these cultural exhibits went into natural history museums along with the animals.*

Imagine if in each of the countries of Asia, Africa and Oceania Ethnographic Museums had been set up to represent white civilisation, and they did it with 18th century European cooking pots and crucifixes, muskets and wigs, kettledrums and playing cards.

Or imagine this. In the American Museum of Natural History in New York, at the beginning of the Hall of the West Coast Indians, there is a display showing how Native Americans indicated prestige and how they placated the spirits. Interesting in itself, but in a reconstructed ethnographic treatment it might be offset by an anthropological treatment of the recent past of the United States. A model of President Reagan, say, his prestige displayed in the presidential lectern, with its totem, the eagle, and his faith in the spirits indicated by the fact that the diorama shows him addressing a breakfast prayer meeting of fundamentalists and creationists.

* * *

Apart from a few places such as the American Natural History Museum, people who have inherited the Euroracist museums now try to make amends. Consider two examples.

One way out, that of good taste, is demonstrated in the

---

* RACIST IS RACIST. I know that in the United States being 'politically correct' in regard to race, ethnic and gender bias can produce absurditites of its own, but there is no reason for not accepting that racism exists, and that in the museum business 'white' civilisations were given a different treatment from black, brown, yellow and red civilisations.

Ethnological Missionary Museum in the Vatican's Museo Paolino. Yellow arrows quietly direct the visitor along marble floors beside plate glass walls to superb artifacts from most of the world's non-European civilisations. One moves past with a sense of the varied colour and texture of human achievement. But there is something missing. It is meaning. No explanation is given. Most objects are not labelled. They are just there—colourful, beautiful ... specimens of 'design'.

In contrast: the grand entrance hall of the Royal Tropical Institute, Amsterdam, with its glitter and marble-inlaid columns, is irretrievably a reminder of old colonial ambition, but everything else in the Institute has changed. The old Tropenmuseum, which began its existence more or less as a museum of the Indies, was shut down in 1975 to be remodelled. Now it is an 'up-to-date visual information centre', concerned with portraying 'daily life and work in the tropical regions', and 'the problems of the tropical world and development co-operation'. With sympathy and skill, its curators have tried to subdue the scholarly colonial approach to departed cultures by adding everyday objects like oil drums, bicycles, street stalls, shanty houses, street noises and political posters to the traditional objects of its old collection—and thereby they have made these old things seem all the more precious.

There is a difficulty with all attempts to reconfigure ethnography museums. In the old museums it was always just *them*. Now one can ask why not also us? The reform of the Tropenmuseum was a great achievement. But if this is appropriate for the former colonies, why not also dump some contemporary junk in Amsterdam's art museums? The better curators now see how ethnography collections can be used to assist the weakening of prejudice. But, however sympathetically objects are re-presented, the continued lumping together of relics of different types of *others* can remain a declaration of prejudice. (Anthropologists were like European explorers: instead of waterfalls or continents, they named people and the things they made.) And the fact that the most curious objects are all out-of-date (this applies to the orientals as well as to the primitives) can produce a panic about 'tradition': these people, as defined by their strange possessions, should go on forever making strange things like those in the glass cases of museums. Any deviation becomes a kind of corruption. It is letting Jean-Jacques Rousseau and the rest of us down.

MIXING US WITH THEM

There are many splendid things in the Euroracist ethnographic museums of Europe and its New World. Apart from just storing these things away (or sending them back where they came from), what can be done with them?

A perfect example of what can be done with old ethnographic stuff was provided when the Australian Museum in Sydney put on an exhibition in 1988, *Pieces of Paradise*, of spirit masks and wooden spirit figures from the Pacific Islands, mainly Papua New Guinea. It showed how to arouse different levels of both delight and curiosity from objects made for supernatural purposes, without degrading either the visitor or the memory of the people who made them. Walking into the exhibition you could be stunned by colour, by a sense of dancing (although nothing was moving) and by the gaze of dozens of pairs of eyes from figures of the spirit world. You could enjoy this kind of civilised *frisson* without knowing what it was all about, but if you looked more closely you found the objects were arranged to tell instructive stories—of the kinds of meanings once held by these marvels, of the destruction of those meanings and of uses now given to these objects.

One of the stories was of the Gogodala people of the Western province of Papua New Guinea. The missionaries persuaded them to abandon their dancing and their communal longhouses and destroy the masks and statues of their spirit world. Now the Gogodala people have returned to some of what was destroyed, reviving cultural forms, although without the supernatural content. In 1975 they reconstructed a communal longhouse: it is used as a cultural centre, where young people learn some of the old crafts and revive some of the old dances, and as a place for selling what they have learned to make, including replicas of sacred ritual paraphernalia with the magic now gone. (The Gogodala line in decorated bags is a popular tourist item in Port Moresby.)

At this exhibition you could look at one object and stand within the presence of five meanings—as a medium for communication with the spirit world, as a heathen idol, as an affirmation of Gogodala cultural identity, as a tourist souvenir, and as an art object. And you could still step back, if you wanted to, and re-create it as dance, in colours, movement and ancestral gaze.

But I can think of only one case for maintaining ethnography museums or ethnography departments as separate collections—turning them into *museums* of ethnography museums. They could be presented just as usual, but with labels added pointing to their prejudices. In fact, even if quite different uses can be given to objects in the main collections, appropriate museums should have at least one room like this. In another room, some artificial European curiosities might be put together and also given the traditional ethnographic treatment, as if Europeans were natives.

It isn't enough merely to rename a museum 'Museum of Mankind' and add some contemporary stuff, as was done in London with the British Museum's collections from 'the primitive people of Africa, America and the Pacific'. If you are going to have a Museum of Humankind it must mix us with them, putting together objects from societies of all the continents in themes that show how alike we all are. All societies have initiation ceremonies, secrets, supernatural beliefs, hierarchies, woman-beatings and masks.

We could juxtapose African icons from, say, the African Art Museum's 1990 exhibition in Washington, with European icons. The Cameroon wooden sculpture of a woman with a baby, symbolising maternity and abundance, could be placed alongside a Raphael *Madonna with Child*. Under the general heading of 'Two as One: the Male and Female Couple', Jan van Eyck's *Giovanni Arnolfi and his Wife* could go next to a Nigerian sculpture of a man and wife sharing a single pair of legs. The terracotta warrior-hunter from Mali, symbolising the forceful male, could be put beside Michelangelo's *David*. In the category of 'Riders of Power: The Mounted Leader', Jacques-Louis David's *Bonaparte crossing the Grand St Bernard* could go next to a Yoruba statuette of a powerful young man on a motor scooter.

MAKING AN EXHIBIT OF YOURSELF IN YOUR OWN COUNTRY

'The Provincial Museum in Hargeisa'. That is a heading in an article in *Museum* which describes what happened when people said they wanted a museum in Hargeisa, capital of Somalia's Northern Province and one of the country's largest towns. In 1976, there was a campaign to collect objects for a building based on the idea of the tent (Somalia having been a predominantly nomad society). Within a year the museum was built and the objects were placed in it, haphazardly, 'by people who wanted their town to have a museum of its own and who made an enormous effort to make their wishes come true'. The things had not been cleaned. There was no protection. There were two 20-metre display cabinets and 23 smaller cabinets, but the glass panels had not arrived. The fluorescent lighting worked badly and it had come in red, yellow and blue tubes, as for a shop window. Later, the fluorescent lights all failed. Apart from two attendants, a gardener and a cleaner, there was no supervision and some of the best pieces were later given to foreign visitors. After four years, swarms of insects and other pests were established inside the cabinets and under the rush matting nailed onto the walls. Windows were broken. Birds perched in the display cases.

In the summer of 1981, carpenters, painters, cleaners and others arrived and the surviving exhibits were taken outside for an airing. The walls were painted white. Simple lightbulbs were put in. There is not much wood in Somalia, so the two 20-metre display cabinets were dismantled and some of the wood was used, along with protective netting, to make frames for the windows to keep out insects and birds while letting in air; the rest went on panels for small objects, displayed on the walls like pictures. The smaller show cases were painted white inside, glassed-in and locked.

Of the 1000 or so objects of national origin, old things produced according to ancient Somali custom were put into the first gallery; objects from contemporary nomadic life took up the next two galleries; the last gallery showed things related to the town life that now transforms Somalia. Somalis could visit the provincial museum at Hargeisa and be among their own things. Then Somalia collapsed into a civil turmoil that destroyed all government and left only armed gangs.

* * *

This is an heroic story, but the enterprising people of Hargeisa (whose progressive aspirations may now mean that they are all dead) were mistaken in wanting to turn themselves into exhibits in a Western-style museum. The Ethnographic Department of the National Museum in Jakarta remains much as the Dutch left it. It is dominated by tall, graceful dark wooden display cabinets in which sparsely labelled objects are scientifically categorised behind glass, but it is as if Indonesians were still 'the natives'.* A basic concern in a Third World country can be to interest both the people of that country, and their foreign tourists, in who they are. But this needs new forms.

Developing a 'living museum' is one way out for a country to avoid putting itself into a glass case. The 'model village' of the West Zone Cultural Centre on the Palace-on-Wheels itinerary was an example of that. Villagers lived there for a while and they could make and sell things, and put on their excerpt performances. They could concentrate on their skills and refresh them, and feel proud displaying them. In our visit all that was wrong were the visitors.

Dr Jyotindra Jain, the director of the Indian Craft Museum, Delhi, sees his museum as exactly what I would describe as a 'cultural genes bank'. In fact, I thought of the phrase while talking to him. The museum is set in a model village which houses village craftworkers who are chosen from a national directory compiled in the museum, and they are paid for the month they stay there. There are three open air theatres and spaces for visitors to watch the villagers at work and buy the things they make. Everything the museum owns is on display in special buildings—where they can be treated as a 'bank' of ideas and information. As Dr Jain put it: "They can consult the work of their forefathers. Conservation of the collection is necessary, of course, but its main purpose is that it can be consulted by people who are making crafts". Those wanting to go on making traditional things can get advice from the museum about how to sell traditional things in a modern world. Those wanting to 'modernise' can learn something about that. Providing support for people who still make crafts is the museum's most important function. It also arranges education programs for children and people interested in craft. Tourists can also come and look—as visitors.

---

* TRANSMUTATION. When some of the items in Indonesian ethnographic museums were sent to Washington in 1990, and arranged by the National Gallery as an exhibition of art treasures, they were transmuted into things of beauty, as part of an 'artistic flowering in Indonesia that lasted more than 700 years'. However, enlightened curatorship also provided a film presenting the myth-system, and its legends and icons of which these objects were an expression. Perhaps they could give a copy of the film to the National Museum in Jakarta.

Another example of what a museum can do if it is seen as a cultural genes bank. When a push to greater Hawaiian self-definition came, the resources of the Bishop Museum were there to be used. The movement began when reaction came up from below in the 1960s and 1970s in the 'Hawaiian Renaissance', and it came up vigorously enough for the state to establish an Office of Hawaiian Affairs. A heritage centre, established as a public facility at the Bishop Museum, became a principal authority on the myth-systems of Hawaiians, their legends, icons, festivals, and some choices in what being Hawaiian might mean.

21.

THE NATIONAL TOURIST SHOWCASE

◆ ◆ ◆

NATIONAL PILGRIMAGES

When we went on the Pretoria City Tour, and ascended the hill to the Voortrekker Monument, it was like approaching a temple where the great truths and values of existence had been cut into stone. A few years earlier Pretoria had become 'the Jacaranda City', and hundreds of flowering jacaranda trees in its streets provided the basis of a springtime tourist promotion. But, to Afrikaner tourist pilgrims, Pretoria remained the city of the Voortrekker Monument. To them, this hilltop shrine in granite and marble celebrating the Great Trek of the 1830s housed the true spirit of South Africa.

The Voortrekker story is a classic legend in the creation of a national spirit. Standing in front of the monument we were told the simple tale of how, to liberate themselves from British oppression, parties of Boer families loaded wagons, hitched up oxen and, despite the treachery and brutality of the Zulu, sought freedom in the wide open spaces north of the Orange River, where they created the two republics later lost in a war with the perfidious British. Then we were asked to examine the symbolic structure. See the iron gates made in the form of *assegais*? Symbol of the threat of Dingane, the powerful and treacherous Zulu. See the circular wall and the *terrazo* designs on it? They represent 64 ox-wagons, drawn up in a defensive *laager*. See the statue in bronze of the mother and child? The civilising Christian spirit of the women of the Great Trek. And the black wildebeeste are Dingane's treacherous warriors. See the granite buffalo head? That reminds us of the bravery and stubbornness of the Boers.

Inside, on a floor of marble, is a cenotaph to all the Voortrekkers who died in their civilising mission. Through an opening in the upper dome, a ray of light falls on the cenotaph at 12 o' clock on December 16 each year, the anniversary of the Battle of Blood River, when scarcely more than 500 Voortrekkers defeated 12–15,000 Zulus without the loss of one Boer.

As in a temple, a basic lesson was to be learned from studying iconic episodes of a fundamental legend—in this case the 27 panels, encircling the central hall, of the world's largest marble frieze. We were taken around these panels one by one, and the Afrikaner foundation epic was laid out, episode by episode, with the revenge at Blood River as the central part of the story. The basic lesson was the correctness of the *laager* mentality: whenever evil struck, ox-wagons could be drawn up in a defensive circle of righteousness, and the determination and rectitude of the Afrikaners would prevail. It was like being taken through the stages of Buddha's life, or of Christ's Passion, or of the wisdom of Lenin.

On the slope of the hill there was an amphitheatre for activities where Afrikaners could celebrate their version of South African virtue, and, closer to the monument, a museum with lifesize dioramas of the rural decencies of Boer family life. We left the monument to pay our respects to the house that Paul Kruger built on becoming president of the Republic of Transvaal in 1883, and from which he presided over the disasters of war with the British. As presented, the Kruger legend had something of both John Wayne (Kruger was aged 10 when he first took to a muzzle-loader in defence of a *laager*) and Honest Abe Lincoln. When he was president of this brief and modest republic, Kruger, like an American sitting on his porch, spent a significant part of the day on a cane settee on the *stoep* of his house, reading documents and talking to the people who came to see him.

* * *

The next day we went to Johannesburg for a tour of a symbol of the moral taxonomies of race segregation—Soweto, the South Western Townships, established in 1954 when government bulldozers destroyed Sophiatown, a relatively free settlement where blacks could own property and were partly in control of their own lives. After government trucks shifted the 60,000 people of Sophiatown to the site of the South Western Townships, the rubble was fumigated and a suburb for whites laid out, to be called Triomf in honour of this victory. At first the government would allow only its own guides on Soweto tours, but by the time we got into our mini-bus only black guides were accepted in Soweto. And not always then.

Near the entrance to Soweto we stood on a bridge spanning a huge mini-bus exchange and looked out over the mass of 'matchbox houses' (familiar to anyone who watches television news). They spilled across to the horizons under a haze of smoke, and floated on an ocean of rubbish—a symbol of resistance to self-improvement under the apartheid system. As in our tours of Harlem and Jaipur, the guide gave us a socioeconomic lecture—on the demography of Soweto (33 suburbs, more than two million people, with ethnic groups intermixed) and its economy (briefly: 25 per cent unemployed). We saw the houses of rich blacks, of middle class suburban standard or thereabouts, but pressed together like large bourgeois vaults in a European cemetery, all within sight of dwellings of the poor, and almost all displaying their sincerity by being surrounded by rubbish. The only section that looked truly suburban were the few streets of 'the Beverly Hills of Soweto', where, said the guide, the sporting stars lived, and the rubbish had been cleared away, and gardens planted. At the other end of the economic scale were the shanty outcrops of the squatters, no worse and no better than the shanty settlements of many Asian and Latin American cities. Then the single men's barracks where, far from their families, men lived in long huts divided into cubicles, reminiscent of the 'concentration camps' that the Nazis named after the word the British used when they built special prisons for Afrikaner women and children during the Boer War.

The dominant structural form was the matchbox house. Three rooms usually, sometimes with a lean-to attached, accommodating up to two dozen human beings. Our guide drove us to the matchbox house where he and his wife and two children lived in a lean-to. The whole household came out and stood behind the wire fence so that we could take a tourist's snapshot. The matchbox house had been the suburban dream of many urban black families in South Africa.

THE NATIONAL TOURIST SHOWCASE   267

After a round of beers and Diet Cokes in a 'perfectly safe' tavern, we left. No postcards. No guidebooks. No souvenir shops. Apart from the division between *them* and *us*, what we had just done was an antitourist experience. Our tour had been a lecture on economic class. Other than the two Mandela houses, we didn't see any famous buildings. No vistas. No picturesque photographs. No art. When it was over we went to a shop and bought a Thames & Hudson book, *Art of the South African Townships*. That made it seem more like tourism.

* * *

In the manner of a public culture, the Pretoria City Tour gave a single and exclusive view of what mattered in the South African nation, and in this world Soweto did not exist. In a nationalist tourist pilgrimage in any country you get a very narrow picture of the national tribe. The Tourmobile in Washington provided aspirations more to democratic taste than the Voortrekker spirit, but it was no complex rundown on the diversity of United States society. There weren't Tourmobiles when the spirit of lynch law terrorised the Deep South, but there were tourists and tourist guidebooks, and they celebrated a United States in which there was one of the great silences of tourism: it didn't include 'the Negro'. And until very recently the hundreds of tourist celebrations in the United States, big and small, of how the West was won told much the same story as the Voortrekker Monument, covered wagons and all.

When modern nationalism was being created, as if all the nation were one tribe, icons and rituals, legends and festivals had to be invented both in new nations and in old. Any nation needed a national flag, a national song, a national day, a national capital, a national dress, a national crest, a national flower, national honours, a national past, a national animal, a national character, a national currency, national postage stamps,* a national poet and a national dish.

It also needed a national tourist showcase. As I said in the chapter on public cultures (Chapter 13), just as with the Great Exhibitions or the grand museums, the development of tourism could be the same

---

* PAPER AMBASSADORS. As Denis Altman shows in *Paper Ambassadors: The Politics of Stamps*, a nation's stamp collection can be seen as a kind of museum of the images that have been cast of the nation—its history, heroes, art, foreign policy, dominant secular and religious faiths, modernisation, economic imperatives and its views of good citizenship.

thing as the development of a public culture. Certain museums, monuments, historic sites and emblematic buildings were essential in fabricating the imagined communal life of a nation. Loyal citizens could make a tourist pilgrimage to them. They would come back better citizens.

For example, consider the part played by tourist pilgrimages to war shrines in Australia and Japan in simplifying these nations down to a travesty of 'national character'.

At the end of the 19th century, when modern Japan was being scripted, the Emperor cult, having lapsed for 1200 years, was revived and restaged as one of the creations of neo-traditionalism. Chinese Buddhism and Confucianism, transmuted, had been the underpinnings of Japanese culture, but now something more specifically Japanese was needed. Shinto was turned into a 'national religion', uniquely Japanese, and four hectares of Tokyo were set aside for the Yasukini Shrine, projected as the national Shinto shrine, and also as the resting place for the souls of dead soldiers. It was a place you were expected to 'do' if you came to Tokyo. The many Japanese who still go there can also visit the attached war museum where there are relics of past war heroes. (Some of them were found guilty as war criminals, but their souls also rest at the Yasukini Shrine along with the other honoured dead).

Until the Great European War of 1914–18 there was no agreement in Australia about what, if anything, should be celebrated about Australia. What then became celebrated was how Australia's 'national character' was formed by the landing on a beach in the Ottoman Empire, on April 25 1915, of an Australian and New Zealand (ANZAC) expeditionary force as part of what was to prove the failed Allied offensive in the Dardanelles. In the public culture this event was instantly declared to have created Australia as a nation. April 25 became 'Anzac Day', the national day. The Anzac cult, celebrated throughout the land in thousands of monuments in granite, bronze, sandstone, marble or stained glass, received its equivalent to the Yasukini Shrine when a National War Memorial was opened in Canberra. In appearance both mosque and fort, the memorial provided a resting place for the memory of the Anzacs and the other war dead, honoured in an arcaded courtyard with a Pool of Remembrance and a Commemorative Stone; in a Hall of Memory and in a war museum (better than most) that became a principal tourist site in Canberra (and one now visited by Japanese tourists).

As with museums, so with nature. Visits to natural features seen as embodying the national tribal character were not only physically refreshing, they were also a regenerative course in citizenship. As John Sears says in *Sacred Places*, '(nature) tourism played a powerful role in America's invention of itself as a culture'. In paying homage to the attractions of Niagara Falls, or 'doing' the Hudson Valley in a steamboat, or going on a guided tour of Mammoth Cave, Kentucky, or, later in the century, in standing in reverence before the sequoias in the Mariposa Grove or the grandeur of Yosemite, some tourists referred to themselves specifically as 'pilgrims'. The tourist landscapes of Europe were created as part of the romantic imagination that invented nations: the Swiss spirit was to be found in the Alps, the Scottish in the Highlands, the Norwegian in mountains and fjords, the Hungarian in the Great Hungarian Plain, and so forth. Every stereotyped geographical feature of New Zealand had a magic circle cast around it as a symbol of national character before it was packaged up as part of a tour to sell to visitors. Sears says of the United States, but it also goes for the other industrialised nations, that tourist attractions 'enabled the members of an emerging mass society to participate in a common national experience'.

As for landscapes, so for other sightseeing. If you look hard enough at the main tourist paths within the modern, industrialised societies you may find that there is very little that isn't nationalist among those 'sights' that are wrapped up as commodities for autonomic tourists to buy. The *Mona Lisa* becomes a French painting because it hangs in the Louvre. It is part of Paris, and of French civilisation. Ironbridge is more about Britain than about the contribution of blast furnaces to the industrial revolution. The Vikings are three different kinds of people depending on whether you go to Oslo for Norwegian Vikings, Roskilde for Danish Vikings or the Jorvik Centre for true blue Yorkshire Vikings. It is an example of the power of the United States that Washington offers as one of its attractions the world's largest elephant. The Maya ruins go beyond being Mayan. They become Mexican—but not as Mexican as Aztec ruins.

In simplifying a nation down to travesties, tourist attractions can be given the patriotic role of leaving out all other possible stories, and even of excluding most of the classes of people and ways of life within the nation. At the Fiji Museum in Suva you get no idea that the descendants of immigrant Indians outnumber the ethnic Fijians. Unless you look at the museum very carefully, you won't discover anything to indicate that there are any Indians at all in Fiji. The National Cultural History Museum in Pretoria, when we saw it, disposed of all the black people of southern Africa in a few glass cases of traditional artifacts, labelled 'ANTHROPOLOGY', and one montage labelled 'CULTURAL CHANGE'. This display ended with a dummy of a near-naked Bushman, looking into the next gallery where the refinements of the colonising civilisation were laid out in detail.

VISITING THE NATIONAL CAPITAL

A national capital city was also an essential element of a modern public culture—and it could also become an essential part of the national tourist showcase.

When Sukarno was president of Indonesia, Westerners were likely to snigger at his attempts to turn a colonial administrative centre (the Dutch Batavia) into a modern national capital (Jakarta). In what had been King's Square under the Dutch, and was now Independence Square, a National Monument was going up, in marble, 137 metres high, topped with a torch flame gilded with 35 kilograms of gold leaf. Alongside, a marble equestrian statue of the 19th century Javanese rebel Prince Diponegoro had his marble horse rearing exactly like that of a 19th century European freedom-fighter. Sukarno was building South-east Asia's largest mosque and what was then one of the world's biggest sports stadiums. Crude monuments to this and that were going up in traffic roundabouts, and a six-lane boulevard, that was intended to become the Champs Élysées of South-east Asia, had been laid down.

Sukarno knew that if a nation was to exist as an idea, it should have a national capital, with open display areas, significant clumps of statuary and large lumps of masonry.

That had been obvious to the Emperor Franz Ferdinand when he decided in 1858 that the old city walls of Vienna should be knocked down, and a Ring Road (*Ringstrasse*) built with impressive new buildings beside it—now making a museum display of grandiloquent 19th century revival styles. It was obvious to Baron Haussman when he knocked down enough of Paris to put in a system of boulevards and a constellation of prestige buildings, and to the Hohenzollerns when they widened and lengthened streets in Berlin and planted monuments and trees. And to Sir Charles Barry when he laid out Trafalgar Square (an example of the creation of an instant historical epoch), thereby beginning the construction of that ceremonial centre of London that was to conclude when the triumphal Admiralty Arch went up. Buckingham Palace was given a more stately face and The Mall was turned into Europe's most spacious (and, later, most televised) processional way. In Rome, the makers of the 'master plans' of 1883 and 1931 gouged through whole quarters to produce wider streets and inspiring vistas, and the Victor Emmanuel monument arose as another declaration of an instant historical epoch.

The need for a national capital was known to the 19th century creators of St Petersburg's central squares, that now provide the greatest monument in Europe to aristocratic self-confidence. It was known also to the Bolsheviks when they made Moscow the capital, knocked down most of the small wooden and brick houses to produce a city of ambitious mediocrity, and turned the Red Square into Europe's most formidable secular cathedral.

It was also known to Pierre L'Enfant when he was asked in 1791 to lay out Washington. In fact, he was probably first in the modern world with an idea of a national capital as a symbolic enterprise. He was sacked after a year and died a pauper but his ambitions in symbolic civic art survived, if in hibernation. At the beginning of the 20th century, the authorities began to drain the swamps that lay to one side of the Mall, removed the railroad track that cut the Mall in half, and decided on a Lincoln Monument. However, it wasn't until after the second world war that the Mall developed into something worthy of the Tourmobile.

Building these boulevards, squares, monuments and collections of prestige masonry was part of the defining of the national capital. But a capital was also defined by what was knocked down. That was the time when it was decided which relics of the past were to survive and be renovated and exalted, and which were to disappear.* The two master plans that restaged Rome destroyed whole quarters of the 'real Rome' (areas where people lived), but they uncovered new stretches

---

* **OLD BATAVIA.** In Jakarta, the oldest part of the Dutch town, once a fortress with a defensive wall and moat, became, for the tourist, 'Old Batavia', with cobbled squares, cream-coloured colonnaded buildings with green shutters, the *Statdhuis* where the Council for the Indies used to meet, and an historic bronze cannon that cures infertility if a woman sits on it. (If you hire a boat at the old port you can float through [authentic] 'living history', past Makassar schooners that are much the same as they have been for hundreds of years.)

of ancient Rome, and made many other old buildings more accessible and more visible. They devised a modern 'old Rome'.

This combination of something-old-something-new created many of the capital cities as the tourist destinations they still are, along with certain celebrated modern buildings—the Eiffel Tower, the Sydney Opera House, the Empire State Building. (Although Sydney is a state capital, New York is neither national nor state capital, but a cultural capital.) The celebrated modern building when I was in Belgrade in the 1970s was the revolving restaurant. When I was first in Jakarta, a decade earlier, it was the department store.

* * *

When the defeated Chiang Kai Shek retreated to Taiwan he proclaimed that, until he returned to the mainland, Taipei would be the temporary capital of China. He had taken with him the bulk of China's most prestigious art treasures and set up in Taipei the National Palace Museum, with the world's largest and best Chinese collection. If this largely Japanese-designed provincial capital was to be declared the national capital of all China until the apocalyptic moment of the 'return to the mainland', it would have to be the national cultural showcase. Temporarily, Taipei would display the cultured past.

Except in federations, the national capital is likely to be the place with the most renowned opera house, the most famous theatres and concert halls and museums (sometimes with the word 'national' in their title). If you were 'doing' Moscow you had to 'do' the Bolshoi. If you were 'doing' Madrid you had to 'do' the Prado. If you were 'doing' London you had to 'do' a West End show.

A national museum had to be 'done' along with obligatory visits to certain other respected museums which provided revelations of culture. From the national museum you learned the national style. Consider the differences, as defined by museums, between the Swiss and the Swedes. The Swiss National Museum was established in Zürich in 1898, because it was Zürich's turn to have a national building. This accident of placing led to the presentation of the typical past of the Swiss as living in solid patrician German comfort, with coffered ceilings, sumptuously carved wall-panelling, opulent furniture and ornately tiled stoves, and, although peasant styles were also given a look in, this became the dominant Swiss museum style. The style spread even into the history museum in French-speaking Geneva, where no-one had ever furnished houses like this either in the city itself or for miles around. In Sweden, because of the national style developed in the Skansen open air folk museum, the Swedes were presented as a nation of peasants. (Proportionately, there may have been no more peasants in Sweden than Switzerland.) Later, almost every town in Sweden projected Swedishness by purporting to recall the verities of a rural past. Yet the differences between Sweden and Switzerland were not as great as these differences in approaches in their national museums.*

If the national capital had a museum containing one of the great archaeological collections of the Ozymandias past that offered civilisation in an afternoon (the British Museum, the Louvre, the Pergamon, etc), the capital gained a special place in human progress because the history of that progress was laid out in this kind of museum. (Even in smaller centres, museums were expected to have, at least, Egyptian mummies and plaster casts.) The grand art museums also gave the national capital a role as witness to human civilisation. The Bolsheviks showed unusual self-restraint in not moving the entire Hermitage collection to Moscow.

All that tourists see of a country may be boulevards and squares in the national capital (laid out within the last century and a half), a few of its selected historical sites (usually designated as historic over the same period) and some of its cultural showcase items. These few sights then turn the capital into a selective museum of the whole nation.

CHOOSING THE NATION'S STORY

All modern states were firmly founded on an ethnic muddle, and national languages did not begin to exist until several centuries ago (at the time of Italian unification in 1861, only one in 40 Italians spoke

---

* **ROMANTIC GERMANY.** Since what it meant to be German was being established before there was a Germany, a specific museum style preceded the creation of Germany by almost 20 years. It came in the romantic declarations of the 100 galleries of the German National Museum at Nuremberg. When the museum was established in 1852, among the half-timbered burghers' houses of Bavaria's most admired medieval city, it appropriated human civilisation as part of the romantic history of the German people, thereby, along with Treitschke's *The History of Germany* and a few other stimulants, providing many murderous dreams.

the new national language). But if a nation was a tribe it had to have its own stories, in the form of legends of a national past. One of the creative opportunities for Europeans in the 19th century came in choosing, in each nation, nation-to-be or nation-within-a-nation, what its national history would be, and one of the destructive opportunities of the 20th century was to carry it out. The 'past' we walk through as autonomic tourists, especially in Europe, can be a story created by 19th century nationalist intellectuals.

Choosing the national heroes

I shall begin with Serbia, because in the early 1990s it became a prime example of the destructive after-effects of one of the inventions of 19th century nationalism. The National Museum in Belgrade has two monumental canvases in soft, bright colours recalling the great days of the 14th century Serbian monarch, Stephen Dušan. One is *The Coronation of Dušan* and the other *The Wedding of Dušan*. The story of their painting is part of the story of how a national past was acquired through decisions made in the 19th century (which could later affect late 20th century Balkan history).

After its two uprisings against the Turks in the first half of the 19th century, Serbia was becoming one of the first of the new nations. In 1844, although Serbia was still only an autonomous region within the Ottoman Empire and still garrisoned by Turks, a small national museum was established in Belgrade. This was on the initiative of a Serbian writer, as one of the ways of proclaiming nationality. Serbian life was expected to be unique and its uniqueness was proclaimed to the romantic intelligentsia by collecting and displaying folk dress, jewellery, woodcarvings and metalwork. (These things were put into a separate museum in 1901. It is still operating, and in the 1970s its curators pioneered new ways of presenting a folk collection.) Relics were also collected, and artists began to accept their role as depictors of both the present and the past of a Serbian nation; their work would be displayed on the walls of the National Museum when it got its own building. Paintings of the present were usually based on the artists' own sketches and notes of Serbian peasant life. Paintings of the past were based on how the history-writers and folklorists were defining Serbia's role in the universe. One aspect of this was pride in the Serbian Empire, which lasted for 20 or so years after its establishment by Stephen Dušan ('Emperor and Autocrat of the Serbs and Greeks, the Bulgarians and Albanians'). Stephen Dušan was an early national hero. That is why you find in the National Museum *The Coronation of Dušan* and *The Marriage of Dušan*.

Many national heroes didn't have faces—there were no portraits of them, or the portraits were not inspirational—and the habit of painting great moments in history had not been invented when most of the heroes were having their great moments. So heroic faces and great moments were created across Europe in a whole flora of history paintings like those of Dušan, improvising a past for each of its nations that is still on the tourist trails, or near them. Monumental canvases of Joan of Arc as royalist saint or as patriot of the people provided a minor industry in France. In Britain, Alfred the Great was produced as a hero and dozens of paintings commemorated him for his law-giving and nation-building battles against the Danes. German princes commissioned paintings that celebrated a past based on tribes who defeated the Romans, and on Frankish kings and characters in Rhineland legends. In Romania, Vlad the Impaler came out as patriot and man of the people.

Just as characteristic of the time was 'statuemania', an obsession that took over middle and upper class Europeans in the 19th century. After the national heroes were chosen, up their effigies went, in bronze or marble statues, in squares and parks and boulevards and at prestigious road intersections. The mounted statue of the 10th century Wenceslas, assassinated Duke of Bohemia, became, when it went up in 1913, a definition of what it could mean to be Czech. In 1875 a statue of beaten copper, 16 metres high, with a sword seven metres long, was unveiled in the Teutoburg Forest in Germany to celebrate the victory of Arminius who annihilated a Roman army in 9 AD. The statue still gets a star and half a page in the Michelin guide.

In Eastern Europe, statues of Serbian, Bulgarian, Greek, Hungarian, Polish and Romanian heroes raised battleaxes, spears, crucifixes, swords and banners against the Ottoman Turks. (Another Serbian example: Belgrade's principal statue is of Prince Mihailo Obrenovic, who managed to get the Turks to withdraw all their garrisons in 1867, and, a year later, was assassinated while on a walk.) When chivalry returned to Western Europe in its 19th century form, statues of Crusaders were erected to advance on the Arabs and Moors. Opposite Zagreb's railway station a statue went up to Tomislav, a *zupan* of Nin, who, in some year like 924, became first chief of the Croats. Female personifications of the nation, with ample breasts—Finlandia,

Britannia, Polonia, Germania, Romania, Hungaria, the French *patrie*, etc—still give an aura of history, in metal or stone, even if in some cities it becomes so faint that we see it, if we see it at all, as some faded memory of the past. (Although on the Tourmobile Tour, no-one fails to notice the Lincoln statue.)

Choosing the national geniuses

When French-speaking élites in the south of the Netherlands revolted against the Dutch in 1830 they set up their own kingdom, calling it 'Belgium' after the Belgae tribes whom Julius Caesar had conquered almost 1900 years before. They brought in a German prince to reign as King of the Belgians, but they also needed a statue. They chose a cultural hero, Peter Paul Rubens, artist, diplomat and scholar, and a statue of him went up in Antwerp in 1840. In response, in the mood of statuemania, Dutch élites also needed to demonstrate that they had a national cultural hero. A year after the Rubens statue was unveiled, the Dutch decided on Rembrandt. Two committees were set up to arrange finance for a statue in bronze. Choosing the national geniuses was as important as choosing the national heroes.

Rubens, Rembrandt, Cervantes, Pushkin, Shakespeare, Beethoven, Ibsen, Yeats and Sibelius all have their statues. In Ljubljana, the muse of poetry holds an olive branch over the head of Franz Preseren, Slovenia's national poet. In a Luxembourg marketplace there is a statue of Michel Rodange, national poet of the Grand Duchy of Luxembourg. In *The Englishman's England*, Ian Ousby traces modern tourism back to literary pilgrimages such as those that went along with the development of the Shakespeare business at Stratford-on-Avon.

National geniuses were culture heroes whose festivals, statues, birthplaces, etc, are still likely to be in the national showcases. But to be a tourist of the national culture of one of the new nations of Europe you also need to know something of philologists, orthographers, grammarians, lexicographers and translators. Even in longer-established states, there were choices as to what a national culture might be. At the time of the revolution, only half the people of France spoke French. But in territories that were to emerge from the dynastic empires as new nations, a sense of nationality had often been almost obliterated.

You can get an excellent idea of what this meant if, on a spare afternoon in Prague, you care to walk through celebrations of much of the invention of Czech national culture. The place to start is the National Museum. It was at the centre of the process of putting together pieces of peasant life—words, songs, proverbs, ceremonies, dress, legends, feasts—and out of these stitching a standardised product to be called Czech culture. Why the peasants? Because they were just about all that was left of being Czech when the Habsburgs ended the 30 Years War—the nobles and the gentry had been killed or expelled or bought over and Germanised. The National Museum's central hall is a pantheon honouring, in bronze and marble, the founders and developers of Czech intellectual and artistic life. On its walls are large 19th century paintings that were intended to provide a laboratory of ideas about what it might mean to be Czech. In front of the museum is the statue celebrating Wenceslas. Around the corner, the neorenaissance Smetana Theatre recalls the new nation-defining music, and, in its name, the first famous national composer. Along another main thoroughfare is the National Theatre, as great a symbol of 19th century cultural definition as the National Museum—and laden with lunettes and statues praising the arts, Czech artists, and 'Our Native Land'.

A quiet side square has a statue of a seated scholar, pen in hand. It is Josef Jungman, after whom the square is named, the philologist who, out of the confusion of peasant dialects, helped create a standard Czech language that could be taught in schools. In Palacky Street, near Jungman Square, a plaque marks the house of F Palacky, one of the historians who created a credible national past for the Czechs. Across the river at the edge of a park on Kampa Island, a bust commemorates Father Dobrovsky, who wrote the first comprehensive Czech grammar. At the foot of the hills, in an old palace, the Ethnographic Museum's collections, first displayed in an exposition in 1895, were part of the basis for defining what it meant to be a Czech. And in the Old Strahov Monastery, a Museum of National Literature shows relics, in books and manuscripts, of the cultural construction of a Czech nation.

Choosing great moments in history

Just as Serb intellectuals chose Dušan's empire as a great moment in their national history, the makers of the other new nations of Europe saw the need to have one or more epochs that could be thought of as the golden age that preceded their subjection. For this, things that looked real were needed as well as 19th century sculptures and paintings. This material past was best provided by on-site relics and authentic objects that could be put into museums. The decisive sorting-out of which old things told the best story of a golden age still defines what we find, as tourists, in the national museums.

To look to the Serbs again. For the Serbs, evidence for the golden age was found partly where you would expect, among manuscripts, coins, jewellery, carved doors and other medieval leftovers. The unique attraction was late in coming, after the second world war, in the cataloguing (and in some cases cleaning and conserving) of 6000 or so frescoes, 'discovered' in medieval monasteries and churches in remote mountain passes. The best were copied for display in the Gallery of Frescoes in Belgrade, and are used in the claim that the Serbs developed the renaissance in painting several decades before the Italians.*

With the assistance of archaeologists, the Irish began their golden past with the loops and whorls and other *motifs* in the passage graves that are one of Europe's greatest provenances of megalithic stone-cut art. Modern Armenians, whose brief empire fell to the Romans in 55 BC, found a golden past in a whole range of historic sites, remains of old forts, burial places, churches, cuneiform tablets and cave dwellings—and in one of them a proof that Armenia was the first Christian 'nation'. When Norway was handed from Denmark to Sweden after the Napoleonic Wars, Norwegians who wanted a Norway of their own began conserving remains of the golden days of medieval Norway and established a Museum of National Antiquities to prove it. In the 1970s, the Romanian government put up a statue in the city of Deva of Decebalus, the last leader of the Dacians before their defeat

---

* **RENAISSANCE IN THE ALTERNATIVE.** Connection with the renaissance can be a high item in national prestige, either the claim to have been there first, or claims for the particular splendours of the golden age of a renaissance queen or prince—Elizabeth of England, François of France, Matthias of Hungary, Sigismund of Krakow, Rudolph of Bohemia and Christian of Denmark remain significant names in the guidebooks. Someone should write a book demonstrating that the renaissance really occurred in the Low Countries. It would begin with the Flemish towns as specimens of early capitalism, Van Eyck as a master of new art and Erasmus of new thought, and it would end with the Dutch seaborne empire of the 17th century, the paintings of Rembrandt and the writings of Spinoza.

by Trajan, showing him mounted on his thoroughbred as a figure of boundless patriotism.

Towards the end of the 19th century the republican French redefined themselves as the descendants not of the Franks, who could now seem too aristocratic, but of the Gauls, who, in the Third Republic, could seem more like 'the people'. At the end of the 20th century the greatest monument to Gallic civilisation had become a new amusement park opened near Paris, Asterix Park, built around a comic-strip hero from ancient Gaul.

The sense of history was sometimes so strong that historical epochs could be declared almost before they were over—there could be a new golden age here and now. In heightened statuemania, the unification of Wilhelmine Germany resulted in more than 1000 statues and other monuments. Later, a standardised monument, the Bismarck Tower, was developed to commemorate Bismarck. Nearly 500 Bismarck Towers were ordered the year after his death.

Choosing a beginning

On our family holiday in Bali, we learned that the world was created out of chaos through meditation, so that Bali could firmly rest on the world turtle. Then we learned that Brahma and Batara Guru (his other self) created the Balinese, having got their skin colour right after some baking experiments with proto-humans in an oven—some came out too dark and some too light, but the gentle brown of the Balinese was perfect. According to the Shilluck, a Nile-dwelling people in the Sudan, the creator produced differences in skin colour by the soil used in fashioning the world's peoples—white loam for the whites, brownish for the Arabs, but for the best people in the world, the black people, the fertile black clay of the banks of the Nile.

There are only two modern nation-states based on a belief of divine origin. The Japanese dynasty was founded by a grandson of the sun goddess Amaterasu, and the Emperor maintained rites of communion with her until Japan lost the Asia-Pacific War. This belief is now in abeyance, but there is still political power in Israel in God's covenant with Abraham that Abraham's descendants would be God's Chosen People, so long as the males went on being circumcised, and in the promise of their own Land, whose territories he then defined.

However, instead of claims to divine origin, a number of nations have legends of secular birth, and these can produce national pilgrimage destinations that take their place on the general tourist routes. Periodically they provide commemorative festivals of national or international significance with re-enactments, Expos and other marvels.

In Europe, chronological beginnings are imagined mainly in Eastern Europe, with dates given to the arrivals of various founders. Those who were doing well out of Hungary at the end of the 19th century thought it important that the nation should have a jubilee. The year 896 was chosen as Hungary's birth year. Patriotic manifestations of various kinds were prepared, including a token re-enactment of the arrival on the Carpathian plain of the 400,000 or so Magyar tribesmen who had been pushed there by the Bulgarians. Although an exhibition in the National Museum in Budapest suggested that the Magyar tribesmen were not so much a 'nation' as clans of cattle raiders, the Millenary Monument, begun in 1896, still demonstrates that in 896 the nation of Hungary was born. In front of a semicircular colonnade bearing bronze statues of Hungary's most famous sons, statues of the conquering Magyar horsemen pause as if surveying Budapest's finest avenue before charging along it to seize the State Opera House.

In several territories the arrival of various Slavs can, like the arrival of the Magyar horsemen, be celebrated as a national beginning. The Bulgarians claim the year 681 for the birth of the Bulgarian nation. That year, a combination of tribal groups signed a peace treaty with Byzantium—and in its honour preparations for 'the Thirteen Hundredth Anniversary of the Bulgarian Nation' in 1981 went on for three years. The Military Museum in Kalegmedan Fortress, Belgrade, shows the story of the Serb nation beginning barbarously as the Slavs fight their way into a place in Europe, across a map lighting up with red to denote the flames of sacked cities. Then, instead of the misty outlines of wild, disastrous invaders, the Serbs take civilised shape, achieving conventional order so that Serbia can bloom into its golden era of empire and Dušan can have his coronation.

* * *

The simplest of all national creation legends are those that begin with the landing of a coloniser. Near the landing where we embarked on our Singapore River 'cruise' is a replica of a bronze statue of Stamford Raffles—who, in 1819, claimed Singapore as a trading post for the East India Company—marking the *exact* spot of the landing site where Raffles looked over the swamps and made his commercial

THE NATIONAL TOURIST SHOWCASE 281

and imperial decisions. The landing of Governor Arthur Phillip, at what was to become Sydney Cove, has been celebrated as the birth of Australia. A site at the confluence of two rivers in Québec City is presented as the birthplace of Canada: it was here that Jacques Cartier spent the winter of 1535–6—a reconstruction of one of his three sailing vessels proves it.

The most magical of the colonial landing sites is, of course, 'Plymouth Rock'. The granite boulder on which the Pilgrims almost certainly did not step when they landed in 1620 has been moved from the beach and put under a granite canopy, and, along with a replica of the *Mayflower* and a reconstruction of the Pilgrims' village, with reconstructed Pilgrims in period dress, it is presented as the spiritual birthplace of the United States. Near Jamestown, Virginia—and it was here, not Plymouth, that the first British settlement was made, in 1607—there is an alternative beginning of the nation, but Jamestown does not have the ethical and rhetorical appeal of Plymouth, nor that emotional appeal that 'America' was truly born in the settlement of the West that produces all those cowboy hats at Republican political conventions.

Only in New Zealand were the indigenous people given early honours of 'discovery'. The landing sites of Abel Tasman (who gave New Zealand its name) and James Cook (who circumnavigated both islands) are part of New Zealand history, and here and there lace-curtained colonial houses recall the landings of groups of European settlers. But the true beginning of New Zealand is imagined in a large history painting in the Auckland City Gallery based in style, although not in theme, on *The Raft of the Medusa*, the painting before which Zola had his party stand dumb and motionless on their puzzling visit to the Louvre on a wet afternoon. It is *The Arrival of the Maoris in New Zealand* and it shows Maoris in their canoes, 1000 years or so ago, swept by a strong wave of destiny towards one of the beaches of Aotearoa, 'the land of the long white cloud', of which they were the true discoverers.

The word 'discovery' may now go out of use as a result of the 1992 Columbus celebrations. Columbus may continue to sit on tops of columns, or rise to heaven from painted ceilings surrounded by allegorical figures celebrating his civilising virtues, but these monuments now have alternative meanings. In its extreme form, this can be a loathing of the whole European conquest of the Americas and the faith that only the indigenous Americans were ecologically sound. In Central America, Mexico and Peru, for some time now, the solid remains of Maya and other civilisations have been used to give the nation-states that came out of the Spanish Empire an alternative perspective on origin—in particular, Peru holds on to this in the midst of its economic and political disasters. From textiles and drawings, several thousand years old, to the granite complexities of Machu Picchu and the nation-making of the Incas, this perspective offers a variety of golden ages that put the Spanish conquerors in their place.

In Australia, archaeological digs show signs of human existence 40,000 or more years ago, and ancient Aboriginal rock carvings have now become tourist sites. Around the world non-Europeans are now, retrospectively, being allowed to enter national history. The Voortrekker monument is no longer the true symbol of South Africa.

Liberations

Liberation can be an alternative birth of a nation. Every Vietnamese schoolchild is expected to know that the Vietnamese nation was created in the second millennium BC by the Hung kings. There is a triumphal presentation of the brilliant culture of this golden age in the Central History Museum in Hanoi—in famous drums, decorated jars and other imposing objects, and in the renowned Viêt Khê coffin, carved from a tree trunk and found with 100 or so objects inside it. The museum's next section shows how, after Vietnam's splendid birth, there is a struggle for independence against Chinese dominance that lasts for 1200 years. Another golden age is manifest in Buddhist texts, elegant ceramics and enamelware, finely-engraved bricks and sculptured birds, but there are also maps and models recalling hundreds of years of resistance, in uprisings against Chinese suzerainty and a medley of invaders. The last section of the museum is devoted to evidence of French colonisation and then of the patriotic struggle against France. The show ends with a diorama of the proclamation of independence after the Revolution of August 1945. The true heirs of the creators of Vietnam are its liberators.

The Irish provide proof of the struggle for liberation in their National Museum—hats with bulletholes, the first typewriter with Gaelic letters, minutes, books, flags, guns. The History Museum in Bucharest solemnises the grand manifestos and the tricolours and swords of the 1848 uprising against the Habsburgs, and the battle paintings, the captured trophies and the tunics of brave men from the war of liberation against the Turks. Part of the tourist trail in southern Serbia was the Tower of Skulls, on the outskirts of Nis—a pyramid of the skulls of 1952 martyred patriots, set up by the Turkish *pasha* of Nis as a warning to others and now a national shrine.

Latin America is as decorated with the statues of liberators as Italy is with statues of heroes of the *Risorgimento*. In China, the liberation of 'New China' from the imperialists is recalled in Sun Yat Sen monuments and special museums. In Guangzhou, the base for the opium trade from which the British drug barons launched two wars to protect their drug-running, eight museums recall the history of liberation from the imperial bandits. One is called, simply, and appropriately, the Museum of Anti-British Struggle. Zimbabwe celebrates its liberation on the outskirts of Harare, in an area of land sacralised as Heroes' Acre, where there are the graves of leaders of the liberation movement out of which Rhodesia was reborn as Zimbabwe.

* * *

The Tourmobile tour is, among other things, a celebration of national birth through revolutionary liberation, as are many of the one-day or half-day tours around Washington—in particular to Philadelphia's Independence National Historical Park, 'the most historic square mile in America', an area of restored buildings, a few replicas, and with grass marking the spots where irrelevant buildings were knocked down. The presentation film in the Visitor Centre includes addresses by the ghosts of revolutionary heroes. ('The War of Independence is over. The revolution has just begun.') Outside Independence Hall ('the birthplace of our nation', where the Declaration of Independence was signed—the silver inkstand remains), pony-carts offer a ride through America's most historic square mile. Across the street from Independence Hall, people stand in line in a modern building of glass and steel set in the gardens of Independence Mall. They are queuing to touch a metal object—the 'Liberty Bell' that was rung in Philadelphia, along with other church bells, on the day that the Declaration of Independence was adopted. It later became an emblem of the anti-slavery movement and has other attached values as well. I watched a woman and her daughter jointly lay hands on it. "The Liberty Bell," she said, "stands for all our American political philosophy." (The Liberty Bell gets bigger queues than the United States Constitution in Washington. It is famous merely for its own fame and it is something you are allowed to touch.)

THE CONSERVATISM OF THE TOURIST PAST

It was in the making of nations that pseudo-traditionalist strands in European public cultures began to form, whether the nations were established by transforming old states or by dividing them up to create new ones. Almost all the 'colourful uniforms' and 'colourful ceremonies' that spice tourist promotions are residues of the 19th century skill for inventing traditions.

New 'living traditions' were needed, as well as legends of a national past. The most colourful, and therefore those most likely to fit into the late 20th century tourist experience, were conservative. Conservatism was one of the significant 'isms' invented in the 19th century, and to mobilise support among the masses it needed flashy traditions justifying the belief that the genius of the nation resided in monarchy, nobility, army and church—not in the people. (Japan went through the same process.)

Some existing monarchies were refurbished more showily, and with appeals to traditions that had just been devised. As new nations were created in the 19th century each needed a new dynasty, or, in the case of Germany and Italy, an old dynasty amplified to give it greater volume (Prussianising Germany, Italianising Italy)—remnants of such theatrical re-stagings can still add tourist charm in Europe, most sympathetically in Denmark. But the big tourist monarchy remains the British, based on '1000 years of tradition' that, in fact, do not exist. As David Cannadine puts it in *The Invention of Tradition*, the 1000-year-old tradition goes back to the refurbishings and additions that began in the 1870s when the British began to catch up with the more vigorous monarchic shows already being put on in other parts of Europe. The Lord Mayor's Show, the Trooping of the Colour and the State Opening of Parliament are all 19th century revivals and the splendour of royal weddings and funerals are 20th century inventions.

As well as being a great era for painters, sculptors and architects, the 19th century had plenty of work for the designers and makers of gaudy uniforms and ostentatious ceremonial robes. There was an overwhelming amount of strutting around and people had to be dressed for it. As the story of the Serbian uprisings against the Turks is told in the Military Museum in Belgrade, the uniforms become more confident. In the first uprising the uniforms are peasants' dress. By the second uprising they show modest pretension, but, as Serbian independence and Serbian territory grow, the uniforms develop all the pseudo-traditional prettiness of chocolate-box soldiers. As it was in Serbia, so it was in other monarchies, to the later benefit of travel posters.

One of the many revivals was of the 'medieval'—restaged as a living tradition. The 'Gothic', a term invented to describe the barbarity of medieval architecture, became a term of praise, both for old cathedrals and for new railway stations. The Gothic revivalists also developed a new interest in the people: the organic sense of community that Scott, Novalis and other romantic writers had found in the middle ages was passed on to the peasantry. The peasantry became essential in creations of the national past. The true traditions of many a nation were to be found in newly-assembled folk museums, such as the Ethnographic Museum in Belgrade. Here, one can still look at the decorations on 19th century Serbian peasant costumes and imagine the reassurance of a communal past—when in fact they were social distinctions, showing the differences between people, that were embroidered or woven or dyed into these costumes or added by ornaments and tassels.

A taste developed for the picturesque quarter of some towns: the genius of the people was to be found in narrow, winding streets, peeling stucco, quiet courtyards, cobbled squares—and especially in an old marketplace. New folk traditions were invented, or old ones restaged. As is demonstrated in *The Invention of Tradition*, the kilt became the 'national dress' of Scotland when it hadn't been in the past. To yodel and to play with *alphorns, zithers* and cowbells became characteristically Swiss. To Europe's folk imagination Norwegian folklorists contributed the *trolls*, mythical beings of the mountains that were intriguing enough for Ibsen to write them into *Peer Gynt*, and for Edvard Grieg to make music around them and to call his house in Bergen after them. Trolls' Hall is on the Bergen tourist agenda and in the souvenir shops of Norway *troll* dolls are lined up to be bought as reminders of what it means to be truly Norwegian.

* * *

How can one imagine tourism without nationalism? Without national landscapes, evocations of national character, the splendours of national capitals and reminders of a national past what would we look at?

But whose nationalism? In the ethnic sense, scarcely any modern state is also a single nation. Instead of speaking of nation-states, we might speak of 'nation'-states. As it turned out, there was no such animal as a 'Yugoslav' and when faith was lost in the political-economic-military complex of Tito's legacy, it was as if the museum exhibits came back to life. Faith in being Serb or Croat or Slovene (or Albanian or Macedonian or Muslim) meant more than being Yugoslav.

Some of the small regional museums of Europe are now becoming 'national' museums, as regional and ethnic groupings challenge the 19th century definitions of nationality. When we were in Inverness, Scotland, they had just rearranged the museum as a story of the greatness and the destruction of the Highland clans. The innocence and goodness of the past offered simplicity, communalism and obligation to a confused Scottish present. And the museum cards had all been translated into Gaelic, so that as you looked at the stuffed animals that were left over from an earlier manifestation of the museum you could decide whether you were examining a stoat or a *neas-beag*, a *sionnach* or a fox.

22.

PATRIOTIC IRONMONGERY

◆ ◆ ◆

THE SILENCES OF GUNS AND UNIFORMS

Most guidebooks to Istanbul don't waste space on the Military Museum, yet, as far as war museums go, it shows how far a national historical imagination can be extended. A good preparation for this unlikely visit is to take the half-day excursion along the European shore of the Bosphorus and photograph the sprawling battlemented fortress of Rumeli Hisar, large enough to span a valley, but built in only four months in 1452 by Mehmet the Conqueror, and given the single use of blockading Byzantium. When the city fell, Rumeli Hisar was abandoned until it was restored by the Turks in 1953 as part of the 500th anniversary of their victory. (In one of the surreal juxtapositions of tourism, Shakespeare plays are now put on in the summer in a stone amphitheatre built out of the base of a cistern.)

As you walk into the museum it is 1526 and full-size statues of Sultan Suleiman II and his generals, on horseback, dominate the entrance hall as if they have seized it. They have just defeated the Hungarian army at the Battle of Mohács, south of Budapest, and killed the king: the Hungarian royal palace will be turned into a barracks and monasteries and churches will be quarried for their stone. At the time there was no reason to believe that the Ottomans would not continue to conquer Europe. Inside the museum, oil paintings commemorate other illustrious Ottoman victories and a large part of the display on the ground floor shows off, on lifesize dummies, the hierarchic ceremonial robes of the Ottoman conquerors.

When I was at the museum it was a time of terrorism and everyday killings. A soldier with a submachine gun followed me around on the ground floor, and whenever I took a note he would lean over my shoulder to look at what I had written, with his gun rubbing unconcernedly against my back. (I began to write things such as 'Take your gun away from my back'.) On the first floor, another soldier, of different disposition, *salaam*ed and walked ahead, smiling and beckoning me to the objects that, in flashback, told the story of Constantinople's capture, beginning with part of the chain used by the Byzantines as a boom across the Golden Horn, and ending with Mehmet the Conqueror, also lifesize, riding across the museum floor in armour into Constantinople, surrounded by opulently dressed officials. A large map, with delicately coloured miniatures that might equally have illustrated a love story, showed the Turks expanding into Europe. After all that, the smiling soldier led me to the relics of the Dardanelles campaign, the last Ottoman victory.

When I was there, a new exhibit was floating in the Bosphorus outside the Naval Museum—a frigate captured from the Greeks in the 1970s war over Cyprus—and at the end of the Military Museum the legend of Ataturk's creation of the Turkish Republic was told in 'The War of Independence'. (It was mainly a story of rapacious Greek invasion after the dismemberment of the empire and the expulsion of the Greeks under Ataturk's leadership.) But the basic feeling I had about this museum was as if I had picked up an old book with many of the pages missing and looked randomly at some evocative pictures. This is the nationalism of nostalgia.

Compare it with the first of 'the military parks', set up in the United States. Established in 1890, Georgia's Chickamauga and Chattanooga National Military Park, in its 3000 hectares, offers more than 1400 monuments, markers and plaques of two Civil War battles, in which 46,000 men were killed as part of the second founding of the United States. The Civil War, the first of the modern wars, was so instantly concerned with nationhood that a national cemetery was dedicated for the fallen of Gettysburg only four months after the battle was fought, and a year and a half before the war ended. It was appropriate that it became the site of the 19th century's most celebrated passage of democratic rhetoric because it was in the Civil War that wars became democratic: once the habit of shovelling soldiers' corpses into a ditch and forgetting them was abandoned, every dead soldier was turned into a martyr. Military cemeteries, at first in the United States and then, after the Great War, throughout the haunted lands of the abandoned Fronts of Europe, became among the most sacred sites in a national tourist pilgrimage. A 'true' war museum purports to be an expression of the nation.

In some countries, as in Japan and Australia, the ultimate shrine, encompassing all the war martyrs, was a single holy museum. Military museums in the Soviet Union became cult-centres of the state religion, as shrines to the memory of the 20 million killed in the Great Patriotic War against Hitler, and evidence of Russian military invincibility. Take Kiev, the capital of the Ukraine. All visitors to Kiev were expected to visit the Ukrainian State Museum of the Great Patriotic War. There, from the 62 metre-high sculpture depicting the Motherland to the grand marble staircase leading to the Hall of Glory, they would be run through the repertoire of a Soviet war museum. There was the Fire of Glory, lit from the eternal flame at the Grave of the Unknown Soldier beside the Kremlin walls (itself lit from the sacred flame at Leningrad's Monument to the Heroes of the Revolution and the Civil War). There were the caskets of sacred soil from other Soviet Union hero-cities (their names cast in bronze on granite pillars); and a statue of Lenin in the centre of the marble hall, with the names of army units and partisan groups lettered in gold all around him. Great Patriotic War memorials and museums were built in all Soviet capitals, and also in other important cities. It was as if the whole Soviet land was held together by sacred flames.

* * *

Washington may be the only national capital of a modern-industrial state without a pilgrimage war museum.* Costa Rica hasn't got one, but Costa Rica abolished its army in 1948. Even the Swiss National Museum has, as its most ambitious display, the Hall of Weapons—a lively glamorisation of the Swiss as fighting man for 1000 years (from 800 to 1800). For some (the Portuguese and the Dutch), national spirit was expressed in sea power, in maritime museums. For nations that didn't fight in the Great War there could be reminders of old dynastic battles, or, in new nations, of the struggle for liberation. After that, as in the Balkans and in Latin America, there could then be reminders of wars the liberated nations fought with each other.

But something happened to many of these museums that denied them the sense of holy sacrifice that could mark Gettysburg, or the Australian War Memorial, or a Museum of the Great Patriotic War, or the Yasukini Shrine. Instead, they made history from pseudo-traditionalist nostalgia for flags and pretty uniforms—and, in particular, of alluringly-designed armour—and from a hierarchic and heroic presentation of the past in which national worth was most effectively declared in orders and medals.

This carnival approach came with the first of the new military museums, the Musée de l'Armée, opened in Paris in 1905, which put on a fashion show of gay flags, bright clothes and gleaming weapons. When the French had to fit the Great War into their museum they turned even this bloodbath into a fashion parade of uniforms. The Italians (in a marble gallery within the Victor Emmanuel Monument) presented the war as an exhibition of design; the treatment of war as pomp was repeated in many other imitations of the Musée de l'Armée. A selling feature for the Royal Army

---

* HOLY SITES. The sites of famous encounters with the British in the War of Independence are also part of national tourist pilgrimages, although not with the same poignancy as the holy sites of the martyred dead of the Civil War. But only in Hawaii, in a six-minute boat ride to the memorial in Pearl Harbour, built on piles over the wreck of the battleship USS *Arizona*, is there a major United States second world war tourist event—and half the visitors to the *Arizona* are Japanese. The forts in the West and the mid-West, from which the European invaders fought the Indians, are also old battlefields but it may be only since *Dances with Wolves* that people see them in that way.

Museum in Stockholm is that, along with regimental flags and banners, 'the trophy hall displays some of the thousands of flags captured by Swedish soldiers in the 17th and 18th centuries'—as if war were an extension of embroidery.

As well as the treatment of war as carnival and the nation as a flag of victory, most of these museums also fit-out war as a technological display, presenting neat arrangements of warfare machinery—field guns, siege artillery, howitzers, rifles, bombs—as if war museums were an extension of industry museums, whose function is to take one into a past of beautiful ironmongery and a future of brilliant technology. The nation becomes a factory.

The silences in war museums, made louder by all the guns and uniforms, can leave out everything else about how people live in times of war. They can become not museums about warfare, but part of the psychology of warfare. (Museums are a way of fighting wars by other means.) In the era of the immense citizen armies of the 20th century, with a few exceptions such as the Australian War Memorial, there is not much recognition of even the life of the common soldier. There is not likely to be any mention of the complexity of the societies that those soldiers were born into and were expected to die for. In their contempt for almost everything about a nation they are as exclusivist as the Voortrekkers' Monument. The nation becomes a society of abstracts.

Insofar as these museums present people, they are robots in uniform. Even the military forces are not presented as complex social formations. We get no idea of why all those people who wore the uniforms did what they were told to do. For example, the trench system of the Western Front in the Great War was not only one of the routinised horrors of the 20th century: it was also an example of the human capacity to quickly invent new kinds of social formations. The trench system became an organised society within a society, with its own rationality. Yet presentation of trench warfare in museums, if it is there at all, is likely to descend either into isolated relics, or into attempted simulation in the form of a reconstructed trench. (For a while the Imperial War Museum in London had a splendid presentation of the society of the trenches. Then they pulled it out. They now have a simulated air raid shelter.)

Because war was put into a social context, some of the communist war museums could seem more intelligent. The best was probably the Military Museum in Belgrade, in its early sections. I remember one object in particular. Behind us were the weapons and maps of the Battle of Kosovo (the famous Turkish victory in 1389 over a Serbian-led alliance of Serbs, Albanians, Croats, Bulgarians and Hungarians). Ahead were the flags and uniforms of the uprising against the Turks (1804–13) of Kara George, a pig dealer whose son was to found one of the two rival Serbian dynasties. The notable object was a *gusle*, a simple one-stringed instrument, presented as a reminder of the *hajduks*, the brigands of the mountains who provided the only continuing (if sporadic) Serbian resistance against the Turks. Serbian minstrels used the *gusle* as background noise to ballads that they chanted during the four and a half centuries of Turkish rule: ballads that recalled the heroic and melancholic past as a remembered way of being Serbian. It was there as a general reminder of the indomitability of the kind of folk memory that could lead the people on to the definitions of 19th century nationalism, and of songs that encapsulated wisdom for those who did the fighting (including the barbarities of the 1940s and the 1990s).

* * *

The 1939–45 war produced a new kind of museum, the Resistance Museum, and a new kind of historic site, the concentration camp. Neither of them lent itself to carnival—but both were also restricted in what they 'told'.

In resistance museums, concealed radio transmitters, maps of escape routes, execution posts, microdots or air-drop containers are reminders of a resistance movement *as a society*—but this society is a closed one of villains (collaborators and Nazis) and heroes, with everyone else left out. The emphasis on equipment can be a temptation, after leaving the museum, to remember most of all the cleverness of the chess sets with false bottoms. In the Danish Resistance Museum, Copenhagen, the theme could have been the daring of a government that, under the guise of co-operation, itself provided the main resistance by political manoeuvring with the Germans. But that doesn't provide exhibits as good as radio transmitters concealed in fishing floats.

What the resistance museums can do is project horror. They all have an authentically reconstructed Gestapo interrogation room, with the crude table, the naked lightbulb, the photograph of Hitler on the bare wall, the whips and clubs. Normally, military museums don't even try to convey the sufferings of war.

Horror is the specialty of concentration camps (which go beyond nationalism, apart from the failed nationalism of those who devised them).* But, as illuminating tourist spectacles of horror, they may fail because they become a strange thing that happened in the past. To save Auschwitz from becoming yet another tourists' chamber-of-horrors, in which from a time-car one might experience the genuine sights, sounds and smells of a concentration camp, its curators found they had to instruct visitors about the actuality of the Nazis. Self-congratulation that the present is better than an aberrant past can save one from seeing the camps as a symbol of one part of the general human potential. Overall, in various ways, 40–50 million people were killed in the Hitler-Stalin period.

---

* **THE NATIONALISM OF HORROR.** There is a kind of nationalism at Yad Vashem, the huge stone hall honouring the Jewish victims of the Nazis in Jerusalem, in that the Holocaust was part of the founding of Israel as a political entity. But there is no nationalism about the tourism of the concentration camps themselves—except perhaps for the dispute between Poles and Jews as to who were the martyrs of Auschwitz. Auschwitz, as a death camp, was created as part of the plan to kill off the Polish intelligentsia, 250,000 of whom died there. Later, it was used as the largest single element in the Nazi's Final Solution, to which it eventually became so symbolically essential that there were protests when, in 1990, after Polish historians studied transport documents only recently made public, the estimated number of Auschwitz deaths was lowered from four million to one–two million. Some Jewish groups then protested against the rewording of inscriptions on memorial plaques. Auschwitz gets about 750,000 visitors a year.

23.

THE CIVILISATION PACKET

◆ ◆ ◆

STAKING OUT THE PAST

Several months after we had been to Chichén Itzá, I was looking over a book of essays about people whose collections (14th century Chinese porcelain, 18th century Limoges enamels, 19th century West African artifacts, and so on) had gone to the British Museum. I noticed a photograph of the 'Nunnery' at Chichén Itzá as it was when it was found in 1889, up to its ears in earth and rubble, palms and shrubs sprouting from its top. The photograph was one of several illustrating an essay on 'Alfred Maudslay and the discovery of the Maya'. (It seems not to have been noticed by whoever wrote this heading that the Maya themselves are still there—what were 'discovered' were the material remains of earlier Maya society.)

Maudslay was one of the archaeologist-entrepreneurs who brought the Maya ruins into the world of scholarship (and later, without knowing it, the tourist business). Heir to an engineering firm that was a flourishing product of the industrial revolution but went broke during his lifetime, he developed an obsession with Mayan 'lost cities' in 1880, after his first encounter with some ruins. For 11 years he regularly returned to a variety of tropical fevers and 'ruined cities' whose cleaning-up he organised—he was at Chichén Itzá for five months in 1889. As well as taking back to the British Museum some sculptures (sawn off their stone bases, with the approval of the Mexican government), he also made a number of plaster casts for the museum. On each expedition he brought out a skilled moulder, and transported by mule-train several tons of plaster and a special kind of Spanish paper made for packing oranges, but also excellent for producing *papier maché* moulds. When the casts arrived in London, Maudslay paid three artists to make drawings of inscriptions and designs as illustrations for a six-volume work he was preparing, that would later provide a basis for the whole field of Maya scholarship.

As a part of their new, nationalist confidence, the grand museums in London, Paris, Berlin, New York and elsewhere were becoming warehouses and showcases of antiquities, but almost any general museum was expected to have at least a few ancient things and, when old buildings were dug out of the ground, or out of surrounding vegetation or rubble, they could provide some of the most inspirational places in sightseeing. Whole touring businesses are still built around prestigious and evocative ruins. Throughout the 19th century, when British, French, German and other Western European and United States scholars, dilettantes and adventurers became archaeologists, they joined the European explorers and anthropologists in inventing new legends of 'discovery' and new processes of naming. Antiquity became another field for staking national and imperial claims.

As they dug things up and put some of them together again, in Greece and Egypt, and then in West Asia, India, China, South-east Asia and parts of the Americas, what they were discovering and giving names to was a large part of the Ozymandias past, of which they were now, in effect, claiming the inheritance. They were the ones who directed the digging and did the grading. They were the ones who decided what the hierarchies of that past were. They were engaged in a great act of creation: they were putting together the principal legend of 'world civilisation', as important to parts of the tourist experience as it was to the editors of *Cassell's Children's Book of Knowledge*.

* * *

Staking out the past could have an effect of cultural vertigo on local people. Interest in classical Greek archaeology had already begun when the kingdom of Greece was inaugurated in 1833 (importing as its king Prince Otto of Bavaria), after the long and intermittent uprising against the Ottoman Empire, but it was an interest of foreigners. Some of the Greek leaders were inspired by Western European classicism, but, for most Greeks, to be Greek was to be Orthodox in religion, Byzantine in art, and Balkan in political imagination. A neo-classical revival style ('Ottonian') was devised for new public buildings in Athens (a Turkish garrison town of only a few thousand before it became the capital), but the driving aspiration from the past was the Byzantine, not the classical. To Greeks impelled by 'the Great Idea' of a Greek Empire that would replace the Ottoman Empire, the geographical centre of being Greek was not the provincial settlement of Athens but 'The City'—Constantinople itself. Even now, the Greece of the tourist imagination is not the Greece of the Greek imagination—that is one reason why the Greek Church formulated a prayer to Christ to save Greeks from tourists.

A similar dissociation between a country idealised as a land of antiquity and the way its own people now see themselves occurred in Egypt. The word 'Egyptology' came into use in the 1850s when the Nile Valley had become the second centre of imperial archaeology, a process begun 50 years before when Bonaparte's expedition to Egypt opened up the first search for a 'lost civilisation'. Before Bonaparte, scarcely anyone cared about Egyptian antiquity. By the end of the century most Egyptians still did not know about it, but Europeans had produced a great dispersal of mummies, sarcophagi, obelisks and statues and other Egyptian things throughout the world's museums, and they had constructed an ancient history for Egypt. Even so, most of Egypt's extensive holdings in world civilisation remained in Egypt itself, perhaps because they were too heavy to carry away (although they lost almost all of their obelisks: only six Egyptian obelisks are left in Egypt—there are 13 in Rome alone). And, in some cases, the Europeans were so ravenous that a papyrus sheet or a stone monument would be divided among several institutions.

The Pyramids, all that had survived of the Seven Wonders of the World (as *Cassell's Children's Book of Knowledge* told me), had become the greatest of all icons of exotic tourism and by the beginning of the 20th century marvels were already being assembled in the Museum of Antiquities in Cairo. Egyptian élites who were not narrowly Islamic, and most of the guides, might later come to see Egypt as central to the legend of world civilisation, but the pharaonic monuments had already long been central to Egyptian tourism. By the 1890s Thomas Cook was the largest single employer of labour in Egypt, with a specialty in cruises down the Nile—24 steamers, their decks dusted with ostrich feathers and their passengers even more protected from the natives (except those who were silent servants in spotless white robes) than travellers on the Palace-on-Wheels.

Greece has beaches, idyllic islands, *souvlaki*, the *bouzouki* and the *taverna* in the tourist showcase, as well as antiquities, but in Egypt the emphasis is almost entirely on the old stones of the pharaohs. Most of present Egypt might as well not be there. Reminders of a past Egypt that has some relation to its present—the material relics of Arab civilisation—have been left to decay: 'Islamic Cairo' is lucky to get half a day on a four-day tour. Masterpieces of Islamic architecture are buckling and drowning from rising damp; the whole unique medieval quarter is rotting and crumbling. And parts of the ancient fortress Coptic quarter, weakened by rising water and broken-down sewage, may collapse back into its Roman foundations.

After French and British archaeologists moved into Mesopotamia and began their treasure hunts, Egyptian, Greek and Roman trophies in the Louvre and the British Museum were joined by winged bulls with human heads, baked clay tablets with cuneiform writing, lions shot by kings, chariots of archers with curled beards—and the kinds of colossal figures that led the visitors to the Louvre in Zola's *L'Assommoir* to conclude that stone carving is 'a damn sight better done these days' than it was by the Assyrians. United States and German teams entered the hunt. The Pergamon Museum, Berlin, produced one of the greatest archaeological reconstructions in captivity from the ruins of Babylon—Nebuchadnezzar II's Ishtar Gate, the ceremonial entry gate into Babylon, and the Processional Way that it led into produced a study in power in the fresh blues and yellows of tiles glazed 2500 thousand years ago.

The big names in 'world civilisation' had become Babylon, Assyria, Egypt, Greece and Rome—and Europe, as civilisation's heir. This is the civilisation packet that a tourist is offered in an antiquities museum, or a general museum of art. The legend of world civilisation is that it arose in Mesopotamia and then passed from Egypt to Europe. The British Museum, with sponsorship by Esso, sent a wonderful collection of treasures to Australia in 1990, from West Asia, Egypt, Greece and Rome. It was called, simply, 'Civilisation'. (The catalogue was able to say: 'Esso Presents Civilisation'.)

It was not that European archaeologists weren't also digging things out of India and China. They were in charge of archaeology there, and it was they who were deciding which monuments mattered. India was given a new (and useful) kind of history for which evidence was found in coins and inscriptions, in lost cities and caves—evidence of a different kind from that in the great Hindu narratives. Large parts of the Buddhist past of India, forgotten for centuries, were found (some by accident—the Ajanta caves, for example, by a British hunting party) and then resuscitated. British scholarship established the enormous extent of Asoka's empire in the 2nd century BC (thereby allowing later Hindu appeals to a continuing tradition of Hindu government). And, although of the cradles of civilisation China has the longest and most systematised written history, it was the European archaeologists who first dug out the bronzes and jades and raided the tombs.

But China was rated, along with India, as not belonging to the grand classical progress that marched onward from Mesopotamia to the Massachusetts State House, Boston, with its Corinthian portico, Doric hall, Greek pediment and Roman dome. There was nothing from India and China in the 1990 'Civilisation' show in Australia.

PERILS OF 'THE CLASSICAL'

The Roman Empire and the Greek ideal still rest heavily on the Western tourist imagination. Apart from those that were Gothic, grand buildings in Europe and North America have never been far from various versions of 'the classical'. (Even the free market theories of the 1980s were 'neo-classical'.) Not only the tourism of fascist relics such as the amphitheatre of the Nuremberg Rallies or the Foro Italico in Rome draws on the classical—Europe has normally used classical forms when it wanted to erect monuments of celebration, triumph and power.

The Babylonian Ishtar Gate and Processional Way were only

preliminaries to the prize attraction of the Pergamon Museum. Its centrepiece provides one of the most surreal moments of the archaeological experience. In a cavernous central hall, under a glass roof, are displayed the resurrected remains of one of the temple wonders of the ancient Greeks. Twenty-eight reconstructed steps, 20 metres wide, lead to the restored friezes and great colonnaded altar. The story of putting this temple together again is one of the legends of archaeology.

In the 1860s, a German engineer building roads for the Turkish government near Pergamon noticed remains of marble reliefs. They had obviously been carved for a temple, but had been used to make part of a fortress wall that the Byzantines had built 800 years earlier as a protection against the Muslims. The Berlin museums sent out an excavation team, and in the Pergamon acropolis it unearthed remains of the rest of the altar building from which the friezes had been stripped, and also thousands of fragments of other friezes. It took 20 years before the last decisions were made about how the fragments should be assembled in Berlin, and even then some scholars weren't convinced they had been put together properly. When the frieze slabs were taken out of safe storage after the second world war, some pieces were put back differently. There is still dispute as to where everything should go.

Nineteenth century German élites were ready to take such trouble because they knew *they* were the true successors of the ancient Greeks, and ready to carry on their civilising mission. The British already knew that *they* were the heirs of the Greeks, a process that had started at the beginning of the 19th century when Lord Elgin interpreted his permit from the Turks to send a party to Athens and 'take away any pieces of stone with old inscriptions of figures thereon' as permission to put into packing cases all that could be moved from the Parthenon. After they were moved to the British Museum in 1816, and somewhere had been found to put them (for a time they were kept in a shed in the garden), there began that rite of standing in the presence of a marble statue from classical Greece and thus of standing in the inner presence of civilisation—although, previously, Greek originals had been almost unknown in Western Europe and were usually seen as of second rank compared with Roman copies.

CRADLES OF HISTORY

With nations liberated from colonial rule, the time came for their own archaeologists to stake claims for a place in world civilisation. Some of these have been added to the tourist trails.

Indian scholars took over when the British left and they followed up the 'discovery' of Asoka (now the name of India's largest hotel chain) by giving priority to other rulers who tried to unite India, and consolidating evidence of the general lustre of their empires. But the largest claim was the creation of the Indus Valley as a cradle of civilisation equal to China, and ahead of Europe—an important matter in the ranking of nations. The two Bronze Age cities unearthed at Harappa and Mohenjo Daro, which survived for somewhere between 500 and 1000 years, were models of geometric town planning—orderly streets and avenues, and brick houses with baths, lavatories, garbage chutes and brick drains. More than 100 other sites of towns and villages from the same civilisation have been found. New ones are still being uncovered. They are not on tourist agendas (in fact they are in what is now Pakistan) and there are no queues lining up to look at the sculptures, inscribed seals, ceramics, bronzes and jewellery that came into Indian museums from these excavation sites. But to be equal to China and ahead of Europe is something, even if the proof is now in Pakistan.

In China, having taken its archaeology over from the foreigners, and with its soil richer than any other in tombs and treasure, Chinese archaeologists continue to demonstrate that, more often than not, China was there first. Apart from objects in museums, the discovery in the 1970s at Xi'an of the 6000 terracotta warriors, that have guarded the tomb of the Emperor Qin Shi Huangdi for more than 2000 years, placed Xi'an in the top 10 of tourist agendas of archaeological sites—and reflected the bigness of China's historical presence: Xi'an for many years had been the world's largest city.

Thailand, not having had a colonial period, took charge of its own past. King Mongkut, in the middle of the 19th century, put together a collection of bits and pieces in the 18th century European 'curiosities' manner, and encouraged the setting up of regional storehouses that later became museums. The National Museum in Bangkok is a Thai, not a Western, creation. To it is appended a Hall of Thai History, with dioramas and paintings of heroic scenes leading up to the modernity of the silver spades used to inaugurate new railways, but with an emphasis also on establishing Thai claims in prehistory, as opposed to the Burmese, the Khmer, the Lao, and, most sensationally, the Chinese. This claim came when the Thais found evidence at Ban Chiang of a well-developed, extensive and long-enduring bronze and iron culture. What became 'Ban Chiang's Lost Bronze Age' was shown as preceding even China's Bronze Age. At least a few hundred Thais are dreaming that Thailand was a cradle of Chinese civilisation.

* * *

In Israel, archaeology became an obsession, as if the digging and burrowing would confirm the God-given right of Israelis to be there.

The Islamic states also made claims to history through archaeology, but for a while some were uncertain about how much of the pre-Islamic past (and therefore of 'world civilisation') they wanted for their own territories. In the secular Iran of the shahs, there were no doubts: they claimed several millennia of Persian civilisation, and archaeology was used to support the extravaganza of the 2500th anniversary celebrations of the founding of the Persian Empire, with half the remaining things at Persepolis being transported to Teheran, where they were easier to look at. But to begin with, the pan-Arab movement was concerned that claiming the inheritance of Egypt and Mesopotamia might defeat their more universal aims. Nationalism won.

After Syria became independent, its 1950 constitution declared that its antiquities were a matter of national importance. Museums were created to display evidence of Mesopotamian pre-eminence. In Iraq, the Baath regime defended its boundaries and unity, with claims to Mesopotamia: archaeologists unearthed Assyrian treasures of gold and jewels, sometimes hundreds of pieces at a time, in their digging and sifting at Nimrud, military capital of the Assyrian empire. But it was Babylon that the regime wanted to be heir to. In support, the techniques of Disneyland were added to those of archaeology— under Saddam Hussein a somewhat miniaturised replica of parts of ancient Babylon was constructed, with every fourth brick saying 'During the period of Saddam Hussein we constructed the remains of this city': in the palace of Nebuchadnezzar, built in the 6th century BC, only every hundredth brick carried the name of Nebuchadnezzar.

The Dutch began restoring Borobudur and established the

archaeological collection in Batavia, but Indonesian élites can now record the presence of powerful dynasties of evident cultural vitality in Java when Europe was coming out of the Dark Ages. The French began restoring the ruins at Angkor and established a Khmer Museum in Phnom Penh, but Cambodians could produce Angkor as evidence of ancient prepotency—before they fell back into their own Dark Ages. It was the British who sorted out 'the ancient cities' of Sri Lanka, ruins of several former capitals in the dry plains north of the hill country. These are still in the guidebooks as evidence of past indigenous power, even if the closest to them that most tourists are likely to get is to Kandy, in the hill country, where there is a 'fabulous' temple containing the Lord Buddha's most famous tooth.

As with the Mayan ruins, relics from the prolific Inca, Aztec and other archaeological sites of central America, Peru and Mexico are now used to evoke lost empires—although, except for Mexico, archaeological reconstruction in Latin America has been almost abandoned and some sites will soon not be worth having. In Mexico the use of themes, styles and *motifs* by modern artists, especially muralists, has provided a sense of continuity and new national meaning. Mexico City's Museo Nacional de Antropologia offers one of the world's most striking expositions of past civilisations—but, as part of the struggle for centrality in the civilisation story, its layout makes the Aztec the central civilisation in the Mexican past. The Mongolian government is using archaeologists in the search for the tomb of Mongolia's greatest son. In the meantime, his name was remembered in Ulan Bator with the opening in 1991 of the Hotel Genghis Khan. In 1991 there came good news for Philistines: excavations in Israel showed that the Philistines were of high cultural achievement.

In Black Africa a past civilisation is a valuable national acquisition. The word 'zimbabwe' comes from the Shona for 'large stone house'. There are a number of ruined zimbabwes, but Zimbabwe got its name from by far the greatest of these—'Great Zimbabwe', a labyrinth of high granite walls, small walls and enclosures and an elaborately fortified hilltop that spreads over nearly 40 hectares and makes up what is probably the largest ancient stone ruin in Africa. The ruins were found by a European hunting in thick bush in 1868, written up in 1872 and then looted and partly wrecked by treasure seekers—and further wrecked in a different style by European restorers.

Since it seemed ridiculous at the time to suggest that this stone complex had been built by Africans, Europeans produced several theories, of which the most ingenious was that it was the ancient Ophir of King Solomon and the most usual that it was a relic of a lost civilisation. (Great Zimbabwe was the inspiration for Rider Haggard's Dead City in *She*.) Africans won a political victory when archaeologists, dating Great Zimbabwe's beginning in the 11th century and its end in the 15th century, associated it with powerful African rulers who benefited from controlling the gold-trading routes. This symbolic connection with past power (and past techniques of dry stone-walling) was prestigious enough to give a new name when white-controlled Rhodesia came to an end. The seven carved soapstone birds found in Great Zimbabwe provided the new nation's national symbol—and the most popular *motif* in souvenirs at the Victoria Falls Hotel.

CIVILISATION IN AN AFTERNOON

Some museums in Western and Central Europe contain exhibits labelled 'Late Iron Age', or 'La Tène Epoch', although these are not attractive terms to tourists, and, without imaginative display, the things themselves could seem a bit dull—except where, among the weapons and tools, there might be magnificent gold jewellery, elegant bronze tableware, aristocratic weaponry or chariot trappings. These artifacts were found in the graves of Celtic chieftains and there is nothing else like them in European prehistory. At the time that the Greeks, and then Romans, were spreading through the Mediterranean, the aristocratic civilisation of the Celts was dominant in Europe, and had been for 1000 years.

The Greeks and the Romans built in stone, and some of what they built lasted. The Celts built in wood and were conquered by the Romans. But that does not make them as insubstantial as they can now seem. From burial sites, from excavations in their hilltop citadels, and even from what the Romans said about them, it is possible to imagine an alternative European culture to the classical.

And it is possible to develop an infinite number of alternative views of 'world civilisation' to the one created so quickly in museums and tourist sites in the civilisation packet of the 19th century. An exemplary anecdote told by archaeologists is of a French resident-general in Tunisia who visited the site of Dougga (where a Roman forum is surrounded by a Byzantine wall) and complained that the wall was blocking the view of a temple. 'You ought to pull down the wall so that the temple can be seen better', he said to the director of antiquities. 'I'm going to pull down the temple so that we can see the wall better', was the reply. Now the Celts seem ready for a revival—in 1991 the Palazzo Grassi in Venice turned one rococo hall into an imitation forest of oaks, and another into a jeweller's workshop, as part of an exhibition called 'The Celts'. The exhibition presented the Celts as 'the first Europeans', and producers of 'the first, the greatest and the most illuminating ornamental art Europe has ever known'.

You can't pick up the story of civilisation just by walking around the British Museum for an afternoon, splendid as the experience may be. For one thing, they have expelled as 'ethnographic' the collections from Africa and the Americas, including the Mayan sculptures and casts that Maudslay gave to the museum. Of the remaining antiquities, the Greek, Roman, Egyptian and West Asian exhibits command most of the space and all the prime positions. Even if the museum had a more comprehensive sample of what has survived, the point is that these just happen to be things that did survive—because they were made of metal or stone. Yet the story of human civilisation is not a matter of the durability of artifacts.

Nor of 'art'. The archaeological rush in the 19th century had followed the belief of humanist collectors that the value of classical antiquities was as symbols of beauty, evoking a desirable set of values; it was this belief that was to give them, and then other art objects, the regenerative power of holy relics. Anything that didn't meet the requirement of beauty wasn't worth keeping. (The greatest destruction of Roman remains occurred during the renaissance, when the humanists were collecting what was seen as beautiful—they had no interest in the rest.) The collecting impulse became less destructively pure, but the basis of archaeology remained in ideas of classical beauty. For a large part of the period when the British Museum was forming its collection, an acceptable reason for collecting all these things was that, by precept, they would improve modern British fine arts. Charles Roach Smith, a London pharmacist (most of whose collection of 5000 objects came from builders' excavations), had to wait for years before the museum would buy what could seem 'merely a historical collection of objects'.

There were other strands developing in archaeology that went beyond beauty. When workmen first dug through the solidified mud that had petrified Herculaneum, and the volcanic rubble that had smothered Pompeii, they burrowed through roofs, frescoes and vaults, smashing anything in the way, looting the past for collector pieces to decorate the palace of the Spanish king of Naples. But a more careful approach to the excavations at Pompeii in the 19th century, and Herculaneum in the 20th, was to produce one of the marvels of the tourism of the past—a walk through ordinary life. In a way, the uncovering of the Darby Furnace and the setting up of Ironbridge were an extension of Pompeii. More pertinent than the Sphinx, whose meaning has crumbled even faster than its stone, was the accidental discovery (when a sewage system was being installed in 1991) of relics of an Old Kingdom town of about six square kilometres, buried beneath a shanty settlement near the Sphinx and Pyramids. From this we may be able to learn something of the people who put up sphinxes and pyramids.

When travelling, some of our greatest senses of wonder can come when we stand in the presence of a relic of the Ozymandias past. But experiencing this is not a way to know the past. To theorise about the past you need to have read books, in which the people who have thought about these old stones and pieces of metal tell us their conjectures.

There can be an instructive resonance if you stand in the presence of the Ishtar Gate in the Pergamon, or the Parthenon sculptures in the British Museum, or the Seated Scribe in the Louvre, but the most realistic echoes one can imagine are not the illusions of knowing Nebuchadnezzar's Babylon, or Periclean Athens, or the Egypt of the Old Kingdom. The past one can recall with a certain accuracy is the 19th century, at the time when museums were becoming part of the newly forming public cultures, open even to people from the Parisian underclass that Zola described in *L'Assommoir*. These exhibits were given modern meaning from a combination of intellectual curiosity, an itch to divide the world into categories, and the *élan* of a developing nationalism.

24. Interlude:

SHOWS WE SAW THAT SUMMER

♦ ♦ ♦

ASPECTS OF THE THEATRICAL

In seven months in the United States and Europe, I kept a journal of incidental observations, which I sent home every week to our daughter and son. Those that were on the shows we saw that summer, if taken together, provide a commentary on some of the tourism of the theatrical—if you extend the boundaries of what you mean by theatrical. They were written not long after we had sat on the floor at Petulu, watching the *Barong* gape and jiggle.

Los Angeles

Sustained by baroque concertos played in authentic period style on original instruments, we float above the palms and rooftops of Los Angeles until the freeway 'lands' our car on a university campus, where a professor of English literature is performing the last of a two-night stand as Mad King Ludwig of Bavaria.

The professor recites some of his own Baudelairean poems and then plays out his fantasies of the fantasy life of King Ludwig. In 18th century dress and wig, he projects handsome youth. Towards the end, he takes off his clothes and we confront a bulky, bald, 60-year-old professor in a white nightshirt.

At the party in the foyer, with cheap wine in plastic cups and sponge cakes decorated with arabesques of cream, the talk is about how we have watched one more scene in the professor's life performance.

Santa Fe

The words 'pueblo' and 'art' dominate the tourist ethos of Santa Fe. Narrow streets are lined by low, brown *adobe* houses bulging out in the Spanish Pueblo style. It is as if we have left the United States, but with all this brownness and lumpiness where have we arrived?

An arts festival is on, but instead of going to the opera, we drive 35 miles to the Cochiti Pueblo, to see a corn dance. We are about to watch a ritual, seen as earlier than art, whose manifest function was to get the gods to do something, but whose latent function (using the famous distinction made by Robert K Merton in *Social Theory and Social Structure*) was to help hold a tribe together. Although the corn dance is advertised as a tourist attraction in the *Albuquerque Herald*, no-one at our hotel knows what it is the gods are being asked to do. Reflecting that we are about to be present at a reminder of pre-'art', at the end of our 55 kilometre drive we find stacks of parked cars.

We walk down a dirt road, towards sounds of chanting and the beating of a drum, into a dusty space that looks like a neglected parade ground. Its boundaries are marked out by tourists, sitting on chairs. Men and women wearing animal skins are shuffling off while 30 or so men remain in the dusty space, standing by. They are wearing trousers and shirts.

This is what happens. A few minutes later, new dancers come out in two long lines, men and women interspersed, stamping and shuffling. The men, stripped to the waist with their torsos painted red, shake rattles. The women swish leaves. The standby group becomes a choir, moving and stamping. The dancers break and reform, shuffling around in a different way. This group goes off.

Another group comes on. We leave. We don't know what we have seen.

The next morning, the *Albuquerque Herald* reports that some of the dancers were local accountants and dentists. Has latent function become manifest, with the Cochiti knowingly dancing not for corn but to go on being Cochiti?

St Louis

I stay in our room in an airport hotel, writing, for three days. When I pull aside the gauze curtains from the grandiose picture window I see a performance (pulling aside the curtain and framing the scene in a window makes it one): two levels of freeways with 'steady streams' of cars and three airport runways with 'steady streams' of aircraft, rising and falling as hypnotically as one of those clockwork displays that department stores used to put in their windows.

At night we watch the telecast of the 1984 Democratic Convention, where anchormen murmur from glass eyries and, as if they were agents from outer space, interviewers on the floor look up at us from beneath their antennae. A favourite shot is to include both the speaker as part of the podium group, and a large image of the same speaker on one of the giant screens. This stamps it as television—real to the participants in this corn dance of thousands watched by millions. A variety of cameos show delegates laughing, crying, thinking, whispering, scratching, wearing funny hats. We are in the presence of the American people.

The pre-eminent television moment on the convention's first night is the keynote speech of Governor Cuomo, both emotional and rational, and presented with a delivery in which when you think he is going to pause—he doesn't, so that there is a sense of athletic excitement. His rhetorical achievement is that his speech means different things to different people. He delivers both conservative values and liberal values as part of a self-portrait of a statesman who has both heart and brain. Perhaps some of the Cochiti still believe that stamping their feet and shaking rattles will make crops grow, but at the Democratic Convention can anyone imagine the result will be affected by what is now happening? What matters is performance and declaration of values.

The next night is Jesse Jackson's. Like the opening performer in a *Topeng* dance acting out uncertainty, the anchormen work up our appetites. Having been confrontationist, will Jesse Jackson now become a man of consensus? There are interviews and flashbacks to the wilder side of Jesse Jackson. An anchorman says: "Go and get your grandmothers and your children and tell them to listen to this. Tell them *history is about to be made.*"

When Jackson speaks, yes, indeed, consensus. Well that was a surprise. 'There is a proper season for everything: there is a time to compete and a time to co-operate.' There is a solemn act of absolution when he confesses he was in error in his statements about the Jews. He reaches a distinctive core of the Christian culture: have pity on us, miserable sinners. The cameras show tear-soaked cheeks. After all the cheering, an African-American sings a spiritual. The delegates sway. They hold hands.

The first main event on the last night is Gary Hart's speech. Its engrossing unreality is brought out by the television treatment of the ovation. It goes on remorselessly, but they have cut out the convention noises and are playing only Hart theme music. As if in a dream, his delegates shout, chant and wave their banners, but no sound comes from their mouths. Hart signals co-operation and, to *Chariots of Fire* music, goes out among his own people. When the New Jersey result is announced and Mondale is ceremonially pronounced the winner, the floor is taken over with Mondale-blue banners, Mondale-blue beach balls, Mondale-blue puppets, laughing Mondale people. The compassionate camera closes in on the tear-stained cheeks of Gary Hart supporters. From the podium, Hart opens out his arms and calls for a unanimous vote. Then some soft rock. The way the camera plays it, all the delegates are now jigging around in solo dances. Jackson blesses Mondale with the will of the people and the will of God. Then, imagine this! A sound-and-light show! Music from the *1812 Overture* with strobe lighting playing over the delegates, and as the *1812 Overture* crashes on—fireworks!

Washington

When we go to a show at the Kennedy Performing Arts Center, the building itself—its very presence and the assertions it makes about Washington—can seem so much part of the performance that I find myself worrying about how small the audience is, as if this were an amateur performance in a country town.

The *Biograph*, a re-run cinema, is just up the street from where we are staying. At the *Biograph* they give big double helpings: the first program we see is a double feature of *Hair* and *Woodstock*, the second a double bill of *La Traviata* and *The Magic Flute*. These reasoned juxtapositions—including a formidable combination of two non-dialogue movies, *Le Bal* and *Koyaanisquatsi*—force us to make comparisons, because we have been brought up like that. We are attending a hidden seminar that makes all of us conventional critics. I am back where I was in high school literature exams: *compare and contrast*.

* * *

The greatest show in town might appear to be Congress, but when we go to the Capitol there are fewer than 10 members in the House of Representatives, and, in the Senate, only Daniel Patrick Moynihan (although that should be enough) and one other. The places to go are the neo-classical edifices where the Committees meet. We walk along a drab corridor to a Committee Room with a high ceiling and wooden panelling. Everything is familiar—members of the Committee seated on a wide, high dais; below them, confronted, the witnesses. All the seats are taken. All the standing space is filled—we are in the doorway. We do not know which Committee this is or, because of the corridor noise outside, what is being said. But it is that thoroughly familiar enactment, a *Committee hearing*. It is like going to a performance in a Balinese village of an extract from the *Ramayana*.

* * *

Each day, one of the Smithsonian museums provides a setting for a lunchtime chamber music performance. When a trio performs in the Hall of Musical Instruments in the Museum of American History, there is an epiphany of musicality. The combination of flute, classical guitar and cello is so odd that the trio had to make new arrangements for everything they play and we are told about each piece in turn. The program is arranged didactically. They tell us about that, too—what is meant by 'renaissance', 'baroque', 'classical', 'romantic', 'modern', 'jazz', a pocket museum of music—the most sensible attempt I have heard to persuade people to listen to the unfamiliar.

SHOWS WE SAW THAT SUMMER

* * *

The last two shows we see in Washington:

The FBI Show. The tour of the FBI Building ends in the basement. The performance begins when a very wide curtain rolls back to reveal an expanse of bulletproof glass, on the other side of which is a shooting range. A man walks onto this glassed-in stage, introduces himself as an FBI agent and explains that he is going to fire at a dummy. He takes out a revolver and silently pumps lead. The dummy is backlit so that we can admire the neat, accurately placed holes. Then the man picks up a tommy gun, fires single shots at first, then, in a couple of bursts, sprays the dummy with bullets. The dummy is again backlit. It is riddled symmetrically. The curtain slides close, covering the wall of bulletproof glass. We have seen a morality play signifying the marriage of technology and individualism.

The Star Spangled Banner Show. In the National Museum of American History are the remains of the colossal United States flag that inspired the writing of *The Star Spangled Banner*. This precious relic has been scientifically preserved by a conservation project financed by a grant from Sears Roebuck. To protect it from the light the flag is concealed behind a large painted curtain, but once an hour it is displayed to the people. This ceremony begins with turning on a floodlight and playing a taped roll of drums. The curtain slowly descends. We hear a recording of a 19th century version of the song. The sacred relic is briefly, like the Holy Mantle of the Prophet, fully revealed. The curtain slowly ascends to a recording of a modern version of the song. Nearby is the hall displaying the Gowns of the First Ladies.

New York

The arts and entertainment industries have done so much stereotyping of New York, for so long, that one can frame almost any scene in New York as if it were on stage and then find it a theatrical cliché. When I was first in New York, in the 1950s, my own stagings seemed 'pure Hollywood' in stereotype, or were based on 1940s and 1950s fiction. Now, in the 1980s, they seem pure *Doonesbury* and, for crowd scenes, early *Hill Street Blues*: in the window of a West Village shop we see a display of 'Games for Gays'—Gay Monopoly, Gay Trivial Pursuit. Elizabeth takes us to what purports to be a genuine Ukrainian restaurant in the East Village, but proves to be a genuine New York diner, filled with punks, graffiti artists, preppies, yuppies, hippies, transvestites, gays and lesbians. The police, we are told, cleared the area by moving through every night like a bulldozer, arresting dozens of junkies until the junkies decided to go somewhere else.

When I visit 'the Tombs', the Criminal Courts Building—an art deco fortress—every one of the accused is dressed to give the worst possible impression. Each case provides a scene in which the prisoner is stood up in front of a judge, while court officials and attorneys speak to each other and the judge so softly that one can watch the lip movements but not hear anything.

I take my notebook and pencil to the New York County Court House, a formidable Roman temple in Corinthian style, where I watch a trial that is, for a while, like the kind of thing I was brought up on in movies. The cross-examiner moves from his table to the box, asks jeering questions, then turns his back (playing scorn) and strides restlessly around the court room, shouting.

"Is it your opinion that this was done?"
"He was sitting there . . ."
"I said, is it your opinion that this was done?"
"But I tell you he was sitting there . . ."
(*Crushingly*) "Do you know what 'opinion' means?"
"No, I don't."

* * *

Even the way we use the subway is more *Doonesbury* than *Daily News*. Although I was first in New York 30 years ago, this is the first time I have seen any reason for taking the subway. In the 1980s it is now the time to make this statement of optimism for the future of New York. We pass a monumental pile of garbage on the pavement and descend the iron stairs, buy a stack of tokens, and pass through the gate as if we are passing through a time-machine into 'Contemporary History'. The scene is as described in all the newspaper articles—rundown, walls smothered in graffiti. Inside and out, the rattling train is covered with graffiti—garish, light-hearted, an amusing thing that has happened to the New York subway.

The stereotype of threat develops when we are sitting inside one of these carnival carriages. A man in some kind of uniform, standing at one end, is armed. One of the passengers is reading a *Daily News* story of a woman cop shot dead while trying to make a subway arrest. A madman jostles me and thrusts something at me.

Then the scene adopts the familiarity of the 'satirical'. What has been thrust at me is a leaflet, advertising a fundamentalist religious event. I throw it on the floor. A woman shouts with New York ferocity. (Is this the one who will shoot me?) She is an environmentalist. She is attacking me for throwing paper onto the floor of a subway train. I am polluting the environment of the New York subway.

Not a 'performance' in itself, but now that I am turning it into a traveller's tale it will become one.

* * *

In a fortnight we have gone to seven shows, five of them museum theatre and two of these 'new interpretations'.

The first of the new interpretations is at the Dance Theater of Harlem, where we see a production of *Giselle* that is set not in Russia but in antebellum United States, and, what is more, in a Louisiana freed-slave society. Mary McCarthy once said that novels can bring you the news: this *Giselle* has brought me the news about antebellum freed slave societies.

However, I don't learn much the next night at the New York City Opera Company's production of *Carmen* at the Lincoln Center. *Carmen* was the first opera I saw—when I was eight or nine I was taken to an Italian production touring Australia, and for years afterwards we used to sing along with *Carmen* around the pianola. At the Lincoln Center *Carmen* is presented as an episode in the 1930s Spanish Civil War, and when I woke up the next morning it seemed that of all the re-presentations of *Carmen* I have seen, this was the only one that was quite silly—a reminder that you do not necessarily know what effect a show has had on you until you've slept on it. The Civil War intrusion was not only a setting: they had written in a whole sub-theme, based on 'the resistance' and *mimed* throughout so obtrusively that this continuing interruption turned one of the successful 'realist' operas into something that is no longer credible.

Malraux was correct when, in *Antimemoirs*, he described a cultural heritage as a 'whole body of resurrections'. By maintaining the art of the past we re-create it. But why is it that in the theatre, in ballet, opera and drama, ever since *Hamlet* was first played in modern dress (although, of course, it was played in the modern dress of the time when Shakespeare first put it on), the inauthenticity of a new production can be part of its merit, while in listening to early music we now demand an entirely new kind of music called 'authentic' sound, procured on replica instruments, in a period style that is only a guess, by recording segments separately, and then editing them together in a studio where engineers produce a volume unimaginable in the rooms or small halls where the piece was first performed? And with a result that could then be played on an authentic early 1980s car transistor as we floated above the palms and rooftops of Los Angeles. An 'authentic' production is as contrived as a 'new presentation'.

At the Metropolitan Opera a well done, routine performance of *Eugene Onegin* was a reminder that the knowledgeable members of the audience for museum theatre in New York can be there for similar reasons as the audience of villagers for a performance of a favourite piece in Petulu in Bali. (Even more so when you watch a conventional production of the ballet *Eugene Onegin*—the ballet of the opera of the book.) You know what's going to happen. It is a question of how well it is going to be done—except that in Bali everyone is knowledgeable.

In any case, 'we have been to the Met'. The very act of going to the theatre makes a declaration about oneself, and about theatricality. *This is opera at the Met* says one thing. *This is opera by the New York City Opera Company* says something different.

* * *

As well as *A night at the Met* we have another kind of museum theatre experience—*A show on Broadway* (two of them). We see a Michael Frayn play that turns out to be a farce from the London West End—in a traditional (1920s) vintage Broadway theatre, that might equally well be a traditional (1900s) vintage West End theatre, packed out and with everyone laughing except me. A couple of nights later we see something called *Hurly Burly*, equally packed out. It has reached Broadway in two moves, appearing first in a small theatre in Chicago (now seen as replacing San Francisco in this function), then a fringe theatre in New York. When the characters say 'fuck', it seems different in this theatre from saying it in the small theatre in

Chicago, or the fringe theatre in New York. Being a New York 'hit' makes new tests of *Hurly Burly*.

* * *

Off Broadway, Sam Shepard's *Fool for Love* seems more at home. It is a short piece set in a tenth-rate motel room and expressed partly in cursing and wall-slamming, but also fanciful. The declaration of the theatre itself is 'small'. It is one of a row of small theatres reconstructed out of what are said to have been porn cinemas, as part of an urban revitalisation scheme in 42nd Street, and is approached by passing through an area (three cops at every intersection) encrusted with the commercialisation of lust. ('STUD BURLESQUE!' 'TOPLESS!' 'BOTTOMLESS!')

* * *

Theme and place come together in one single parody when, on our second-last day in New York, we take Elizabeth to see *RapMaster Ronnie*—a song-and-dance satire written by Gary Trudeau. For us it is an emotional purging after months of watching the nightly television news comedies and corn dances. There is a difficulty: *RapMaster Ronnie* maintains the upbeat mood of the Reagan presidency with all its cheerful emptiness, so everybody is happy and laughing, even the character of the deadbeat sleeping in the subway who, to capture the spirit of the age, has moved upmarket and now sleeps under Park Avenue. It ends with Reagan running the economy as a bingo game. Everyone wins a prize.

RapMaster Ronnie is put on in a club in Greenwich Village so that performers and audience seem to come together, as part of what I heard one of the fundamentalist radio stations describe as 'the satanic force of liberal humanism'. Among the audience are some Woody Allen caricatures.

London

We have been to only two 'West End shows'—similar plays in similar theatres to those we experienced on Broadway—and at both we are surrounded by much the same kinds of United States tourists. It is two other productions that 'tell us the news'. For one we go to 'the *Royal Court* upstairs' (an act that in itself is its own kind of self-declaration) to see the Black Theatre Co-operative perform, before a packed house of 40, *Money to Live*, a piece about women and about West Indian life in Britain. The dialogue is loose, at times the acting sticks, and the ending is a mess, but this play by a 22-year-old West Indian woman, performed in front of 40 people, 'told' us more than the large, commercial productions.

The other play, *Six Men of Dorset*, tells the news, obliquely, about an imaginative construct now spoken of as 'Mrs Thatcher's Britain'. It is a revival of a social realist drama written 50 years ago for the centennial of the Tolpuddle martyrdoms, an heroic story in the development of trades unions, but it is reconceptualised, with a Brechtian sprinkling of 19th century working class songs, and split into tableaux that give it a simple morality-play significance. What makes it especially significant is that the national coal strike is on, and the miners are losing. There are fund-raisers for the miners in the foyer. The theatre company itself, a lively, radical group, has just had its government grant cut. As each song or tableau of early 19th century struggle is given late 20th century meaning, you can feel spasms of recognition from most of the audience. As with the corn dance, they are expressing their communality—although it is not clear what it is they expect the gods will do in response to the ritual act of sitting in this subsidised theatre with faith that reason will prevail.

* * *

Four more pieces of London museum theatre:

At the National Theatre we see a Feydeau farce, *A Little Hotel on the Side*, which we saw in Sydney some years ago. Why did I like this and dislike the Michael Frayn farce in New York? An ingenious answer comes from a useful piece of criticism in the program, which suggests that a large part of the pleasure in watching farce is seeing the bourgeois world dismantled, only to be put back as it was. Michael Frayn begins with a society and characters already in disintegration, and all that can be added are pratfalls, puns, breakages and, finally, for climax, the falling down of the scenery.

At the Colosseum we see the English National Opera's production of Richard Strauss's *Arabella*. The program notes for the first act are so confusing that instead of the notes illuminating the performance, the performance illuminates the notes. The words are sung in English but they might equally be Eskimoan. Should I return to the theatre and buy the libretto to find out what I enjoyed? That we are engaging in a *night at the opera* is emphasised by being official guests, a small play of its own as we are taken to the theatre in a limousine, given the best seats and, subsequently, dinner at a famous restaurant while the car driver waits outside, building up his overtime. When I wake up the next morning I am deeply ashamed of my ignorance of *Arabella*.

At the Barbican we watch a production of *Henry VIII*—a play not often seen, and, when produced, usually put on as a projection of courtly spectacle. This time it is done with visual bleakness and played out with clipboards, bits of committee business, and so forth, to provide a modern 'power game' perspective. Unlike use of the mime show for *Carmen*, this technique works. Half the point of moving a classic into contemporary dress is to draw attention to the contemporary.

When we go to a performance of *Imeneo*, the last opera that Handel wrote, we enjoy the music, but there is a puzzle: are the performers remaining 'faithful to the original' with their exaggerated gestures? There are a number of laughs at their excesses. Are they being authentic? Or are the performers saying: *Look, there are some absurdities, but if you listen to the music itself you can get a lot out of it?*

Amsterdam

Lunching on two excellent Chinese dishes, and sitting at a window that frames the street, we notice a young man walking along without his shirt. He takes off the rest of his clothes, pisses on them, and walks off naked (*left*) with a determined meaning that is not obvious. Oh well, we think, this is Amsterdam. The woman running the restaurant says she never thought she would see such things in Amsterdam.

After our lunch we go to the Mickery Theatre, where foreign plays, mainly English, are presented (thereby, it is said, helping to get some of them off the ground in their homelands). The atmosphere is the same as 'the *Royal Court* upstairs'. We go up much the same kind of stairs. What is intended as discussion becomes 'pure theatre'.

Richard Foreman, director of the New York Worcester group, plays the despair of the *avant-garde*—that all good theatre must fail, because of its essential impenetrability, the only choice being either such necessary failure or the failure of being co-opted into the system. (He says specifically that all traditional theatre should cease to exist, and adds despondently that the Worcester group is probably all that is left of the *avant-garde*.) A woman from *Village Voice* comes in with almost equal despair. That Richard Foreman is in Amsterdam, expenses paid, between appearances (for which he is also being paid) at Bordeaux and at Milan is discussed privately during the interval.

After the interval the audience turns on him. They change this into a drama of the generations. A young Dutchman says Foreman still believes in words, whereas in the Netherlands what matters now are not words but movement. A young Dutchwoman says these two New Yorkers sound like her parents, who are always talking nostalgically of the aspirations of the 60s. Another young Dutchman attacks the *Village Voice* woman for displaying the lack of faith of an older person. An American says the two lead performers represent the inadequacies of a United States now past its prime, and they know nothing about theatre in an enlivened Europe. An Italian says that, unlike Italy, the United States didn't even have terrorism in the 60s. Yes we did, says the *Village Voice* critic, who is then instructed in the difference between terrorism and random violence. Another Dutchman quotes the vitality of two shows he saw recently on Dutch television—one of Welsh folk performance and the other of Australian Aboriginal dance. The two New Yorkers maintain their monopoly on despair. I speak. The *Village Voice* woman dismisses me as concerned with 'agitprop' when I say how *Six Men of Dorset* and *Money to Live* at least told some news. I have been cast as an aging Dutch Stalinist with a strange accent.

* * *

I have never much liked the idea of classical ballet and I have had practically no experience of modern dance, but travel in foreign-language countries encourages interest in movement performance. In New York at the Dance Theater of Harlem, before *Giselle*, there were some pieces choreographed by Balanchine to Stravinsky music—'abstract', with nothing, as it were, but their own geometrical message. That seemed interesting. When we visit the Municipal Theatre in Amsterdam to see the National Ballet perform three pieces are we again watching modern dance? *Watching* is not the word: our seats offer a view of only half the stage, and there are no program notes. With hesitations, I imagine that I like what

I can see of the first piece (mainly abstract dance, to *gamelan* music) and the third (ostensibly about hotel guests, but also a ballet about ballet, a meta-ballet). Almost all of the middle piece is performed on the side of the stage we cannot see.

At the Amsterdam Theatre Institute we spend most of a morning watching yet another variation on the corn dance—some videotapes of movement theatre. The first piece, *The Square Dance*, uses bars of lights along with dancers, producing squares, rectangles and cubes but, as the dance becomes more complex, it abandons Euclidian geometry until, at the end, both dancers and lights return to squares. In the second, a group called GRIFT uses a slaughterhouse as background to horror sequences. Then we watch a solo dancer and drummer whose drums consist of microphones concealed in various parts of his clothes. After that—minimalist dancing, with a simple set and small varieties of movement. The young man who plays these and other videos for us is enthusiastic about 'inter-arts'— mime, dance, words, music, slides, video, all together in the one thing. What I like about movement theatre is that it has no plot.

Tourism can be a kind of cultural window-shopping in which one finds new things to try out.

* * *

We go to the Oude Kerk, to see a 'movement' show put on by BEWT, a group that has some relationship with GRIFT. We arrive early and walk past unintentional street shows in the red-light district surrounding the church. At the Oude Kerk the audience of 20 sits on a small grandstand. We wonder whether the single tone that has begun to sound is intended to begin the performance. It is. The sounds which come and go are either single or alternating notes, or sticks clicking. Performers walk, or run, in different parts of the church, with no concern for each other or for us. They stand still, in what at first seem individual studies in solitude. What they are making us do is *look at the church*. The group are making their act not out of themselves, but out of the space of the church and its wood and stone. The grandstand itself moves and stops, strategically, here and there. The individual performers move, and stand. Occasionally, a ball rolls then stops. At the end we know more about the church than if we had gone around it with a guidebook.

Rome

We go to a ballet performance at the Giulio Cesare, a large theatre designed to be unremarkable, where we watch, among other things, an authentic reconstruction of *Parade*. With music by Erik Satie, the Dada musician, a *bricoleur* and minimalist before his time, and a roll of credits that includes Cocteau, Massine, Picasso and Diaghilev, it is one of the monuments of modernism. *Parade* is a substantial museum piece, and apart from the Picasso designs, that is its only interest: it is a 'novelty' rather than a 'classic'. It is not rich in possibilities of re-interpretation to suit changing times. But now we know what *Parade* was like.

Our last opera for the season is *La Traviata*. I enjoy it as a series of tableaux, but when I wake up next morning and become the critic giving it a mark, it goes down a grade because these days opera, like other things, must be treated as drama but that information hasn't reached this part of Rome. One of the greatest delights in opera can now be one of those rare productions when the whole thing works. This judgment would puzzle them at Petulu, where the idea of *La Traviata* as a series of scenes would seem quite obvious. You could walk in and watch the scenes you liked, assess the performance, then walk out or talk through the rest.

* * *

We go to concerts. I agree with Nietzsche that music goes beyond rational understanding. So can dance (I have now discovered) and so can some of the visual arts. Listening and looking are different from talking and writing. We can *use* sights and sounds in criticisms of existence, but only in their own 'language'. When we appear to use them in the written language it is as metaphors, or literary co-relatives: they are saying something else. That would seem to put an end to criticism of the arts.

* * *

In Rome we have been listening to secular music played in small old churches. There may have been some relation between performance and place when the Martini Musical Society put on, in the church of San Marco, a program of concertos by the baroque composer to whose name it is dedicated: this church was restored in a sumptuous style in the 18th century. But dissonance began to appear with a strange little playalong by a guitarist-composer, in a church whose confidently severe style was juxtaposed against the informality and uncertainty of the performer.

The sense of juxtaposition became surreal in a concert put on by the Accademia Italiana di Musica Contemporanea in the church of Sant' Agnese in Agone, with the first half consisting of music by Schoenberg, Stravinsky and Berg, and the second of pieces by three Italian composers, each of whom took his bow after the clapping. In this ancient little church, thoroughly re-done in baroque style in the 17th century, each of the seven altars was floodlit and surrounded with so many ferns that we seemed to be in a temple of the arts constructed in a greenhouse.

Other than this, apart from a Rachmaninoff recital at the Concertgebouw, Amsterdam (*We are at the Concertgebouw*) and a mass sung by the Vienna Boys Choir in the Brompton Oratory, London (which became a concert hall), the settings of musical occasions don't seem to have impinged as they have on other kinds of performance. Perhaps this is because the circumstances in which one listens to recorded music have become so bizarre. I have heard songs of the Crusaders on the car radio on the way to a dinner party, and, in the middle of the night, have turned on the radio and heard a recital of the music of Tibetan stone bells.

Paris

We go to the Palais Chaillot to see an Argentinean performing group, Le Grupo Accion Instrumental, present *L'Empire Dadi*. The group's program notes say: 'We wish to abolish frontiers, in uniting all the elements of dramaturgy and the theatrical imagination: instrumental music, dance, song, slide-projection, image and sound'. Their technique is 'opera collage', developed in '*la simultaneité et l'intemporalité*', by which they mean different things happening at once, irrespective of normal considerations of time and space. 'Past and future mingle in a common present created by musical, visual and literary combinations.'

This particular opera collage, *L'Empire Dadi*, is inspired by the music and career of Erik Satie, whose nickname of 'Dadi' combined 'Satie', 'Dada' and 'Daddy'. It is a 'spectacle', learned and droll, ironic and sensitive, clown-like and serious. The first part has three kinds of action. In one, Satie, in Dada style, is at the piano performing a kind of simplified extension of himself. In another, musicians and comedians, along with singers dressed in rich pieces from the theatrical wardrobe, give a sense of the creation of music, both mystical and parodic. Then there are enactments of small family tales of Satie and his mother and father in a museum collection of theatrical styles. The opening scene has 'characters' from opera and high drama—most in silent agony, cast in roles for which they cannot find the tunes or the words. At times they groan; one woman sings. In the second part (the whole thing is over in one hour, forty minutes) Satie, in life 'un buffon derisoire' becomes jubilant clown, and there is a medley of 'spectacles', all cheerful. The overall impression is of the theatrical gone mad.

But it is not 'mad'; rather something well known to sociologists of knowledge: the frailty of coherence.

PART FIVE

♦ ♦ ♦

How to be a tourist

25.

BALI NOW—AND WHAT IT CAN TEACH THIRD WORLD BRITAIN, ETC

◆ ◆ ◆

HAS TOURISM SPOILT BALI?

Sanur has grown 20 times over since we were there on our family holiday in 1971. The Segara Village Hotel, which was a few bungalows around a courtyard, now seems like a small suburb and there has been a strip development of hotels, restaurants, pizzeria, bars, discos, art shops and souvenir boutiques.

Has tourism spoilt Bali? People have been asking that question for 60 years. Bali was already considered 'spoilt' when we were there. The answer to the question is—as these things go—no. Or, at least not yet.

It depends on what you mean. If Bali is expected to perpetuate forever all the ways of life that prevailed at the turn of the century, well then, yes, it is 'spoilt',* although not by tourism: it has television and schools and soccer fields; widows are no longer burnt. Yes, it is part of the international tourist industry, but, as Adrian Vickers points out, its economy depends less on tourism than many other communities of two and a half million, and its cultural tradition is stronger: 'Balinese own motorbikes and fax machines, while at the same time going to trance seances or obtaining holy water from Brahman high priests . . . The traditional and the modern in Bali are two aspects of a complex social system'. Vickers suggests that Balinese culture is strong *because* of tourism, not despite it . . . in a rough century, tourism has defined Balinese culture and it has defined Balinese identity within Indonesia.

Tourism in Bali is not seen just as a matter of making a fast rupiah. Governments in both Denpasar and Jakarta know tourists can kill the things they are supposed to love. They also know tourism can be a positive force. One result is that the Bali experience can teach something to those decaying cities in Europe and North America whose industries have been gutted, and whose controlling bodies turn to tourist exploitation of 'culture' as the gambler's last desperate throw.

There are absurdities in Balinese tourism, but it is the tourists who are absurd, and the Indonesians have an enclave policy that confines most of them.

People who want the resort holiday experience in Bali, untouched by contact with what goes on in the rest of the island, can now live in cultural quarantine—an enclave of luxury beach-resort hotels, including a Club Med, has been established at Nusa Dua in a dry, sparsely populated peninsula in the south-west. It is joined to the rest of the island by a coral isthmus which many of the quarantined tourists cross only once, in a half-day coach tour beginning with a *Barong* dance and ending with the Elephant's Cave. Apart from that interruption, tourists live in hotel palaces decorated with images reminiscent of traditional Balinese art, with visits from Balinese

---

* HAS DEMOCRACY SPOILT PRAGUE? After the departure of the communists from Czechoslovakia, I was ashamed to find myself wondering if Prague would now be 'spoilt'. We had the privilege of 'discovering' Prague, the most architecturally 'pure' of the capital cities of Europe, when the presence of the communist regime meant that the streets were relatively free of tourists.

BALI... AND THIRD WORLD BRITAIN

performers who draw on the repertoire of excerpts; there are plenty of postcards and souvenirs. The centre of life is likely to be found around a baroque swimming pool: tourists can imagine Bali as a luxury swimming pool set in the South Pacific.

Unplanned events in the 1960s at Kuta, just north of the isthmus, produced an earlier enclave whose visitors also did not much concern themselves with what went on in the rest of the island. In the 1930s Kuta, which had been a port and a metalsmith village, began to be re-defined, because of its surf as a *beach*; in the late 60s it also became a pilgrimage place for the laid-back. The original Kuta Beach Hotel has been followed by the spreading out, within a labyrinth of lanes between the beach and a fearsome main road, of several hundred home-stays and *losmen* (cheap and often pleasant *pensions*), restaurants (most of which don't serve Indonesian food), Bali beach-fashion shops, *warungs* (food stalls), art shops, pubs, nightspots, soul food cafes and fruit juice bars. Kuta attracted several generations of the laid-back—hippies, drug freaks, swingers, surfies, singles, and so many Australians that Australians staying elsewhere on the island sometimes go to Kuta to look at their fellow citizens. Part of the earlier charm of Kuta for visitors was feeling that they were getting close to 'the people', but for most who now stay there for a sun, surf, sand, sex* (and, often, booze) holiday, the 'people' are those who work for the service industries—waitresses, *losmen* servants, hawkers, the staff in the shops and the masseuses on the beaches.

These two tourist enclaves are part of a damage-control system. Indonesian and Balinese authorities planned the peninsular cultural quarantine. Kuta just happened, but it matches the plan.

Other enclaves are developing, but the bulk of 'tourist Bali' at present consists of two areas. They are both in the south-west, one based on Sanur and the other on Ubud, 'the painters' village'—with routes for day-trips extending to a dozen or so villages. Most of Bali

---

* **SEX.** Tourist sex in Bali is mainly between the tourists themselves. For women, there are some (Balinese) 'Kuta cowboys' but it is not a big business. For men, such prostitutes as there are in Bali are likely to be Javanese. There have been some famous cases of homosexuals living in Bali, but the main homosexual trade in this part of Asia is in Penang, in the north of Malaysia, and Thailand of course, where there is something of everything.

is not tourist country, although its villages provide a kind of resource bank of tourist services. Almost all the performers that tourists see still live in their villages, and although villagers move to tourist enclaves to work in the hotels, it is often as part of village networks. Most of the 100,000 or so people who have moved to Denpasar and nearby settlements are still likely to go back to their villages for the important temple ceremonies and family festivals.

Sanur is part-enclave. It is overgrown with the holiday trade but it is still recognisably Bali. The bungalow has become the characteristic hotel architectural form and even the Bali Hyatt, with its low buildings, fits into a landscape of coconut palms. Although they do it more expensively, some of the Sanur visitors, like those in the Kuta enclave, are there for the sun and the sand—they have to be satisfied with sea, rather than surf, because of the reef. But others move into the hinterland to seek bits of the Balinese experience in air-conditioned coaches, *bemos* (small pick-up trucks in which one can 'meet the people'), mini-buses, motorbikes, bicycles or hired cars. Some even walk through the rice fields on the edge of Sanur.

Those seeking the Balinese experience have been more likely to go to the hills of the Ubud district, which became defined as the cultural centre of Bali. Ubud was not an enclave. Despite some fast selling in the main street, it became a place where local people accepted travellers not just as tourists but as visitors—although some of the visitors attracted by new bungalow hotels are now proving to be enclave people. Ubud is a frontier. If it is 'taken over', another Ubud might have to be found.

Within these areas, tourists have been able to find the Bali they want: luxury Bali, or sun-and-sand Bali, or the cultural Bali of temples, art shops, cremations, monuments and, in particular (because it comes out best), performance. They could combine this, according to taste, with rides in *bemos*, strolls through villages or walks across rice fields. Most of the Bali of the Balinese is somewhere else (and few visitors move into it). To keep it like that, the authorities are limiting expansion to further tourist enclaves.

* * *

The West Zone Cultural Centre in Udaipur that we saw on our Palace-on-Wheels pilgrimage was an Indian attempt to maintain artistic and ceremonial traditions and relate them to tourist policy.

In Bali, because the tourist selling of Bali is as a place of culture, this becomes a matter of social and economic betterment.

One vexation has been that so much of the visual art of Bali was so determinedly imitative that it might as well have been produced by machines. An art that was previously important mainly in the structure of temples and palaces was abruptly secularised and democratised—because tourists wanted paintings to hang in frames, and sculptures to display on shelves. But since this innovation took place in a society in which imitation was the basis of art (viz, it was a 'traditional' society), no sooner did an artist think up something new than commercial imitations were being run off in their hundreds. Anything new at once became 'traditional', ie: distinctively Balinese. We went to the village of Kamasan where two masters have formed schools that draw inspiration from classical painting. Although ignored by the tourist trade, these paintings are bought by the hotels and by rich Balinese and, to some extent, Javanese (who have become important in Bali tourist statistics). Now the paintings are imitated by the cartload for street souvenir stalls.

If you keep your head above the trash and recognise that almost none of the cheapest things are worth buying, and if you don't trouble yourself about authenticity (which, in this situation, has no meaning unless you are going for old stuff—and, if that is what you want, there is scarcely any chance you will know what you are doing), you can buy much better in Bali than in those holiday places in the United States that provide an 'artists' colony', where visitors acquire paintings to remind them of where they have been. I'm not writing this as a useful tip, but as a reminder that in Bali policy for community welfare is also policy for art-making. Recognising the stagnation of Balinese visual art, the authorities established, in the 1960s, a secondary school for visual art and an Institute of Fine Arts and Architecture in Denpasar. In architecture, a professional and bureaucratic push developed a neo-Balinese revival style; there are controls for the design of new buildings and incentives for the owners of Western-style buildings to redesign the facades—not in imitations, but by developing new styles within Balinese traditions.

Many of the present dances performed in Bali came out of a radiant season of creativity in the second half of the 19th century, prompted mostly in the rajas' courts. Then, for most of this century, dance was in the control of the village dance masters, along with several exceptional village choreographers. They transformed village performance. They invented the tourist medleys. Beginning with the Paris World Festival in 1931, they put together troupes for international shows. They also produced new dance forms. Now the development of dance is (probably necessarily) partly bureaucratised.

KOKAR, the school of music and dance that was preparing for Queen Juliana's visit when we were in Bali on our family holiday, was also established in Denpasar in the 1960s, and so, later, was ASTI, the National Academy of Dance which now has an international reputation. Its director in the 1980s was Dr I Made Bandem, the son of the celebrated dancer who, in 1936, created the tourist version of the *Barong* dance. But the village dance masters are still there: unlike most Western societies, there is still a mutual relationship between élite culture and folk culture. Even in neighbouring Java traditional dance is a matter for intellectuals and experts, but in Bali the village communities and the Academy professionals influence each other. What is wanted in the villages partly shapes what is done by ASTI. They can be branches of the cultural genes bank.

Things aren't as good as that sounds. *Drama gong*, an entertainment form without dance, developed in the late 1960s, and began to pack them in in the villages; it provides a high-rating show on television. In Denpasar, and sometimes elsewhere, some Balinese prefer adaptations of the tourist excerpt medleys to their own stuff. So, in reaction, ASTI helps conserve and stimulate certain kinds of dance. The village of Batuan is now the refuge of the *Gambuh*, a proto-dance form that may be 1000 years old. But ASTI is also concerned with moving things along from the static and from the degenerate elements in the excerpt culture of the tourist performances. When he spoke to us, Bandem preferred to be optimistic about how providing for tourists affects performance, but only if villagers were persuaded to become less standardised in what they do. Our talk finished with him speaking about the relation between art and ceremony: the future of the arts in Bali depended on maintaining respect for family and religious ceremony.

An artistic stocktaking now occurs every year in the six weeks of the Bali Arts Festival. The main events are held in a large arts complex in Denpasar with its stages and exhibition halls. Over several visits we saw displays of Balinese contemporary dance (on a quiet afternoon with a small élite audience); tryouts of *Legong* variations, with new instrumentalisation and new types of song (held at night, and packed out, partly by coachloads from the dancers' villages); a presentation of the possibilities of a Bali revival style in architecture; a competition in palm leaf arrangements for temple offerings; sales of craft and exhibitions of Balinese-styled abstract paintings. We also bought some excellent spiced duck.

There were traffic jams on the night of the biggest show, which had an audience of about 8000. It was a presentation of an episode from the *Ramayana*, done in the music-dance-drama form developed in the 1960s in which the actors mime, while a *dalang* (traditionally a shadow play puppeteer), with great virtuosity, speaks all the parts and provides all the narration. It was the premiere performance but everyone knew the story. There was a lot of laughing where it was played for laughs, applause for passages of KER-POW! action, talking among the audience when it seemed to be lagging, and startlingly long and loud clapping after the recitation of a famous passage on the principles of good government that is more than 2000 years old. We had seen a presentation of part of the same episode put on by an élite Javanese group in Yogyakarta a few days before— pure dance, somewhat abstract, no laughs, hardly any audience, but preferred by some visitors (including, as it turned out, me).

IN THIRD WORLD LIVERPOOL

Compare the attitude towards tourism in Bali with attitudes towards tourism in another Third World area—Liverpool, England. Once a great city of the British Empire, made rich by cotton and slavery, and in the days when Britain commanded the waves, as a port, second only to London. At first look there is still imperial grandiloquence in neo-classical buildings, in sweeps of Georgian merchants' houses and in the dreaming commercial domes and towers at Pierhead, on the banks of the Mersey. But many buildings are unused. Shopfronts are boarded. Grandiose streets are half-empty. Pubs have closed down. Since the early 1960s its population of Lancashire-born and Irish, Scots, Welsh, Africans, West Indians and Chinese has almost halved. Parts of the city seem hastily abandoned in the face of the enemy. Factories were closed and the confident complex of docks stretching along the Mersey, once a symbol of British global assertion, looked like a grand battle fleet that had been scuttled. The docks were silted up. Grass grew on the sides. The walkways were luminous with smashed glass.

The exception was the 19th century Albert Dock, which had been restored. Granite quays and colonnaded brick warehouses looked as bright as in the 19th century; the water was quiet and clear. Within the buildings were shopping plazas selling tatt at higher prices than in town, an interesting emigration museum, a maritime museum and—of all things—a northern branch of London's Tate Gallery. When we had lunch in the Atlantic Tower with authorities of the Merseyside Development Corporation they told me they had come up with a 'Leisure, Culture-Type Investment' as a last resort for the Albert Dock. I began to put forward the theory that this development must be part of a wider cultural plan; that tourism can be culturally devastating and not even have much economic return. They cut me short before I could tell them about Bali. They said they were not interested in 'the arts'. In any case, what Liverpool itself had to offer was too parochial. The lunch would have ended earlier if I had told them what they could learn from Bali.

After lunch we drove to Bootle, a devastated dockland with 50 per cent youth unemployment that lies next to the wastelands of Liverpool. It is known as the Merseyside's smack city and as we walked to a community arts centre where we were to have a cup of tea there were patches of broken glass to crunch across and, in the gutter, syringes. SADOL (Sons and Daughters of Liverpool) was a group of several dozen young women and men, all unemployed, working together with some assistance from the regional arts organisation as a community arts group. The conventional youth clubs were part of a world to which they didn't belong. Their co-ordinator (also on the dole) was an artist-evangelist who, although he kept on talking me down (literally—he sat us on the floor and sat himself on a chair), was a kind of Merseyside holy man. They had made a video to give us an ironic view of the way they lived. Several weeks before, the 'star' of the video had tried to kill himself. He discussed that with us. When I asked them what they thought of the beautifying of the Albert Dock and the setting up of a branch of the Tate Gallery I sounded like someone from a youth club, speaking of a world to which they didn't belong. Who was I? What did I know? However, when I told them about the Bali Cultural Service they saw this as part of their world.

A few months earlier, we had spent several days moving around Bali with the director of the service, Dr Ida Bagus Rata. At Kuta, Balinese were asking for help in at least copying some of the cultural life of Kuta before it became a beach resort. At Batuan, villagers had formed a craft co-operative. At several villages where Dr Rata was arranging for artists to spend weekends as art advisers, he made speeches saying he would work only with the consent of the villagers, but they should understand that the Bali Cultural Service supported the new as well as the old—with the idea of expressing the Balinese spirit in contemporary forms. In Denpasar he was arranging a pop music contest to offset the Jakarta monopoly. At the small beach resort of Candi Dasa (which is now becoming an enclave) he talked about how in just a few years the village had been changed by the culture of beach tourism. What could he do? The villagers were under shock, but they hadn't asked for help.

On the north coast we went on a day's expedition up a dusty road through very steep hill country to Tigawasa, a pre-Hindu village. Behind our car was a bus containing a task force of 10 members of the Cultural Service—an archaeologist, an expert in the use of the leaves of the palmyra palm (*lontar*), a dancer, a social anthropologist, a woodcarver, etc, all with degrees or diplomas. (Graduates are easy to hire because of unemployment.) We sat around in the village office, with a litter of documents and tape recorders, while Dr Rata and his staff talked with the headmaster of the village school, along with the village secretary (a young lawyer who was the only graduate in the village) and other village activists. Some months had been spent setting out the social rules of the village, especially those concerned with the communality of land. Now they were going through records made by the Dutch of the customs of the place in the 1930s. The villagers were asked to speak into the tape recorder. Which customs had survived? Which did they wish to restore? At the end of the day it was decided that for a start they would have a supply of books, a dance-music teacher and a teacher of religious meaning.

* * *

The Sons and Daughters of Liverpool said they wished the Bali Cultural Service would come to Liverpool.

WHAT DO YOU DO FOR A DAY IN DENVER, COLORADO?

The airport at Denver, Colorado, is the sixth busiest in the world, but a lot of it is busy with people changing flights to go somewhere else. If you do get out at Denver, you pass almost at once from the baggage claim area into a suburban street. You stay in suburban streets until, hey presto, downtown Denver. Suburban houses on one block. High-rises the next. What do you do if you have a day in this city where the suburbs lap against the latest high-rise?

You can evade that question by going on the Rocky Mountain One-Day Big Circle coach tour, 'thrilling for 225 miles to the unequalled beauty of panoramic splendour', or by taking the coach to Georgetown, 'Silver Queen of the Rockies', and boarding a narrow gauge train for 'an unforgettable scenic trip that turns back the hands of time'. But the authorities at Denver hope for more than that.

As the Queen City of the Plains, Denver still offers the chance to go West. The world's largest rodeo brings in 400,000 people each January, and available at any time of the year are the last resting place of Buffalo Bill, a herd of 40 genuine plains buffalo (maintained in a natural setting) and cowboy-sized steaks at the Buck Snort Saloon or the Lazy H Chuckwagon. If you want to take the West more seriously, there is a quite good museum of the art of the United States West—and, slightly out of town, a museum that gives evidence of how African-American cowboys, soldiers and outlaws contributed to the winning of the West.

Denver is also the Mile High City ('A mile high and climbing'). For some time now its PR people have had figures to establish that Denver has more hours of annual sun than San Diego or Miami Beach. They also have demographic and other figures to demonstrate that it is the city with 'the youthful flavour'. But what Denver's promoters now want is for tourists to appreciate the city's architectural, cultural and heritage development, products of the Urban Renewal Authority's Skyline Project and the city's cultural and heritage plans.

If you want heritage on your day in town, the Western Whip Company offers 'an elegant horse-drawn carriage for an historic downtown tour', and the Historic Denver company a two-hour tour of the homes of 19th century mining millionaires, real estate boosters and industrialists, in architectural styles ranging from Beaux-Arts Mansion to Dutch Colonial Revival Cottage. At Four Mile Historic Park you can see the oldest frontier home in Denver. Pausing on the thirteenth step of the golden-domed State Capitol you can stand exactly a mile above sea level. If you visit the 'quaintly facaded' Molly Brown House you will be visiting the home of a survivor of the sinking of the *Titanic*, and in 16th Street you can stand in front of a replica of the *campanile* of St Marks in Venice. But they also have in Denver, in the Colorado History Museum, a heritage centre that is more intelligently presented than in most cities anywhere, and one that does almost all the things that I think a museum should do.

Denver's promoters would also like you to admire what they have been doing to the place lately. In 1969 they had only three buildings higher than 20 floors, and one of them was the imitation of the St Mark's *campanile*. Now a couple of dozen modest skyscrapers huddle together, and their photograph makes a favourite postcard. You are invited to admire the office towers of the financial district—this should take about five minutes—but where your real attention is required is for the Shopping Centers, which, in the manner of Shopping Centers, are not only places where you buy things or eat and drink; they are also areas of sociability and declarations of value and hope. To keep its shopping areas lively, the Denver Chamber of Commerce has a special program of cultural events and celebrations.

We began our odyssey of hope with 16th Street, a mile of which was turned into a successful-looking city mall at a cost of $76 million when it was re-paved in a chequered pattern of red and white granite blocks, planted with dozens of trees, provided with 11 fountains, a number of plazas and outdoor cafes and what seemed enough benches (with a bit of rostering) to seat the unemployed who became the victims of Denver's collapse as an 'energy city'. Walking all the 14 blocks of the Mall was too detailed a research project, so we took one of the 'European-built' shuttle buses that leave each end of the Mall every 90 seconds—in the evening you can ride up and down the Mall in a Western Whip horse and carriage.

The 16th Street Mall is one of the many attempts to restore to a United States city some of the sociability that used to be found in Main Street before the Main Streets fell into urban decay. (When Main Streets flourished it was not as symbols of nostalgia but as a journey into modernity. A Main Street displayed some of what was new and possible.) It has Shopping Centers both vertical and horizontal, as well as department stores, supermarkets, boutiques in restored Victorian buildings, restaurants and office towers of glass—which seem to go well with the imitation St Mark's *campanile*. Part of the Skyline Project was building Tabor Center, a two-block glasshouse galleria, with a skyway marketplace and its precious burden of chichi, as well as its own atrium with a fountain and indoor trees.

To offset modernity, 18 Victorian buildings were restored in what had been a rundown relic of Denver's first Main Street ('one of the finest examples of historic renovation anywhere in the nation') and, to match, the sidewalks were extended and there was a general distribution of arcades, fountains, courtyards, arts events, walking tours, carriage rides and gas lamps. If you have spent the afternoon with the delights of the Mall and its environs you might have dinner in a restaurant in Tivoli Denver. This 19th century brewery with a palatial facade was declared an historic landmark in 1973 and converted by 1985 into a six-level 'shopping, entertainment and dining facility', in which metal parts of the old works have been polished and turned into large, gleaming toys.

There are other new shopping districts that they would like you to look at in Denver, with boutiques, galleries, restaurants, professional offices and specialist businesses placed, along with high income condos and a few large stores, in restored 19th century streets. But the cultural jewel, and what could be the pride of Denver, is the Tattered Cover bookstore, largest and best bookstore in the United States and one the most comprehensive and best in the world. And while the Tattered Cover now has customers from all over, its inventory was developed over 10 years to meet the interests of the people of Denver itself. As Jason Epstein said in 'The Decline and Rise of Publishing', this 'suggests something hitherto unsuspected by book publishers about the capacity of typical American readers to take control of their cultural lives and decide for themselves what books to buy'.

It also suggests that there is more to Denver (and more to tourism and to the human potential) than the Buck Snort Saloon and the 16th Street Mall. So do the excellent history museum, the intelligently-done museum of the art of the West and the museum of African-Americans in the West. And so does the Denver Art

Museum (which we also visited during our day—to be exact, our day and a half—in Denver). It may have been the first museum in the United States to re-define Native American artifacts as art. It was one of the first museums to be housed in a building that is 'a work of art in itself' but, despite that dreadful start, it is easy to work through and there is good question-raising and follow-up material to encourage people to have a think about what they are looking at. There is also the kind of cultural assemblage that now becomes part of a city like Denver—a Performing Arts Center with three theatres, a concert hall ('the nation's first symphony concert hall in the round'), dance, drama and opera companies, symphony orchestra and chamber orchestra.

* * *

I bought a copy of Ian Ousby's *The Englishman's England* at the Tattered Cover bookstore and on the way to Los Angeles I came across this passage about 18th century tourists: 'The suspicion that life used to be more happy or humane, more comfortable or kindly, is a characteristically modern anxiety. Before the advent of Romanticism people believed confidently in their superiority over their ancestors, especially their superiority when it came to comfort, efficiency and taste. So when they turned tourist and visited country houses, they sought modernity and admired improvements. They were drawn to . . . houses that had often been built within their lifetimes and, indeed, were sometimes still being built, extended or further improved.'

Tourists in the United States still want to see 'the past', whether it is Monticello or Colonial Williamsburg, or the Molly Brown House, Denver, but, like 18th century tourists, they can also seek modernity and admire improvements. They can be drawn to palaces of art built within their lifetime—and to new commercial palaces like the galleria of the Tabor Center, or a new ceremonial concourse like the 16th Street Mall. And a 19th century brewery polished up and turned into a 'shopping, entertainment and dining facility' can also meet the taste for modernity and improvement. It shows how much better we know what to do with the past than did the people who lived in it.

Visiting national parks used to be the top United States tourist activity. Now the largest source of tourist revenue is likely to be spending a few days in someone else's town—where, as well as paying tribute to heritage, art, sport and minor feasting, you can look at the townspeople and see what they have been doing to their town.

This process began with the 'revitalisation' of Boston. Faneuil Hall, 'the cradle of liberty', was cleared of its commercial litter and the invention of 'Faneuil Hall Marketplace' made Boston the cradle of urban regeneration in North America. Then Quincy Hall and two other big, old, rundown and partly abandoned market halls built next to Faneuil Hall in 1826 were recommissioned. Now, surrounded by brick and cobblestone pavements, these marketing halls are eating, drinking and shopping places that are boosted as bringing in more visitors a year than whatever they compete with.

The 'revitalisation' of an inner city has become an important tourist pitch in the United States—from Baltimore, whose central disaster area was transfigured by a Mies van der Rohe glass tower and two huge glass pavilions, to Seattle, where decrepit buildings of 19th century brick were born again as the galleries, boutiques and restaurants of 'Pioneer Square'.* Why does this 'revitalisation' attract tourists? Fame, as ever. But also familiarity. It fits the visitor's experience. Going to a town to see how it has been improved can be done with an informed, critical interest. There has also been a reverberant relief among some middle class citizens that a way out might have been found from the collapse of the inner cities into demolition sites not worth demolishing, or nine-to-five business areas so deserted at night that all that is left are the muggers and their victims.

Is there also some desire for cities to go back to being cities? I spent a few days in 1984 in Fresno, in the San Joaquin Valley, a town of 250,000 or so in the heartland of those irrigated Californian farmlands that can seem a monument to high productivity and

---

* HIDING THE DROPOUTS. One should remember that a criticism of 'inner city revitalisation schemes' is that they sweep off to somewhere else the city's discards, derelicts and dropouts, in the same way that the police harassed junkies away from parts of the East Village in New York. The result of this was that on our stay (Chapter 24) we could eat safely in the company of punks, graffiti artists, preppies, yuppies, hippies, transvestites, gays and lesbians. However, this is a fault not in urban regeneration plans, but in a collapse in the practical conscience of United States citizens.

rugged individualism, unless you know the cost of irrigating them.*
It was the week when results were published of a survey of 277
United States cities in terms of desirability as living places. Fresno
had come last. It wasn't crime rates: they had put together a small,
new, clean downtown. It wasn't ethnic tension: the Vietnamese had
replaced the Armenians at the bottom of the scale (William Saroyan
had been born there), but not with any notable disasters. There
were seven freeways running through Fresno and they seemed to
have emptied it of urban content. No-one I met had been to the
new downtown. Occasional complexes of neon-lit heraldic signs
along the freeways denoted shopping centers, supermarkets, eating
places, takeouts. Fresno offered the civilisation of the motel strip.
The way to have handled it as a tourist would have been with
notebook and pencil, exploring a new version of the mundane.

A BELIEF IN PEOPLE

In 1991, the United States Travel Data Center reported a promising
outlook for 'cultural tourism'. The baby boomers are now
approaching middle age, and many of them have college degrees.
'Seniors' ('a strong and growing market') also have a predisposition
towards 'cultural activities'. And, because vacations are becoming
shorter but more frequent, theatres and museums are useful for
hotels that put together weekend packages.

At Denver, as with so many other United States cities, years
before the tourist industry had thought of a name for cultural
tourism, civic wisdom had gone about building museums and

---

* **THE INDIVIDUALISM OF THE COWBOY** is
celebrated in the tourist experience of the West, from the
National Cowboy Hall of Fame in Oklahoma City, to Knott's
Berry Farm, Los Angeles. ('with lusty can-can dancers, Indian
chiefs, spirited fiddle music and shoot-outs between the good
guys and the bad'). But the West was won very largely through
immense government subsidies that brought water
uneconomically to semi-arid deserts, and that continue to
waste resources. Celebrations of rural folk heroes can also
serve special interests in Europe. When visiting an open air
museum dedicated to the self-reliance of the peasantry, it is
worth remembering that the farmers of Western Europe are
protected by such heavy subsidy and quota systems that they
have threatened the future of world trade.

performing arts centers and selective resurrections of the past. Tourism is part of the Denver cultural plan. (Nearly 100 US cities now have cultural plans.) In a new kind of boosting that would have terrified George F Babbit, but would have seemed self-evident in Bali, *Cultural Denver* says: 'As cities compete with one another—for economic development, for progressive and energetic citizens, for the attention of the world—careful nurturing of the arts becomes paramount'.

But *Cultural Denver* also expresses the wish for the arts to meet the wants of residents. It says that the communities of Denver—Native American, Hispanic, African-American, Asian and European—are diverse, and 'are faced with growing educational and social problems that a stable economy alone cannot solve. These include functional and cultural illiteracy, high drop-out rates and homelessness . . . All of the financial arts-support systems in Denver—public, corporate, foundation and individual patron—have not reached a desirable minimum level of contribution to the artistic and cultural life of the community.'

The concern that is expressed here (I don't know what is actually happening) puts Denver closer in cultural and tourist policy to Bali than to Liverpool. Re-doing the Albert Dock and setting up a colony of the Tate didn't do anything for the dispossessed youth of Bootle, except insult them.

In *City of Quartz*, his report from the battlefront of civil war in Los Angeles, Mike Davis recalls that the arts acropolis boom in LA ('buying Culture straight off the rack of the world market') was accompanied by cutting spending on school board financing for music and arts instruction, and closing key community arts workshops and jazz venues. 'Black dance has been shut out in the cold, community theatre has withered, Black and Chicano film-makers have lost much of their foundation support, the world-famous East LA mural movement has almost disappeared. The inner city has been culturally hollowed out.' The cultural tourism of Bali is related to what is happening among the Balinese themselves and cultural development policy in Bali is to enliven local culture. In LA—and Liverpool—cultural development policy is to distract attention from local culture.

There is no logical contradiction between a local cultural development program and a local tourist development program. In Third World countries, and the Third World sections of prosperous societies (Bootle, South-central LA), tourist development can be part of a cultural development program, and a cultural development program can be essential to a new self-confidence.

* * *

This argument can be extended to post-industrial societies generally. But we can't yet know what 'post-industrial' might mean.

On the positive side, it is supposed to open up possibilities for a more lively and creative society with a high productive culture, and with an economic as well as a cultural emphasis on the necessity for service, leisure and quality-of-life industries.

For the moment, we are more likely to see deficits, crises, unemployment and junk jobs.

People at the top still see as their norm some return to the long, relatively assured postwar boom, when policy could be a matter of responding to a few trusty economic indicators. But the indicators have gone mad and they will never work again.

We now need quality of life indicators, dramatising a new moral dynamic that could also be an economic dynamic. And, in this, cultural development programs and tourist programs can be one of the tryouts, so long as they are part of the same thing—the belief that, given the opportunity, people can expand their potential.

Until it happened, no-one knew that in Denver there was the potential to support one of the world's best bookstores.

26.

VISITORS IN OUR OWN LIVES

◆ ◆ ◆

LOOKING AT THINGS

At the Temple of Karnak, the largest surviving religious complex from antiquity, I decided that as well as wandering around forecourts, pylons, statues, halls, chapels, shrines, sanctuaries, sacred lakes and the cafeteria, I would spend some time observing a guided tour group. The guide I picked out seemed very good. At some celebrated parts we had to press up to hear his voice above the other guides shouting in French, Arabic, German, Japanese and Italian, but if there were too many rivals he had a repertoire varied enough to revise his script and we would go somewhere quieter for a while. (The groups clustered like flocks of birds, so that for some minutes a particular area was crowded; then it was empty.) I found the guide particularly good at picking out the shape of things (using a torch instead of pointing a stick), helping me to see things I might have missed. There was also a flowing lecture on the meaning of this and that, which I found it best not to listen to, getting on instead with walking around to get a feeling for this old stone.

We reached our crisis in the Great Hypostyle Hall, which, at

5000 square metres, is said, in itself, to be larger than any Christian cathedral and, with its 134 columns in 16 rows, with capitals so large that 100 people could stand on each of them, it seemed more remarkable than the Great Pyramid, because it achieved such a complex composure that you didn't notice its size until (as in the Mariposa Sequoia Grove in California) you saw, in contrast, a human being.

I was wandering among the columns but I heard the guide, distantly, quite usefully, explaining who built it, but then describing the content of an occasional relief: 'Seti I is making an offering to Amun-Re accompanied by Mut and Khonsu-Neferhotep . . . ' and so forth. Then he swept his torchlight in circles over several columns, as if absolving them from the need to provide any further information, and said to the group: 'Now you can go around and feel the hypostyle hall for yourselves'. Some of the group had already wandered off to measure their own significance against the size of the columns. About half the others joined them. The rest stayed with the guide, stuck together as a group. They didn't want to feel the hall for themselves. The guide, politely, went from one column to the next, explaining various offerings to various gods as the little group watched the spotlight fall.

* * *

What is the point in going to some historic site, or a noted landscape, or a market square, or a museum, unless it is to have a look? The rational explanation for going to all that trouble to see something for ourselves is to gain experiences that cannot altogether be expressed in words, or that cannot be expressed in words at all. You don't have to fly to Cairo and then take a train, plane, coach or ship to Luxor to learn about Khonsu-Neferhotep. You can do that by reading a book.

Why go to a museum or an historic site or a famous view except to *look*—with the prospect of wonder, of an exalted attention that can come from regarding a thing in itself, and of curiosity, the desire to know a bit more? Even if one's motive is to 'do' Luxor, to acquire it as a conquered site, there can be an interest in finding out 'what it is really like'.

There is another thing. In our ordinary lives, how much looking do we do?

In a relatively prosperous commercialist society what are the kinds of things that people usually look at in an organised manner? Things for sale, mostly, or things other people have bought. Objects of desire. We may look at such objects critically, estimating their usefulness, or how they would look in the sitting room. But we are also likely to see them given meaning and drained of meaning by the general magic of marketing. In commercialist societies, shops are the main exhibition centres. One of the values of tourism is that if we can get away from the shopping and the tour packaging, it can organise us to look at things we don't usually see and pay a special kind of attention to them.

But in this process we may merely pass from the litter of empty symbols in our public culture to seek relief, as sightseers, in hyped-up simulations—symbols of symbols. And if that is what we want, we might as well just stay in the hotel admiring the empurpled stereotypes of the travel brochures, the fantasies of the more lavishly styled guidebooks and the appeals of the hotel's video program about its services for guests. (If, on the other hand, we go to an historic site simply to listen to the guide, or to a museum simply to read all the labels, we might be better off reading a book.*)

The fetishes of authenticity and the idea of sightseeing as a flight from the false into the real don't stand up in logic. But they gain some meaning if one considers them as an exercise in looking.

* * *

The Girard collection, the basis of the Museum of International Folk

---

* WORDS IN MUSEUMS. Not that it is necessarily wrong to read labels. Bitter struggles of conscience still go on in the museum business about the place of words in museums. Some purists believe that in all cases words distract people from looking. In the leanest view, an exhibition should be prepared so that it gives meaning for illiterates. Others don't mind words, but they warn of 'museum fatigue'. Papers are given on how lengthy the captions and text should be. Should they be in language comprehensible to an 11-year-old? A 12-year-old? A 13-year old? Research is conducted into the use of different sizes and shapes of typography to allow multi-level use for different kinds of readers. More conversational styles are suggested. For others, the words can be poetic. One answer is that information can be provided without cluttering up the inspection site, with cheap takeaway leaflets and back-up from videos and the museum shop.

Art in Santa Fe, New Mexico, was put together by an architect-designer who, with his wife, had collected 100,000 dolls and toys—not just traditional Western dolls, but dolls of all kinds. In the museum presentation he wanted to avoid the categorising and linear approach. In his words: 'I've often felt that objects lose half their lives when they are taken out of their natural settings. To me, nothing can be worse than an exhibition in which a number of objects are just lined up in cases . . . We rarely see single things in life—we see crowds of people, or the sea, or cities, or buildings . . . While many of the objects are, to a number of people's minds, great, to most people they are meaningless. I've listened to and watched people in exhibitions and I see they get bored quickly. Any rhythmic thing like case after case after case after case, or even labels in the same format, can be hypnotic. You have to distract people into looking at things.'

The way Girard got out of this predicament was to put all his dolls and other stuff together so that they told stories. He wasn't providing a taxonomy of dolls. And he wasn't providing any explanations. He just put them together as a child might, so that they are doing things together. This has an extraordinary effect. It makes you see the objects. By putting them together in clusters of stories, he made people have a sense of actually *experiencing the object*.

One of the functions of museums in the future can be to help us reclaim the capacity to *look*. But not just by laying things out in the old style. Nor just by 'telling stories'. There must be techniques of juxtaposition, of estrangement, of surprise. Objects should be presented in museums with the kind of imperative that drives sculptors and painters to make the viewer 'see'.*

This could be part of the wider change that Neil Postman spoke of when he said in *Museum News*: 'What we require are museums that tell us what we once were, and what is wrong with what we

---

* **EXHIBITIONS AS POEMS.** Some of the things we look at can be 'arranged in disorder', as Inger Sjørslev suggests in an essay, 'Communicating Objects', so that we can look at them in a different way. She says that creating an exhibition should be like creating a poem. 'As in a poem we find the playing on metaphors and symbolic expressions and the freedom from grammatical rules of ordinary language. The ideal of the exhibition should be the creation of powerful images, the playing with symbols, and the exploitation of the freedom from ordinary sequentiality.'

are, and what new directions are possible . . . A museum must be an argument with its society'.

That is an appeal to the liberal and critical strand in public life. But much of the noise now surrounding museums can be a distraction from considering how they can fulfil new moral and cultural tasks.

How can a museum become 'an argument with its society'? How can museums provide what cannot be provided by television and video? How can they continue to offer the possibility for changes in perception so that visiting a museum may provide an illuminating life experience? How do they accommodate themselves to the change from classifying objects? How can the museum movement be used for local participation and identification? Or to assist the self-definition of groups who don't get a place in the public scene? In Third World countries, how can museums be used in sustaining cultural confidence? In restoring traditional (and marketable) skills? In assisting a modernisation that is sympathetic to local cultures? In modern-industrial states, how can they again teach us to look?*

Many museum people are now changing their museums in ways that may be as important as the creation of museums in the first place. As for the rest of us, we can begin the reform of museums by reforming them in our own minds.

This means we must resist being classified into immobility by being described as 'the public'. We are many 'publics'. And we are all participants. We all negotiate meaning in museums, even as Zola's characters did, out of what is already in our heads.

As critics of existence, we can approach a museum not on its terms, but on our own, seeking from it material for our general

---

* NEIGHBOURHOOD MUSEUM. A classic example of a museum in a situation of argument in its own society was the idea of 'the neighbourhood museum' that came when the Smithsonian Institution acquired a small disused cinema in the black neighbourhood of Anacostia in Washington DC, where there was an active community group. The neighbourhood museum opened in 1967 (with an 84-piece local band) with display objects chosen by neighbourhood residents. The museum was used as a means of developing local issues—the first ecology exhibition (1969), *The Rat: Man's Invited Affliction*, dramatised awareness of a local problem and also offered information and solutions—but it did this and others with such flair that some Anacostia Museum exhibitions now go on national tours.

construction of views of existence. This is a reminder that, finally, the reform of museums is up to the people who go to them. We should teach ourselves how to 'read' museums as we are supposed to read books—critically, and from our own interests and perspectives.

OUR OWN RANGE OF EXPERIENCES

If one is concerned with learning to look, this can (as suggested in Chapter 15) include contemplating everyday things from the past that have special attention brought to them by being placed within a magic circle in a museum or a heritage site or, as we did at Bali and at Denver, one can find wonder in what to other people is their mundane.

Why not begin deploying the attentive looking of tourism to things and places not of the distant *other*, but from our own range of experience—and find in these familiar things some of the strangeness that can attract us to other people's lives? The way out for sightseeing tourism may be to begin at home. We can become visitors in our own lives.

By casting magic circles, we can learn to walk around our own area and see *that* as a tourist experience. We can make discoveries and declarations about ourselves and we can share with visitors our interest in our own lives, in our past and our present, and in our social and natural and cultural environment. And the particular impetus of tourism may lead to culturally enriching plans that we couldn't get away with otherwise, because they could seem economically unworkable. Then when we go to other people's places, or look at exhibitions of other people's things, we can be not tourists but travellers and guests.

The whole idea of 'heritage' can play a more useful part in liberal-pluralist societies when people learn the arts of conserving some of their own places and collecting some of their own things. In Australia, the Snowy Mountains are a Mount Olympus of the myth of the Australian as long, lean horseman, rounding up the cattle: they are the setting for the legend of the ballad *The Man from Snowy River*. On the slopes of the Snowy Mountains, at Tumbarumba, a settlement of less than 2000 people, some women decided at the end of the 1970s to collect their own old things, and to ask other country women for some of theirs, so that they could provide material evidence for a quite different legend of European pioneering in Australia. Instead of stockwhips and branding irons they offered tomato sauce bottle covers, washtubs, kitchen utensils made from kerosene tins, furniture made from butter boxes, dress patterns, clothes pegs—and doileys, the small ornamental mats and covers (crocheted, knitted, beaded, knotted, netted and tatted) that could be the one symbol of refinement and gentle aspiration in a rough bush hut.

The best of this collection is now exhibited in 'The Pioneer Women's Hut' just out of Tumbarumba, and the things there are seen as part of the national collection. Local people bring visitors to the museum and explain their lives to them. Coach parties are let in only if they are not too big, and only if they take the museum seriously enough to stay in it for some time. As a result of this rule, it is difficult to 'do' the Pioneer Women's Hut as quickly as some people 'do' the Louvre.

With an interest in greater cultural engagement among ordinary people, the Swedish National Council for Cultural Affairs began to encourage people to collect and assemble their own stuff, as an important element of self-definition in a diverse society. In Denmark (where they told me that it was really in Denmark that the emphasis on community collecting was strongest), the belief is that collecting itself is what matters most. I was told about collections connected with leisure, with the development of kindergartens and with the 'summer house' (viz holiday house) subculture of North Zealand.

In Oporto, Portugal, the central museum began encouraging people in small regional towns to put on their own shows made up of their own things, some of which might then go to the central museum's permanent collection. Calabria is a region depleted by more than a century of immigration and is losing both a sense of its past and a sense of its future, but most of the objects in the Museum of Farming and Crafts at Monterosso Calabro have been given by local people, reaffirming by their collections memories of being and identity. In these, as in other participatory museums, collecting things and presenting them can widen out beyond thinking about who you are ('identity'); it can also help people think about their local economy and the local ecology—and, as 'tourism', it provides a chance to tell other people who you are by showing them some of your things.

The intellectual credit goes to the French—in their conceptualisation in the 1960s of the *éco-musée*, the eco-museum, a term at first applied to rural areas where fragments of traditional culture still had meaning. In an eco-museum there would be a museum building, to encourage focus, but most of the material would be scattered around a district—houses, farming tools, domestic equipment, appropriately 'traditional' animals. The concern was that the people who still lived in a region should understand something of where they came from. Tourists mattered only within the context of the needs of the locals. As Kenneth Hudson describes it in *Museums of Influence*, the Musée Camarguais, in the Camargue district near Arles, provided an ideal of a mutually productive relationship between people who lived in a place and 'their guests'.

The development of community collecting can have a socially therapeutic value for the kinds of victims of the post-industrial age that we now call 'the underclass'. Hugues de Varine, one of the pioneers of eco-museum theory, was also a pioneer in developing participatory exhibitions as part of a 'Neighbourhoods in Crisis' program operating in some socially devastated areas in France with large, unemployed ethnic minorities. People are assisted in making exhibitions out of their own things that increase both their own self-esteem and esteem from others. Shared culture, even of an externally degraded ethnic minority, can represent one of the last resources of appeals to self-confidence. How can there be action without a 'cultural factor'? In Glasgow we visited the Springburn Community Museum, in an area whose industrial base (mainly locomotive making) had been annihilated. From the start, local people were desperate for anything to help maintain some sense of being themselves.

* * *

If we can begin to respect the shape of the ordinary in our own lives, we can learn to be intelligent visitors in the societies we invade. We can understand that the whole world is a museum. It's there to be looked at. If we understand that, we have cured ourselves of one of the sicknesses of tourism.

27.

COMING OUT OF THE CULTURE BUNKER

◆ ◆ ◆

TURNING THINGS INTO ART

A large part of the rest of the trial balance on tourism can be struck by assessing art museums—because they are so rich in resources and also because they are so rich in follies. One way of beginning might be this: in the Tumbarumba Pioneer Women's Hut there are tomato sauce bottle covers, dress patterns, furniture made from butter boxes and clothes pegs—what is there in art museums?

Sacred things—taken from sepulchres, sanctuaries, altars, places of sacrifice and worship. Low reliefs and statues prised from their bases, mosaics lifted from floors, frescoes stripped off walls, painted wooden panels pulled from their frames, masks and vestments, and supernatural utensils of stone or wood or metal. Randomly surviving treasures of palaces and mansions—china, paintings, furniture, scrolls, sculptures, painted screens, jewelled ornaments in precious metal, coins and medals, armour and weapons, carpets and tapestries. Produced to display prestige and power, these are now laid out like lots in an auction, along with statues and portraits of the powerful, depictions of great events or exemplary scenes, 'oils' in extravagant frames, and modern works of art, some of them miraculous because although neglected at the time they now sell for millions of dollars. And almost all of these fabrications in wood, stone, metal, clay, pigment and fibre have become glorified in ways that would have astounded those who made them (except for artists who produced work specially for museums; sometimes even them).

In themselves, these transmutations are simply one among the many magic encirclements of tourism. Australian women who crocheted their doileys didn't know they would become 'exhibits' in the Pioneer Women's Hut at Tumbarumba. Anything celebrated in a guidebook is cast into a different order of reality from the rest of experience. But art museum objects have gone through greater transformations than that.

One of these transformations has been an exaltation in classifying and *naming*. At Tumbarumba they classify their things under headings. 'Making do' (seating made from sheep-dip boxes, clothing made from flour bags) . . . 'A stitch in time' (sewing machines, buttons, dress patterns) . . . 'Washdays' . . . 'Cooking' . . . 'Fancy work' (teapot holders, aprons with artistic scenes sewn into them, ornamental teapot cosies). In some of the more specialist areas—doileys in particular—there is the beginning of a system of naming. (If this kind of collecting catches on, scholars will be classifying doileys, as was done with Singapore shophouses. They may create a taxonomy of Australian doileys.) However, art museums were cursed by a particular system of classifying and naming.

It came when art museums were configured within the historical chassis that began in 1810 when the Musée de la République Francaise reopened as the Musée Napoléon and its director divided art into the four national 'schools'—Italian, Flemish, Dutch and French—that provided a basis for the scholarly framework that was then slightly extended and tacked together in the German world of art scholarship.

Nothing in the material itself demanded that things should be presented chronologically, and in territories: all these things could have been arranged and thought about in different ways. But the shadow of the chronological hang in national schools was cast over everything, and all the grand art museums became museums of art history.*

Even where a collection had no historical substance, to those who were in the know it could nevertheless be seen as a fragment of some celestial chronological hang—just as the smallest splinter of a tooth might be imagined by a dentist as part of an imaginary great mouth.

Like effigies in a procession, paintings that happened to have been collected in an art museum were arranged in a certain order, aloft, on a wall. Knowledgeable visitors could pass through and tick off the categories. Those who were not in the know could feel they were in the presence of something greater than them, even if they did not know what it was.

Art museums also became a special case because awe of the expert and the authentic can still ravage more visitors' minds in art museums than in all other museums combined. And expertness has gained greater authenticity with the special glow given to works of art by lavish bidding in the art markets. The lavishness of art museums adds to their emotional dazzle. Old art museums were reminders of the past as a palace. New art museums are reminders of the present as a luxury hotel.

But what is unique to the alchemy of art palaces is that they not only transmute things into exhibits. They also transmute them into 'art'.

The special magic of art objects compared with all the other things we look at as sightseers is that art objects seem to have no origin.

---

* BAD HISTORIES OF GOOD ART. If this was art history, it was bad art history—if art history means something more than going back through relics of the past and sorting them, by classifications, into chronological order. There was no concern with showing the meanings of paintings in terms of the meanings that were around in the society in which they were painted. Usually, no idea was provided even of what else was going on in visual design. And in any case, no art museum can be comprehensive. There is always something missing and the curatorial subculture doesn't permit showing visitors copies of some of what is missing. If art history *were* nothing more than a systematic presentation of the canon, the only rational policy would be the suggestion I made in *The Great Museum*: break up all the great collections and re-sort them as a series of smaller, intellectually comprehensible exhibitions, placed in a number of small museums.

COMING OUT OF THE CULTURE BUNKER 353

The Tumbarumba Pioneer Women's Hut does not keep it secret that the doileys were made for a use other than being admired in a museum. Nobody has illusions about the origin of a neolithic flint when they see it in a museum, or a stuffed bird, or an old steam engine or an ancient cannon. But the belief that everything that appears in an art museum has lost its origin and been transmuted into 'art' can have blinding effects on those who are contaminated: they may see 'art' only when they go to an art museum. 'Art' will have nothing to do with ordinary things or ordinary life.

Objects in art museums have nothing to do with anything except themselves. And the more recently they have been produced, the more remote from us they become. Jean Clair, chief curator of the Musée Picasso in Paris, published a pamphlet in 1988 in which he said that establishing so many new museums of contemporary art means that people no longer believe in contemporary art. He said their proliferation was like the proliferation of temples in Rome, at the time that the Romans were ceasing to believe in their gods. They accepted so many deities of their subject peoples, and built temples to them, that there was a pantheon of 30,000.

A first step in making art museums more accessible to the imagination might be for the people who run them to let their visitors know how the objects on display were used when they were first made, and how and why they got into an art museum.

But the remoteness of art museums is only a worst-case example of the more general alienation effect of sightseeing, in which the things we look at can seem out of this world. For intelligent sightseeing, all museums, all historical sites and monuments and, with modifications, all celebrated natural views, should be seen in context. What were these things like before they were encircled by the magic of sightseeing? Under what circumstances did those transmutations happen? What changes have occurred in their magic since the initial transmutations? If I can do this every time I go for a walk in the Blue Mountains (end of Chapter 19), it can't be that hard.

* * *

To art historians and a few knowledgeable tourists, one of the Vatican Museum's wonders is a Roman copy in marble of a bronze Greek statue. It is of a man with a papal figleaf over the genitals. One arm is missing, and the hand of the other is broken off. It is the Apollo Belvedere, discovered in the 15th century and for 300 years one of the world's most adored statues: a cult object. It was described as art's highest ideal by Johann Joachim Winckelmann, the greatest 18th century publicist for the neo-classical revival, at the time when art objects were being transmuted with the power of holy relics. Winckelmann believed that this broken statue was an image of divine nature in which a 'celestial spirit courses like a sweet vapour through every part . . . His lofty look, filled with consciousness of power, seems to rise above his victory and gaze into eternity . . . in the presence of this miracle of art I forget the whole universe'. The reason people are now likely to seek out this statue is to wonder at how it had once been seen as a message from the universe.

Messages in marble, or in paintings that made flesh look like marble, were seen to offer human redemption. Although marble has gone out of fashion for divine communication, redemption is still on offer from Art—and from the Past and from Nature and from the People, sightseeing's other redeemers. In a very difficult book, *The Culture of Redemption*, Leo Bersani argues that art can still falsely be presented as saving us from the catastrophes of history, redeeming our lives, making life whole, correcting its errors. He is writing about modern literature and those who theorise about it, but we can be equally wary of a cult that imagines that redemption of this kind is achieved by entering a temple of art (or through communion with nature, the people, or the past). Regeneration, yes. We can come back from an art museum, or a walk in the Blue Mountains, or a stroll through the Great Hypostyle Hall of the Temple of Karnak, or after talking to some people in Bali or Bootle, and feel refreshed from the sense of wonder or discovery, or extended in our minds, or pushed in a new direction by changed perspectives. But a redemption that saves us from the world is not of this world.

THE RIGHT TO LOOK

In attacking the celestial chronological hang I have been arguing against my own experience. One of the imagination-openers of my life came from a special exhibition of Impressionist and Post-Impressionist paintings that came to Australia when I was a 17-year-old student. I went to it day after day. (It was a year of imagination-openers, but all of the rest came from books.) But later I took my untutored vision to the grand museums. When I was working at a boring job in London in the early 1950s it left me hours of spare time, much of which I spent working my way through the National Gallery, picture by picture, room by room, century by century, country by country. (Not that there were many countries. Most countries were seen as not having art.) I would have long looks at each painting. I would read about individual painters, schools and periods. Then I would go back for another look. After a year of this I had walked the whole course, from Italian Primitives to French Impressionists. Having absorbed the chronological hang in national schools into my bone structure, I started all over again, for revision, back among the Primitives* (although visiting other kinds of art museums—particularly the Jeu de Paume and the Museum of Modern Art—produced counter-revelations).

* * *

The traditional art museums are enormous repositories of cultural resources. How can they be better used, so that they have functions other than confronting visitors with presentations of art as the curators see it? How can they open out their resources to multiple uses?

As ever, the autonomic tourist agenda is to blame for many of the things that go wrong, but tourists and other visitors who are able to break away could construct their own museums in their own minds. Why imagine, for instance, that in one visit you should exhaust the potential of a large art museum by appearing in each

---

* RE-ORDERING THE UNIVERSE. The National Gallery in London announced in 1990 that it was going to modify the rigidities of the 'hang' in national schools, so that the gallery is presenting the development of European, rather than national, painting—although still not recognising much European painting as painting. For a great gallery to engage in a 're-hang' is like the Creator deciding to re-order the universe.

room and exposing yourself, briefly, to the presence of its objects?*

In Penza, a Russian city of about 400,000 people on the banks of one of the largest tributaries of the Volga, there is the One Picture Gallery, established by the regional art museum in a sympathetically restored postmaster's house of the 19th century. The One Picture Gallery shows only one picture at a time, borrowed from one of the major museums and displayed for a season of several months in 'the picture room', an upstairs room with armchairs for 35 people. Visitors book in advance and there are six shows a day, six days a week. Each 40-minute session begins with a slide and tape show—which is not a lecture in art criticism, but an indication of the life of the artist and what things were like when the picture was painted. When the slide and tape show is finished, curtains open and people can spend the rest of their time looking at the picture.

* * *

Of course, people do not have to stand in an art museum, or in front of any other sightseeing object, and go through what I happen to consider the proper responses to what is in front of them. But if people *do* go to art museums 'knowing nothing about art', and come out in the same condition, then the controllers of those museums should be thinking more radically about how to encourage their visitors to look at the things on show (preferably, fewer of them), and feel free to use them as part of their general criticisms of existence. So that visitors no longer stand in awe of conspicuous money value, as if they were bankers, or worship celebrity, as if they were travel agents, or deride the unfamiliar, as if they were clowns on a tour from outer space, but enter into some kind of cultural engagement.

---

* DOING THE LOUVRE. You can gallop through the Vatican museums along the green, the yellow, the purple or the orange route, and not stop until you get to the Sistine Chapel. Some museums offer a quick menu of a dozen or so pictures. (Perhaps they should also list some of the pictures that most people don't see.) In the new Louvre, if the queues for the *Mona Lisa* or the Winged Victory of Samothrace are too tedious, you can go back to *le hall Napoléon*, under the *Pyramide*, with its boutiques and cafes, have a cup of coffee and buy yourself a souvenir. Three-quarters of the six million or so visitors a year are foreigners, in town for a few days, so most of the people who 'do' the Louvre will be making these kinds of decisions.

COMING OUT OF THE CULTURE BUNKER   357

A good art museum offers a prodigious concentration of resources for looking at things which provide a sense of wonder that can't be put into words, and which broaden our vision of the human repertoire and of the repertoire of 'realities'. But, at their most abused, art museums, articulated around fragments of the celestial chronological hang, can represent one of the greatest fiascoes of autonomic tourism. Visitors to art museums need help to free them into understanding that they have the right to *look*.

Unfortunately, that is likely to mean that people may be content to stand before anything famous, and otherwise maintain their existing tastes. ('I like this. I don't like that.') They need some information about the potentials of looking. Yet that goes against the curatorial wisdom that art needs no explanation: it would impede communication between art object and visitor to tell visitors anything, or anything much, about what they were looking at. There's the painting. Stand in front of it. React.

But art doesn't speak even to the curators through itself. It speaks to them through a multitude of scholarly publications, many by other curators. The whole profession of art scholarship would be impossible without books, prints, slides, and now computers. Curators don't fly somewhere every time they want to look at a picture. They consult some form of reproduction.

We *learn* to look at art paintings, just as we learn to look at anything else. Only in the physical sense are most of us born to see. When we open our eyelids, electromagnetic waves bend through five different parts of the eye to focus on the retina, where light-sensitive pigments go through chemical changes to 'translate' these waves into electrical activities that then pass on to the brain, which causes us to 'see'. But these processes do not give meaning to what we see. And they are a simple process compared with cultural (which is to say human) seeing.

To acquire meaning, what we see must pass through the mind's cultural refraction system. And painting, like anything else we look at, has its peculiarities. If we are looking at a painting of a woman sitting at a table with a small glass and a cup and saucer, we denote its constituents in simple elements. Woman. Table. Small glass. Cup and saucer. But, simultaneously, we add emotional connotations to these elements, according to how we feel about women, cups, glasses and tables. But this woman is sitting at a *cafe* table, the cup is *empty*, the glass holds some *brandy* and she holds in one hand a half-finished cigarette. How do we feel about cafes, empty cups, small glasses of brandy and half-finished cigarettes? And about a woman like this one, garishly made-up, with huge blue circles around her eyes? If the woman is dressed in a way that we recognise, establishing period and class, and the table matches these perceptions, we may be able to finish with the picture. But the top of this table is tilted towards the viewer (although nothing falls off) and the woman is naked apart from blue stockings and a fur tippet. Colour her head of hair orange and her pubic hair light brown. Yes, you're right: this is a German expressionist painting.*

In saying that we learn how to see, I am not suggesting that we shouldn't use things in art museums (or anywhere else) as we wish. But if we want to get more out of them, we should recognise that it requires skills to find ways of looking at these things that avoid merely laughing at them, or standing in awe of them, because they are unfamiliar.

One of the great things to learn about looking at art objects, for example, is in itself quite simple. It is to know that there can be more to a painting or a sculpture or whatever than meets the eye. In this it can be essential to apply the principle of intelligent superficiality, because so much art scholarship and analysis can be so useless. You don't have to know about, say, verticals, central zones, diagonals and the rest of the geometry of paintings. Not in detail anyway—you don't have to sit for an exam. But it can be useful to understand how the now thoroughly familiar might once have been an affront to convention.

We no longer need to know that Degas achieved his effects with close-up techniques and off-centre emphasis, and that he often cropped figures and objects at the edge of the picture. It can add technical interest to observe this, but it doesn't add to wonder or discovery. However, it can be useful to know this as an example of how what now seems 'natural'—as natural, in fact, as photography—once did require explanation.

It is easy, in any kind of sightseeing, to be frightened off by strangeness. Looking is never as easy as it sounds. For most of us, serious sightseeing of any kind must at some stage become a reading experience (or a video-watching experience, if that's the way you

---

* **'BEAUTY** I shall praise thee', from Georg Grosz's *Ecce Homo*.

feel), inspired by the principle of intelligent superficiality. Reading about a place after you have been there, and going on doing this, now and again, for the rest of your life, can be one of the lasting and intellectually useful pleasures of travel. (Not just guidebooks, however; they are usually too restricted, and 'travel writing' is usually an exercise in literary sensibility. What's wrong with reading history books, and social, cultural and economic critiques?) And it can be useful to know that strangeness, not only in art museums and in sightseeing generally, can be important in discovery and wonder.

WONDER, RESONANCE, AWE, CURIOSITY, SCEPTICISM

One function of a great work of art (but this can also be true of great survivors in architecture and natural landscape) is to be produced as witness, generation after generation, to give authority to particular purposes that come up, generation by generation. Goya's *The Shootings of the Third of May, 1808, in Madrid*, one of the first, and still the ultimate, painting of execution by firing-squad can have a message of terror to anyone who looks. But in what context? How do we explain it? What else is it saying? As Robert Hughes suggested in *Nothing If Not Critical*, this painting can be seen as the work of Goya the Romantic, Goya the Man of the People, Goya the Proto-Marxist, Goya the Surrealist, Goya the Existentialist or Goya the Liberal. These are some of the 'Goyas' invented to suit passing purposes (although, through these various cultural refractions, the painting remains wondrous and memorable).

This is part of what Malraux meant when he said in *Antimemoirs* that art was first and foremost a vast resurrection: 'Art consists of the works that have been resuscitated: one of the objects of culture is the whole body of resurrections (but) the thing resuscitated is not the same as when it was alive . . . The statues in (Indian) caves and those of European cathedrals are not what they were for the men who sculpted them. Greece for us is not what it was for itself, obviously . . . The past of the world consists of all the cultures different from our own . . . brought together for the first time through that metamorphosis'.

To stand in front of some work of art, or to engage in some

other notable sightseeing experience, can give sensory and intellectual texture to existence. But not only from the meaning you give it. You can also stand in its historical presence.* We may not be able to bring back the past, but we are not helpless. If we know nothing at all (the Ozymandias factor) we can at least stand in the presence of our ignorance and contemplate that. If we know something about contemporary styles when the object was made, and something about the myths that may have permeated the society in which it was made, we can still interpret it as we wish, giving new meanings, but we can do so knowing it wasn't seen like that at the time (although we can also recognise how little we may know of what it *did* seem like at the time). If we know enough we can stand in the presence of its history of meanings. That might be the way for the intelligently superficial tourist to use Stephen Greenblatt's 'resonance'.

'Resonance' is the feeling we get when we stand in the presence of some old thing and 'feel' what we can imagine to be its past, and also 'feel' the history of the meanings that have been given to it by succeeding generations. (Including our own. Understanding the role of the guide in the group tour is now part of the Great Hypostyle Hall experience.)

But what of the way in which we can also find in art objects ways of experiencing meanings that cannot be put into words? That goes for all the things we look at as tourists—but the best in art museums seem more than most other things to be too deep for words. (Of course words go on in their millions and millions. But words are words and looking is looking.)

This kind of feeling, applying to all the objects of sightseeing, is different from 'resonance', and the intelligent sightseer needs a word for it. Reworking Stephen Greenblatt's 'wonder' may do it, if by 'wonder' one means the feeling that can accompany an arresting sense of a thing-in-itself, its 'whatness'. In fact, things come to us

---

* **ART AS HISTORY.** But if we are interested in works of art only as part of cultural history we don't need to go to museums (although some special art exhibitions have been very good at putting paintings in a wider context). In fact, some of the art historians who are best at putting visual images into a social context (and to whom one painting is as good as the next) may go to museums only to analyse them as places where bourgeois controllers of cultural capital affirm their power.

not in themselves but through cultural refractions, but some of them provoke in us such an exalted attention that we can have a feeling of revealed presence. In sightseeing, this probably occurs most widely in the form of 'views' of nature, and then of certain buildings, art objects and social displays, but if we exercise the right to look we can make 'discoveries' throughout the sightseeing experience that can make the world seem that much wider.

I have usually, in this book, used the term 'awe' with the meaning that the journey was worthwhile (Michelin's three stars) if one wanted to stand within the aura of a famed object or situation. However, that may not go much beyond satisfaction at having been there and photographed it. In any case famed objects or sites can sometimes disappoint us by being less than we expected—or by being exactly as we expected. 'Awe' might be reserved for the occasion when the famous object or site has provoked a wonder that makes the experience more than expected. And it might be given the extended meaning that John Passmore suggests in *Serious Art*— that it has a magnitude which does not lose control and become merely grandiose (an approach that he suggests can also be applied to scientific, historical and philosophical writings).

To wonder, resonance and awe—the grand experiences of tourism—one can add *curiosity*, an experience that can seem lesser but that can wear more easily and is more versatile. A wondrous thing or scene can provide a charge to the imagination and one can want to know something more about it, or it might affect (marginally or grandly) one's view of existence generally. But so can an 'ordinary' thing. Even in the middle of an awestruck experience it may be some ordinary unexpected little thing that most arouses curiosity. Unless we are all going to go down with Stendhal's Syndrome, curiosity can be our greatest comfort as intelligent travellers.

And, without falling into the Loud-Mouthed Yank's Syndrome (Chapter 12), we can find, as I suggested in Chapter 3, that *scepticism* must also be the intelligent traveller's aid. Travelling can be a great question-raiser as, from what is told to us and from what we experience ourselves, we build up our own particular criticism of existence. But, like anything else, this requires training: some of us become more particular than others.

A WORLD WITHOUT ART MUSEUMS

In a better world we would not have art museums except as cultural genes banks, and we would not tolerate the imprisonment of collections in closed repositories.* Everything would be on show. Many things might be dispersed among public places, with a real effort to have contemporary art in particular as part of public life. What was left of the art collections would be displayed in open repositories which people could walk around: if they found something of interest, they could look it up in the reference area.

That would be the end of 'art'.

In this better world, there could still be specialist exhibitions of the kind so well developed over the last decade or so and that have some point to them. But there could be Visual Image Museums that went beyond art and brought together images of all kinds. Some of them could provide contemplations of design. Others could be related to particular themes and cultural conditions. Objects could be put together that are not usually grouped together in museums, art objects among them, so that there was a projection in material remains of a general cultural movement. (But this is something that people can also do in their own neighbourhoods and communities.)

The Pompidou Centre in Paris had an exhibition in 1978–9, *Le Temps des Gares*, that was a study in the imagery of the great railway station era. This began with engineers boldly creating metal and glass 'halls' to cover platforms (thereby expressing faith in progress through technology), while for the passenger buildings architects constructed memories of Roman baths and Benedictine monasteries, Mughal palaces and Greek temples which were megalomaniac in size but timid in imagination. They expressed a nervousness towards the future that changed direction in the 1920s, but only to neutral styles that pretended a building wasn't really there, apart from its material

---

* **PERPETUAL STORAGE.** A report from Italy's state auditing office in 1990 estimated that several million artworks are kept 'perpetually in storage'—without even a national inventory. The report suggested that all duplicate pieces and most 'lesser works' should be sold—to other Italian museums, and some of them to foreign museums. This would mean that more things would be on display, and that the museums who sold some of the works they did not display would be able to improve their care for what they retained, and improve their presentations.

functions. (Now, in the epilogue, a partly-abandoned railway station can be seen as a centre for 'urban renewal'.)

To develop its theme of railway stations revealing 'the myths and realities of the epic times we have lived in' the exhibition showed photographs of the stations themselves and of the profusion of instructive imagery cast up in the statuary, frescoes, emblems and symbols in their facades and halls. It showed the posters with which they cast seductive spells; the uniforms with which they graded their officials and the signs with which they graded their waiting rooms; the signal systems and the famous station clocks; the use of stations in the movies for images of theatricality and mobility; the enduring icons of brief encounters, sad *adieux*, holidays (and other adventures), troop departures, funeral cars—and, at Auschwitz, the end of the line.

'Our artists must find the poetry of stations as their fathers found forests and rivers', Émile Zola had said and the exhibition showed how, from Impressionists to Futurists, from Expressionists to Surrealists, the railway station had engendered (in a new display of modern imagination) 'manifestations which changed and enlarged our vision of the world', helping define the essence of pictorial modernism. Some of these paintings were part of the exhibition.

They made up the part that was 'art'.

* * *

The catalogue said: 'The railway station is one of the last great picture-books offered to the consumption of the public'—a strangely fatuous statement from the people who organised such a perceptive exhibition. If we learn to see, everything is a picture book.

28.

HOW TO BE A TOURIST

◆ ◆ ◆

YOU CAN'T DO THE WORLD

Why bother with travel when you can celebrate the world's cultures and peoples in the 11 exciting countries that lie along two kilometres of promenade in Orlando, Florida, at Disney World's 'World Showcase', and at the same time admire the calm beauties of a body of water the size of 35 football fields? As you would expect from a Disney creation, you can do all this comfortably, in a single morning, at a leisurely pace—with time for a pleasant lunch in an authentic national cuisine that will in no way offend American taste. If you haven't a whole morning, you can circle the world in a quaint double-decker bus in less than half an hour.*

---

* AMERICA'S GREATEST HOLES. Why tour the United States to play its most famous golf courses when a new course, opened at Houston in 1993, offers a replica of 'America's Greatest 18 Holes' in one round. Each hole is an almost exact replica, made out of grasses, shrubs and trees brought in from a range of courses stretching from Florida to California. In playing the famous hole from Pebble Beach, California, the ocean breeze and the sound of the surf are missing, but on one of the Georgia holes you can walk over genuine Georgia pine needles.

HOW TO BE A TOURIST   365

Imagine a full morning, in-depth tour. The first country across the entrance bridge from Future World is Mexico, where you can thrill to the grandeur of an ancient pyramid rising from a tangle of tropical forest. You then stroll past the shuttered balconies of a typical Mexican *plaza* (where it is always dusk) and enter the quaint cobblestoned town square of a typical Norwegian town, with its picturesque stave church, its *trolls* and its 14th century castle—don't miss the hand-knitted woollens in the castle shop. Nearby, there is all the colour of China in the famed Temple of Heaven, and all its serenity in an authentic garden with a century-old mulberry tree to marvel at. In contrast is Germany's beerhall and *weinkeller* bustle beside a cobblestoned *platz* so full of charm that it might have come out of a fairytale. (Try to arrange your visit so that you are there on the hour, when a *glockenspiel* chimes with a specially composed melody.)

You are then drawn irresistibly to Italy by the sight of St Mark's *campanile* set beside a *piazza* where fountains and a sea wall are stained with an authentic simulation of age. Your journey is nearly half over. Now you are in the centre of the world: you are in the United States. Before you is an imposing colonial mansion with 110,000 bricks, each hand-made from soft, pinkish-orange Georgia clay. Conveniently placed on the other side of this mansion is the exquisite simplicity of the Katsura Imperial Villa, converted into a small *yakitori* house where you can drink gently warmed *sake* from a large, hygienic plastic cup, while looking out on an authentic Japanese garden with boulders (brought from North Carolina) that represent the enduring nature of the earth.

Within sight is the delicate tracery of the Koutoubia Minaret: you are now in Morocco—and beside the minaret a shaded courtyard has a fountain gently playing in its centre; beyond are the traditional alleyways, surrounded by tourist shops, of the Medina (Old City)—do not miss the shop selling Casablanca carpets, near the ancient waterwheel. As you might expect, the Eiffel Tower is within sight of the minaret, and heavenly aromas from a sidewalk cafe announce the presence of fresh croissants. Beyond is a traditional English pub serving genuine English afternoon teas, and an elegant London square leads into a busy English street with gas lamps and scarlet letterboxes. You enter a Red Indian trading post sheltering beneath the majestic peaks of the Canadian Rockies. Your journey is at an end.

Not only can you encompass what really matters in the world in one pleasant morning: within each country, usefully compressed, is all that matters in that nation's experience. Norway itself doesn't have one town square where you can admire, all at once, the architectural styles of Bergen, Alesund, Oslo and Setesdal. (For that matter, where else in the world can you position a gas lamp and a coconut palm within the one photographic frame?)

Consider other advantages. In each country the water is safe to drink, and the ice-cream to eat. Restrooms are presented, externally, in authentic national styles, but within each there is familiar American comfort. Altogether there are 42 separate shops, but if you don't buy any pre-Columbian artifacts, Norwegian pewter, German beer *steins*, Italian leather, French perfume, Scottish tartans, or whatever, there are convenient souvenir barrows selling a quick T-shirt or baseball cap in national design that will show you have been there.

* * *

On the face of it, Disney World presents one of the best emergency policies for holding back the hordes which, by their very numbers, must help destroy what they have come to see. Instead of restricting access by unfair devices such as visitors' taxes, or by fair devices such as advance bookings, or by limiting devices such as nearby replicas*, some of the hordes can be kept away with alternatives. I prefer the Bali-style enclaves (which don't pretend to be much more than they are), or resort areas, such as Australia's Gold Coast with its 'Surfers' Paradise' (which boast of what they are), but Disney World, as an emergency measure in dreamland, may help keep millions of people away from historical sites like Venice that, unless something happens, won't survive. (In a spare part of Florida, Disney World has created a city with a million residents, 70,000 hotel rooms and its own international airport.) And well-engineered

---

* **REPLICAS** can be unavoidable. The Lascaux Caves in France's Dordogne had to be closed down because the breath exhaled by 200,000 visitors a year, and the bacteria they brought with them, were destroying the cave paintings. In these circumstances a replica is the best that can be done. I don't think it would work for the Taj Mahal, although the replica element in the Acropolis is increasing.

enclaves—for example, Benidorm, the most physically rational of Spain's concrete costas—keep down the physical pollution.

If everybody really wanted to see Venice there would be a democratic problem. But many people, when they go to Venice, do not go there to see it. They go there to do it because of its celebrity status in the hysteria for 'doing' certain sights. Short of setting a small exam to see whether people want to see Venice or *do* it, part of the short-term answer to the problem of the invasion of Venice is to build up a greater desire to 'do' pseudo-replica theme parks like Disney World. In fact, at a conference on saving Venice held in February 1992, it was suggested that since the main problem was day-visitors who weren't much interested in Venice apart from its celebrity, the easiest way out might be to construct a Disney-like essence-of-Venice on the mainland nearby, so that tourists could 'do' a pseudo-Venice in an hour or so and enjoy some rides as well.

People should be able to enjoy their holidays. But some people would enjoy their holidays more if they were saved the tedium of queuing to be in the presence of celebrated objects or sights that may not interest them. (The train buff on the Palace-on-Wheels preferred to look at the Agra city railway station rather than the Taj Mahal.) This is where 'commodification' becomes an intellectually useful term of abuse. There is nothing wrong with people planning travel and paying for it. There is everything wrong with simplifying the world into a set of categorised prestige items to be acquired in cash transactions.

Coaxing people into enclaves is a necessary emergency measure—necessary because there aren't enough obligatory sights to go around, and emergency because something may have gone wrong with all of us and we don't yet know what it is. This gives us time to find out. It's easy for me to say this. I have been to most of the sights I first learned about from *Cassell's Children's Book of Knowledge*, and in ways that, in many cases, are no longer available. But that doesn't alter the fact that if we continue to want to 'do' the sights, there are not at present enough of them to go around. It is physical necessity that demands that we have to extend our ideas of what we can look at when we go sightseeing. We can only 'do' the world in one lifetime if we reduce human variety to a very restricted list. It is possible when visiting a city not to 'do' its most celebrated features, but to choose others—or even to spend part of the time just walking around. My favourite industry museum became the Quarry Bank

Mill at Styal because its Great Wheel is its only significant piece of machinery. You have time to look at it.

Since I think that a critical curiosity is one of the best things one can find in human beings, I am not saying that we shouldn't have a wide interest in the world. But we don't have to 'do' (viz visit) a large number of celebrated sites in the world to know (viz speculate about) it. Most of our speculation about the world is prompted second-hand by reading, looking and listening to what other people have to say. It's true that going out and having a look for ourselves can be one of the sharpest ways of giving us new ideas. (If new ideas are what we want; otherwise, of course, this merely confirms old prejudices.) But that doesn't mean concentrating on doing the sights, unless we find the contemplation of tourism itself a main interest. In *Riding the Iron Rooster*, Paul Theroux says he never looks at famous sights.

A PLACE FOR THE INTELLIGENT TOURIST

Some last words on the disasters of tourism. Many of these disasters come from the nationalisms that helped frame each nation's tourist showcase. With a bit of sensitivity, it is not hard to realise when you *are* inside a tourist showcase. Fort Bowie, Arizona, a centre for the military onslaught on the Apache Indians, can be seen as national prejudice in *adobe*. In Serbia, you can see that what is offered on the tourist schedule is part of the 19th century creation of Serbia, just as the Louvre is part of the 19th century creation of France. It is what can *not* be seen that provides the disaster: whole parts of a nation, past and present, are not there at all, or there only in the grossest caricature.*

Consider the moral calamity that came to England when the most significant part of England's past was evoked by the country houses of the aristocracy and the gentry—or the even greater calamity when

---

* **PRESERVING THE TOURISTS** During the elections for Governor of Louisiana at the end of 1991, in which a favoured candidate was a former Grand Wizard of the Ku Klux Klan, the New Orleans authorities banned political advertising and shut down the TV sets in corner bars in case the realities of the present frightened tourists away from the nostalgia of the French Quarter, of Créole food and conserved honky-tonks.

South Africa was represented by the Voortrekker Monument. There are also the art disasters, in which the past is valued principally as an aesthetic experience; the nostalgia disasters, in which the past is seen as ranging between the idyllic and the cosy; the disasters of the positivistic irrefutability of museums; and the disasters of 'the exotic' (of which racism is only one of several subsets), in which *they* are all different from *us*.

But for millions of the mass tourists of the last century and a half sightseeing was a liberating and enlightening force—especially if they brought to their experiences something that was already in their own heads. It could excite sharpness of perception. It could give new ways of looking at people and things. It could be part of the search for building a general intellectual critique of existence. It could be a reminder that all things decay, that the past can be sought but will never be found (although we can speculate about the material fragments that survive, and thereby reflect on the insubstantiality of knowledge). Tourists treading through fragments of old myths could realise they were close to the remains of supernatural beliefs, to past legitimations of power and to the legends and icons that gave meaning to existence. Some could recognise that they were also treading through the live myths of modern societies, in which all these old things had been transmuted and now played new roles that their makers could not have imagined. And they could draw on the 'cultural genes banks'—the restorations of narratives and ceremonies, of dance, music, drama, and visual images, of bodies of knowledge and wisdom and habits of speculative observation and inquiry—that provided more plentiful repertoires of what it might mean to be human than could ever before have been imagined. There was the special encouragement to *look at things* (which in our other lives we may not do). And, however superficially, there was the chance to get out among people different from us, and places different from where we lived, and not see them as the alien 'other', but as alternatives.

I have put these benefits into the past tense. They still hold, of course, if mainly for those I have called the intelligent tourists, of whom there are still many. What has changed is that for a large part of the beginnings of modern tourism sightseeing was declaredly and unashamedly seen as edifying. Now it is not. If you seek edification, you may have to pursue it as a secret pleasure.

For the future it might be better if, for a while, the enlivening approach of taking tourism seriously went public, as a matter of public (including government) concern, even if (or because) it is only a minority market (if still a large market). For those who do not share it, there are the enclaves. People should understand that they can lead very good lives without feeling they have to 'do' the Sistine Chapel, the Pyramids, the Grand Canyon or the Great Wall of China. Ideally, these places should be for those who have an interest in them not for their celebrity, but for what they are celebrated for. (In fact, seeing the Pyramids or the Great Wall can subtract from their potential awe. They can become interesting mainly as a specimen of the tourist experience.)

Is what I have said 'elitist'? Well, it isn't possessively elitist. One of the curses of culture critique in this century, sometimes coming from the Left as well as the culturally conservative Right, has been a panic that if things are 'popularised', in the sense of being widely seen, used and read by masses of people, then they lose their value. As contrasted with that, I still have a 19th century liberal faith that the great repertoires of world culture are a common human possession that should be available to anyone for their enlightenment. In going out and having a look at things for themselves I wish more people wanted to see things rather than *do* them and knew more about what they were doing. But while it doesn't matter how many people read or look at or listen to reproductions of a particular work, it *does* matter how many of us tramp around a site or crowd out a city or a museum.

And it isn't financially elitist either, with all the good things going only to those who can afford to pay for them. (In fact, because they don't like queues, the rich have very largely been got out of the way—in the enclaves of luxury hotels and exclusive resorts—although there is still a disposal problem with those of the middling well-to-do who want to achieve a high score in *doing* the world.) It is a minority policy for the benefit of the enormous numbers of intelligent tourists—most of whom are not rich and many of whom are not well-off. That should mean that while private firms do what they like (within the safety, pollution and other regulations), public money should substantially serve serious purposes.

For example, the policy of developing alternatives would encourage intelligent attempts—in a process that has already begun—to spread interest beyond the few most celebrated exhibits in a national showcase (some of which are not worth queueing for). Denver is one example. Another is the suggestion in Britain (at the time, it made almost everyone laugh) that towns like Wigan Pier that have been dumped by progress could be cleaned up a bit and made an occasion for a visit to the industrial past. Another is that the tourist authorities in national capitals should try to spread interest around more widely. The French and Swiss idea of 'green tourism' may be another: that you stay with local people in their homes, and learn something about them and the places where they live, perhaps going back for refresher courses. Better guidebooks would be a help—guidebooks that go beyond obligatory agendas and that recognise diversity. Providing a multiplicity of 'heritage trails' on the Boston model is an essential antidote to the monopolies of the public culture.

Greater control by governments of their own advertising could be of some use in suggesting that their countries are not as idiotic as many ads suggest. Why is it in the national interest of a country to produce cartoon versions of itself? Or, if they feel they have to do it for commercial reasons, can't they also run some alternative ads for people with wider interests?

Some correction is needed of the errors of what is probably the most corrupt section of the media—the travel supplements which trade in lies so that their publications can get ads and the writers can get free trips. Another area for immediate treatment is the special kind of inanity that usually infests the across-the-counter staff of government tourist agencies and hotel lobbies—who often seem to know nothing about their own country or city, apart from the departure time of the next package tour.

* * *

Museums are an obvious example of taking sightseeing seriously, but we should recognise that there is a difference between respect for things in museums and obsequiousness. A sense of heaviness and inflexibility weighed down the idea of the museum from the time of its birth, in contrast to the flexibility, lightness and showiness of the concurrent idea of the Great Exhibition. Making museums accessible and enjoyable is both sensible and democratic, and it is also sensible to make some extra money out of them, so

372   THE INTELLIGENT TOURIST

long as it does not subvert a museum's distinctively museum-like functions.*

However, one can overdo making museums fun places. Museum shops can be an intellectually useful follow-up to a museum visit, and they may be the most useful part of a science centre, but they can also degrade museums into mere stopovers for tourists who want to demonstrate that they have 'done' a museum by buying not even a postcard, but a T-shirt. Museums should be places of excitement— but it should be the imagination and the intellect that they excite. Museums are not just funfairs or adventure parks. To justify their special status they must be places of enlightenment, appealing to our imaginations; to our desire to see what things look like; and to our desire to find something out. (We should be particularly wary of press-buttons. As science centres can show, just as visitors might once have been so baffled by scholarship that they might not see the exhibits for the labels, they can now be so distracted by fun that they might not see the exhibits for the press-buttons.)

Something of a seminar industry has now developed around museums as a problem in marketing. The big question can be: at the bottom of the line and the end of the day, how can we get down to basics and attract the tourist dollar? But there are other ways of attracting the 'tourist buck' than preparing programs for the devastation of museums. Museums should be run efficiently and their economies should be studied. But it is *museums* that should be studied, and this means beginning with a belief that there are things that a museum can do that Disneyland can't. Some people who want to make museums more efficient really want to kill altogether the traditional edifying function of museums—because it affronts the crasser kinds of commercialism.

---

* FUN PLACES. Museums can now be planned right from the start with spaces to hire out for parties. In Stockholm, there is the 17th century warship, the *Wasa*, built with such baroque top-heaviness that in 1628 it keeled over and sank as it sailed from the naval yard. Its carcass lay in an aluminium intensive-care ward for 16 years after it was salvaged in 1961, while they put 14,000 pieces together again. The new Wasa Museum, to which it was floated in 1988, includes a restaurant where people can dine at night, with the harbour on one side and the floodlit *Wasa* on the other. Why not? Is having a party in these surroundings any more or any less absurd than putting a baroque warship into a museum?

What we should now be talking about when we discuss museums is changing how things seem. Traditional divisions of subject, when museums were making classified inventories of the world, made museums a modernising force, but they no longer serve our views of the world—or, if they do, they shouldn't. The grand museums of each metropolis should have regular carnivals in the form of combined, interdisciplinary exhibitions on some common theme, put together by choosing from among all their collections—thereby demonstrating how arbitrary the present divisions are. Now that we see a need for better husbanding of resources and for understanding the connections between things, Natural History Museums* should become Ecology Museums or Environment Museums. And now that we live at a time when the problems of production have been solved, but most of the world does not benefit, Museums of Science and Industry, established as expressions of faith in materialism and uncontested views of reality and the inevitability of progress, might also become places of warning.

Museums, seen by many as so boring, can uniquely throw up new ways of looking at things—at times simply by changing things around. One can't rearrange Victoria Falls or the Acropolis, but one can rearrange a museum.

In 1992 Fred Wilson, a New York artist, was given the running of the Maryland Historical Museum in Baltimore and asked to do something new with it. He juxtaposed things that would never have been imagined together (a whipping post was labelled 'Cabinet-making, 1820–1960' and four comfortable Victorian chairs were placed round it, for better viewing); he arranged a row of dime-store Indians so that they faced a wall of photographs of real native Americans, staring back. He left spaces with labels showing some of the things that were not there in the museum; one cast-iron artwork was a 'Naughty Nellie' bootjack, of a black woman

---

* THE SPECIAL CASE OF NATURAL HISTORY MUSEUMS. Classifications are essential as a research function in natural history. Collecting specimens in an orderly way and grouping and comparing them (taxonomy) provides the main way of learning what is going on among living things—and, in particular, how they are changing. But most of this is a research activity: it should not be the basis for display. What the taxonomists should do is to give us examples of change, especially changes occurring in the local region, or devote some space to demonstrating how taxonomy works.

stretched out with her legs spread apart. The Historical Museum attracted the African-Americans and Hispanics who live around it, but would not have imagined themselves inside it. Fred Wilson was booked up by other museums whose managements felt it was time they had some visitors among their exhibits.

* * *

In general, as a pleasure, sightseeing should be taken more seriously. Digby Anderson, an English travel writer, has suggested that intellectually successful tourism is like a liberal education: if it's worth having, it's worth working for. That was what I had in mind with 'the principle of intelligent superficiality'—good sightseers can't be experts on everything, since no-one can be an expert on everything, but that doesn't mean that they don't have to do any preparation on what they are going to look at.

This shouldn't be just a matter for the self-improvement of individuals (although assisting that process should be the beginning of public policy—since one of the most effective openings of a reform movement is to sustain those who are already halfway there anyway). Some of the world's worriers should lend their worries positively to analysing the excesses of autonomic tourism as if it were a mass drug problem. Inhaling doses of hallucinogenic tourism *is* a drug problem.

Come back to 'World Showcase' and see it as an opium den. What a moral disaster it is that people can enjoy such rubbish. The official guide itself gives the game away: it praises World Showcase for offering the *essence* of each country, 'much as a traveller returning from a visit might remember what he or she saw'. Disney World saves you from the nuisance of doing your own remembering. That is what is hallucinogenic about it. It means, not simply, as in our imagined nature tour of New Zealand, that you buy a packet of clichés. In New Zealand, if you know how to, you can look at the scenery despite the clichés and find out what comes into your own mind. In World Showcase you are looking at symbols of clichés. According to the guidebook, nothing else need come into your mind. To get the best out of World Showcase your mind has to be taken over.

And there is a special nastiness about these symbols of clichés and the fatuous suggestion that each collection of these pseudo-replicas 'represents' a culture. Apart from the gardens and the shops and the eating places (most of which are good) there is not the 'hyper-reality' that Umberto Eco found in the United States, but a thoroughly researched *subreality*. With the exception of the United States mansion, which is larger than any mansion has ever been, everything is brought down to less than size and clearly faked. The world is put in its place, as toylike and quaint. What are real are the Disney World contrivances.

In an essay, 'The Semiotics of Tourism', Jonathan Culler sees postmodern travellers as 'interested in everything as a sign in itself . . . All over the world the unsung armies of semioticians, the tourists, are fanning out in search of the signs of Frenchness, typical Italian behaviour, exemplary oriental scenes, traditional English pubs'. But, for those who are on autonomic control, 'interested' is too active a word. Semiotician tourists can go, say, to the Royal Military Museum in Brussels, look at the uniforms and flags, banners and swords, and see them as the signs which maintained order and apparent coherence and see the museum itself as exhibit, a reminder of the tourism of nationalism. Or if they go to the Revolutionary Museum in Hanoi, where the show begins with a big bronze war drum that is about 4500 years old, they can see how this is used as one of the symbols of what is presented as a long revolutionary tradition in Vietnam. People like that can agree with me that a principal use of museums and other forms of exhibition can be to help us see objects as cultural symbols. But I don't recall all that many tourist semioticians of that kind on the Palace-on-Wheels.

One of the refreshments of sightseeing is to see places and things and people for ourselves. We can read about them in books or look at them in videos, but when we go there we can 'see what they are like'. Instead of contemplating familiar emptied symbols we can *look*, and experience a sense of discovery and wonder and curiosity. And we can experience the silence of the things we are looking at. They don't speak to us. If any speaking is being done it is us speaking to *them*. But we can learn to experience them by looking rather than speaking. We can give up sight*seeing* for sight-*experiencing*.

KEYWORDS

♦ ♦ ♦

ART MUSEUMS
What unites all the disparate objects in these arbitrarily assembled collections is, that by the very fact of being displayed in an art museum, they have become 'art'. They therefore have nothing to do with anything except themselves.

AUTHENTICITY
One of the special magics of sightseeing tourism is that an object can cast a spell of moral and material value by being the real thing. In fact, authenticity must always be contrived. It is the *idea* of authenticity that many tourists want.

AUTOBAHNIA
A word invented by Frank Moorhouse, in *Room Service*. A special form of autonomic tourism in which the principal interests are the motorways, their facilities (motel strips, service stations, food outlets) and the signs pointing to famous tourist sites you need never see.

AUTONOMIC TOURISM
A kind of tourism that is as involuntary as the functions of the autonomic nervous system of the human body. We become autonomic tourists if in our sightseeing we don't move beyond whatever the tourist industry has prefabricated for us, in conceptualisation or itineraries. A deadly symptom of autonomic

tourism is an over-riding interest in travel facilities—a process that reaches its depths in AUTOBAHNIA, see above.

CIVILISATION PACKET
Some of the grand museums of Europe and the United States offer a civilisation packet in which there is presented a 'world civilisation' which you can pick up in an afternoon. This civilisation begins in Mesopotamia, passes through Ancient Egypt to Greece and Rome, then spreads throughout Europe, which is where it stays. It is seen as consisting predominantly of 'art'.

COMMODIFICATION
An approach in which sightseeing is something to be bought, piece by piece, as if sightseeing consisted of acquiring a number of packaged goods.

CULTURAL GENES BANK
In the cultural storehouses of modern-industrial societies—the museums, historical sites, libraries and archives, the reprints, reproductions and compact disks, and the places used for re-presentations of performance—there are preserved for us to use as we wish more varied repertoires of what it might mean to be human than could ever before have been imagined. These make up a kind of 'cultural genes bank', which is one of the greatest wonders of our age and one of the greatest justifications for sightseeing.

DARSHANA
The feelings that tourists can have when confronted by a famous landscape or historic site or celebrated object may be compared to the Hindu concept of *darshana*, the mysterious ecstasy generated in the presence of a holy place.

DISCOVERY
In tourism this can mean maintaining the myth that no part of the world existed until a European found it. It can also mean a sudden exciting of our curiosity or wonder when we see something for the first time that can make the world seem that much wider—sometimes only a little wider, sometimes with such a change in perception that it becomes a life experience.

'DO'
You 'do' an object, or place, or city, or country when you can tick it off on your itinerary.

ENCLAVE TOURISM
A tourist settlement almost completely cut off from the surrounding society. In Third World countries this can be seen as revival colonialism. Nevertheless, for people who are not much interested in finding out something about the country they are visiting, a well-run enclave can enable them to enjoy themselves without crowding out the sights or making a general mess.

ETHNOGRAPHIC MUSEUM
A treatment of the artifacts of lesser breeds.

EXCERPT CULTURE
'Excerpts' from performances are the parallel of the 'exhibit', as something taken out of context. As seen in cultural shows, excerpts may be entirely degraded—or they may be illuminating introductions.

EXHIBIT
A thing becomes an 'object' when it is acquired by a museum, evaluated for its authenticity, named, catalogued and conserved. If it is placed on view it becomes an 'exhibit'. As an object it enters a realm of authentic purity. As an exhibit it is magically detached from the rest of the world.

EXORCISING TOURISM
One hope for sightseeing as an intelligent and useful pastime is that we can exorcise the spells cast around celebrated objects and see them in some other way.

FESTIVAL
A festival is a ritualised break from routine in which participants are defining certain values in an atmosphere of fellowship. Group touring is a festival: it is at its worst if it displays how different *we* are from *them*.

FRAMING
This is a process in which you are told how to look at something so that it becomes isolated from the rest of the world, and you see it in the way that a guidebook suggests you see it.

GUIDEBOOKS
One of the functions of guidebooks is to obliterate everything in a society that is not framed in a magic circle and *named*.

ICON
An image that carries an immediate conceptual and emotional weight in illustrating a myth. Icons of tourism such as the Taj Mahal, the gondolier, the Statue of Liberty, or the grass skirt, can pass from being emblems of themselves to becoming worn-out symbols of symbols of tourism.

INDUSTRY MUSEUMS
Collections of old machines which usually suggest that industrialisation occurred without people.

INTELLIGENT SUPERFICIALITY
Becoming a generalist is a specialism of its own. In tourism, if you want to be enlightened you have to learn how to be intelligently superficial. There can be advantages in knowing a little about a lot. The alternative is to know nothing about a lot.

ITINERARY
A ceremonial agenda of obligatory rites; an agenda of magic circles similar to those on a pilgrim's progress.

LANDSCAPES
Tourist landscapes such as the Swiss Alps, the Grand Canyon, or Victoria Falls were created by the romantic imagination, which offered to the tourist-pilgrim regeneration and even redemption by standing in their presence. Guidebooks then encircled them by fame. Certain landscapes—Mount Fuji, for example, or Ayers Rock in Australia—became parts of the national tourist pilgrimage, revealing national character. Landscapes are entirely a human concept. There are no landscapes in nature.

LEGEND
A simple story that helps perpetuate a myth. The legends of tourism are found in travel books, guidebooks, travel brochures and the stories we bring back home.

MAGIC CIRCLE
One of the wonders of the enchanted journeys of tourism is that certain objects and places are framed within such a radiance of celebrity that they are magically transmuted into something they were never intended to be. These are all you have to 'do'. This is the major sorcery of tourism.

MONUMENTS
Objects that were developed for one purpose can be transformed so that they 'stand for' some idea that would have astounded their creators. One of the enchantments of tourism is to turn inanimate matter into meaning by transforming it into a museum exhibit or an historic site.

MUSEUMS
These were institutions founded to bring order to the universe by classifying it and laying things out in a straight line, from entrance to exit. People who found doubt in the churches could find certainty in the museums. However, many of them could also become modernising agents. Now they can again become agents for change.

MYTH
A belief held in common by a large group of people that can, by a kind of magic, explain almost everything. As sightseers we tread through the material relics of other peoples' myths, but we may not know what they were. The special myth of tourism is the possibility of regeneration or redemption through the tourist pilgrimage.

NAMING
When Europeans 'discovered' a natural feature they performed an act of conceptual appropriation: they 'named' it. Naming can be one of the essential parts of tourism. The people who decided what to put in the guidebooks were the 'discoverers' of the world of tourism.

NATIONAL CAPITAL
All that tourists see of a country may be the boulevards and squares in the national capital (laid out within the last century and a half), a few of its selected historical sites (usually designated over the same period), and some of the most celebrated items in the national cultural showcase. These few 'exhibits' then turn the national capital into a selective museum representing the whole nation.

NATIONAL PAST
As the modern nation-states were formed, there was invented for each of them a 'national past' that gave a strong sense of historical meaning to help justify the existence of the state. The 'past' presented to tourists is usually a simplification of these simple legends, put together by 19th century nationalist intellectuals.

NATIONAL TOURIST PILGRIMAGE
The development of tourism could be the same thing as the development of a public culture. Certain natural features, museums, monuments, historic sites and emblematic buildings were essential in fabricating the imagined communal life of a nation. If loyal citizens made a tourist pilgrimage to them, they would come back better citizens.

OZYMANDIAS
Shelley's sonnet about the ruins of a monumental statue in an antique land should be the special sonnet of tourists, as a reminder that all things pass.

PAST
The 'past' is an invention of the present. Despite the inside stories told by the guides, we can never 'know' the past. We can, however, examine relics of the past, speculate and provide stories.

PILGRIMS
Sightseeing can become a pilgrimage in which certain secular objects are given properties similar to holy relics. What the tourist-pilgrims seek is physical, mental or cultural regeneration.

PRADAKSHINA
A tourist itinerary can be similar to the Hindu idea of *pradakshina*, of walking around a holy place and meditating—except that the meditating may be done for us by guides.

PSEUDO-TRADITIONALISM
In the 19th century in Europe conservatives tried to mobilise the masses around newly invented 'traditions'. Pseudo-traditionalism seems a better word. Since then it has become a kind of neo-pseudo-traditionalism, a revival of a revival.

PUBLIC CULTURE
There is projected in every modern-industrial nation-state a public and visible culture which purports to be the national life and to provide the national version of the certainties of existence. The principal tourist programs are usually part of this illusionary projection.

'READING' TOURISM
Tourism becomes more intelligent if whatever it is you are looking

at can be seen in relation to myth-systems. We can 'read' the 'language' of tourism by asking what views of the world some particular tourist experience suggests. And then ask: who benefits from that?

RELICS
By the second half of the 18th century art objects were being given the veneration previously reserved for holy relics. This veneration then spread to other objects (exhibits or historic sites) which had the special magic of authenticity. It is the idea of authenticity that unites the different objects from which tourists seek regeneration.

RESONANCE
The feeling we get when we stand in the presence of some old thing and 'feel' what we can imagine to be its past and the history of the meanings that have been given to it by succeeding generations.

RITUAL
This is an action that we perform with our bodies to get something done, according to a basic myth. The ritual of tourism is to achieve regeneration by moving our bodies in a predetermined pattern in proximity to celebrated objects of sightseeing.

SIGHT-'EXPERIENCING'
One can distinguish between 'sightseeing', which, at its crudest, can just mean looking without seeing so that you have scored another sight, and 'experiencing' a sight, so that you have a sense of its past and how it is now being used. You get something of your own out of it.

SIGHTSEEING
For the purposes of this book, this includes: looking at historic sites and monuments or significant buildings, villages, town squares, boulevards, marketplaces, picturesque quarters, new architectural developments or engaging in other kinds of edifying rubbernecking; visiting museums and other exhibitions, with or without a special interest in 'art', and going to theatres, concerts and other kinds of performance ranging from a Palestrina mass to an African rain dance; standing in the presence of (or taking a helicopter flight over) magic landscapes of nature, filled with cultural messages; getting to know something about the ways of other peoples, whether at the ends of

the earth or the next town. Sightseeing can include going to the Kentucky Fried Chicken in Beijing.

'SILENCES'
What is significantly missing. A public culture is full of 'silences'. So, often, is a museum, or any other tourist experience.

STATUEMANIA
A 19th and early 20th century European obsession for putting up statues of the heroes of the national past in squares and parks, boulevards and prestigious traffic intersections.

'STENDHAL'S SYNDROME'
A tourist condition characterised by a loss of sense of reality and identity, insomnia, paranoia and guilt, named for the occasion when Stendhal wrote in his diary after first seeing the Giotto frescoes in Santa Croce: 'I had palpitations of the heart . . . Life was drained from me. I walked from the fear of falling'.

TARZAN VILLAGE TOURISM
Edgar Rice Burrows Inc once considered purchasing The Gambia so that they could build a series of 'Tarzan Villages' in it. Tarzan Village tourism is enclave tourism in which, within the enclave, there is put together a fake tourist version of the surrounding society.

TOURIST
I am a traveller. You are a tourist. They are a coach party.

TOURIST SHOWCASE
In a whole city, or perhaps a whole nation, only a few views and vistas, a few buildings, monuments or museums (and only a few objects within these museums) are all you have to 'do'. These are the city's, or the nation's, tourist showcase. The rest does not exist.

'TRADITION'
Is what you want peoples other than your own (especially in the Third World) to maintain so that you can have a picturesque holiday. If they begin to move away from the past, as a holiday place their country is being 'spoilt'.

TRAVEL BOOK
A travel book is an exercise in refined sensibility that provides sensations of acuteness of observation that none of us (including the author) is ever likely to experience.

VIEW
A 'view' is a way of looking at a landscape in a tight, preordained 'frame'. The classic views were 'sublime' (a theatrical sense of awe) or 'picturesque' (simple harmonies). In the 19th century 'views' became romantic. Nature was a vital force that could instruct and ennoble the human soul. It is now essential that a 'view' should look like a photograph.

WAR MUSEUMS
Collections of weapons, flags, uniforms, etc which usually suggest that wars were fought without people.

WONDER
The feeling that can come from an arresting sense of a thing-in-itself. In fact, things come to us not in themselves but through cultural refractions, but some of them provoke in us such an exalted attention that we can have a feeling of revealed presence.

SELECTED BIBLIOGRAPHY

◆ ◆ ◆

All the works referred to in this book are listed here. I have added some other works on tourism that are worth reading, and also a few of the books that have proved useful in working out some of the more general assumptions in this book.

Judith Adler, 'Origins of Sightseeing', *Annals of Tourism Research*, Vol. 16 No. 1, 1989.

Denis Altman, *Paper Ambassadors*, Sydney: Angus & Robertson, 1991.

Malcolm Andrews, *The Search for the Picturesque: Landscape Aesthetics and Tourism in Britain, 1760-1800*, Aldershot: Solar Press, 1989.

Ulla Arnell, Inger Hammer & Gøran Nylöf, *Going to Exhibitions*, Stockholm: Riksutställningar, 1976.

Auckland Committee on Racism and Discrimination, *The Souvenir Trade; Debasing a Culture*, Auckland: 1988.

Todd Barr, *No Swank Here? The Development of the Whitsundays as a Tourist Destination to the early 1970s*, Townsville: James Cook University of North Queensland, 1990.

Roland Barthes, *Mythologies*, London: Granada, 1973.

Roland Barthes, *The Eiffel Tower*, New York: Farrar, Strauss & Giroux, 1979.

Walter Benjamin, *Illuminations*, London: Fontana, 1973.

Tony Bennett, *Out of Which Past? Critical Reflections on Australian Museum and Heritage Policy*, Brisbane: Institute for Cultural Policy Studies, 1988.

John Berger, *Ways of Seeing*, London: BBC and Penguin, 1972.

Peter Berger, *Invitation to Sociology*, Harmondsworth: Penguin, 1963.

Peter Berger & Thomas Luckman, *The Social Construction of Reality*, Garden City: Doubleday, 1966.

Leo Bersani, *The Culture of Redemption*, Cambridge, Mass: Harvard University Press, 1990.

Stephen Birnbaum, *Birnbaum's United States*, Boston: Houghton Miflin, 1992.

Marshal Blonsky (ed.), *On Signs*, Oxford: Blackwell, 1985.

Robert Bocock, *Hegemony*, London: Tavistock, 1986.

Carl Boggs, *Gramsci's Marxism*, London: Pluto Press, 1976.

Piers Brendon, *Thomas Cook: 150 Years of Popular Tourism*, London: Martin Secker & Warburg, 1991.

Asa Briggs, *Iron Bridge to Crystal Palace. Impact and Images of the Industrial Revolution*, London: Thames & Hudson, 1979.

Paul Carter, *The Road to Botany Bay: An Essay in Spatial History*, London: Faber & Faber, 1987.

Jean Clair, *Paradoxe sur le conservateur, précédé la modernité conçue comme une religion*, quoted in *The International Herald Tribune*, October 28 1989.

Peter A Clayton, *The Rediscovery of Ancient Egypt: Artists and Travellers in the Nineteenth Century*, London: Thames & Hudson, 1990.

Stefanja Cobelj, 'The Provincial Museum of Hargeisa', in *Museum*, No. 151, 1986.

James E Combs & Michael W Mansfield, *Drama in Life*, New York: Hastings House, 1976.

Jennifer Craik, Resorting to *Tourism: Cultural Policies for Tourist Development in Australia*, North Sydney: Allen & Unwin, 1991.

Malcolm Crick, 'Representations of Tourism in the Social Sciences: Sun, Sex, Sights, Savings and Servility', *Annual Review of Anthropology*, 1989.

Jonathan Culler, 'The Semiotics of Tourism' in *The American Journal of Semiotics*.

Howard Daniel & John Berger, *Encyclopedia of Themes and Subjects in Painting*, London: Thames & Hudson, 1971.

Mike Davis, *City of Quartz*, London: Vintage, 1992.

H D Duncan, *Symbols in Society*, New York: Oxford University Press, 1968.

Umberto Eco, *Faith in Fakes*, London: Secker & Warburg, 1986.

Umberto Eco, *Semiotics and the Philosophy of Language*, London: Macmillan, 1984.

Maurice Edelman, *Politics as Symbolic Action*, New York: Academic Press, 1971.

Allen Ellenius, *Den offentiga konsten och ideologierna*, Stockholm: Almqvst & Wiksell, 1971 (English summary).

Jacques Ellul, *Propaganda*, New York: Vintage Books, 1965.

Jason Epstein, 'The Decline and Rise of Publishing', *New York Review of Books*, March 1 1990.

Stuart & Elizabeth Ewen, *Channels of Desire: Mass Images and the Shaping of American Consciousness*, New York: McGraw Hill, 1982.

Michel Foucault, *Discipline and Punish: The Birth of the Prison*, Harmondsworth: Penguin, 1977.

Paul Fussell, *Abroad: British Literary Travelling Between the Wars*, New York: Oxford University Press, 1982.

Herbert J Gans, *Popular Culture and High Culture*, New York: Basic Books, 1974.

Jean Garrigues, *Images de la Révolution: l'imagerie républicaine de 1789 à nos jours*, Paris: Éditions du May, 1989.

Alan D Gilbert, *The Making of Post-Christian Britain*, London: Longman, 1980.

Erving Goffman, *Frame Analysis: An Essay on the Organisation of Experience*, New York: Harper & Row, 1974.

Heinz Gollwitzer, *Europe in the Age of Imperialism*, London: Thames & Hudson, 1969.

Andre Gorz, *Farewell to the Working Class: An Essay on Post-Industrial Socialism*, London: Pluto Press, 1982.

Suresh Goyal, *Chittorgarh, the Land of Chivalry and Heroism*, Udaipur: Goyal Brothers, 1989.

Stephen J Greenblatt, *Learning to Curse: Essays in Early Modern Culture*: Routledge, 1992.

Robert Hewison, *The Heritage Industry: Britain in a Climate of Decline*, London: Methuen, 1987.

Eric Hobsbawm & Terence Ranger (eds.), *The Invention of Tradition*, Cambridge: Cambridge University Press, 1983.

James Holloway & Lindsay Errington, *The Discovery of Scotland; The Appreciation of Scottish Scenery through Two Centuries of Painting*, Edinburgh: National Gallery of Scotland, 1978.

Donald Horne, *The Great Museum: The Re-presentation of History*, London: Pluto Press, 1984.

Donald Horne, *The Public Culture: The Triumph of Industrialism*, London: Pluto Press, 1986.

Kenneth Hudson, *Museums of Influence*, Cambridge: Cambridge University Press, 1987.

Robert Hughes, *Nothing If Not Critical*, London: Collins Harvill, 1990.

John A Jakle, *The Tourist: Travel in Twentieth Century North America*, Lincoln: University of Nebraska Press, 1985.

Richard Jenkyns, *The Victorians and Ancient Greece*, Cambridge, Mass: Harvard University Press, 1980.

Orrin Edgar Klapp, *Heroes, Villains and Fools*, Englewood Cliffs, NJ: Prentice Hall, 1962.

Orrin Edgar Klapp, *Symbolic Leaders*, Chicago: Aldine, 1964.

Herman Kühn, 'The Restoration of Historical Technological Artifacts, Instruments and Tools' in *The International Journal of Museum Management and Curatorship*, 8–4.

Susan Langer, *Feeling and Form: A Theory of Art*, New York: Charles Scribners, 1953.

Charlie Leadbeater, 'In the Land of the Dispossessed', *Marxism Today*, April 1987.

Eric J Leed, *The Mind of the Traveler*, New York: Basic Books, 1991.

Walter Lippmann, *Public Opinion*, New York: Free Press, 1965.

Marie-Claire Llopès, *Le Temps des Gares*, Paris: Pompidou Centre, 1978.

David Lowenthal, *The Past is a Foreign Country*, Cambridge: Cambridge University Press, 1985.

Robert Lumley (ed.), *The Museum Time Machine*, New York: Routledge, 1988.

Trevor Lummus & Jan Marsh, *The Woman's Domain: Women and the English Country House*, London: Viking, 1990.

Dean MacCannell, *The Tourist. A New Theory of the Leisure Class*, New York: Shocken Books, 1976.

Ann McGrath, 'Travels to a Distant Past: the Mythology of the Outback', in Julia Horne & David Walker (eds.) *Travellers, Journeys, Tourists*, Geelong: Australian Cultural History, 1991.

André Malraux, *Antimemoirs*, London: Hamish Hamilton, 1968.

Robert K Merton, *On Theoretical Sociology*, New York: The Free Press, 1967.

Karl E Meyer, *The Art Museum: Power, Money, Ethics*, New York: William Morrow & Co, 1979.

Frank Moorhouse, *Room Service*, Melbourne: Viking, 1985.

Meaghan Morris, 'Sydney Tower', in *Island Magazine*, 9/10, Hobart: March 1982.

George L Mosse, *Fallen Soldiers. Reshaping the Memory of the World Wars*, New York: Oxford University Press, 1990.

Ian Ousby, *The Englishman's England*, Cambridge: Cambridge University Press, 1990.

Maurice Pianzola, *Paysages Romantiques Genevois*, Geneva: Museé d'art et d'histoire, 1977.

J H Plumb, *The Death of the Past*, London: Macmillan, 1969.

Griselda Pollock, *A Feminist Looks Round the City Art Gallery*, Manchester: Manchester City Art Gallery, 1987.

Karl Popper, *Conjectures and Refutations*, London: Routledge & Kegan Paul, Fourth Edition 1972.

Neil Postman, 'Museums as Dialogue', in *Museum News*, September/October 1990.

Michael R Real, *Mass-Mediated Culture*, Englewood Cliffs, New Jersey: Prentice Hall, 1977.

Jean-Jacques Rousseau, *The Social Contract*, London: Dent, 1973.

Carl P Russell, *100 Years in Yosemite: The Story of a Great National Park*, Berkeley: University of California Press, 1968.

John F Sears, *Sacred Places: American Tourist Attractions in the Nineteenth Century*, New York: Oxford University Press, 1989.

Inger Sjørslev, 'Communicating Objects. Towards a Theory of Exhibition Language' in *Folk* Vol. 33, Copenhagen, 1991.

Peter Sutton (ed.), *Dreamings: The Art of Aboriginal Australia*, Melbourne: Viking, 1988.

Alan Swingewood, *The Myth of Mass Culture*, London: Macmillan, 1977.

Paul Theroux, *Riding the Iron Rooster: By train through China*, New York: Putnam's, 1988.

Julian Thomas, '1938: Past and Present in an Elaborate Anniversary', in *Making the Bicentenary*, a special issue of *Historical Studies*, Melbourne: University of Melbourne, 1988.

Gaye Tuchman, *Making News: A Study in the Construction of Reality*, New York: Free Press, 1978.

Louise Turner & John Ash, *The Golden Hordes: International Tourism and the Pleasure Periphery*, New York: St Martin's Press, 1976.

Mark Twain, *The Innocents Abroad*, New York: Harper & Row (originally published 1869).

Susan Vogel, 'Always true to the object, in our fashion', in Ivan Karp & Steven D Lavine, *Exhibiting Cultures*, Washington: Smithsonian Institute, 1991.

Marina Warner, *Joan of Arc: The Image of Female Heroism*, London: Weidenfeld & Nicholson, 1981.

Marina Warner, *Monuments and Maidens: The Allegory of the Female Form*, London: Weidenfeld & Nicholson, 1985.

Max Weber, *The Theory of Social and Economic Organisation*, trans. Talcott Parsons, New York: The Free Press, 1964.

Judith Williamson, *Decoding Advertisements: Ideology and Meaning in Advertising*, London: Martin Boyars, 1978.

Felicity Woolf & Michael Cassin, *Bodylines: The Human Figure in Art*, London: National Gallery Education Department, 1987.

Patrick Wright, *On Living in an Old Country: The National Past in a Contemporary Britain*, Thetford: Verso, 1985.

Gavin Younge, *Art of the South African Townships*, London: Thames & Hudson, 1988.

INDEX—PLACES

♦ ♦ ♦

f = footnote

AFRICA: African railway, 17
  Black Africa, 181;
  museums of, 130f, 181;
  religion in, 67; ruins in, 302;
  sorcery in, 73; tourism in,
  250; **Southern Africa**, 72,
  272; **West Africa**, 7
ALBANIA: 204; nationalism in,
  286
AMAZON RIVER: 26
AMERICA:
  Central America, 282;
  archaeological sites in, 302;
  Latin America, 290;
  archaeology in, 302;
  museums of, 130f;
  nationalism in, 283; religion
  in, 67, 70; sorcery in, 73
AMERICAS: archaeology in,
  295; conquest of the, 281–282
ANDES, THE: 25, 74
ANTARCTICA: 26, 104
ARGENTINA:
  Buenos Aires, 35; La Boca,
  104; **Tandil**, 70
ARMENIA: nationalism in, 278
ASIA:
  East Asia, Buddhism in, 66;
  South-east Asia,
  archaeology in, 295;
  Buddhism in, 64; Hinduism
  in, 69; temples in, 64; **West
  Asia**, archaeology in, 295
ASSYRIA: 297, 301
AUSTRALIA: 26, 127, 128f;
  Aboriginal art in, 75–77, 133;
  Aboriginal culture/history in,
  75–77, 131, 220, 282;

INDEX—PLACES

museums in, 131, 221f; nationalism in, 268, 272, 281; open air museums in, 200; painting in, 26; war memorials in, 268, 289, 291

Blue Mountains, 244, 353, 354; **Cairns**, 128f; **Canberra**, 53; Australian War Memorial, 268, 290, 291; **Gold Coast**, 366; **Great Barrier Reef**, 10f, 104; **Hobart**, 32; **Melbourne**, 51; **Monkey Mia, WA**, 10f; **Olgas, The**, 181; **Perth**, Western Australian Museum, 221f; **Port Arthur**, 32; **Shark Bay, WA**, 10f; **Snowy Mountains**, 347; **Surfers Paradise**, 366; **Sydney**, 281; Australian Museum, 259; Opera House, 272; **Tumbarumba**, 347–348, 350–351, 353; **Uluru** (Ayers Rock), 26, 180, 379; **Western Desert**, 76

AUSTRIA: Habsburgs, monuments to, 46
Vienna, 46, 270; reconstruction of, 123; St Stephen's Cathedral, 46

BABYLON: 31, 297, 301
BALKANS, THE: 204, 274, 290
BELGIUM: 29, 276; festivals in, 29; nationalism in, 276, 375; war memorials in, 49
Aalst, 29; **Antwerp**, 276; **Brussels**, 49, 236; Royal Military Museum, 375; **Flanders**, 192f; **Flemish towns**, 278f; **Ieper**, 29, 192f; **Yvoir**, 29
BELIZE: 38
BLACK SEA: 119
BOLIVIA: painting in, 25, 26
Andes, The, 25; **La Paz**, Museo Nacional de Arte, 26
BRAZIL:
Rio de Janeiro, 71, 104
BRITAIN: (see also ENGLAND, SCOTLAND, WALES); nationalism in, 275
BULGARIA: 30, 75; museums in, 204; nationalism in, 30, 280; religion in, 75; revolution in, 204
Sofia, 30, 31; Alexander Nevski Cathedral, 75, 76, 77; Museum of the Revolutionary Movement, 204, 224; St Petka's Church, 30, 45

CAMBODIA: archaeology in, 302
Angkor Wat, 40, 103, 302; **Phnom Penh**, 224–225; Khmer Museum, 302
CANADA, museums in, 221f; nationalism in, 281; painting in, 26; pioneer museums in, 201; science museums in, 195–197
Alberta, 218; **Montreal**, Maison des Sciences et des Techniques, 196, 197; **Niagara Falls**: see separate entry; **Ontario**, Ontario Science Centre, 195; **Québec City**, 281;

Vancouver, Museum of Anthropology, 221f
CARIBBEAN: 38
CASPIAN SEA: 119
CHINA: 106; archaeology in, 298, 300; industrial sites in, 218; museums in, 224, 283; nationalism in, 283; painting in, 28; revolution in, 224; theatre in, 159–160; tourism in, 35; zoos in, 128f
  Beijing, 8, 383; Great Wall, 35, 370; Ming Tombs, 35; Museum of Chinese History, 130; Tiananmen Square, 124, 230; **Guangzhou**, 283; **Hainan Island**, 8f; **Shanghai**, The Bund, 106; **Tonglushan**, 218; **Xi'an**, 300
COLOMBIA:
  Bogotá, 70
COSTA RICA: 90
CROATIA: nationalism in, 275, 286; statues in, 275
  Zagreb, 103, 275
CZECHOSLOVAKIA: (see also CZECH REPUBLIC); communists in, 326f; nationalism in, 275, 276–277; revolution in, 233
CZECH REPUBLIC: tourism in, 326f
  Prague, 49, 233, 276–277; Ethnographic Museum, 277; Museum of National Literature, 277; National Museum, 125, 277; National Theatre, 277; Smetana Theatre, 277

DENMARK: 278; museums in, 348; nationalism in, 269, 284; war museums in, 292
  Copenhagen, Danish Resistance Museum, 292; Labour Museum, 199, 203; Little Mermaid, 74; National Museum, 127; **Roskilde**, 118; **North Zealand**, 348

ECUADOR: 6
  Galapagos Islands, 6
EGYPT: 34, 35, 62, 208, 297; Ancient Egypt, 131, 207–208, 296; archaeology in, 207–208, 295, 296–297; temples in, 62–63, 64, 103; tourism in, 34, 40, 208, 297, 342–343
  Abu Simbel, 40; **Aswan**, 40; Temple of Isis, 62; **Cairo**, 34, 297; Islamic Cairo, 297; Museum of Antiquities, 297; **Deir el Medina**, 208; **Dendara**, 63; **Giza**, Pyramids, the, 34, 112, 296–297, 305, 343, 370; Sphinx, the, 34, 74, 305; **Karnak**, 64, 342–343, 354; **Luxor**, 34, 343; al-Uqsur, 207–208; **Nile River**, 64, 208, 297; **Nile Valley**, 296; **Sakkara**, 34, 35; **Thebes**, 207, 208
ENGLAND: 119; aristocracy in, 172, 181; country houses in, 181, 184; heritage in, 217; industrial sites in, 185–190, 197, 203; monarchy in, 29, 172, 284; museums in, 202, 206; nationalism in, 269,

INDEX—PLACES 395

270–271, 284; science museums in, 190–193, 196; tourism in, 181; war museums in, 291

Bournemouth, 236; **Kent**, Leeds Castle, 32; Walmer Castle, 51; **Kew**, Royal Botanical Gardens, 128; **Liverpool**, 331–333, 340; Bootle, 332, 340, 341, 354; Mersey River, 331; Museum of Labour History, 205–206; Tate Gallery, 332; **London**, 29, 32; Barbican, The, 317; British Museum, 31, 40, 260, 273, 294–295, 297, 298, 299, 304, 305; Buckingham Palace, 29, 271; Greenwich Maritime Museum, 21f, 124; Highgate Cemetery, 224; Imperial War Museum, 291; Mall, The, 271; Museum of Mankind, 260; Museum of Natural History, 120, 196; museums in, 295; National Gallery, 355, 355f; National Theatre, 316; Piccadilly Circus, 32, 74; Science Museum, 186–187, 190–192; South Kensington museums, 167, 195; theatre in, 315–317; Tower of London, 29, 74; Trafalgar Square, 270–271; West End, 272, 315; Westminster Abbey, 48; **Manchester**, City Art Gallery, 178–180, National Museum of Labour History, 206; **Shropshire**, Blists Hill Open Air Museum, 188–189; Coalbrookdale, 185–186, 185f; Ironbridge Gorge Museum, 185, 305; Severn Valley, 187; Telford, 186; **Stratford on Avon**, 276; **Styal**, Quarry Bank Mill, 189–190, 197, 367–368; **Wigan**, 371; **York**, 117, 119; Jorvik Viking Centre, 117–119

EUROPE: 127, 297; Celtic history in, 303–304; museums in, 181, 377; nationalism in, 284; revolutions in, 229–230, 232–233; tourism in, 104–105, 172, 231, 274; war in, 291, 292; war memorials and museums in, 50, 289, 292

Central Europe, museums in, 303; **Eastern Europe**, 232; museums in, 275; nationalism in, 275; revolution in, 224, 226–227, 233; **Western Europe**, museums in, 303; nationalism in, 275; theme parks in, 181

FIJI: 28, 251; nationalism in, 269–270; tourism in, 28, 29
Suva, Fiji Museum, 269–270
FINLAND:
Helsinki, National Museum, 125
FRANCE: art museums in, 123, 351–352, 353, 356; folk museums in, 202; military museums in, 290; museums in, 123, 349; nationalism in, 47, 269, 272, 275, 279, 290; revolution in, 44, 49, 226f,

228–230, 228f, 232, 233;
science museums in, 190, 195;
tourism in, 371; war museums
in, 219
  Arles, 349; Musée
  Camarguais, 349; **Karnac**,
  218; **Lascaux Caves**, 366f;
  Lourdes, 43, 71, 172;
  Paris, 123, 229, 232, 270;
  art in, 126; Asterix Park,
  279; Cité des Sciences et de
  L'Industrie, 195–196; Eiffel
  Tower, 170, 232, 272; Jardin
  des Plantes, 128; Louvre, 34,
  121–123, 269, 273, 297,
  305, 348, 356f, 368;
  (Louvre/Musée de la
  République, 123, 351);
  (Louvre/Musée Napoléon,
  123, 127, 351); Musée
  Carnavalet, 229; Musée de
  l'Armée, 290; Musée des
  Arts et des Traditions
  Populaire, 202; Musée en
  Herbe, 220; Musée National
  des Techniques, 190; Musée
  Picasso, 353; museums in,
  295; Père Lachaise Cemetery,
  49; Pompidou Centre,
  362–363; theatre/
  performance in, 321–322;
  Péronne, 219

GAMBIA, THE: 250, 383
GERMAN DEMOCRATIC REPUBLIC: 233
GERMANY: 50; industrial
museums in, 194, 203;
museums in, 208–210, 224,
273f; nationalism in, 273f,
275, 284; revolution in, 233;
science museums in, 190
  Bavaria, 44; art museums in,
  44, 123; **Berlin**, 224, 270;
  Berlin Wall, 233; Museum of
  German History, 208–210;
  museums in, 295; Pergamon
  Museum, 31, 273, 297, 299,
  305; **Leipzig**, 233;
  Munich, 103, 123;
  Deutsches Museum, 103,190;
  Nuremberg, 169, 298;
  German National Museum,
  273f; **Rüsselsheim**,
  Municipal Museum (Opel
  City), 194, 203, 235;
  Wittenberg, 180
GILBERT ISLANDS: 251
GREECE: 297; archaeology in,
295, 296; tourism in, 249, 297
  Athens, 51, 296; Acropolis,
  366f, 373; Parthenon, 31,
  32f, 103, 299; Plaka, 103
GREENLAND: 119
GUATEMALA: Mayan sites in,
38
  Tikal, 38

HONG KONG: 7
HUNGARY: nationalism in, 25,
269, 280; revolution in, 233
  Budapest, 233, 280;
  Museum of Contemporary
  History, 224; National
  Museum, 125, 280; **Lake
  Baloton**, 25

ICELAND: 119
IGUAÇU FALLS: 26, 27
INDIA: 12, 138–159;

archaeology in, 298, 300; dance in, 159; Hinduism in, 28, 66, 69, 377, 381; museums in, 218–219; religion in, 67, 71; temples in, 103; tourism in, 35

Agra, 64; Taj Mahal, 46, 74, 366f, 379; **Ajanta**, 66, 298; **Amber**, 141–143; Jaigarh Fort, 141; **Bombay**, 3, 4, 5, 114f; **Chittaurgarh**, 145–147; Tower of Victory, 145–146; **Delhi**, 64, 139; Indian Craft Museum, 262; **Elephanta**, 66; **Ellora**, 66; **Fatehpur Sikri**, 64; **Ganges River**, 28, 71; **Great Thar Desert**, 151–152; **Indus Valley**, 300; **Jaipur**, 140–144; Jantar Mantar, 143–144, 154, 156; Nahargarh, 143; Palace of Winds, 141; Rambagh Palace, 143; **Jaisalmer**, 152–153; **Jodhpur**, 153; **Kanchipuram**, 64; **Khajuraho**, 66; **Mewar**, 145, 147; **New Delhi**, 53; **Old Delhi**, 225; **Rajasthan**, 138–159, 237, 250; **Udaipur**, 147–150, 153; Lake Palace Hotel, 147; West Zone Cultural Centre, 148, 154, 156, 158–159, 262, 328; **Varanasi**, 71, 172

INDONESIA:
BALI: 79–97, 340, 347, 354; art in, 92–93, 95, 329; Australians in, 327; dance/performance in, 81, 82–83, 87, 88, 93, 96–97, 314, 329–331, 333; festivals in, 95–96; nationalism in, 270, 279; religion in, 83–84; sex in, 327f; tourism in, 79–97, 252–253, 325–331, 340; **Batuan**, 78, 330, 333; **Candi Dasa**, 333; **Denpasar**, 83, 85–86, 88, 91, 94, 96, 328, 333; Bali Arts Festival, 96, 330–331; Institute of Fine Arts and Architecture, 329; Kokar Conservatorium of the Arts, 85, 88, 330; Museum Bali, 85, 91; National Academy of Dance, 330; **Kuta**, 327, 328, 333; **Nusa Dua**, 326; **Sanur**, 78, 82, 325, 327, 328; **Ubud**, 78, 79, 90, 327, 328

JAVA: 302; **Batavia**, 270, 271f, 302; **Borobudur**, 40, 103, 301; **Jakarta**, 270, 271, 272; National Monument, 130, 270; National Museum, 261–262, 262f; **Yogyakarta**, 331

IRAN: archaeology in, 301
Persepolis, 301; **Teheran**, 301

IRAQ: archaeology in, 301
IRELAND: 119; nationalism in, 282
Dublin, 50; National Museum, 282

ISRAEL: (see also PALESTINE); archaeology in, 301, 302; nationalism in, 60, 279, 293
Jerusalem, 61, 64–65;

Brook of Sidron, 57; Church of the Holy Sepulchre, 57, 58; Dome of the Rock, 60; Garden of Gethsemane, 57; Haram al-Sharif, 60; Holocaust Museum, 65; Islamic Museum, 61; Mount of Olives, 57, 58; Mount Zion, 58; Old City, 57, 60, 61, 104; pilgrimages to, 172; Via Dolorosa, 59; Western Wall, 59, 60; Yad Vashem, 293f; **Tel Aviv**, Museum of the Diaspora, 65

ITALY: archaeology in, 305; artworks of, 362f; nationalism in, 271, 273–27, 283, 284; pilgrimages to, 41–43; war memorials in, 290

Calabria, 348; Museum of Farming and Crafts, 348; **Florence**, 45; Santa Croce, 45, 48, 383; **Herculaneum**, 305; **Mount Vesuvius**, 42f; **Naples**, 41, 72, 305; **Northern Italy**, 77; **Pompeii**, 305; **Ravenna**, 77; San Vitale, 77; **Rome**, 271, 272 (see also VATICAN CITY); Foro Italico, 298; Forum of Vespasian, 77; music/ performance in, 320–321; obelisks in, 296; Victor Emmanuel Monument, 271, 290; **Southern Italy**, 41, 42; **Venice**, 6, 180, 366, 367; Correr Museum, 192f; Palazzo Grassi, 304; tourism in, 366–367

JAPAN: civil war in, 33; gardens in, 33; museums in, 124, 206–207, 218; nationalism in, 279; science museums in, 191; theatre in, 160–161; war memorials in, 50, 268, 289

Hakodate, Hakodate City Museum, 254; **Hiroshima**, 50; **Kyoto**, 124, 231f; Ginkaku-ji, 231f; Ryōan-ji Temple, 33; **Mount Fuji**, 28, 104, 379; **Nagasaki**, 50; **Nagoya**, Toyota City, 193; **Nara**, 124; **Tokyo**, 28, 124, 268; department stores in, 176; Disneyland, 166; National Science Museum, 191; Shitamachi Museum, 206–207; Ueno Park, 206–207; Yasukini Shrine, 268, 290

KOREA: see NORTH KOREA, SOUTH KOREA

LAOS: 17, 64
Khong Falls, 17; **Vientiane**, Wat Sisaket, 64
LATVIA:
Riga, 103, 200
LUXEMBOURG: nationalism in, 276

MACAU: 7; tourism in 7
MACEDONIA: nationalism in, 286
MALAYSIA:
Penang, 249; sex in 327f
MALI:
National Museum, 125

MESOPOTAMIA: 297, 298, 301

MEXICO: 49; archaeology in, 37–38, 302; Aztec culture/sites in, 302; Mayan civilisation in, 282; Mayan Indians in, 37–38; Mayan monuments in, 37–39, 250, 269, 294–295, 302; museums in, 127, 219; nationalism in, 38, 269, 282; tourism in, 38

   Acapulco, 8, 10, 38; **Mexico City**, 49, 51; Museo Nacional de Antropologia, 302; **Yucatan**, 10, 37, 38; Cancun, 10, 38, 250; Chichén Itza, 38, 39, 294; Mérida, 10, 37; Palenque, 38; Progreso, 10, 37; Uxmal, 38

MONACO:
   Monte Carlo, 9

MONGOLIA: archaeology in, 302
   Ulan Bator, 302

NEPAL:
   Mount Everest, 33

NETHERLANDS: 278f; nationalism in, 276

   Amsterdam, 9, 317; Maritime Museum, 21f, 124, 290; Oude Kerk, 319; Royal Tropical Institute, 258; theatre/performance in, 317–319; **Haarlem**, Teylers Museum, 128; **Hague, The**, 236

NEW ZEALAND: 238–244, 374; Maoris/Maori culture in, 254–255, 281; nationalism in, 269, 281; tourism in, 237–244, 254–255

   Auckland, Auckland City Gallery, 281; Auckland Museum, 254; **Bay of Islands**, 240; **Milford Sound**, 238, 239, 243; Milford Track, 239, 242–242; **North Island**, 239, 240; **Queenstown**, 238–239; **Rotorua**, 238; **South Island**, 240; **South Pacific Ocean**, 239; **Tasman Sea**, 239, 240

NIAGARA FALLS: 15, 43–44, 113, 175, 180, 269

NIGERIA: museums in, 125
   Kano, 32

NORTH KOREA: museums in, 224; revolution in, 224

NORWAY: industrial sites in, 187; nationalism in, 269, 278, 285

   Bergen, 285; **Bygdöy**, 118; **Kristiansund**, 187; **Oslo**, 49; Museum of National Antiquities, 278

PACIFIC ISLANDS: 251, 259

PAKISTAN: 152, 153; archaeology in, 300

PALESTINE: 58 (see also ISRAEL)

PAPUA NEW GUINEA: 259
   Port Moresby, 259

PARAGUAY:
   Asunción, 70

PERU: Inca culture/monuments

in, 31, 282, 302; nationalism in, 282
  Lima, Museo Historico Nacional, 130; **Machu Picchu**, 31, 282
PHILIPPINES: 35
  Manila, 104
POLAND: communism in, 168; museums in, 224; revolution in, 234; war museums/memorials in, 293, 293f
  Auschwitz, 293, 293f, 363; **Cracow**, 51, 104; **Warsaw**, 51, 224; restoration of, 107
PORTUGAL:
  Lisbon, 21, 21f; Alfama, 103, 104; Maritime Museum, 21f, 124, 290; **Oporto**, 348
PRUSSIA: art museums in, 44

RHODESIA: 283, 303 (see also ZIMBABWE)
ROMANIA: 232; nationalism in, 275, 278, 282–283
  Bucharest, 105; History Museum, 282–283; Palace of The Republic, 105; restoration of, 105; **Deva**, 278
RUSSIA: 25 (see also LATVIA, SOVIET UNION, UKRAINE); museums and galleries in, 225, 356; revolution in, 222–223, 225, 227–228, 235, 235f; war memorials in, 50
  Ekaterinburg, 48f; **Leningrad**, 73, 223 (see also Petrograd and St Petersburg); Museum of the Peoples of the Soviet Union, 124; Revolution Museum, 227; **Moscow**, 174, 223, 225, 230, 271; Bolshoi Ballet, 272; History Museum, 182; Kremlin, 32, 74, 174; V I Lenin Museum, 225; Pushkin Fine Arts Museum, 124; Red Square, 9, 124, 271; Revolution Museum, 223, 225, 230; State Historical Museum, 130; Tretyakov Gallery, 25; **Novgorod**, 65; **Penza**, 356; **Petrograd**, 223, 227–228 (see also Leningrad and St Petersburg); Winter Palace, 222, 227–228, 233; **St Petersburg**, 31, 48, 271 (see also Leningrad and Petrograd), Hermitage, 124, 273

SAUDI ARABIA:
  Mecca, 172
SCANDINAVIA: 25, 202 (see also DENMARK, FINLAND, NORWAY, SWEDEN); museums in, 206
SCOTLAND: industrial sites in, 188; museums in, 207; nationalism in, 269, 285, 286
  Edinburgh, 49; The People's Story Museum, 207; **Glasgow**, Glasgow Green, 186; People's Palace Museum, 207; Springburn Community Museum, 349; **Inverness**, 86; **New Lanark**, 188, 189
SERBIA: 274–275, 292, 368; nationalism in, 274–275, 277,

278, 280, 283, 284–285, 286, 292; tourism in, 368
  Belgrade, 51, 272; Ethnographic Museum, 285; Gallery of Frescoes, 278; Military Museum, 280, 284–285, 291–292; National Museum, 274–275; **Nis**, 283
SINGAPORE: 108–111; cuisine of, 157; nationalism in, 280; restoration of, 108–111
  National Museum, 110; Raffles Hotel, 16, 157; Singapore River, 108, 110–111, 119, 280; Singapore Science Centre, 195
SLOVENIA: nationalism in, 276, 286
  Ljubljana, 276; Slovene National House, 125
SOMALIA: 260–261
  Hargeisa, 260–261
SOUTH AFRICA: 264–267; nationalism in, 200, 264–265, 270, 282
  Cape of Good Hope, 21; **Johannesburg**, 265–267; Soweto, 266–267; Triomf, 266; **Pretoria**, 51, 72, 264, 267; National Cultural History Museum, 270; South African Museum, 254; Voortrekker Monument, 264, 282, 291, 369; **Republic of Transvaal**, 265; **Table Mountain**, 35
SOUTH KOREA:
  Yongin, Korean Folk Village, 200
SOVIET UNION: 223, 224, 289 (see also LATVIA, RUSSIA, UKRAINE); communism in, 63f, 168; Lenin cult in, 48, 63f, 204, 223–224, 225, 235, 235f, 289; military museums in, 289; museums in, 130; revolution in, 223–224, 226; war memorials in, 289
  Ulyanovsk, 223
SPAIN: 8; guidebook to, 24; tourism in, 8, 366–367
  Benidorm, 8f, 367; **Costa Blanca**, 8f; **Madrid**, Museo de America, 124; Prado, 272
SRI LANKA: archaeology in, 302
  Kandy, 302
SUDAN: nationalism in, 47, 279
SWEDEN: 278; folk museums in, 200, 203–204; industrial sites in, 187, 193–194; military museums in, 291; museums in, 210–211, 273, 372f; nationalism in, 47, 273; science museums in, 190–191
  Bergslagen, 187; **Norrköping**, 210; **Österbybruk**, 193–194; **Stockholm**, City Museum, 199, 203; National Museum of Science, 190–191; Nordic Museum, 210, 254; Royal Army Museum, 290–291; Skansen Folk Museum, 200, 200f, 273; Wasa Museum, 372f; **Uppsala**, Uppsala Cathedral, 47
SWITZERLAND: 19, 20, 25; museums in, 210, 272;

nationalism in, 269, 272, 285, 290; tourism in, 19–20, 371
  Alps, 25, 112, 269, 379; Jungfrau, 104; **Bern**, 106; Bernese Historical Museum, 210; **Central Plateau**, 106; **Geneva**, 272; **Zürich**, Swiss National Museum, 272, 290
SYRIA: antiquities in, 301

TAIWAN: 7, 272; nationalism in, 272; tourism in, 7–8, 9
  Peitou, 7; **Taipei**, National Palace Museum, 272
THAILAND: 29, 64, 301; archaeology in, 300–301; customs in, 136f; folk museums in, 205f; nationalism in, 205f; sex in, 253, 253f, 327f
  Bangkok, 28, 64, 71; Muang Boran Museum, 205f; National Museum, 300–301; Temple of the Emerald Buddha, 64; **Pattaya**, 253
TOGO: 250
TUNISIA: archaeology in, 304
  Dougga, 304
TURKEY: archaeology in, 299
  Bosphorus, 287, 288; **Constantinople**, 288; **Dardanelles**, 288; **Istanbul**, 64; Blue Mosque, 64; Haghia Sophia, 64; Military Museum, 287–288; Naval Museum, 288; **Rumeli Hisar**, 287

UKRAINE: war memorials in, 289

Kiev, 65; State Museum of the Great Patriotic War, 289
USA: African-Americans in, 213–214, 214f, 267; civil war in, 50, 288–289, 290f; cultural literacy in, 135, 135f; food in, 157–258; guidebooks to, 47, 188f; industrial sites in, 185f, 187; military parks in, 288–289; museums in, 214f, 219, 373–4, 377; national parks in, 6, 26; nationalism in, 47, 267, 269, 271, 272, 281, 283; Native Americans in, 181, 216–217, 219, 256, 290f, 368; painting in, 26; pioneer museums in, 200–201; politics in, 54, 308–309; religion in, 72; revolution in, 185, 212–213, 216, 226, 226f, 283; science museums in, 195–196; theatre/performance in, 305–315; tourism in, 43, 52–56, 73, 334–341, 364–367, 368f; war memorials in, 50, 54–55, 288–289, 290f
  MAJOR CITIES: **Boston**, 73, 212–128, 338, 371; Faneuil Hall, 213, 216, 217, 338; Massachusetts State House, 298; Museum of Fine Arts, 133, 135, 216; Native Americans in, 216–217; Quincy Hall, 213, 338; **Chicago**, Dusable Museum of African-American History, 214f; modern architecture in, 106, 231–232; Museum

of Science and Industry, 195; **Denver**, 334–337, 339–341, 347, 371; Colorado History Museum, 335; Denver Art Museum, 336–337; Four Mile Historic Park, 335; **Los Angeles**, 339f, 340, 341; Forest Lawn Cemetery, 69; Hollywood, 114f; theatre/performance in, 306–307; **New York**, 63, 311–315; American Museum of Natural History, 116, 255–256, 257; Broadway, 314–315; East Village, 312, 338f; Empire State Building, 170, 272; Greenwich Village, 315; Harlem, 63, 77, 250, 255; Lincoln Center, 313; Manhattan, 6, 202–203; Metropolitan Opera, 314; Museum of the American Indian, 219; museums in, 295; performance in, 311–315; South Bronx, 104; Statue of Liberty, 74, 230–231, 379; West Village, 312; zoos in, 128f; **Philadelphia**, 212, 283; Independence Hall, 283; Liberty Bell, 283; **San Francisco**, 3, 4, 32; Fishermen's Wharf, 32; San Francisco Exploratorium, 195; **Washington DC**, 51, 52–56, 63, 124, 168, 171, 217, 237, 267, 271, 276, 283, 290, 309–311; Anacostia Museum, 214f, 346f; Arlington National Cemetery, 53, 54; Capitol, 47, 53, 310; Capitol Hill, 53, 54; Center for African Art, 221f; FBI Building, 311; Freer Gallery, 56; Hirshorn Museum, 56; Jefferson Monument, 55; Kennedy Center for the Performing Arts, 56, 309; Lincoln Memorial, 53, 55, 217, 271, 276; Mall, The, 53, 54, 217, 271; National Air and Space Museum, 195–196; National Gallery of Art, 55, 262f; National Museum of African Art, 56; National Museum of American History, 182, 182f, 310, 311; National Museum of Women in the Arts, 182; Pentagon, The, 53; Smithsonian Institution, 310, 346f; Supreme Court, 53; Washington Monument, 55, 225; White House, The, 53

STATES AND AREAS: **Arizona**, Fort Bowie, 368; **California**, 3, 27; Disneyland, 6, 21, 54, 165 167, 171, 176, 195, 200f, 301, 372; Fresno, 338–339; Mariposa Sequoia Grove, 27, 45, 269, 343; Sacramento, 3, 4; San Diego, 334; Sierra Nevada; 27; Yosemite Valley, 6, 113, 269; **Colorado**, Georgetown, 334; Grand Canyon, 104, 370, 379, Rocky Mountains,

334; **Florida**, 26, 114f; Disney World, 195, 199, 364–367, 374–375; Everglades National Park, 26; Florida Keys, 26, 114f; Miami Beach, 334; **Georgia**, National Military Park, 288–289; **Hawaii**, 10, 250–252; Bishop Museum, 251–252, 263; Honolulu, 252; Pearl Harbour, 290f; Polynesian Cultural Centre, 251; tourism in, 250–252; Waikiki, 251; **Illinois**, Springfield, 47; **Indiana**, New Harmony, 188f; **Louisiana**, New Orleans, 368f; **Maryland**, Baltimore, 338; Maryland Historical Museum, 373–374; **Massachusetts**, Plymouth, 212, 216, 281; Salem, 73; **Minnesota**, Minneapolis, 9; **Missouri**, St Louis, 308–309; **Nevada**, Las Vegas, 9; Caesar's Palace, 9; Nevada Desert, 9; **New England**, 215, 216; **New Mexico**, Pueblo Cultural Centre, 214f; Santa Fe, 307; Museum of International Folk Art, 345; **New York State**, Seneca Falls, 182; **Niagara Falls**, see separate entry; **Oklahoma**, Oklahoma City, 339f; **Pennsylvania**, Gettysburg, 289, 290; Hopewell Furnace, 185f; Pittsburgh, 187; **Texas**, Houston, 364f; **Virginia**, Jamestown, 281; Mount Vernon, 47; Williamsburg, 31; **Washington**, Seattle, 338; **Yellowstone National Park**, 26

VATICAN CITY:
Museo Paolino, 258; Sistine Chapel, 45, 104, 356f, 370; Vatican Museums, 353–354, 356f
VENEZUELA: 17, 26
Angel Falls, 17; **Caracas**, 26, 225
VIETNAM: museums in, 224; nationalism in, 282; revolution in, 224, 375
Hanoi, Central History Museum, 282; Revolutionary Museum, 375; **Ho Chi Minh City**, 8, 9

WALES:
Cardiff, 200
WEST INDIES: 127

YUGOSLAVIA: 286 (see also CROATIA, SERBIA, SLOVENIA)

ZAIRE: 17
ZAMBIA: 16
ZIMBABWE: 16–17, 302 (see also RHODESIA); nationalism in, 283, 302–303; Shona culture of, 125, 302; Tonga people of, 20; tourism in, 15–22

Bulawayo, 17; **Great Zimbabwe**, 302–303; **Harare**, 17, 283; National Gallery, 125; **Victoria Falls**, 15–22, 23, 36, 72, 104, 116, 177, 250, 303, 373, 379; **Zambesi Gorge**, 17; **Zambesi River**, 16, 17, 18, 20, 21, 22, 37, 176, 237

INDEX—PEOPLE AND THEMES

◆ ◆ ◆

f = footnote

Aborigines – see AUSTRALIA
Abraham 60, 69f, 279
Ah Kinchil 68
Ahmed I, Sultan 64
Albert, Prince 166, 167, 167f, 176
Alexander Nevski, Prince 75, 77, 176
Alfred the Great 275
Allen, Woody 315
Altman, Denis 267f
Amaterasu 279
American Express 19
Amish sect 201f
Amun-Re 343
Anderson, Digby 374
Anglo-Saxons 117, 119

ANZACs 268
Apollo 180
archaeology and tourism 294—305
architecture and tourism 9, 63–64, 106–111, 231–232, 359
Arkwright, Sir Richard 189, 190, 197
Arminius 275
art and tourism 65–66, 74–78, 178–180, 182, 362f
art museums and tourism 25, 44–45, 69, 71, 127, 129, 176f, 350–363
Asoka, Emperor 298, 300
Ataturk, Kemal 225, 288
Athena 103
authentic/authenticity 36,

INDEX—PEOPLE AND THEMES

44–45, 55, 76, 101–120, 240–241, 251, 314, 329, 352, 365
Autobahnia 155f
'autonomic tourism' 155, 168, 175, 224, 239, 269, 274, 355, 374, 375
Aztecs, the – see Mexico

Babbitt, George F 340
Badung, Raja of 85
Bakunin, Mikhail 227
Balanchine, George 318
Bandem, Dr I Made 330
Barry, Sir Charles 270
Barthes, Roland 24, 62f
Bathsheba 180
Baudelaire, Pierre Charles 307
Baudin, Nicolas 126
Beethoven, Ludvig van 276
Benjamin, Walter 175
Berg, Alban 321
Berger, John 179
Bersani, Leo 354
Bismarck, Prince Otto von 279
Bohemia, Duke of 275
Bolívar, Simón 130
Bolsheviks, the 222, 227, 235, 271
Bonaparte, Napoléon 34, 47, 174, 296
Bond, James 147
Botticelli, Sandro 179
Brahma 89, 279
Brecht, Bertolt 316
Brendon, Piers 43
Brezhnev, Leonid 9, 191, 225
Briggs, Asa 167f
Britten, Benjamin 160
Brown, Molly 335, 337

Buddha 48, 62, 68, 77, 135
Buddhism 33, 62, 63, 64, 66, 268, 298
'Buffalo Bill' 334
Bulgars, the 31

Caesar, Gaius Julius 276
Canaletto, Antonio 107
Cannadine, David 284
Carol, King (of Romania) 105
Carter, Paul 22
Cartier, Jacques 281
casinos and tourism 7, 9
Ceaucescu, Nicolae and Elena 105, 232
celebrity (in tourism) 16, 33–35, 36, 338, 367–368, 370–371
Celtic Football Club 207
Celts, the 303–304
Cervantes, Miguel de 276
Chaucer, Geoffrey 48
Chiang Kai Shek 272
Chopin, Frédéric 51
Christ 48, 49, 57–59, 65, 68, 69, 70–71, 77, 133, 223, 249
Christianity 41–42, 50, 57–59, 62, 63, 65, 66, 66f, 69, 69f, 70–71, 72, 74–75, 104, 180, 278 (see also Christ, pilgrimages, Saints)
Christoff, Boris 75
'civilisation packet' 294–305
Clair, Jean 353
class (social) 136, 203–204, 210–211, 231
classical, the 103, 296, 298–299
classification (in museums, etc) 21, 126–131, 346, 351, 373
Cleopatra, Queen 180

Cocteau, Jean 320
Columbus, Christopher 54, 281
commodification of tourism 175, 239, 244, 367
Communards, the 49
Communist Party, the 168, 226
community participation 206–207, 218, 260–261, 347–349, 362
Constantine, Emperor 54, 57, 58
Cook, Captain James 281
Cook, Thomas 18, 34, 43, 166
Cook, Thomas & Son 19, 208, 229, 297
Coward, Noel 106
Cranach, Lucas 180
Crick, Malcolm 249f
'critics' culture, the' 172–173, 236
Crusaders, the 59, 275, 321
Culler, Jonathan 375
'cultural genes bank' 262–263, 330, 362, 369
cultural shows 28–29, 68, 153, 158, 250–251
cultural tourism 28–29, 92–93, 232, 328, 339–341
Cuomo, Governor 308

Dadaists 34, 320, 321
da Gama, Vasco 155
Daley, Mayor (of Chicago) 232
Dali, Salvador 256
Danae 180
Dante Alighieri 48, 166, 215
Danton, Georges Jacques 222
Daphne 180
Darby, Abraham 185, 186
'darshana' 28, 52, 166, 223, 242

Darwin, Charles 6, 130, 196
David, King 180
David, Jacques-Louis 260
Davis, Mike 340
Davy, Sir Humphrey 190
Decebalus 278
Degas, Edgar 358
Delacroix, Eugène 230
Della Sala, Dr Georgio 42
de San Martin, José 130
de Varine, Hugues 349
Diaghilev, Sergei 320
Dimitrov, Georgi 30, 48
Dingane 265
Diocletian, Emperor 54
Diponegoro, Prince (of Java) 270
'discovery' 16, 17, 20–21, 21f, 26, 33, 155, 221, 281, 295, 361
Disney, Walt 165, 166, 176, 364
Dobrovsky, Father 277
Donald Duck 166
Dušan, Stephen 274–275, 277, 280

Eastman, George 113
Eco, Umberto 375
ecology and tourism 16, 36
eco-tourism 6, 26, 104, 218, 244, 371
Edgar Rice Burrows Inc 250, 383
Eisenstein, Sergei M 227
Elgin, Lord Thomas Bruce 299
Elizabeth I, Queen 181, 278f
enclave tourism 250, 326–328, 366–367, 370
Epstein, Jason 336
Erasmus, Desiderius 236, 278f
ethnography and tourism 71, 124, 171, 181, 218, 256–263

Euclid (euclidian) 319
Europa 136, 180
excerpts/excerpt culture 157–161, 262
'exorcising' tourism 35–40, 56

fame – see celebrity
Farwell, Jerry 72f
FBI 311
festivals and tourism 29, 70–71, 74, 95–96, 169, 280, 307–308
Feydeau, Georges 316
folk museums and tourism 200, 202–203, 204–205, 339f
Fonteyn, Margot 81
Fonzie 55, 56
food and tourism 110f, 146, 157–158
Foreman, Richard 317–318
Foucault, Michel 191
'framing' in tourism 18, 23, 31f, 33, 112–114, 156, 237, 242
François (King of France) 278f
Franz Ferdinand, Emperor 270
Frayn, Michael 314, 316
Frederick William III of Prussia 44
Fussell, Paul 154

Gainsborough, Thomas 179
Galileo Galilei 48
Gandhi, Mohandas K 225
Garibaldi, Giuseppe 222
Garton Ash, Timothy 233, 234
Gautama – see Buddha
Genghis Khan 302
Giereck, Edward 168
Giotto 45
Girard (collection) 344–345

Godwin, William 236
Goebbels, Paul Joseph 174
Goffman, Irving 24
Gordon, General Charles 65
Goya, Francisco de 359
Goyal, Suresh 146
Great Exhibition, The 124, 166–170, 167f, 176, 186, 195, 371
Greenblatt, Stephen 133, 156, 360
Gregorios V, Patriot 51
Grieg, Edvard 285
Grosz, Georg 358f
group tourism/guided tours 5, 24, 52–56, 74, 94, 138–156, 229, 242–244, 250, 252, 342–343, 360
guidebooks 19, 23–24, 33, 47, 52, 70, 74, 80, 175, 238, 267, 275, 319, 344, 359, 361, 371

Habsburgs, the 46, 277, 282
Haggard, Sir Henry Rider 303
Handel, Georg Friedrich 317
Hanuman 86
Hart, Gary 309
Hatshepsut, Queen 208
Hausa, the (of Nigeria) 32
Haussmann, Baron Georges 123, 270
Hazelius, Artur 200
Helena, Empress 57, 65
Henry the Navigator, Prince 21
heritage sites and tourism 209, 212–218
Herod, King 59
Hewison, Robert 217
Hilton, Conrad 7
Hinduism 28–29, 52, 61–62,

66, 68–69, 71, 79–97
Hirsch, E D 135f
historical sites 30–32, 115
history museums and tourism 45, 69, 71, 114–115, 121–131, 174, 201–202
Hitler, Adolf 54, 171, 217, 289, 292, 293
Ho Chi Minh 48, 224
Hohenzollerns, the 270
Holguin, Melchor Perez 25
Holmes, Oliver Wendell 215
Homer 62f
Hudson, Kenneth 191, 208, 349
Hughes, Robert 359
Huss, Jan 49
Hussein, Saddam 301

Ibsen, Henrik 49, 276
icons (of tourism) 70, 74, 169, 230, 260, 263, 296, 369
Imperial Airways 18
Incas, the – see PERU
industry museums/sites 102–103, 129, 171, 182, 184–194, 203, 234, 373
'intelligent superficiality' 132–137, 159, 161, 177, 358–359, 360, 374
Isaac 69f
Islam 60–62, 68, (see also Muhammad)
Ivan the Terrible 32

Jackson, Jesse 308–309
Jain, Dr Jyotindra 262
Jefferson, Thomas 55, 55f, 63f
Jesus – see Christ
Joan of Arc 275
Judaism 59–62, 64–65, 68

Juliana, Queen 85, 330
Jungman, Josef 277
Juno 180
Jupiter 67, 69f, 180
Justinian, Emperor 64

Kamehameha, King (of Hawaii) 252
Kara George 292
Karadzic, Vuk 51
Kelly, Ned 51
Kennedy, John F 56, 215
Kennedys, the 54, 55
Khmer Rouge 224–225
Khonsu-Neferhotep 343
Kim Il Sung 224
King, Elspeth 207
King, Martin Luther 53
Kossuth, Louis 229
Krishna 48, 68–69, 77
Kruger, Paul 51, 265
Krum (of Bulgaria) 30, 31
Ku Klux Klan 368f
Kühn, Herman 103

landscapes 24–28, 174, 175
picturesque 23
romantic 16, 25, 36, 237–238, 244, 269
Langer, Susan 50
Lavoisier, Antoine 190
Lazarus, Emma 231
Leadbeater, Charlie 209
Leda 180
Lee Kuan Yew 108
Leed, Eric J 58, 127
legends 68–69, 74, 169, 223, 229, 369
L'Enfant, Pierre 271
Lenin, Vladimir Ilich 48, 50,

INDEX—PEOPLE AND THEMES 411

63f, 222–228, 226f, 235, 265, 289 (see also SOVIET UNION; Lenin cult in)
Lincoln, Abraham 47, 53, 54, 55, 55f, 63f, 265, 271, 276
Linnaeus, Carolus 191
Lippmann, Walter 112
Livingstone, David 17, 20, 21, 22, 23, 36, 37, 176
Louis XIV, King 229
Lowenthal, David 51
Lucretia 180
Ludwig of Bavaria, King 306–7
Lumms, Trevor 181
Lupescu, Madame 105

MacCannell, Dean 31f, 105
McCarthy, Mary 313
McCoy, Elijah 214f
McGrath, Ann 180
Machiavelli 48
magic of tourism/'magic circles' 23–40, 173–174, 352–353
Magyars, the 233, 280
Malraux, André 313, 359
Mandelas, the 267
Mao Zedong 48, 224
Maoris – see NEW ZEALAND
Marsh, Jan 181
Marx, Karl 62f, 63f, 188, 224, 226, 226f
Marxists 226f
Massine, Léonide 320
Matthias of Hungary, King 278f
Maudslay, Alfred 294–295, 304
Mayans, the – see GUATEMALA and MEXICO
Mehmet the Conqueror 287, 288
Merton, Robert K 307

Michelangelo di Buonarroti 45, 48, 103, 260
Mickiewicz, Adam 51
Mihailo Obrenovic, Prince 275
military museums 129, 287–293 (see also war and tourism)
Mondale, Walter 309
Mongkut, King (of Thailand) 300
Moorhouse, Frank 155f, 376
Mormons, the 251
Mosse, George 50
Moynihan, Daniel Patrick 310
Mughals, the 64, 143, 362
Muhammad 48, 60, 62
museums 121–131, 174, 202, 218–221, 234, 255–263, 272–273, 278, 286, 344–347, 344f, 345f, 356f, 371–374, 372f (see also art museums, ethnography, folk museums, history museums, industry museums/sites, military museums, natural history museums, pioneer museums, science centres/museums, war and Places Index)
Muslims, the 299
Mut 343
myths 67, 74, 169–170, 217, 225, 233, 236, 263, 360, 369

Nagy, Imre 233
'naming' 22, 295, 351
national
 capital (tourism of) 52–56, 270–273
 heroes/geniuses 274–277
 past 184–185, 201, 223, 273–286
 showcase 7, 264–286, 368, 371

nationalism 46–51, 123–126, 173, 190–191, 195–196, 205f, 249–263, 264–286, 287–293, 294–305, 368, 375 (see also under country name in Places Index)
natural history museums 116, 118, 196, 373, 373f
nature and tourism 6, 8, 10f, 15–16, 25–28, 180–181, 237–245, 269, 359, 361
Nazis, the 50, 51, 65, 107, 172, 194, 266, 292, 293, 293f
Nebuchadnezzar II, King 31, 297, 301, 305
Nicholas II, Tsar 48f
Nietzsche, Friedrich 320
nostalgia 182, 184–198, 203, 205, 225, 231, 335, 369
Novalis (Friedrich von Hardenberg) 285

Obregon, General Alvaro 49
Ohm, George Simon 190
Opel Manufacturing Company 102, 194
Osiris 68
Otto of Bavaria, Prince 296
Ottomans, the 30, 58, 274, 275, 288, 296
Ousby, Ian 43, 276, 337
Owen, Robert 188, 188f
Ozymandias past/factor 37–40, 56, 102, 273, 295, 305, 360

Palacky, F 277
Pascal, Blaise 190
Passmore, John 361
people, the (proletariat) 172, 199–211, 216, 226, 226f

performance and tourism 90–93, 96–97, 159–161, 306–322, 329–330
Pericles (Periclean) 305
Petöfi, Sandor 125
Philistines, the 302
Phillip, Governor Arthur 281
photography and tourism 6, 15, 23–24, 25, 35, 59, 90, 91–92, 103, 112–115, 141, 142, 148, 156, 239, 242, 243, 266
Picasso, Pablo 106, 320
pilgrimage
    religious 41–43, 57–59, 104
    tourist 41–51, 54, 74, 76, 104, 217, 223, 24, 225, 244, 264–270, 279–280, 289, 290, 290f, 328
Pilgrims, the 281
pioneer museums 200–201
Pol Pot 224
Postman, Neil 196, 345
postmodernism 170f, 233, 375
'pradakshina' 52
Preseren, Franz 276
proletariat – see people, the
public culture 165–177, 182–183, 185, 197, 201, 202, 205f, 212–218, 222–236, 267, 284, 305, 344, 371
Puritans, the 216
Pushkin, Aleksander 124, 276

Qin Shi Huangi, Emperor 46, 300

Rachmaninoff, Sergei 321
racism 168, 171, 254–258, 265–267, 269–270, 369
Raffles, Sir Thomas Stanford 280

INDEX—PEOPLE AND THEMES

railways and tourism 17–18, 19, 41
Rajputs, the 142–144, 150, 154
Rama 28–9
Ramaccini, Dr Franco 42f
Ramses II 40
Raphael (Raffaello Santi) 260
Rata, Dr Ida Bagus 333
'reading' tourism 173–177, 178–183
Reagan, Ronald 53, 257, 315
Real, Michael 165
relics and tourism
 religious 41–44, 42f, 354
 secular 46–51, 48f, 76, 171, 177, 224, 231, 250, 254, 271, 311
religion and tourism 57–78, 172 (see also Buddhism, Christianity, Hinduism, Islam, Judaism, pilgrimage, Saints)
Rembrandt van Rijn 44, 276, 278f
replicas in tourism 8f, 364–366, 364f, 366f
'resonance' 133, 305, 360–361
restoration of cities/
 tourist sites 104, 105–111, 332, 335–338, 338f
revolution and tourism 222–236
Rhodes, Cecil 18
ritual 71–73, 169
Rivière, Georges Henri 202
Roach Smith, Charles 304
Rodange, Michel 276
Roman deities 42
Romans, the 59, 65, 119, 150, 275, 278, 303
romanticism 273f, 337 (see also landscapes, romantic)

Röntgen, W C 190
Roosevelt, Franklin D 55f
Roosevelt, Theodore 255
Rousseau, Jean-Jacques 27, 170, 258
Rubens, Peter Paul 276
Rudolph of Bohemia, King 278f
Russell, Carl P 113

Saints 42, 68
 Agatha 180
 Gennaro 42, 72
 James 69f
 Joan 275
 John 69f
 John the Baptist 104
 Paul 42
 Peter 42
Saroyan, William 339
Satie, Erik 320, 321–322
Sawai Jai Singh II 143
scepticism in tourism 40, 361
Schoenberg, Arnold 321
science centres/museums 129, 186–187, 190–192, 194–198, 218–219, 373
Scott, Sir Walter 285
Scottish Labour Party 207
Sears, John 43, 175, 180, 269
Seti I 343
sex and tourism 7, 9, 253, 253f, 327, 327f
Shaftesbury, Earl of 32
Shakespeare, William 62f, 232, 276, 287, 314
Shelley, Percy Bysshe 40, 381
Shepard, Sam 315
Shiva 89
shopping and tourism 155, 175–176, 335–336, 344, 366

showcase
national – see national showcase
tourist 238, 297, 368
Sibelius, Jean Julius 276
Sigismund of Krakow, King 278f
'silences' of tourism 182–183,
   201, 217–218, 267, 287–293,
   375
Sjørslev, Inger 345f
Slavs, the 30, 31, 280
Smetana, Bedrich 277
Solomon, King 303
Southern African Caledonian
   Societies 20, 37, 176
souvenirs 7, 51, 72, 92–93, 94,
   175, 229, 233, 243, 252, 255,
   259, 267, 329, 366, 372
Spinoza, Baruch de 236, 278f
Stalin, Joseph 224, 293
Stalinists 50, 174
'statuemania' 222, 275–277,
   279
Stendahl, Marie Henri 45, 383
Stendahl's Syndrome 45, 361
Stephenson, George 190
Strauss, Richard 316
Stravinsky, Igor 318, 321
Sukarno, Achmed 270
Suleiman II, Sultan 287
Sun Yat Sen 283
supernatural, the, and tourism
   66–67, 71–73, 76–78, 369
Susanna 180

Tasman, Abel 281
Telford, Thomas 186
Tell, William 47
Thatcher, Baroness 202, 316
theme parks and tourism 6, 111,
   165–167, 195, 200f, 218,
   364–367, 374
Theroux, Paul 115, 368
Third World tourism 15–22,
   79–97, 138–161, 249–254,
   256, 262, 325–333, 340–341,
Thoreau, Henry David 26
Titian (Tiziano Vecellio) 122
Tito, Marshal Josip Broz 286
Tomislav, Zupan of Nin 275
Trajan, Emperor 279
travel
   agents 19–20, 41, 371
   books – see guidebooks
   literature/postcards etc 10, 19,
      23, 31f, 91–92, 238, 294f,
      344, 371
   photography – see photography
      and tourism
   writing 115–116, 116f, 359,
      371
Treitschke, Heinrich von 273f
Trotsky, Leon 51, 228
Trudeau, Gary 315
Tutankhamen, King 46

van der Rohe, Mies 338
van Eyck, Jan 260, 278f
Vasa, Gustav 47
Vespasian, Emperor 77
Vickers, Adrian 91, 326
Vikings, the 117–119, 269
Villa, Pancho 49
Vishnu 68, 69
Vlad the Impaler (Prince of
   Romania) 275
Vogel, Susan 221f

war and tourism 50, 54–55,
   219, 234, 265, 268, 287–293
   (see also military museums)

Washington, George 47, 51, 55, 225
Watt, James 186, 187, 190
Wayne, John 146, 265
Weber, Max 171
Wellington, Duke of 51
Wells, H G 181
Wenceslas, King 275, 277
Wilson, Fred 373–374
Winckelmann, Johann Joachim 354
Windsors, the 29
Wollstonecraft, Mary 236
women and tourism 168, 171, 178–183, 214, 218, 347–348, 351
'wonder' 143, 152, 156, 343, 347, 359–361, 375
Wordsworth, William 26

Yeats, William Butler 276
Yeltsin, Boris 225, 235, 235f
Yoshimasa, Ashikaga 231f

Zeus 68, 69f
Zhou Enlai 226f
Zola, Emile 121, 200, 281, 297, 305, 346, 363
zoos 128, 128f